American Heart of Darkness

American Heart of Darkness

Volume I:
The Transformation of the American Republic into a Pathocracy

Michael and Nuhad, It has been such a pleasure to meet all of you! Thanks for your interest in the book, and I hope you enjoy it.

Bob Kirkconnell

Robert Kirkconnell

Copyright © 2013 by Robert Kirkconnell.

Library of Congress Control Number:		2013902568
ISBN:	Hardcover	978-1-4797-9322-8
	Softcover	978-1-4797-9321-1
	Ebook	978-1-4797-9323-5

All rights reserved. No part of this book may be reproduced or transmitted in any form or by any means, electronic or mechanical, including photocopying, recording, or by any information storage and retrieval system, without permission in writing from the copyright owner.

This book was printed in the United States of America.

Rev. date: 07/12/2013

To order additional copies of this book, contact:
Xlibris LLC
1-888-795-4274
www.Xlibris.com
Orders@Xlibris.com
124469

Contents

Foreword 9

Chapter One
The Body Bag Case 21

    The Case 21
    Analysis 27
    The First Contact—Michael Levine 29
    Reflections 33
    The State Department's Explanation 35
    "Airgram" Analysis 38
    Second Contact—Alex Constantine 41
    Third Contact—Michael Marr 49
    Conclusions 50

Chapter Two
William Herman Jackson and
the Rest of the Crew at "Jack's Place" 52

    Background on William Herman Jackson 53
    Additional Press Reports 61
    Conclusions 71

Chapter Three
Who Are We? 72

    The Science of Evil 73
    Psychopaths at the Helm 74
    Ponerology in Recent History 80
    The Ponerological Process 81
    Ponerology Comes to the United States 83
    Pathological Personalities, Let's Start at the Top 85
    The Bushes 87
    Alberto R. Gonzales, US Attorney General 90
    Two Lackluster Secretaries of State 93

The Rest of the Pathocracy Players 97
Conclusions 98

Chapter Four
How We Got Here—a Short History of the International Drug Trade 100

The Portuguese 102
The Dutch 102
The British 102
The French...104
Here Comes the Americans-Vietnam Was First 105

Chapter Five
The CIA, War, and Drugs in Southeast Asia 110

Witness Number 1: DEA Agent Mike Levine.............................113
Witness Number 2: Captain Jeffery MacDonald 114
Witness Number 3: Dois "Chip" Tatum....................................115
Actor in the Heart of Darkness Play: L. Fletcher Prouty 117
Letter of the Month October 1996..118
Actor in the Heart of Darkness Play:
    Paul Lional Edward Helliwell 132
Actor in the Heart of Darkness Play:
    Major General Edward Geary Lansdale 134
Actor in the Heart of Darkness Play: Theodore Shackley............136
Actor in the Heart of Darkness Play: Richard L. Armitage..........144
Actor in the Heart of Darkness Play: David Sanchez Morales 145
Actor in the Heart of Darkness Play: Richard V. Secord.............147
Conclusions and Reflections..148

Chapter Six
The JFK Assassination 149

JFK's Plans to Withdraw from Southeast Asia 150
The War and Drugs...151
John Fitzgerald Kennedy's Place in World History....................152
The Cover-up Primer 155
Who Had the Motive?...157

The Trial of Clay Shaw 159
Possible or Likely? 164
Oswald as the "Patsy" 165
So Who "Done" It? 168
Who Confessed Involvement,
   Had Firsthand Knowledge, or "Talked"? 173
Joseph Milteer 174
Army Private Eugene B. Dinkin 176
Robert Wilfred Easterling 182
Rose Cheramie 185
"Grassy Knoll" Witness Gordon Arnold 187
Lyndon Baines Johnson, Scandals, and Confessions 190
LBJ's Confession 194
Marita Lorenz and Operation 40 197
Operation 40 199
Cuba and the Drug Trade 204
Other Anti-Castro and Assassination Groups 205
Sylvia Odio 210
More Than One Oswald? 211
ZR/RIFLE 213

Chapter Seven
A Likely JFK Assassination Scenario 222

LBJ's Role 226
Hoover's Role 228
Richard Helms and the CIA 231
The Media 233
Organized Crime 236
William Harvey's Role 243
James Jesus Angleton 245
The Assassination Plot Goes Into Action 248

Chapter Eight
The JFK Assassination—Democracy to Pathocracy 259

JFK and Narcissism 259
Reflections on Greatness 262
Operation Northwoods 265

Domestic Achievements and More Enemies 266
Definition of Pathocracy 270
JFK—Cold Warrior to Peace Ambassador 273

Chapter Nine
The Age of Fanaticism: Jamestown to World War I 277

Racism 282
Militarism 287
Genocide...292
The Presidents...301
American Holocaust..306
The Civil War 317
William Tecumseh Sherman 321
Calvinism and Puritanism 326
Manifest Destiny Past Western Shores 329
Woodrow Wilson 336
The Anglo-American Empire 339
Conclusions 352

Chapter Ten
The Age of Greed: World War I to the
John F. Kennedy Assassination 361

Enemies in Battle, Friends Everywhere Else 361
Anglo-American Corporations 363
Fascism and America 367
Fascism in the Aftermath of World War II 384
Nazis Among Us 389
Ends Justify the Means—Allen Dulles Personified...................396
The Rockefellers, Greed Personified 398
The Foundations 402
The Carnegie Institution and Eugenics 413
Hidden History...420
Reflections 424

Afterword..427
Acknowledgements...439
Index 441

Foreword

Today, most Americans seem to know that things are not as they should be. It is becoming more and more evident that there is "trouble in paradise" so to speak. Liberals and conservatives, whatever those terms mean these days, both seem to agree that the Constitution is in shreds. Further, we have families sending their children to college and the end result is that they graduate but cannot find a decent job. Add to this that many owe so much in student loans that they are often worse off for having gone to college in the first place. Inability to pay back student loans is now the number one reason for loan default. Further, the richest country in the world cannot afford decent health care for its people. Something like 40 million Americans are without health care. The cost of medical treatment is the main reason for bankruptcy. Cubans are now living longer that Americans and have a much lower infant mortality rate. Cuba is a poor country. We now have a government that is telling us that we cannot afford Social Security and Medicare benefits, at least not like we have had in the past. If this is the richest country in the world then where is the money going? How is it possible that we cannot afford what much poorer countries are able to afford?

And why is it that every country that we "liberate" ends up in far worse shape than before we got so interested in their welfare? Iraq was and is a total disaster, and it turns out that there was no justification what-so-ever for the US invasion of a country that had done absolutely nothing against us. Add to this that Iraq was far from the first country to have been invaded and occupied "for its own good" and certainly will not be the last. Something is wrong here, and it is becoming more and more evident to more and more people.

The author's first exposure to the idea that America might not be what it purports to be occurred in Vietnam. Even at the age of twenty there were things happening that seemed out of place. Ostensibly we were there fighting to "contain communism" and as our president at the time Lyndon Baines Johnson stated we were there for the "self-determination of the Vietnamese people." Lofty goals, but the facts on the ground were much different. It did not look like anyone was being freed in Vietnam, including us. The appearance was that all Vietnamese were considered the enemy. The author also saw rampant corruption. Many, many, Americans and Vietnamese were involved in black market activities, selling military exchange goods for profit and just about anything else they could get their hands on. What was this war really about? No one seemed to be talking about winning other that the likes of Secretary of Defense Robert McNamara and he did not seem very convincing. Most of the conversations among the troops were about surviving and getting back to the "world" in one piece. Everyone knew that the war was not going to end on your tour anyway. We did, however, know who was getting rich off the war and it was not us. Even at a young age it looked to us like "endless war for endless profit," and we, the young GIs were the losers.

There were also the obvious questions about the Air America transport planes flying all over the place. "What was Air America and what were they doing there?" was the obvious question, which was answered by the old-timers with, "Well, that's the CIA's airline." "Well, what are they carrying?" was the next question. "Prostitutes, drugs, weapons . . ." came the reply. "Why does an intelligence agency need to transport anything, much less stuff that anyone else would go to jail for?" was the next obvious question. "Don't know . . ." would usually be the reply, followed with "It just beez that way . . ." or some variation thereof. These were only some of the imponderables that existed then and still have not been answered to this day, at least not by the power structure anyway.

These questions still haunt the post war baby-boom generation, along with many others. Why were most of the anti-war, anti-racism moral leaders of America assassinated during the 60's? Is America really "spreading democracy" and freedom around the world? Why is America the biggest user of illegal drugs? Why does America lead the world in violence and incarceration? And the list could go on . . . Over and over again what we say we stand for is in marked contrast to what we do.

There are many great things about the United States of America, but there are also many not so great things. Most of us know the good, but the bad is not so well understood. It has been hidden from us. This book is about the hidden dark side of America. It looks at what America actually does and not what it says that it does. It explores the "why" of the ugliness that is not in your average history book. It is not a pretty story. It is, however, what the author believes every American needs know if we are to steer an effective course in the challenging days ahead.

The author is writing this the day following the November 6th, 2012 election results, and has mixed feelings. One is a sense of profound relief that voter suppression and massive corporate spending could not sway the election. The Republican platform and the candidates were a real threat to the survival of mankind and the planet. Their positions on myriad issues were frankly, outlandish. The fact that over sixty percent of White America voted for and supported the reactionary agenda put forth by the Republicans is sobering.

But it was deeply inspiring that a majority of the American people would not allow the above reactionaries to steal and buy the presidency. To see New Yorkers standing in lines for many hours in the freezing cold was inspirational. It was also inspirational to see one state in the Deep South vote for a Black president. These examples give us hope and not just a little hope at that. Also uplifting was the fact that even in a bad economy most voters were concerned with more abstract issues and did not just want to just roll the dice. The economy was a major factor in making the Carter and the George H. W. Bush administrations one-term. This time America recognized that values and principles matter. This author is very proud of the American people.

Having said that it also is evident that we are, again, at an important point where we are struggling with what direction we want the country to go. It has become clear to this writer that the choice is now and has been in the past a choice between a democratic republic and a pathological empire. It is also clear that we are not the first people to be in this situation. From ancient Rome on, this has been the dilemma. As in the past we cannot have it both ways, for the above two options are mutually exclusive. A republic is commonly accepted as a system of government whereas the power is derived from the people and not from an elite ruling class. This is codified in the U.S. Constitution.

An empire is a different matter, and the best definition this writer has found was put forth by John Perkins in his book, *The Secret History of the American Empire: The Truth About Economic Hit Men, Jackals, and How to Change the World*. Perkins came up with what college students on several campuses had put forth during his book tours which he compiled into common elements as stated below:

> **Empire**. Nation-state that dominates other nation-states and exhibits one or more of the following characteristics: 1) exploits resources from the lands it dominates, 2) consumes large quantities of resources—amounts that are disproportionate to the size of its population relative to those of other nations, 3) maintains a large military that enforces its policies when more subtle measures fail, 4) spreads its language, literature, art, and various aspects of its culture throughout its sphere of influence, 5) taxes not just its own citizens, but also people in other countries, and 6) imposes its own currency on the lands under its control.

Renews your faith in college students, doesn't it? "One or more of the above characteristics would qualify us as an empire?" Why, we just hit an empire grand-slam home run! With the exception of, arguably, "taxes people in other countries," we clearly are guilty of all of the above, and even that one hold-out could be debated. For example, any oil rich country that refuses to trade in U.S. dollars, which are devaluating at a steady rate, gets invaded. Iraq and Libya are the most recent examples. The constant devaluation could be considered a tax. That aside, the U.S. is clearly, and has been for quite a while, an empire.

Now we are able to see how a republic and an empire cannot coexist. In order to create and maintain a military force large and powerful enough to exploit more and more resources, further and further away, the basic needs of the people have to be deprived. Resources that need to go into infrastructure, education, and healthcare in order to maintain a strong, vibrant society have to be diverted to the increasing use of force needed to subjugate peoples in foreign lands. There is no end to it and eventually it collapses of its own weight. It has happened over and over again and this is exactly where we are at right now. We have to choose one or the other but we cannot have both.

The Republican party would have been the choice America would have made had we wanted to continue with an empire. At this time the United States is spending more on "defense" than the rest or the world put together, and even this picture has been parsed. For example, spending for the nation's nuclear arsenal comes mostly under the Department of Energy and not the Department of Defense. When the money shell-game is deciphered the figures are staggering. The U.S., in real terms, is spending the majority, that is slightly more than fifty percent, of the treasury on "defense," and the republicans want to spend even more. We now have the capacity to destroy life on earth as we know it hundreds of times over, and we need more? And the most preposterous thing about it is that the resulting huge deficit that has been accrued is being blamed on Medicare, Social Security, welfare, food stamps, you name it, when in reality all of these together are a tiny sliver compared to defense spending. The American people are starting to wise up to this, and good on us! When one puts one's life savings into a dream house, works for ten, twenty years to get it, and then loses it, this is what is referred to as an "attention-getter."

So America rejected the empire scenario in favor of voting for a republic, right? Well, it's not that easy. The democrats want to make you think you can have it both ways, that is an empire *and* a republic which will not work either, as we have just discussed. This also is not new. America was at cross-roads once before and actually not very long ago. Post WW-II, President Eisenhower warned in his farewell address of the growing power of the "Military Industrial Complex" that he cautioned threatened the very foundations of the republic and democracy. He left it to his successor to deal with this. His successor, John F. Kennedy, did deal with it and as we shall see, got his head blown off, and the hyper-military state continued to sail on its course of self destruction. The realistic and workable new direction laid out by John F. Kennedy could have set the example on how to manage human and environmental resources toward a vision that had been defined by the founders of the republic a little less than two hundred years ago.

Of course we know that this was not to be, and he was removed from office with "extreme prejudice." His successor, Lyndon Baines Johnson, tried very hard to have an empire and a republic which resulted in the failure of both. Having served only one elected term, Johnson died a broken man. His successor, Richard Nixon, thought he had the formula right, but he also failed and was removed from office

his second term. He also died a disgraced and broken man, and the man who replaced him, Gerald Ford, also a proponent of the arms and defense industries, assumed the Presidency but could only get elected once. Jimmy Carter was next, and he tried also to have it both ways resulting in another one-term presidency. Next, Ronald Reagan went for empire and spent more money, borrowed from our future, than anyone in recent history and possibly more than anyone before him. All he did was prolong the inevitable. George H. W. Bush was next and continued in Reagan's footsteps, but the checks Reagan had written started to come due. The economy failed miserably and he also was a one-term president. William Jefferson Clinton probably did the best at trying to juggle empire and a democratic republic but did not quite get there. He did nothing about defense spending and cut social service drastically which got him through two terms but the republic vs. empire dilemma remained. Basically he treaded water for eight years.

Then came George W. Bush and we had the most insane squandering of resources on militarism imaginable. Add to this that his administration spent money it did not have. Deficit spending during his administration made Reagan look like penny-pincher. He broke the bank and further squandered America's future on dominating the oil rich Middle East. Add to this his all out frontal assault on human rights and the Constitution and we are left with an America that is now both financially and morally bankrupt. America cannot recover from this trail of destruction since WW-II which reached a crescendo during the last Bush administration. The score sheet is not in yet on the Obama administration but it looks like he is also trying to have it both ways, a la Clinton. Of course this is not going to work.

How did it come to this? Where did all of this militarism come from and how did "life, liberty, and the pursuit of happiness" become war, racism, and genocide? How we came to the critical point in the Kennedy administration where the United States needed endless enemies and endless spending to defeat them, while having to deprive our citizenry of basic human needs is the subject of this book. The fact that a president actually had to be murdered to stay on this increasingly destructive course is the reality that has to be exposed. Other authors have explored this subject, but none to this writer's knowledge have gone all the way back to the very beginning, back to the little colony at Jamestown in 1607, identified the seeds of destruction in its very foundation, and traced it to the post WW-II dilemma that John F. Kennedy faced. General Douglas MacArthur once told J.F.K. that "Some of Eisenhower's chickens are coming home to roost, and you (Kennedy) are in the chicken coup." Seems that President Eisenhower was an active player in the same "military industrial complex" that he whimpered about during the last days of his administration.

To tell this story the author needed to tell his story about how he became aware that there was something seriously wrong in the "land of the free." This began with a bizarre case of drug smuggling that took place toward the end of the Vietnam War. The author "fell down the rabbit hole," so to speak, in what is sometimes referred to as the "Body Bag Case." As outlandish as it may seem, there was an investigation into smuggling heroin using the bodies of GIs out of Vietnam. The case happened in December, 1972 and was widely reported throughout the US Media. The prosecutors in the case issued many press releases detailing the case and giving specifics on how the smuggling was done and by whom. For whatever reasons, however, no one was charged or prosecuted for smuggling drugs using human remains. This case and others did, however, expose the fact that enormous amounts of heroin were coming into the US through military channels, perhaps most of it.

To insure that the reader is not overly skeptical that something as bizarre as this might have happened even if the individuals that were accused of it were not involved, this author will take the unusual step of front-loading some information about this. Award winning investigative journalist Jonathan Kwitny, front page editor for the *Wall Street Journal* for much of the 1980's, wrote several excellent investigative non-fiction books. One of these books was *The Crimes of Patriots: A True Tale of Dope, Dirty Money, and the CIA*, in which Kwitny went into some detail about heroin smuggling out of Vietnam using the bodies of G.I.'s, which is quoted below from page 52 of the above book.

> Another former officer from the army's Criminal Investigation Division recalls a mammoth heroin scheme he and his colleagues investigating corruption in the sale of supplies to commissioned—and noncommissioned—officers' clubs. The corrupt U.S. and Vietnamese officers they caught tried to bargain away jail terms by describing the heroin

traffic involving Vietnamese politicians and senior U.S. officers. The reports checked out, the investigator says.

The investigator, now a stockbroker, says that his investigation group filed reports to the Pentagon revealing that G.I. bodies being flown back to the United States were cut open, gutted, and filled with heroin. Witnesses were prepared to testify that the heroin-stuffed soldiers bore coded body numbers, allowing conspiring officers on the other end, at Norton Air Force Base in California, to remove the booty—up to fifty pounds of heroin per dead G.I.

The Army acted on these reports—not by coming down on the dope traffickers, but by disbanding the investigative team and sending them to combat duty, the former investigator says. Other reports corroborate the use of G.I. bodies to ship dope back to the United States via military channels.

The late Jonathan Kwitny spent his entire life in the profession of journalism, and he was well aware of the need for validity of the story and the reliability of sources. This author has to seriously consider Kwitny's comments and the possibility that they contained some basis in fact, and that he also must have had good reasons for not identifying his sources. In the case outlined in this author's chapter one, no one was convicted or charged of anything having to do with heroin and bodies; however, it is a matter of record that there was an investigation into this and that evidence disappeared out of official government channels. Further, the author's supervisor, at Kadena Air Force Base, Okinawa, had briefed him that "a whole shipment of bodies had been discovered that had been gutted and stuffed with heroin." That said, it was apparent that this sordid episode was not fully investigated, and certainly not publicly reported. The possibility does exist that a shipment of bodies with heroin in them *did* arrive at Kadena Air Base, Japan, in December of 1972, but that the individuals indentified as couriers for the bodies had nothing to do with it. By their own admission they were smuggling heroin, and quite a bit it, but they have stated that they had it in bags with false bottoms and had nothing to do with bodies. It was clear, however, that something had happened involving organized criminals from within or associated with agencies of the U.S. Government. This certainly was not the work of relatively low ranking enlisted personnel of the military services. It had to have been high ranking personnel in the military, Department of Defense, or even higher.

Although the above mentioned investigation did not yield solid evidence that smuggling heroin using bodies actually happened, it was evident someone was hiding something; that is for sure. There is a mountain of evidence that a lot of heroin and other drugs were coming into the U.S. on government owned and controlled aircraft. The possibility exists that a thorough investigation into the "body bag case" would have negated this premise but exposed other just as explosive alternatives. Tons of heroin coming into the country on U.S. military aircraft is bound to make someone look really bad, and that "someone" would not be low ranking enlisted personnel, for sure. The possibility also exists that the individuals suspected of smuggling heroin in bodies had inadvertently crossed paths with an unrelated criminal operation that was actually doing this. Whatever happened appeared to have been suppressed. There were no public disclosures either confirming or denying this explosive subject.

This left the author with life long, lingering questions. There were two suspects in the above case, and the logical questions that should have come to the forefront of investigative agencies would have been who were they, who were they connected to, where did the heroin come from, where was it going, and how was it getting there? Investigators call these the "five "W's." Well, the five W's never happened in this case, so in chapter two we take a "five W's" approach to this heroin smuggling situation. This lead to a bar in Bangkok, Thailand, sometimes called "Jack's place," and although the author found no evidence that anyone at that bar had anything to do with bodies they certainly moved a lot of heroin out of that location. Over roughly a ten-year period the fellas at Jack's Place moved tons of over eighty percent pure heroin worth many billions of dollars through military channels to the United States. As we shall see, the FBI, CIA, and other law enforcement organizations knew of them, and it is inconceivable that these organizations did not know about the heroin trade as well. The fact that the author was able to find messages, the subject of which were activities at Jack's Place, that went directly from the FBI director to the CIA director tells us that this was not a low level criminal operation. This author concludes that these agencies were at the very least complicit in this, while ostensibly fighting a ferocious "war on drugs."

In researching how drugs come into the United States the author found drugs linked to the Vietnam war and also to government agencies that promote and support wars. Further, there were also large corporations linked to the illegal drug trade. The further this writer dug into these connections the more the pieces to a very ugly picture started to come into focus, and the people who really called the shots from the top were not the so-called "drug lords" that we see pictures of in the news. Invariably the captured or killed drug lords ended up to be thugs that had lost their power and so had outlived their usefulness to the real power structure that needed the enormous profits that illegal drugs can produce. What corporate America needs these profits for is to boost the bottom lines of their companies, make their stocks appear more desirable, and so forth. Government agencies use and have used drug money to overthrow governments that they deem "unfriendly" to the United States, pay for assassinations, and other illegal "black operations" that are classified because they are illegal under US and international law. Drug money is off the books and the perfect way to pay for illegal activities that you do not want to pay for with traceable money. Add to this the fact that what is a private corporation and what is a government agency tends to get a little fuzzy at times, and so we now have what some call the "corporate-government" fueled by drug money to support an ever expanding empire.

Without drug money the empire collapses, and this has been true throughout history. The subject of pathological personalities that have invariably ended up running empires throughout history is explored in chapter three, and the history of the connection of drugs to empire is covered in chapter four. The mechanics of how war, drugs, militarism, racism, and genocide came together in building the American empire is explored in chapter five. In chapters six, seven, and eight we see how John F. Kennedy stood in the way of all of these factors and therefore had to be eliminated. Along with the question of why, we also cover the rest of the "five W's" in chapters six, seven, and eight.

In the last two chapters we explore how a people presumably in search of freedom ended up creating possibly the most murderous and oppressive empire in history. To do this we go all the way back to the very beginning and that would be Jamestown in 1607. As we shall see the seeds of destruction were sown in the foundation of the republic from the very beginning, and we will trace not only the growth of the empire but also the growth of the destructive forces that have come to fruition in modern times. From that little colony in Jamestown to the Revolutionary War and on to the Civil War and through both World Wars I and II, the country had an unalterable course toward genocide against mostly Native Americans, racism toward mostly African Americans, and militarism to project these two objectives from sea to shining sea and beyond. John F. Kennedy was also squarely in the way of these unmentioned but powerfully driven forces on the dark side of America.

The last chapter will discuss the rise of US industrial might and the concentration of power that ended up in the hands of a few. The hands of the power elite became especially dirty around the turn of the 19th to the 20th century manifesting itself into what was referred to as the "eugenics movement." Supported and fostered by known and respected names such as Carnegie and Rockefeller, this movement stated that its goal was to create a "master race" by eliminating the most undesirable ten percent of Americans to begin with and keep doing this until all undesirable "germ plasm" in the country had been eliminated. This idea caught on with a guy over the Atlantic ocean named Adolph Hitler. The rest is history, but the fact that the origins of the Holocaust sprang forth from "the land of the free" certainly has not been very well publicized. Further, it is not well known that the titans of US industry were avid supporters of the Nazis.

Another imponderable was the massive post war effort to bring thousands of the worst war criminals the world has ever seen into the United States and South America. Not only bring them here but put them in charge of massive government, medical, and educational programs. This is almost beyond belief, and we are still dealing with the effects of this today, as we shall see.

Along the way we try to understand the why of all of this. The answers will shake the foundations of the reader's belief systems, and this is a good thing. It is time we looked at ourselves and asked the hard questions. What is the American dream, and are we headed in that direction? National leaders do not even speak in these terms anymore. Another idea to ponder is the fact that even in the recent past this nation led the world in many wonderful things. Polio was virtually eliminated in the United States and this was shared with the rest of world. In what areas do we lead the world today?

Whether conservative or liberal that list is likely to contain at least some of the following: incarceration, military spending, drug use, depression, suicide, murder, international violations of human rights, invading sovereign nations, and the list goes on . . . Is this the legacy that we want to share? The author does not think so. What to do about it will be the subject of the author's next books, but in this one we will get a clear picture of a people with some wonderful goals but got lost along the way. We will end at the assassination of John F. Kennedy which is seen by most Americans today as a coup. In fact some surveys show that over eighty percent of Americans do not believe the government's account of what happened in Dallas on the 22nd of November, 1963.

In writing this, it is the author's firm belief that given the facts the American people have it within their power to not tolerate what has happened in the past. We cannot afford it any longer. The first step is to become aware of our hidden past, and reading this book is an excellent beginning.

The Author

Chapter One

The Body Bag Case

Over forty years have passed since I researched the logistics portion of an investigation into heroin smuggling into the US. What made this case unique was that the smugglers were suspected of using the corpses of US military deceased out of Southeast Asia. Yes, there was an investigation into this, late in 1972. This incident would profoundly change my fundamental belief systems, and since then, I have been looking for and compiling information that would explain the whole picture. This case leads to some shocking realities that are almost beyond belief. First, let us take a look at what happened.

The Case

I was an air transportation supervisor in December of 1972, stationed at Kadena Air Base, Okinawa, Japan. My position was noncommissioned officer in charge, flight data records processing. I was a staff sergeant in the air force assigned to the 603rd Military Airlift Support Squadron. During that month, we had an air force C-5 come in from U-Tapao, Thailand, that was only scheduled for a few hours servicing, and then on to Travis Air Force Base, California. This plane contained a number of transfer cases containing human remains presumably killed in action, KIA, out of Vietnam. Although some of our personnel told me that it was a large number of human remains, I do not recall the exact number. When it arrived, the plane had a maintenance problem, and our aircraft maintenance personnel had to order parts that would take over twenty-four hours to receive.

On in-transit aircraft, Japanese customs normally did not get involved unless the plane was on the ground more than twenty-four hours, which was the case with this C-5. After the plane was fixed, our personnel noticed that the two couriers for the human remains could not be located. This was highly unusual. Actually, it was unusual for a shipment of human remains to even have escorts. I had never seen a shipment of bodies with escorts or couriers or anything of that sort. The only time you would see this was when a military person from the deceased's outfit was escorting a body back to the USA for a funeral and internment. These escorts were code-named Blue Bark. This was not the case in this incident.

These two couriers were nowhere to be found. As I recall, one of the couriers was an army captain, and his name could have been Beaudreau or something similar to that, although I could be off on both the name and the rank. I do recall that this person was a commissioned officer. The other was an army master sergeant, and his name was Thomas Edward Southerland. I am sure of this name because it was not only the name I remembered over forty years later but was also the name cited in a *Time* magazine article published January 1, 1973, about this incident. I did not know that this article existed until I was researching this incident over thirty years later and found it in the *Time* magazine archives.

Our people started looking for these two army personnel and notified Japanese customs that something was very suspicious. Our passenger service, terminal reservations personnel discovered that Master Sergeant Southerland had taken a flight off the island of Okinawa, using his travel orders, and had gone to Hickam Air Force Base, Hawaii. From there, he had apparently caught a KC-135 to the continental United States. We found no trace of what happened to the captain.

I was told by my immediate supervisor that Japanese customs opened the transfer cases and found that the bodies had had their internal organs removed and that they were stuffed with bags of pure heroin. I was not a witness to this, so I do not have firsthand information as far as how many of the bodies had been prepared this way. An Air Force Office of Special Investigations (OSI) agent contacted me and told me "not to release any documents pertaining to the incident to anyone but him." One of my responsibilities was for processing and storage of all cargo and passenger documentation.

He told me that he would let me know when he needed the documentation at a later date. I passed this info on to our people working the night shift. That night, an army investigator from Criminal Investigations Division (CID) came to the records section and demanded these records. Our personnel refused to give them to him. He then threatened to put our personnel in jail for obstructing an investigation and so forth. The shift supervisor again refused to give him the records, and eventually he went away. The next day, this supervisor described to me that the CID agent was very belligerent, demanding, and threatening. At the time, I thought what was happening was a case of interservice rivalry of two investigating bodies, namely army CID and Air Force OSI. I now believe there might have been more to it. From information that I have gained since this incident, I believe that this was likely a case of Army CID trying to tamper with evidence. Later, the evidence in this case did disappear and is missing to this day.

The next day or so, the same OSI agent came to my office, identified himself, and explained the case he was working on in some detail. I knew this OSI agent because I had researched several other cases of drug smuggling on military aircraft for him. He always operated in the above fashion. I did not ask him questions other than what I needed to know in order to do whatever it was he was asking me to do. Although this case piqued my interest, I resisted asking too many questions that might cause him to wonder why I was so curious. There is something about military service that causes you to think and act like this on an official level. Military people tend to get suspicious when you pepper them with questions. Besides, I usually found out more by just listening anyway. People like to talk and about how much they know. The less you talk, the more others are inclined to do so.

He had me get all the travel documentation out pertaining to this case, and we went over these documents. These documents included travel orders, Transportation Control and Movement Documents (TCMDs), and aircraft manifests. The OSI agent and I went over the meaning and significance of every code in these documents pertaining to the case. There was no question that whoever prepared these documents were military logistics personnel; my guess would be Air Force Specialty Code (AFSC) 60571 (air transportation supervisor) or a related career field.

Whoever it was knew every code and every nuance of military logistics. For example, Transportation Control and Movement Documents (TCMDs) contain codes that identify who are shipping, receiving, and paying for the shipment. The same is also true of travel orders on passengers. I had done a lot of research into questionable travel, fraudulent travel, and also drug smuggling cases. This area was a big part of my job, and it did not take me long to identify cases where a cargo shipment or passenger travel was other than what it was supposed to be. After a while, it just jumps out at you.

Every document and every code in these documents was perfect. There were no mistakes and nothing suspicious at all. The only thing suspicious was the fact that there were couriers with a shipment of human remains, and also the fact that these couriers left the shipment. Our personnel believed that if these couriers had stayed with the shipment, no one would have ever been the wiser. Further, it was felt that these "couriers" panicked when they realized that Japanese Customs might find the drugs, investigate the case, and prosecute them under Japanese law. The Japanese have very harsh penalties for drugs, and it is likely that they knew they probably could not influence or control the legal system. They could and did influence the US legal system, as we shall see.

Another possibility put forth by the eventual prosecutor in this case, Michael Marr, was that Southerland went to Hickam Air Force Base, Hawaii, because it might have been a transshipment point, sometimes referred to as a hub, where he picked up another "shipment" and continued on to the Continental US.

After the OSI agent and I spent several hours going over these documents, he again told me to lock them up and not give them to anyone but him. As I recall, he took notes of what we talked about, but he did not ask for or take copies of these documents with him. He did take with him computer-generated copies of the information contained in the flight folders that we had reviewed. The agent asked for the file copies a week or two later.

Master Sergeant Southerland, or the individual traveling as Master Sergeant Southerland, was apprehended at Andrews Air Force Base, Maryland, a few days later and was charged with several offenses. It is noteworthy that the above investigation commenced *before* Southerland was apprehended and, therefore, could not have been initiated by information received during or subsequent to his arrest.

There was a very interesting article connected to the above that appeared in *Time* magazine, January 1, 1973. *Time* still has this article in their archives. In the "CRIME" section under the heading "Coffins and Corruptions," *Time* explained what was suspected to have happened on the last leg of Southerland's trip that started in Thailand, went through Okinawa and Hawaii, and was headed for Dover Air Force Base, Delaware. Based on informant information received by federal authorities The air force KC-135 with a total of 64 passengers and two coffins was diverted to Andrews Air Force Base, Maryland. Apparently authorities were looking for 20 kilos of heroin which they did not find. What they said they did find was that one of the bodies had been recently restitched. Authorities concluded that heroin had been stitched into the abdomen and that it had been removed in Hawaii. This information had been obtained from Assistant U.S. Attorney Michael E. Marr. Federal authorities could only charge Southerland with impersonating an army sergeant and using fake military documents to travel on military aircraft.

The article also stated that federal authorities suspected that Southerland was a part of an international drug ring that had been operating for eight years smuggling millions of dollars worth of heroin into the U.S. They further indicated that using G.I. cadavers was the primary method this group used to do this. Authorities also estimated that this ring was buying heroin at $1,700 a kilo and reselling it for as much as $250,000. The article ended with assurances that there were full-scale investigations going on in the U.S. and Southeast Asia. It is noteworthy that we shall see these same assurances that also came from the Department of State about this very same drug ring, and that was the last anyone would hear about it. As far as this author could tell neither *Time* nor the Department of State publicly commented on the results of these follow up investigations in any way shape or form. Nothing more was said about it.

Also in the crime section was another article that was titled "Missing Evidence." There was a famous case that occurred in New York which was the basis for the movie *The French Connection,* and apparently all of the heroin that was taken from a major supplier was stored by the New York City Police Department. Evidently almost all of the heroin disappeared from the evidence locker, and no one seemed to know what happened to it. We will be discussing the French Connection incident further, but for now it is interesting to note that this affair had been hyped as an enormous amount of heroin when the totality of it was only a few hundred pounds. This was a small fraction of what was coming into the U.S. at that time, but if one watched the movie, *The French Connection,* one would think that a major portion of the drug trade had been shut down. Not only was it not shut down but the little bit of heroin confiscated ended up back on the streets anyway. These two articles and virtually all of the reporting done in the U.S. lead one to conclude that illegal drugs have been coming into the U.S. only as a result of the actions of organized crime, rogue elements of the military and law enforcement, drug cartels, and many small groups of amateurs. This is the subject that we shall explore further.

Comparing the information in this article to what was alleged to have happened in Okinawa, Japan, over forty years ago one has to ask the following questions:

How did Southerland get from Kadena Air Force Base, Okinawa, Japan, to Andrews Air Force Base, Maryland? The one stop at Hickam Air Force Base, Hawaii, is known, but we do not know where he went and stopped from there.

If the above article is accurate, where did he allegedly get the two bodies? Did he take them from the ones he was escorting that arrived on the C-5 in Okinawa, or did he pick them up at Hickam?

Where was the heroin allegedly removed from the body?

Although the flight originated in Thailand, were the bodies out of Vietnam? If so, how did they get to Thailand? Is it possible that wounded in action out of Vietnam were treated in military hospitals in Thailand and died there? Another possibility is that the bodies came out of Vietnam, stayed over twenty-four hours in U-Tapao, and picked up a new mission number showing the flight as originating from U-Tapao, Thailand.

Southerland was tried in federal court in Baltimore, Maryland a few weeks or perhaps months later. A captain from our organization, the 603rd Military Airlift Support Squadron, testified at the trial. The OSI agent in Okinawa came to me before the trial and signed for all related documentation (orders, aircraft manifest, etc.). He informed me that he sent them via US registered mail, signature service required, to the federal prosecutor in Maryland.

The evidence never got to the court. It disappeared out of US mail! I know this because I was concerned that the records needed to be returned to the files, and I inquired about them on a regular basis. The OSI agent eventually told me that the records had disappeared, and he signed a statement that they were missing and could not be returned. I put this statement in the files. He also told me that Southerland was convicted of only charges relating to unauthorized wear of a US military uniform and unauthorized travel on military aircraft. None of the other charges were proven because of lack of evidence. He further stated that neither Southerland nor the captain with him had ever been in the army.

I might add that this OSI agent seemed to have this casual smile and also a knowing demeanor about him that I had never seen in him before. I had seen him pursue an investigation of a few thousand dollars worth of stolen watches to the ends of the earth. In that case, he went as far as even recalling people back to active duty that had left the service and courts marshaling them. Now he seemingly gets a case that is "magnitude ten" on the Richter scale, the evidence disappears, and he has this casual, whimsical smile on his face. I did not know what to make of this then and do not know what to make of it now, over forty years later.

Analysis

This author spent many years wondering and thinking about this case. Of course there was "scuttlebutt" about this all throughout the outfit, and even now one ponders about what information received was absolutely accurate. This writer's memory is not absolutely accurate and has faded some over the more than forty years since this happened. One forgets things over that period of time. Add to this the likelihood that some of the information reported at the time also was not precise or could have been exaggerated or understated.

However, it is an absolute certainty that an investigation took place into heroin smuggling using the bodies of US servicemen at Kadena Air Base, Japan, on or about the above date. It is also certain that a man named Southerland impersonated a US serviceman and was involved in the incident. This writer was not privy to the results of this investigation, and it appears that the investigation was not pursued to the extent that it could have or should have been. Why the disappearance of evidence was not the subject of an intense investigation is a question this writer cannot answer. What were the results of the investigation into the use of human remains to transport heroin at Kadena Air Base, Japan? These are questions that need to be answered, even today.

The noncommissioned officer in charge of the branch mentioned that we were all whispering when we talked about this as if we should not be discussing it. I must admit that it was eerie. Who could have the power and connections to do something like this? And if true, who would use the bodies of these poor unfortunate young GIs like this? Anyone even remotely associated with this would have to be someone with no sense of remorse or guilt whatsoever. After I came back to the US, I did not talk about this much for fear that people would doubt my credibility. It was so bizarre that it was almost unbelievable even for me, but the questions continued to gnaw at me.

It also occurred to me that millions of dollars of heroin being removed from bodies at Hickam Air Force Base would not be as easy as the *Time* article stated. You just cannot go out on a flight line or into a warehouse and do that. It is possible that Hickam was being used as a hub or a transshipment point, but I do not believe it is probable that the drugs were removed from the bodies at Hickam unless the smugglers had co-conspirators stationed there.

Even at the age of twenty-five, my intuition told me that this was not the work of some Sicilian with a big moustache. That the Mafia or even a small group operating within the military, or government, could do something like this just did not add up. All the details carried the marks of people who knew exactly what they were doing, and the connections that these people had to have had were obviously extensive. This had to be an inside job at least involving military law enforcement and quite conceivably people in high places. Powerful and influential people and institutions had to have been at least complicit in the scheme.

The First Contact—Michael Levine[1]

I kept this incident in the back of my mind and continued to look for any information that would make sense out of this. When the Internet came up, I began searching, but I did not find much. A few years ago, I found the following article on Fred Burk's web site, www.wanttoknow.info.[2]

Michael Levine is a twenty-five-year veteran of the DEA turned best-selling author and journalist. His articles and interviews on the drug war have been published in numerous national newspapers and magazines, including the *New York Times*, *Los Angeles Times*, *USA Today*, and *Esquire*.

When President Nixon first declared war on drugs in 1971, there were fewer than five hundred thousand hard-core addicts in the entire nation, most of whom were addicted to heroin. Three decades later, despite the expenditure of $1 trillion in tax dollars, the number of hard-core addicts is shortly expected to exceed five million. Our nation has become the supermarket of the drug world, with a wider variety and bigger supply of drugs at cheaper prices than ever before. The problem now not only affects every town and hamlet on the map, but it is difficult to find a family anywhere that is not somehow affected (pp. 158-159).

---

1. Photo courtesy of *The Expert Witness Radio Show*, http://www.expertwitnessradio.org/about.html
2. This is a condensed version of Michael Levine's testimony in, *Into the Buzzsaw: Leading Journalists Expose the Myth of a Free Press,* by Kristina Borjesson. The references to page numbers correspond to pages in the book.

The Chang Mai factory the CIA prevented me from destroying was the source of massive amounts of heroin being smuggled into the US in the bodies and body bags of GIs killed in Vietnam (p. 165).

My unit, the Hard Narcotics Smuggling Squad, was charged with investigating all heroin and cocaine smuggling through the Port of New York. My unit became involved in investigating every major smuggling operation known to law enforcement. We could not avoid witnessing the CIA protecting major drug dealers. Not a single important source in Southeast Asia was ever indicted by US law enforcement. This was no accident. Case after case was killed by CIA and State Department intervention and there wasn't a damned thing we could do about it. CIA-owned airlines like Air America were being used to ferry drugs throughout Southeast Asia, allegedly to support our "allies." CIA banking operations were used to launder drug money (pp. 165-166).

In 1972, I was assigned to assist in a major international drug case involving top Panamanian government officials who were using diplomatic passports to smuggle large quantities of heroin and other drugs into the US. The name Manuel Noriega surfaced prominently in the investigation. Surfacing right behind Noriega was the CIA to protect him from US law enforcement. As head of the CIA, Bush authorized a salary for Manuel Noriega as a CIA asset while the dictator was listed in as many as forty DEA computer files as a drug dealer (pp. 166-167).

The CIA and the Department of State were protecting more and more politically powerful drug traffickers around the world: the Mujahedeen in Afghanistan, the Bolivian cocaine cartels, the top levels of Mexican government, Nicaraguan Contras, Colombian drug dealers and politicians, and others. Media's duties, as I experienced firsthand, were twofold: first, to keep quiet about the gush of drugs that was allowed to flow unimpeded into the United States; second, to divert the public's attention by shilling them into believing the drug war was legitimate by falsely presenting the few trickles we were permitted to indict as though they were major "victories" when in fact, we were doing nothing more than getting rid of the inefficient competitors of CIA assets (pp. 166-167).

On July 17, 1980, drug traffickers actually took control of a nation. Bolivia at the time [was] the source of virtually 100 percent of the cocaine entering the United States. CIA-recruited mercenaries and drug traffickers unseated Bolivia's democratically elected president, a leftist whom the US government didn't want in power. Immediately after the coup, cocaine production increased massively, until it soon outstripped supply. This was the true beginning of the cocaine and crack "plague" (pp. 167-168).

The CIA along with the State and Justice Departments had to combine forces to protect their drug-dealing assets by destroying a DEA investigation. How do I know? I was the inside source. I sat down at my desk in the American embassy and wrote the kind of letter that I never myself imagined ever writing. I detailed three pages typewritten on official US embassy stationary enough evidence of my charges to feed a wolf pack of investigative journalists. I also expressed my willingness to be a quotable source. I addressed it directly to Strasser and Rohter, care of *Newsweek*. Two sleepless weeks later, I was still sitting in my embassy office staring at the phone. Three weeks later, it rang. It was DEA's internal security. They were calling me to notify me that I was under investigation. I had been falsely accused of everything from black-marketing to having sex with a married female DEA agent. The investigation would wreak havoc with my life for the next four years (pp. 168-171).

In one glaring case, an associate of mine was sent into Honduras to open a DEA office in Tegucigalpa. Within months he had documented as much as fifty tons of cocaine being smuggled into the United States by Honduran military people who were supporting the Contras. This was enough cocaine to fill a third of US demand. What was the DEA's response? They closed the office (p. 175).

Sometime in 1990, US Customs intercepted a ton of cocaine being smuggled through Miami International Airport. A Customs and DEA investigation quickly revealed that the smugglers were the Venezuelan National Guard headed by General Guillen, a CIA "asset" who claimed that he had been operating under CIA orders and protection. The CIA soon admitted that this was true. If the CIA is good at anything, it is the complete control of American mass media. So secure are they in their ability to manipulate the mass media that they even brag about it in their own in-house memos. The *New York Times* had the story almost immediately in 1990 and did not print it until 1993. It finally became news that was "fit to print" when the *Times* learned that *60 Minutes* also had the story and was actually going to run it. The highlight of the *60 Minutes* piece is when the administrator of the DEA, Federal Judge Robert Bonner, tells Mike Wallace, "There is no other way to put it, Mike, [what the CIA did] is *drug smuggling*. It's *illegal* (author's emphasis)" (pp. 188-189).

The fact is—and you can read it yourself in the federal court records—that seven months *before* the attempt to blow up the World Trade Center in 1993, the FBI had a paid informant, Emad Salem, who had infiltrated the bombers and had told the FBI of their plans to blow up the twin towers. Without notifying the NYPD or anyone else, an FBI supervisor "fired" Salem, who was making $500 a week for his work. After the bomb went off, the FBI hired Salem back and paid him $1.5 million to help them track down the bombers. But that's not all the FBI missed. When they finally did catch the actual bomber, Ramzi Yousef (a man trained with CIA funds during the Russia-Afghanistan war), the FBI found information on his personal computer about plans to use hijacked American jetliners as fuel-laden missiles. The FBI ignored this information, too (p. 191).

Learn about Mr. Levine's books and radio show at http://www.expertwitnessradio.info.

I e-mailed Fred that I had some additional information for Mike Levine about heroin smuggled in bodies during Vietnam. I sent him the information I had, and he passed it on. Mike and I talked on the phone, and the information that we both had matched up. In fact, it fit like a glove. Mike and I did an hour on his *Expert Witness* radio program in New York. It was emotional for both of us and, from my point of view, cathartic to know that someone other than myself who was, and is, as shocked and dismayed as I am to realize that there are people high up in our government that are capable of creating the conditions where ghastly deeds such as this can flourish. Mike understood and sensed everything I said, and I also could feel Mike's deep disillusionment. There is no greater sense of betrayal than when someone has developed a deep appreciation for our democratic institutions and is then confronted with the fact that these same institutions have been corrupted by what can only be described as psychopaths.

Reflections

It goes further than that. When we as humans are confronted with information that is threatening to our fundamental belief systems, most of the time we simply disregard it. Psychologists call this "cognitive dissonance." It is just easier to reject inconvenient information, no matter how true it is, than to go to all the trouble to rethink and restructure our belief systems; and it does not matter how smart you are. I know this feeling. This cognitive dissonance has lingered with me for all these years, and even today, I sometimes find it difficult to see things with my mind's eye that are not emotionally safe, but I just cannot leave information alone that I cannot make sense out of. It just bounces around in my head until I figure it out. I just have nowhere to put it, so it just keeps buzzing in my head. I sensed that Mike Levine was also wired like this.

I have found that there are many people like this, but certainly they are not the norm. This book is filled with people that have a keen intellect, uncommon analytical skills, and the character to rise up against injustice. I deeply admire Mike Levine and people like him; they are a special gift to the world. In my search for some of the answers to the body bag case, I have found many people who are a gift to humanity. Their courage is almost beyond belief, and they are rarely rewarded. Actually, they are often criticized, scorned, vilified; and sometimes, even worse things happen to them.

Another barrier to processing threatening information is the fact that you have to come to terms with cold reality. Eventually, you have to face the fact that your "service" to the country was an illusion. You have devoted your life, and sometimes risked it, for something that never existed. Further, that all the Americans that died in Vietnam gave their lives for naught; that the Cold War was a bill-of-goods. Basically, one has to come to terms with the reality that for most of your adult life, you were a chump. Although this is difficult, I would rather be a chump for most of my life than spend my whole existence as one. I sensed that Mike also felt this way.

Finally, when I found Mike Levine, I had found somebody and something that made sense of this case. As farfetched as it would seem, who else could have been behind this hideous crime? The forged documents, US Army impersonators, placement of heroin in bodies and retrieval of them in the States, evidence that disappeared out of US mail, and the list goes on. I disagree with the author of the *Time* magazine article. Having spent many years in logistics, I do not agree that "the grisly logistics are not as difficult as they may appear to be." It is highly unlikely that this was the work of an organized crime syndicate, no matter how sophisticated. Only someone that is able to act under the veil of secrecy and authority could tamper with registered mail and all the other mechanizations involved. Can you imagine someone walking into a mortuary in Saigon, Danang, or anywhere else and saying, "Excuse me, but would you mind if I stuff these bodies with heroin?" No, this was not the Mafia, the Crips, or the Bloods. It had to be the work of a government agency, or agencies, most likely as Mike plainly points out, the CIA. Also as we shall see, the State Department had to be at least complicit in this macabre enterprise.

My mind went back to Vietnam, and some of the things I saw that just did not make sense. I recalled that the CIA had a whole fleet of cargo and passenger airplanes, clearly marked "Air America." Why would an intelligence agency need hundreds of relatively large cargo planes? If they were moving food and passengers and so forth, wouldn't it make more sense for the Air Force to do this? I also recalled that when a town was put off-limits to American military, Air America would fly the bar girls from the off-limits city to one that was on-limits, free of charge. Why would an intelligence agency be doing that?

Before finding Mike, I looked for any official explanation for the questions I had. I found a virtually nothing. That small article in *Time* magazine was all that I was able to find until very recently. Much later, I found out that there were many newspaper articles about this, but the fact remains that all legal actions only resulted in low-level people having been held accountable. This adds credence to Mike Levine's statement that the CIA has virtual control of the media and the courts.

The State Department's Explanation

A few years ago, I found the following Department of State, Congressional testimony, from 1972.[3]

> Foreign Relations, 1969-1976, Volume E-1, Documents on Global Issues, 1969-1972
> Released by the Office of the Historian
>
> DEPARTMENT OF STATE
> AIRGRAM
> TO: All Diplomatic and Consular Posts
> FROM: Department of State
> SUBJECT: Congressional Testimony by Nelson Gross on International Narcotics Control.
>
> Attached for your information is the text of a statement on United States Government efforts in Inter-national Narcotics Control made by Nelson Gross, Senior Adviser and Coordinator for International Narcotics Matters, before the Subcommittee on Drug Abuse, Committee on Armed Services, U.S. Senate. The statement while dated February 29, 1972, was submitted into the record on March 2.

[3.] US Department of State, Office of the Historian, File Designation A-2333, E.O. 12958, Amended June 22, 2004, http://history.state.gov/historicaldocuments/frus1969-76ve01/d220

Mr. Chairman:

The President has made drug abuse control a national objective of first priority in our foreign relations. In his message to the Congress on June 17, 1971, he stated:
"No serious attack on our national drug problem can ignore the international implications of such an effort, nor can the domestic effort succeed without attacking the problem on an international plane..."

The Department of State has the primary role in mobilizing and coordinating U.S. efforts to deal with the foreign supply and international trafficking elements of the drug problem. The Cabinet Committee on International Narcotics Control, established formally in September 1971, is chaired by Secretary of State William Rogers.

Southeast Asia is the world's largest source of illicit opium, with an estimated annual output of 700 tons grown in the upper reaches of Burma, Thailand, and Laos—in the so-called Golden Triangle area. The bulk of the supply is consumed by Asians, but as is well known to this committee, a portion of it has been reaching US troops in Vietnam in the form of #4 heroin. Our short-term goal is to stem the flow of illicit opium and opiates both to our military forces in Southeast Asia and to the continental United States. In the long-term, we would like to see the elimination of poppy growing. To achieve these goals, we must stimulate local government action. Let me cite a few examples.

Burma—Burma is the largest producer of opium in Southeast Asia, accounting for an estimated 400 tons annually...

Thailand—In August 1971, our ambassador to Thailand signed a joint statement with the Thai Foreign Minister, which publicly expressed concern over the growth of drug addiction and drug abuse... Several rings involved in smuggling heroin to American consumers—including US servicemen—have been smashed, and we have made a start in our objective to make life sufficiently risky for the traffickers to discourage others who may be tempted to smuggle illicit narcotics.

Opium growing in Southeast Asia, its processing, and transport out of the Golden Triangle area apparently have not involved American citizens. However, the illegal onward movement of opium and its derivatives, especially heroin, to the big cities of Southeast Asia and the distribution in South Vietnam and to other American consumers in East Asia and the United States has been sufficiently profitable to attract American traffickers, mostly ex-servicemen. For example, on January 21, 1972, an ex-GI, Andrew Price, was arrested in Bangkok while almost simultaneously William Henry (sic) Jackson, a long-time American resident of Bangkok, and Sgt. Jerald Ganius were arrested in the United States. The arrests followed many months of investigation by the Thai police and BNDD agents in Thailand and were the consequence of a shipment of 17 pounds of high-quality (No. 4) heroin from Thailand via U Tapao Airbase to the United States, using forged military documentation. Price and Jackson were mentioned in the Murphy-Steele report of last May.

Laos—Attention was first focused on Laos as a source of heroin supplied to U.S. forces in South Vietnam early last year when on two occasions, smugglers arriving from Vientiane were apprehended with heroin at Tan Son Nhut airport in Saigon . . .

Concrete results so far have included several important seizures of opium and heroin and acetic anhydride, the main catalyst in refining opium into No. 4 heroin. Our intelligence sources indicated a virtual halt in the movement of heroin through Laos. In addition, a refinery near the Burmese border, which apparently supplied much of the heroin smuggled to South Vietnam, has been abandoned.

The most recent development directly affecting the supply of heroin to South Vietnam occurred on January 6 when Lao police, acting on information developed by BNDD agents, arrested a dealer who admitted he had supplied the heroin seized at Tan San Nhut early last year. Ten kilograms of heroin were in his possession when he was arrested . . .

Vietnam—Vietnam is, of course, a victim nation—not a producer of opium and its derivatives. Despite the government of Vietnam's obvious preoccupation with political and military matters, it is actively engaged in a nationwide antinarcotics campaign under the leadership of Admiral Chung Tan Cang . . . The effort has paid off: in 1971, arrests of narcotics violators increased 70 percent over 1970; the confiscation of heroin rose from 5 kilos in 1970 to 123 kilos last year.

On the American side, steady and encouraging progress has been made . . .

"Airgram" Analysis

There are several points in this Department of State Congressional Testimony that are questionable. The first of which is that the total output of opium for all of Southeast Asia in 1972 is quoted at about 700 tons. Alfred W. McCoy, in his blockbuster book, *The Politics of Heroin: CIA Complicity in the Global Drug Trade*, on page 285, states the following:[4]

> In addition to growing over a thousand tons of raw opium annually (about 70 percent of the world's total illicit opium supply), [7]Southeast Asia's Golden Triangle region has become a mass producer of high-grade no. 4 heroin for the American market. Its mushrooming heroin laboratories now rival Marseille and Hong Kong in the quantity and quality of their heroin production.

This was in 1971, and the output was increasing. If the output according to McCoy was over a thousand tons of opium in 1971, and was increasing how could the total output for Southeast Asia be 700 tons in 1972? Further, the Department of State Congressional Testimony states that "the bulk of the supply is consumed by Asians,

---

[4.] McCoy's reference 7 cites the following sources: *Report of the United Nations Survey Team on the Economic and Social Needs of the Opium-Producing Areas in Thailand* (Bangkok: Government House Printing Office, 1967), pp. 59, 64, 68; *The New York Times,* September 17, 1963, p. 45; June 6, 1971, p. 2.

but as was well known to this committee, a good-size portion of it had been reaching US troops in Vietnam in the form of #4 heroin." This implies that almost all of the output did not reach the United States, which is deceptive. The facts are clear that a large amount of no. 4 heroin was being produced specifically for this very profitable market. Further, the amounts talked about as being major interdiction are almost laughable. A few hundred pounds a year in Vietnam was touted as a major reduction, and nothing was said about the fact that most of the leadership in Vietnam was in the drug trade! In Thailand a big to do was made of a seizure of 17 pounds! In Laos the claim was made that trade in heroin had been reduced to a "virtual halt!" Southeast Asia was putting out about 100 tons of heroin a year, much of which was reaching the U.S., and this report talked about a few pounds being seized as major progress.

Also misleading is the sweeping claim that the heroin entering the United States got there at the behest of "ex-servicemen" implying that a few rogue GIs were largely responsible for the import of the largest and most lucrative heroin market in the world. This was simply preposterous.

After searching for years, I found a related appeals case that referenced a William *Herman* Jackson. I also found reference in a Congressional hearing that referred to William *Henry* Jackson that stated the following.[5]

> " . . . 1972, an ex-GI, Andrew Price, was arrested in Bangkok while almost simultaneously William Henry Jackson, a long-time American resident of Bangkok, and Sgt. Jerald Ganius were arrested in the United States. The arrests followed many . . ."

This incident and the resulting trials should have been plastered all over the national news. A story like this one should have been front page of every major newspaper, and the "big story" for every television news outlet. But we heard nothing except for a few paragraphs in *Time*

[5.] Drug Abuse in the Military, Hearing, Ninety-Second Congress, Second Session, By United States Congress. Senate, Committee on Armed Services, Subcommittee on Drug Abuse in the Military; 1972, 577.

magazine and several articles in local papers. Perhaps I missed it, but this author does not recall any reports on national TV news concerning these events at all, and I think that I would have noticed. I have seen stories about a dog caught on an ice flow get more coverage. You can bet that when you do not see wide coverage of a story like this it is something that is threatening to very powerful people and institutions.

Going back to the "French connection" article in *Time* magazine, I wondered how approximately a few hundred pounds of heroin, which was a drop in the bucket considering the many tons entering the United States annually, could receive so much publicity. After all, the movie received all sorts of awards and was highly publicized all over the world. For years everybody was talking about "Frog One" and "Popeye." There are hundreds of tons of cocaine and heroin entering the United States every year worth hundreds of billions of dollars. Why the fuss about a piddly few hundred pounds?

Why are there virtually no investigative journalists, documentaries, or even movies about the other hundreds of tons? Where is that bastion of truth and liberty namely the free and independent American press? Oh yes, there was *American Gangster*, and it portrays an Afro-American gangster that is responsible for major importation of heroin, in bodies no less, into the United States. How much heroin? And how does the rest of it come in? And have you noticed that almost exclusively, the Hollywood version of a big-time drug smuggler is a person of color? Well, I think there is more to it than that.

The image of minorities, gangs, etc., responsible for the US drug trade has been carefully cultivated. On the face of it, this hypothesis is absurd. Although figures vary widely and one could argue about any amount stated, it is safe to assume that the total US drug trade is roughly three hundred billion dollars a year. If African American and Latino male gangsters were making this money, you would not be seeing them in jail. Are we to believe that American institutions dominated by Anglos do not have any control of this money?

Where are all these drugs coming from? Why are there no movies, documentaries, or news reports about hundreds of tons of heroin and cocaine entering this country? Of course the obvious question is, How can hundreds of tons of drugs be moved thousands of miles across oceans without it being transported on airplanes or ships? Is there a fleet of thousands of Piper Cubs somewhere that can fly thousands of miles across oceans? We are led to believe that the drug trade is dominated by organized crime and gangs, but I have yet to see a ship or a plane with the word *Mafia*, or *Crips*, or *Bloods* anywhere on it. These are the questions that kept rattling around in my head. It just does not make sense. This had to be the work of large organizations and institutions.

Second Contact—Alex Constantine

Some time ago, I came across and read Alex Constantine's book *Psychic Dictatorship in the USA*. In chapter 7, I found the most information related to the body bag case to date. With the author's written permission, I have quoted large portions of chapter 7 below. Keep in mind that this happened *before* the State Department's analysis above:

> The "Fatal Vision" murders & the Nomenclature of an American Death Squad[6]
>
> The Army's Body Bag Heroin Connection and a Triple Murder in Vietnam Era North Carolina
>
> Dr. Jeffrey MacDonald's prospects appeared far from grim. At 26, the Princeton graduate had attained the rank of Captain in the Army medical Corps at Fort Bragg, 10 miles northwest of Fayetteville, North Carolina. He was a talented physician; his contributions to emergency medicine had been adopted by paramedics and from the units across the country. Acquaintances maintain that he doted on his family. Colette, his wife, was pregnant with her third child when her life ended and his was coldly dismantled.
> On Feb. 17, 1970 Colette MacDonald and Kimberly age five and Kristen age two where bludgeoned and stabbed to death. Military police responding to MacDonald's call for help found him unconscious and multiple stab wounds, one of which, examining physicians later testified, collapsed

---

[6.] Alex Constantine, *Psychic Dictatorship in the U.S.A*, Feral House, (Portland, Oregon, 1995), pp. 121-129. Permission to reprint chapter 7 given to author by Alex Constantine, November 7, 2008.

a lung. He was hospitalized for ten days. Despite the severity of his injuries, the government concluded they were "superficial" "self-inflicted." MacDonald was charged, tried and acquitted in 1970 in an Army hearing. He was retried in the summer of 1979, found guilty, acquitted by an appellate court a year later, and sentenced yet again by the Supreme Court decision in 1982. He is currently serving three life terms in a medium-security prison in Sheridan, Oregon . . .

"Malignant narcissism," drugs and "rage of the female sex" aside, another perspective of the case begins with a young criminology student police informant from Nashville, Tennessee—Helena Stoeckley.

In 1968 Stoeckley, whose information on the narcotics underground resulted in over 200 arrests of the Fort Bragg area (though she was ruled not credible by Judge DuPree, who presided over the MacDonald case), was transferred by her police contact, Lt. Rudy Scuder, to the office of detective Everett Beasley, a new cop on the narcotics squad. Beasley didn't know it, but Stoeckley had fallen in with a circle of Vietnam vets running heroin into the Fort Bragg area.

On one occasion, Stoeckley told Beasley, "Drugs, primarily heroin, were being smuggled into this country in the body cavities of casualties returned by air from Vietnam. She named Ike Atkinson[7] as the ring leader." Atkinson was assigned to Seymour-Johnson Air Force Base in Goldsboro, North Carolina. He was "in the service," Stoeckley said, "but subsequently got out and continued his business in drugs with the same contacts."

In a 1985 deposition, Beasley stated that a shaken Helena Stoeckley contacted him after the murder of Jeffrey MacDonald's family. She told him that she had been in the MacDonald House in the early morning hours of February 17th. She also provided him with details about the drug operation. The recipients of the heroin, she said,

---

[7.] This is the same Leslie "Ike" Atkinson portrayed in the movie *American Gangster* thus connecting these two drug smuggling operations allegedly using KIAs out of Vietnam. http://en.wikipedia.org/wiki/Ike_Atkinson

had contacts in Vietnam who placed it in the bodies of war casualties. The bodies where re-stitched and shipped to Johnson Air Force Base and other installations around the country. When the bodies arrived in the U.S., they were met by a military contact and the heroin was removed. The bodies were then sent to their final destinations.

"The person who met the bodies at the respective air bases knew which bodies to check, based on a predetermined code," Beasley says. "Helena told me that the people who handled the assignments in Vietnam, and those who met the planes in the United States, where military personnel. She also told him that the couriers made their pickups at Fort Bragg. Distribution was handled by enlisted man, civilians, police officers, "Local attorneys and Army officers as high as generals were part of the operation. She stated that she would name and identify the people if given immunity by the U.S. Government."

Beasley believes the workings of the drug operation were part of the "bombshell" she promised to drop at the trial of Jeffrey MacDonald. But the government would not offer her immunity. (Facing a conviction for participation in the killings, she admitted later, Stoeckley overdosed herself with drugs before appearing in MacDonald's trial. She was reeling under the influence when she recanted on the stand, and was dismissed as a witness.)

If granted immunity, Stoeckley's testimony would have surely drawn national attention to an obscure chapter of the war in Southeast Asia. Had she lived, Stoeckley might well have toppled an international empire.

During the war in Vietnam and after, small contingents of American soldiers settled in Thailand to enter the world heroin trade. Among the Yank opium gangs was a syndicate of GI's known as the Black Masonic Club, led by Leslie "Ike" Atkinson, nicknamed "Sergeant Smack." they called Jack's American-style bar in Bangkok, a favorite watering hole for black GI's on furlough and a notorious drug dispensary, their home.

Atkinson was identified by Helena Stoeckley as the leader of the umbrella group linked to the MacDonald killings. Atkinson had no role in the killings, but a subgroup in Fayetteville reportedly did. One of this group, Cathy Perry, confessed to the FBI in 1984 that she took part in the killings. The word "cult" surfaced much earlier.

In December 1970, Perry confided to a friend that she had "killed several persons." She complained that "the cult" had pressured her to do "things" against her will.

On the East Coast, said Stoeckley, the heroin was unloaded at Fort Bragg and Seymour-Johnson Air Force Base. The heroin was distributed along the eastern and southeastern states. According to a 1973 issue of *Time*, casualties of war were indeed used as couriers. The opiate was stuffed into coffins, body bags and internal organs. The *Time* report described the scandal as "the most vicious case of war profiteering" in American history.

Military police, looking into the black market in stolen supplies and narcotics, periodically snagged an enlisted man or petty officer. Pressured to plea bargain, they often named senior officials. One team of drug agents filed reports at military bases around the country. Eyewitnesses at Norton Air Force Base in California agreed to roll over under immunity and testified the incoming bodies stuffed with as much as 50 pounds of heroin each, were surgically relieved of the contraband. *Wall Street Journal* reporter Jonathan Kwitny reports in the *Crimes of Patriots*, published in 1987, that "corrupt U.S. and Vietnamese officials" arrested for complicity and heroin pipeline turned evidence on "senior U.S. officers."

"These reports check out," Kwitny affirmed (leaving the identities of said officials a lingering mystery).

The Army acted quickly—not by rounding up the ringleaders, but by dismantling the investigative team and packing them off to combat duty in Vietnam. Skittish military officials, alleges Ted Gunderson, former agent in charge of the FBI's Los Angeles office and a long-time MacDonald's supporter, only pursued lower-level couriers in the drug transfers. "High-ranking Army officers," he says, "were in charge of this drug ring (and) have never been identified. Informants have advised that the

Army investigation of the operation was controlled and manipulated to conceal its magnitude and the extent of (official) participation."

This gruesome successor to Air America began to fall apart in 1972 when federal agents were tipped off that 20 kilos of heroin could be found aboard a KC-135 bound for Delaware's Dover Air Force Base. The plane was ordered to land in Maryland, and the agents searched the transport. Search proved futile until one agent noticed the body in the cargo hold had been freshly stitched. The agents arrested Thomas Southerland[8], an Army veteran from North Carolina. His bail was set at $50,000. The jury was informed that Southerland was an operative in an international opium ring.

The DEA soon made the arrests of Ike Atkinson, currently serving a forty-year prison sentence. Federal authorities are convinced that he still has $85 million cabbaged away in offshore accounts. (Atkinson has since changed his name. He told fellow prisoners that he was used in CIA mind control experiments. He was, apparently, a pawn, not a true insider. Federal documents released under FOIA have since established that the agency used the military as cover for experiments in behavior modification.) The stiff sentence is inconsistent with the fate of James Smedley, who directed the Thai end of the operation. Smedley spent two years in a Bangkok prison and was released to enter a guilty plea in a Raleigh, North Carolina courthouse. He walked away with a reprimand and parole. Jasper Myrick, a courier, did not fare so well—he was arrested in Bangkok and sentenced to 33 years in a maximum security cell.

In Fayetteville, an accused drug dealer, Spider Newman, consented to turn state's evidence on his suppliers. The case was heard in federal court. During a break in the trial,

---

8. This is the same Thomas Edward Sutherland who allegedly left a shipment of KIAs out of Southeast Asia that had been stuffed with heroin, at Kadena Air Base, Okinawa, just prior to his apprehension described above.

Newman disappeared. His body was found in his car, behind his house. He'd been shot in the head. Police ruled the death a suicide.

But in 1970 the Atkinson syndicate was still operating undetected. Some of the local distributors feared and loathed one Dr. Jeffrey MacDonald. The primary aim of any murder investigation is the establishment of a motive. The prosecution, and later McGinnis, smeared MacDonald by falsely attributing the murders to amphetamine abuse . . .

Among the details that Stoeckley gave Beasley in 1970 were the names of police officers entangled in the body bag operation. One of them was Lt. Rudy Studer, the informant's former contact. Shortly after the MacDonald murders, Studer was promoted to captain, chief of detectives. The promotion was short-lived, however. Studer was soon forced to resign after "misappropriating" pornographic material seized in a police raid. Stoeckley said Studer supplied her with heroin for sale in Fayetteville. His partner in the drug trade was allegedly William Ivory of the Army's criminal investigations division (CID).

Detective Studer's partner, Lt. Sonberg, disappeared immediately after the murders. It was bruited around the Fayetteville Police Department that he had double crossed a ring of drug dealers. A police informant, Joseph Bullock, had stated that Fayetteville police on more than one occasion had witnessed Studer and Ivory exchanging envelopes at the local Dunkin' Donuts shop. Shortly after talking to police Bullock was ambushed in his home and, like Spider Newman, received a fatal bullet to the head.

City officials fingered by Stoeckley in the body bag drug syndicate also had a direct role in the prosecution of Jeffrey MacDonald. "Helena once mentioned the name Proctor to me," Beasley recalled in a signed statement, James Proctor, a prosecuting attorney in the MacDonald case, was the former son-in-law of Judge DuPree, a certain conflict of interest in a case this sensitive . . .

Among them a file of Greg Mitchell, a G.I. placed by Stoeckley at the crime scene, one of several mysterious "Fatal Vision" casualties. His wife recalls that Mitchell once explained to her how drugs were smuggled into the country in the body cavities of soldiers killed in Vietnam . . .

MacDonald passed a polygraph. He submitted to five independent forensics examinations. The government's own lab specimens linked Fort Bragg's body bag ring to the crime scene, including a long synthetic blond strand corroborating MacDonald's contention that Stoeckley wore a blond wig the night of the murders. A bloody syringe found in his home was "lost" by the prosecution.

In fact, Government files released since the trial verified William Ivory, the CID investigator and alleged body bag drug courier, misplaced or destroyed most of the evidence corroborating Dr. MacDonald's version of events . . . All evidence that could reverse a conspicuous case of malicious prosecution is systematically rejected upon appeal—very comforting for the coterie of military officers and public officials connected by CID investigators, Stoeckley, Perry, Mitchell and others to the importation of heroin from Southeast Asia by casualty-courier to Fort Bragg.

But another motive was rough sketched in 1987 by Melenda Stevens, a tenacious supporter of Jeffrey MacDonald, in *I Accuse: the Torturing of an American Hero*, a self-published debunking of the government's case. Suspects described by MacDonald "all existed," she observes, "all know each other and all have motive to kill . . . drugs. The Army had a motive for covering up their crimes, stemming from the fact that they were government informants involved in illegal LSD experiments at Fort Bragg." Her source of information was Major Jim Williams, MacDonald's colleague and a witness at the 1970 hearing and testified that he feared MacDonald had carried his investigation of drugs on the base too far, and had thereby exhorted disaster. Williams also stated on the record that the confessed "Fatal vision" killers were "Government informants."

As noted, Ike Atkinson has alleged that he was used in a CIA mind control operation involving brain telemetry.

All of this is consistent with CID investigator William Ivory's recruitment of Dr. James A Brussel, a mental health commissioner for the state of New York, Brussel has claimed to be an agent of the CIA and an adviser to the CID's counter-espionage division. He also, according to Potter and Bost, was "an innovative researcher into novel methods for controlling inmates in psychiatric institutions. Lamenting the frustrations of managing unruly patients and the cost of housing them in the late 1940s, Brussel and an associate instituted electric shock experiments on the brains of female inmates." Dr. Brussels' early ECT "treatments" were performed on 50 female mental patients, in some cases at the rate of 40-50 sessions per patient. Brussel also experimented with amphetamines and methedrine on depressed patients. He was recruited by Ivory in 1971 as a secret consultant to the government.

Yet another CIA mind control researcher brought into the MacDonald case was the infamous William Kroger, author of *Hypnosis and Behavior Modification* (1963), with a preface by MKULTRA's Martin Orne and H. J. Eisenck. Kroger's work for the agency involved hypnosis as an espionage tool. Of particular interest to Kroger was the development of the drug assisted, hypnotic means of programming intelligence operatives to carry out an assignment and obscure any memory of it. Whether these mind control specialists had a direct role in the killings is not clear, but the confessions of Helena Stoeckley and Cathy Perry both mentioned dim recall of events of February 17, 1970, as if they'd dreamed the killings.

They have provided MacDonald's defense team with a wealth of details, confirming that the only "Fatal Vision" in the case is the government's own. McGinnis's version of events has had the effect of drawing attention from the body-bag connection and the CIA's attempts, in violation of repeated congressional injunctions, to commandeer the mind. *Fatal Vision* is their cover story.

A comparison of these two documents quoted above, the Department of State's airgram and the MacDonald case, yields some astounding facts. In the MacDonald case, we have reference to "Jack's place," also known as the Five Star Bar in Bangkok, Thailand, which was the drug ring's base of operation. Although the State Department identified the owner, or manager, of the bar as William *Henry* Jackson, his given name apparently was William *Herman* Jackson. This mistake, if it was a mistake, caused this author not to find anything on Jackson for many years. The information that finally did come forth was revealing. Jackson had drug convictions that started well before any of the above. Further, he apparently was able to run the operations at Jack's place even while in confinement for many years.

The MacDonald case happened in 1970. Then we go to January 21, 1972, and we have William Henry (Herman) Jackson and "Jack's place" still in operation, and we have the State Department stating that the case was "being prosecuted" in Thailand and also in the United States. In fact, Jack's place stayed open and was smuggling drugs for about ten years. If this case was being aggressively prosecuted then, how is it possible that "Jack's place" is apparently in full operation again about one year later, and beyond? We know this because we have the same people involved in the MacDonald case and also mentioned in the *Time* magazine article January 1, 1973.

Obviously, people in high places had to be complicit in this operation—very high places. We are looking at a drug ring that could easily move through branches of the military, apparently had access to mortuaries, could manipulate evidence in trials, and could control the outcome in military and civilian courts. Let's keep in mind that the MacDonald case went all the way to the Supreme Court, which overturned the dismissal of the case. So we have MacDonald who has been found not guilty once and also was successful in appealing for a dismissal, in jail to this day. Who has the power to do these things? Generals in the military? I would think that if these incidents only went as far as generals they would have been covered in much more depth than the media coverage that was seen. This would've been an outrageous scandal that virtually all Americans would have known about and demanded justice. There would have been high-ranking military and civilians taken away in shackles, frog-marched for the cameras!

Third Contact—Michael Marr

After reading *Psychic Dictatorship*, I was able to contact the lawyer that prosecuted the case. His name is Michael Marr, and he has a private practice in Baltimore, Maryland. I e-mailed him, and he responded. I asked him about the case, and he replied that he clearly remembered it and that Southland had received a twenty-year sentence. I responded with another e-mail and asked a series of questions. I wanted to know more details about the case. I never received a reply from him. I e-mailed him one more time and mentioned that he was probably busy, but that I was very curious about some details of the case. He also did not respond to this e-mail, and I have not heard from him since. I do not know if he just did not want to be bothered, or whether something had made him fearful. At any rate, he would not respond to any further e-mails.

Conclusions

There was an investigation into heroin smuggling using human remains. The investigation took place toward the end of 1972 and the beginning of 1973. The results of this investigation have not been made public. No one was charged with using bodies to smuggle heroin. Evidence disappeared in this case. There are three possibilities here. The first is that there was no heroin being smuggled using human remains. The individuals involved in this case have admitted that they were smuggling heroin in "AWOL bags" with false bottoms that were not discovered. They adamantly deny that anything else was going on, and this is certainly possible. Another possibility is that someone else was smuggling heroin using bodies and that Southerland and his associate had nothing to do with it. The last possibility is that there was not enough evidence to charge or convict anyone in this case.

It was becoming increasingly clear to me that this was a major heroin smuggling operation, and I was beginning to suspect that many influential people in the US military, government, organized crime, and even the US media were somehow complicit. The author could not believe that a handful of GIs could carry out operations of this magnitude all by themselves without protection. When you are talking about the potential for smuggling tons of a substance that is many times more valuable than gold illegally into the United States, the author is inclined to believe that power and influence from high places is necessary, or at least some sort of protective umbrella. Of course, most people in law enforcement are honest, hard working, and dedicated people. What we are talking about is complicity and a system constructed only to catch the lower levels of the international drug production and distribution system.

Finally, I was starting to find information about this under-investigated and under-reported case. This writer was starting to compile names and associations that were beginning to show a bigger picture and one that was leading to high places. "Jack's place" was starting to become bigger and bigger, and the obvious question of, If true, was this the only time bodies were used to smuggle heroin? And further, were there other methods being used? And what else could be going on at Jack's place, and beyond? Let us have a look.

Chapter Two

William Herman Jackson and the Rest of the Crew at "Jack's Place"

Years after writing the first chapter, I found more information about the Five Star Bar in Bangkok. I did not get better at research, Google did. I now had Google Scholar, Google Books, and so forth at my disposal. Also, newspaper archives became more accessible online. I just love Google!

Apparently, Jack's place, and/or the people associated with it were in operation for about ten years. The more I found out about this, the more I realized that this was a top logistics channel for heroin importation into the United States, perhaps the number one operation. The story started to become clearer as time went on. Over and over again, lower-level people were arrested, but the operation kept going on and on. And over and over again, the stories were sporadically reported in newspapers, and the dots were not connected.

Some of the news reports about the body bag case that I was involved with were in the Fort Bragg/Fayetteville, North Carolina, area that should have set off alarms because of the Captain Jeffery MacDonald, "Fatal Vision," case that occurred there two years earlier. As mentioned earlier, Captain MacDonald said that massive quantities of heroin were coming into the area in the bodies of killed in action out of Vietnam. The army's Criminal Investigations Division and local law enforcement should have easily made the connection. That is, unless they were more concerned with covering it up.

Background on William Herman Jackson

Because government agencies repeatedly identified him as William *Henry* Jackson, it took me years to find anything on him. It seems there was an artist of the same name, and every search came up with only information on the artist. An archived court appeals case identified him as "Herman" for the middle name, and within minutes, I found a lot of information on Jackson, none of it nice. Perhaps the State Department made an error, but I have seen several instances where official agencies make these subtle "errors" and make it difficult to research criminal activity. Readers might notice that some agencies had Lee *Harvey* Oswald listed as Lee *Henry* Oswald in their records. One can easily say that it was a "clerical error."

The first official record this author found was from the Federal Bureau of Investigation in a series of reports, dated late in 1967. These reports are from the Mary Ferrell Foundation and are archived from the House Select Committee on Assassinations and are listed under a JFK Assassination System Identification Form with the record number of 124-10291-10364. It is interesting that the same individuals accused of smuggling heroin in bodies are also, somehow, connected to the JFK assassination. Of course it does not mean that they did it or were involved in it, but there must be some connection. Passages from these investigative reports are provided below.[9]

[9.] FBI—House Select Committee on Assassinations Subject File: William Herman Jackson http://www.maryferrell.org/mffweb/archive/viewer/showDoc.do?docId=73950&relPageId=1

UNITED STATES DEPARTMENT OF JUSTICE
FEDERAL BUREAU OF INVESTIGATION
Charlotte, North Carolina
September 12, 1967

In Reply, Please Refer to
File No.

    LESLIE ATKINSON, also known as
    Ike Atkinson;
    HERMAN JACKSON, also known as
    Jack Jackson;
    UNKNOWN SUBJECT, also known as
    Smitty;
    UNKNOWN SUBJECT, also known as
    Red
    MISCELLANEOUS - FALSELY MAKING OR
    FORGING NAVAL, MILITARY, OR OFFICIAL
    PASS

    A confidential source who has furnished reliable information in the past and does not desire identity divulged, advised that recently he was in Bangkok, Thailand. At that time he became acquainted with some individuals who he believes are illegally wearing the military uniform, impersonating military personnel, and illegally using fraudulent military identification.

    Source explained that American servicemen in Saigon, Viet Nam, are not paid in American money, but in P.C.'s. The servicemen use these P.C.'s to purchase items on the economy. Servicemen who wish to have American money or send the equivalent to their relatives in the United States may do so by going to any one of the many exchanges in Saigon and buying money orders. These exchanges are run by the American government.

    THIS DOCUMENT CONTAINS NEITHER
    RECOMMENDATIONS NOR CONCLUSIONS
    OF THE FBI. IT IS THE PROPERTY
    OF THE FBI AND IS LOANED TO
    YOUR AGENCY; IT AND ITS CONTENTS
    ARE NOT TO BE DISTRIBUTED OUTSIDE
    YOUR AGENCY.

ENCLOSURE

RE: LESLIE ATKINSON;
    HERMAN JACKSON;
    UNKNOWN SUBJECTS

A serviceman is not entitled to buy as many money orders as he pleases, but the dollar value he may purchase depends on his rank and rating. Money orders are sold in $50, $100, and $250 denominations. The $50 and $100 denominations are handled by the American Express, while the $250 denominations are handled by the Chase Manhattan Bank. In order to buy money orders, the serviceman must display his military identification card. Records are kept by the exchanges as to the amount of money orders each serviceman buys.

For an unknown reason, a $100 money order can be purchased with only $69 worth of P.C.'s. The other denominations of money orders can also be purchased in P.C.'s for about two-thirds their value. The money orders can be purchased any time during the month, but more are purchased during the latter part of the month since this is when the serviceman is paid.

If an individual has more than one military identification card, he may purchase a larger quantity of money orders. The illegal operations in this case take place because many civilians have illegally obtained military identification cards or else they have forged cards. With these cards and after obtaining a quantity of P.C.'s, they can buy almost as many money orders as they wish, and with each purchase realize a 33 percent profit. Source believes that this activity is wide-spread in Saigon, but he only has good information regarding three individuals.

The individuals are LESLIE ATKINSON, also known as Ike; HERMAN JACKSON, also known as Jack; and an individual called SMITTY. All three individuals are American Negroes. JACKSON and ATKINSON are believed to be retired military personnel. ATKINSON is about 5'7", 190 pounds, grey eyes, medium brown complexion, about 42 years of age, and a fast talker who always smokes cigars. He is married and has seven children. His home in the United States is at 127 Neuse Circle, Goldsboro, North Carolina. ATKINSON is currently home in Goldsboro, North Carolina, with his wife and children, but is expected to return to Bangkok in the near future.

RE: LESLIE ATKINSON;
    HERMAN JACKSON;
    UNKNOWN SUBJECTS

      HERMAN JACKSON is about 5'10", 180 pounds, dark brown complexion, about 46 years of age. He claims to have been born in Alabama. JACKSON drives a 1961 black Cadillac in Bangkok.

      SMITTY is about 6'2", 240 pounds, medium brown skin, and about 46 years of age. SMITTY is married to a German girl and claims to be retired from the military. He resides at 229 Soi 55 Road, Bangkok, Thailand. ATKINSON also makes his residence at this same address. JACKSON's address is unknown.

      ATKINSON, JACKSON, SMITTY, and a Chinese man whose name is unknown, own and operate Jack's American Star Bar near the Bangkok Hotel in Bangkok, Thailand. This bar is the front for the illegal operation and serves as a reason for the three Americans being there. Many of the persons who frequent the bar are aware of this illegal operation. One such individual is a Negro male called "RED." He is about 22 years of age, 5'11", 160 pounds. RED has several military identification cards and purchases money orders illegally.

      The base of the illegal operation is at 229 Soi 55 Road, Bangkok, Thailand, the residence of JACKSON and ATKINSON. At this address, these individuals have numerous identification cards, a polaroid camera to make the identification photographs, a laminating machine to laminate the cards, as well as a mimeograph machine and stencils to cut military orders which will support the military identification cards. The purchased money orders are kept at this address also. They are cashed as needed anywhere in Bangkok. The identification cards and the money orders are kept in locked dresser drawers and in a wall locker at this residence. It is customary for these individuals to meet at this address each morning about 11 a.m., either to socialize or discuss the illegal operation. The residence also has a caretaker and maid who are natives of Thailand. These individuals are probably aware of the illegal operation, but are not participants.

After reviewing the above documents and many more on file, it appears that several agencies, including the US Army, the FBI, and the CIA, knew quite a bit about the illegal activities of Jackson and his associates as far back as 1967. They also knew a fair amount about the illegal activities going on at the American Five Star Bar in Bangkok, Thailand. Of interest is also the fact that J. Edgar Hoover personally knew of this operation and that drugs were involved. Jackson's FBI rap sheet shows that he was arrested four times in 1969 on federal drug charges.[10] Hoover also knew the names of most of Jackson's associates which were the following: James Warren Smedley, Rudolf Valentino Jennings, Luchai Luwiwat, Leslie Atkinson, William Kelly Brown, William Thomas, James McArthur, William King Wright, Charles Murphy Gillis, Monroe Lorenzo Martin, Freddie Clay Thornton, Jerald Ganius, Andrew Price, Johnny Trice, Series (last name only), and George Hoover Pratt.

Of particular note is the name Leslie (Ike) Atkinson who was also involved in the case that the movie *American Gangster* was based on. Now recall that Atkinson was reported by Helena Stoeckley as involved in heroin smuggling into the Fort Bragg, North Carolina area. Further, the fact that Stoeckley said that MacDonald's inquiries into this situation directly led to the murder of his family. Virtually, all of Stoeckley's testimony was disregarded because she was not considered credible; however, everything that this writer has reviewed that was said by Stoeckley has turned out to be very accurate.

Further, any investigator could have easily checked out her story. The US Army, CIA, FBI, and the Bureau of Narcotics and Dangerous Drugs all had extensive records on much of what she said. There is no way that these agencies, and in particular the director of the FBI at the time, J. Edgar Hoover, could not have known about these connections. This writer knows, firsthand, why the Criminal Investigations Division of the US Army did not provide this information; they were complicit in it. They hid and destroyed evidence in this case as they did in the case in which I was involved. It is also more than probable that the

---

10. William Herman Jackson's FBI "Rap Sheet" is available at http://www.maryferrell.org/mffweb/archive/viewer/showDoc.do?docId=76182&relPageId=1

other agencies mentioned did not provide evidence that they were required to provide for the same reason.

In the following document, we have the director of the FBI informing the director of the CIA about the activities of Jackson and his associates. The note that Hoover added, in which he explains that his agency, the FBI, had been previously informed by the CIA that one of the members of this group was training "these people" in the "Black Movement" and then shipping them to the United States, is interesting. Also note that the subject on the communication contained the words *racial matters*. Could it be that Hoover and the CIA were more concerned about this issue than they were with the possibility that this group was shipping tons of heroin into the United States? Also noteworthy is the fact that this communication took place just one month after the MacDonald murders at Fort Bragg in which Atkinson and Southerland were named by Stoeckley as involved in the drug trade that resulted in the murders.

EX-106 REC-35
(RI) 163-1504

SECRET

1 - Mr. Michela

Date: March 20, 1970

To: Director
Central Intelligence Agency

CIA HAS NO OBJECTION TO
DECLASSIFICATION AND/OR
RELEASE OF CIA INFORMATION
IN THIS DOCUMENT. Except for
Brackets on pg. 2
KP 10-10-97

Attention: Deputy Director for Plans

From: John Edgar Hoover, Director

Subject: GEORGE HOOVER PRATT
INTERNAL SECURITY - LAOS
RACIAL MATTERS

1-17-98
CLASSIFIED BY 5668 SLD/KSP
DECLASSIFY ON: 25X
(JFK)

ALL INFORMATION CONTAINED
HEREIN IS UNCLASSIFIED
EXCEPT WHERE SHOWN
OTHERWISE

Reference is made to your request dated March 10, 1970, and to my letter dated November 21, 1969, concerning captioned individual, your file B-956.

There is enclosed one copy each of the fingerprint cards of captioned individual and James Warren Smedley, who may be identical with the James Warren Smedley mentioned in your request of March 10, 1970.

It is noted that you were furnished two copies of the Federal Bureau of Investigation Identification Record concerning George Hoover Pratt, by my letter dated November 21, 1969. A review of the files of this Bureau disclosed no Identification Record identifiable with James Warren Smedley or William Herman Jackson, also known as Jack Earl Lantern, who were also mentioned in your request of March 10, 1970.

SEE NOTE PAGE TWO

JCM:djw/ekv
(4)

Director
Central Intelligence Agency

SECRET

While no Identification Record concerning James Warren Smedley was located, the enclosed fingerprint cards concerning Smedley and Pratt may be of assistance to you in making record checks through ▓▓▓▓▓▓ sources. (S) 77
The enclosed fingerprint cards and the copies of the Identification Record which were furnished to you by my letter dated November 21, 1969, may be utilized by you 77
in checking ▓▓▓▓▓ sources concerning the (S)
individuals mentioned above. In making such checks, you
must insure that the ▓▓▓▓▓▓ clearly understand (S) 77
that it is your Agency which is making the record checks
and that such checks are not in any way being made for
this Bureau.

Enclosures - 2

NOTE:

Central Intelligence Agency (CIA) previously checked the names of Pratt, Jackson, and Smedley through Bureau files. CIA has advised that Pratt had reportedly attempted to get people out of Vietnam into Laos where these people could be trained and shipped to the United States to assist in the "Black Movement." By memorandum dated 3/10/70, CIA furnished additional identifying information concerning Jackson and Smedley and requested copies of fingerprint records. CIA requested to be advised if those
records could be provided to ▓▓▓▓▓ sources in (S) 77
order to facilitate checking certain ▓▓▓ records which
would otherwise be unavailable. (S) 77

- 2 -

Source: Mary Ferrell Foundation, House Select Committee on Assassinations Subject File: William Herman Jackson
http://www.maryferrell.org/mffweb/archive/viewer/showDoc.do?docId=76183, accessed February 13, 2013."

Additional Press Reports

Years ago, the *Time* magazine report was all that I had to go on as far as press reports are concerned. Recently, I found more, a lot more, about this "Jack's place" operation. Below are summaries of significant facts obtained recently. In the *Times Daily,* Alabama, December 23, 1972, first page, under the heading "IN THE NATION" we have the following.

> AN FBI AGENT HAS TESTIFIED that a 31-year-old man accused of being part of a smuggling ring which sewed heroin into the bodies of Vietnam war dead "Was not a member of the Armed Forces" as he had claimed. Agent Joseph Stehr testified Friday that the defendant, Thomas Edward Southerland of Castle Hayne, N.C., travelled with unauthorized documents, some of which were issued in Baltimore. Agents feel the mysterious organization shipped heroin into the country from Southeast Asia in $20,000 lots sewn into bodies and removed either at Ft. Lewis, Wash, or Dover, Del. Southerland was arrested last week when federal agents intercepted a military plane at Andrews Air Force Base. The plane was flying two war dead to Dover.

Note the agent appears to distance this from the armed forces and recall that most of the evidence in this case disappeared from military channels before the trial. Also note that the above information was released by an FBI agent who named specific military installations involved.

Next we have an article in the *New York Times,* January 3, 1973, page 7, by Ben A. Franklin, with a very interesting title.

> **U.S. JURY INDICTS HEROIN SUSPECT; But Doesn't Mention Alleged Smuggling in G.I. Coffins**
> A Federal grand jury indicted today a 31-year-old North Carolina man who the Government has said was "a functionary" in a conspiracy to smuggle Asian heroin into the country in the coffins or in the cadavers of American servicemen killed in Vietnam . . .

A "functionary" is an odd reference to an individual on a military aircraft, in uniform, escorting a body suspected of having been stuffed with heroin. I also found a consistent trend of not mentioning anything about bodies used to smuggle drugs in indictments and also appeals when government agencies said that this was the case.

A UPI article appeared in the *Ellensburg Daily Record*, Washington, January 4, 1973, page 8 that added some interesting information.

Heroin Investigation Centers Near Army's Fort Bragg

> WASHINGTON (UPI)—Investigation of a smuggling operation in which heroin allegedly was shipped to the United States inside the bodies . . . focused on Fayetteville, N.C., Army sources say.
>
> Ft. Bragg, one of the largest Army bases in the country with 38,000 troops, is located just outside Fayetteville. But the sources said Wednesday the alleged operation so far appeared to have been civilian . . .
>
> Drug use among troops at Ft. Bragg was the subject of a Senate subcommittee hearing in 1970 . . . U.S. Attorney Michael E. Marr said in a Baltimore hearing that informers had reported 44 pounds of heroin left Thailand inside one body . . . . Army sources said the investigation was "a very large operation and that so far the Army has been involved only in its fringes." They said nothing had turned up so far to cause the Army to launch its own investigation . . . . The Washington Post Wednesday quoted "well-placed sources" as saying the investigation was nearly over and likely to result in indictment of more than a dozen persons. The Greensboro (N.C.) Daily News reported confidential informers in Fayetteville were credited by federal agents "with tips that led to the dramatic arrest Dec. 11 and the indictment in Baltimore Tuesday of a North Carolina man. Thomas Edward Southerland 31 . . ."
>
> Southerland, a Greensboro resident, was indicted on nine counts of using false military orders . . .

We have another article from the *Tuscaloosa News*, Tuscaloosa, Alabama, January 3, 1973, front page, written by Philip A. McCombs of the *Washington Post*, that adds a few more interesting facts. This article confirms that Southerland was in a U.S. Army uniform, and also had an interesting partner with him.

Fort Bragg, North Carolina: Heroin Probe Hits Army Base

> . . . Also on the flight with Southerland but not arrested was a retired Army sergeant who was dressed as a civilian. In a bond hearing, Marr identified this man as "Leslie Atkinson who we knew to be part of the conspiracy." Marr said Atkinson and Southerland "were seen in Honolulu acting in a friendly fashion together. They were also staying in the same hotel in Honolulu."
>
> Marr declined to comment Tuesday on Atkinson's whereabouts, but it was learned that he lives in the Fayetteville area.
>
> The indictment does not specify when the bodies were loaded on the airplane but says that Southerland left U Tapau Air Base in Sattahip, Thailand, on Dec. 9. The flight then went to Kadena Air Base in Okinawa. Then Southerland changed planes, taking an Air Force C141, to Honolulu that was scheduled to go on to Dover.
>
> Public information officers at Ft. Bragg and the U.S. attorney's office in Raleigh declined to confirm that major breakthroughs in the case or grand jury indictments are expected.

This is incredible! Almost three years after Green Beret Captain Jeffrey MacDonald stands accused and convicted of murdering his entire family, and the above smuggling operation was alleged to be involved, we have the same individuals still operating in exactly the same manner. Recall that military physician Captain MacDonald found indications that heroin was coming into the Fort Bragg area in the bodies of killed in action out of Vietnam. Also recall that that is exactly what Helena Stoeckley testified to, testimony that was ignored by the courts.

This incident should have sent shock waves all through the media and also the courts. Prosecutors should have jumped all over this. This case should have led to an "endless can of worms." Stoeckley's testimony that there were people in high places involved should have been bird-dogged in both cases.

Another reoccurring theme was that the military was not involved. How is it that we have Southerland in a US Army uniform, Atkinson who was retired from the US Army, and both on a US Air Force air plane, but we have no military involvement? excerpts from the next article further illustrates this. This article was again in the *Tuscaloosa News*, January 11, 1973, page 5, and was also written by Philip A. McCombs of the *Washington Post*.

Heroin Smuggling Ring Infiltrates Military Morgues

Washington—An alleged heroin smuggling ring infiltrated U.S. military morgues in Vietnam to place 40-pound heroin packets inside the autopsied bodies of dead American Servicemen for shipment home through what was one time a major heroin supply system for the Washington-Baltimore area, according to federal sources . . .

Federal investigators have for more than two years tracked the ring, said to include up to 100 conspirators—some of them posing as servicemen—in one of the 10 largest drug smuggling operations in the world. Several ring members, including alleged leader Herman Jackson, were convicted and are in prison—but the investigation is still under way.

Federal authorities have produced no evidence of heroin shipped inside bodies . . .

Sources said autopsied bodies, which are cut open and then sewn shut, were used by the alleged ring because any other cuts on bodies would be noticeable and could arouse suspicion.

Assistant U.S. Attorney Michael E. Marr said in court that Southerland wore medical insignia on his uniform and that his false military orders were issued from the Fifth Field General Hospital in Bangkok.

Southerland has been a member of the alleged ring for five years and has traveled to Southeast Asia several times on smuggling missions, Marr said.

Significant is the comment that federal authorities did not have evidence of heroin being smuggled using bodies. The simple answer to this is the fact that the same federal authorities, specifically the US Army's Criminal Investigations Division, that were supposed to be gathering evidence were actually involved in hiding and "losing" evidence. Also noteworthy is Southerland's ability to move with ease through military channels. He apparently was able to use a variety of military functions and also pass himself off as a member of a medical services unit in Thailand; some feat for a civilian.

Also noteworthy is the above information pertaining to Southerland wearing medical insignia and that he was traveling on orders from the Fifth Field Hospital in Bangkok. There are some who claim that Southerland was flying space available or, in other words, on leave. There is a big difference between traveling on falsified orders issued from an army hospital and traveling "space A," on leave. If he had been in a space available status, there would be nothing to connect him to the human remains on the aircraft. This author recalls him being on orders when he came into Kadena. Also, the fact that he was wearing a military uniform with medical insignia and passed himself off as being on official orders from a military hospital lead one to question the claim that he was merely smuggling drugs.

We next have an article in the *Milwaukee Journal*, January 10, 1973, and again by Philip A. McCombs, that adds the allegation of murder associated with this heroin smuggling. Despite the headline, the article does not appear to confirm the use of corpses.

Heroin Ring's Use of Corpses Confirmed

> . . . New York trial of several people caught with 25 pounds of heroin failed to get a single conviction in 1969 after a key government witness was found dead with six bullets in his skull the day the trial began.

We also had the situation in the MacDonald case where one detective was shot in the head, ruled a suicide under suspicious circumstances. We further had in the same case a witness for MacDonald shot in the head during a court recess, which was also ruled a suicide.

Next we have an appeals case in 1973[11] that sheds light on the extent of this group's operation. Also, it illuminates the inner workings of what appears to resemble a large drug cartel that employs many people and a variety of drug smuggling strategies.

United States of America, Plaintiff-appellee, v. William Herman Jackson et al., Defendants-appellants

United States Court of Appeals, Tenth Circuit.—482 F.2nd 1167

Argued and Submitted April 9, 1973. Decided July 23, 1973. Rehearing Denied in Nos. 72-1792 and 72-1793 Aug. 21, 1973. Rehearing Denied in No. 72-1653 Aug. 31, 1973.

1. Appellants Jackson, Price, and Gainous, together with one Serles were indicted on two counts of smuggling heroin into the United States. The first count charged the illegal importation or aiding and abetting in the importation of heroin into the United States. The second count charged them with conspiracy in commission of the abave stated offense. A jury convicted appellants Jackson and Price of Count One and all three appellants of Count Two. The defendant Serles previously entered a plea of guilty to the indictment.

2. The attempted smuggling was first observed at U-Tapao Airfield, Thailand. Upon Reaching Travis Air Force Base, California, customs authorities opened the smuggled package and discovered over 7800 grams of 85 percent pure heroin hidden inside. The package was then sent to its destination point, Lowry Air Force Base, Colorado, where powdered soap was substituted for most of the heroin. Finally it was placed in the appropriate warehouse until picked up by unknown

---

[11.] Public.resource.org, *US v Herman Jackson et al.*, Tenth Circuit Court of Appeals. Typographical errors have been left as is.

persons on January 11, 1972. Subsequently four persons were arrested, three of whom are appellants in this case.

3. Serles was the prosecution's chief witness. His testimony is crucial to the government's case and thus will be recited extensively. While stationed at U-Tapao Airfield, Serles became friends with Johnny Trice. These two men discussed shipping contraband into the United States on military flights, but as Trice was later transferred to Tinker Air Force Base, Oklahoma, the discussions went no further.

4. In June or July, 1971, Serles suggested to appellant Jackson that he knew a way to ship goods into the United States. Jackson's reply was "stay cool" and contact him later. Their next visit was in September, when Jackson contacted Series. He handed Series a paper containing instructions for shipping cargo to Tinker Air Force Base, and questioned him on his understanding of the instructions. Convinced that Serles understood shipping procedures. Jackson suggested they meet again later in the day at Jackson's "American Star Bar." When they met later that day, the conversation centered on shipping goods to the United States on military cargo flights. Jackson stated he would like to ship a package weighing over seven Kilos and worth more than its weight in gold. Jackson promised the package would be packed airtight to prevent discovery by dogs, and if Serles would help out he would be paid $15,000 for his efforts. Serles accepted the offer but first wanted to ship a test package to discern whether it would pass customs inspection.

5. The Following night Serles met Andrew Price at Jackson's tavern. Price assured Serles that Jackson had told him everything, so it was all right to proceed with the planning. At the end of their conversation Serles was given $300 in Thai money to bribe Thai workers loading the military cargo.

6. In the latter part of September Serles and Price began executing the plan. They picked up the test package from Jackson's house. Serles then typed up false shipping documents to be sent with the package. This package was delivered to a Thai national at Dong Muong Airfield outside

Bangkok. From there it was flown to U-Tapao where another Thai worker forwarded it to Tinker Air Force Base.

7. At this point we shift to Trice's testimony. Trice testified he informed appellant Gainous of the discussion with Serles concerning smuggling goods into the United States. Later Gainous suggested Trice visit the "big man" at Jackson's tavern, but Trice declined. When Trice was back in the United States on a thirty-day leave, Gainous contacted him by telephone and suggested he come to a party in the south. All expenses would be paid if Trice would make the trip, but ultimately Trice decided not to go.

8. After his leave, Trice was stationed at Tinker Air Force Base. In August Gainous journeyed to Tinker for the purpose of offering Trice $10,000 to pick up a package sent from Thailand. Gainous also wrote down shipping instructions to aid Trice in identifying the package and urged him to write Serles concerning the shipment. In the early part of October Gainous sent Trice more instructions by special delivery. He also met with Trice to find out the best method for shipping a package from Thailand to Tinker.

9. It was during this time that Serles sent the test package to Tinker. Because Trice did not pick up the package, Gainous visited him again, this time to offer him $15,000 to go along with the scheme. Apparently all plans concerning Trice were thereafter discarded, as the next time Gainous contacted him was January, 1972. This call was to inform Trice that Series had been picked up for questioning. Trice was cautioned to "be cool" and only tell the authorities that he had known Gainous since 1966.

10. Serles testimony explains the rest. Because the first test shipment was not picked up, all parties were told to "freeze." Only in December, 1971 did they proceed with their original plans. A second test package was shipped, this time to Lowry Air Force Base. Price instructed Series on how to send this package and gave him another $300 to pay the Thai workers. Once again the package made it through customs inspection, but once again it was not picked up at its destination point. Nevertheless, on December 24 or 25, Price and Serles completed the smuggling scheme.

> Serles typed up false shipping documents from information supplied by Price. The real package was then picked up at Jackson's house and delivered to Thai workers who forwarded it to Lowry Air Force Base. As mentioned earlier, appellants and Serles were arrested for the attempted smuggling and subsequently convicted . . .

The above information illuminates the enormity of the operation that centered around "Jack's place." We now have a variety of shipping methods and destinations. So far, we allegedly have heroin in bodies, although this has never been proven, and certainly have it in military household goods shipments. We also have air force and army personnel using military logistics resources, including air force aircraft, to smuggle large amounts of heroin into the United States. Further, we have heroin smuggling channels set up, or being set up, at and around Fort Bragg, North Carolina, area probably using Pope and Seymour Johnson Air Force Bases as the ports of debarkation. We also have similar systems at Tinker AFB, Oklahoma, and also Lowry AFB, Colorado. The point of origin of these channels appears to be U-Tapao Air Base, Thailand, not to mention many military transshipment points in between. How many other military bases had similar heroin smuggling operations going on?

Later we also had a lot of heroin coming into the United States using military mail. Military mail is US mail that mostly is handled by military personnel in overseas areas. This is mainly mail going to and from military personnel in overseas locations, and it merges with other mail in the United States. From reviewing court cases, it is evident that the drug smuggling operation associated with "Jack's place" used this extensively to smuggle heroin into the United States. It is hard to say how much heroin came into the United States using the mail, but it is evident that it was a lot. Some of the testimony and conclusions of investigators and federal prosecutors establishes that it was easily hundreds of pounds per year and possibly many tons per year.

It also has been established that this smuggling ring also used aircraft maintenance personnel that were going from Thailand to the United States, for training, as transporters of large amounts of heroin. They carried bags that military people call AWOL bags that had as much as two kilos, about 4.4 pounds, of almost pure heroin concealed by a false bottom sewed into the bags. This heroin that was coming out of Thailand was the most pure in the world. Virtually, all of it was over 90 percent pure, and some of it was close to 100 percent pure. Although estimates of the street value of heroin vary substantially, it is safe to say that at that time, a pound of this nearly pure heroin was worth at least a half of a million dollars. Some estimates the author has seen approached a million dollars. So one air force aircraft mechanic carrying two kilos would amount to millions of dollars of heroin.

This is what this author refers to as "the enormity" of these events. Court records show that this ring operated for about ten years. Court records also show that the total amount of heroin smuggled into the United States by this group that can be proven in court is over $500,000,000. It is safe to say that this figure is only a fraction of the total amount, as probably most of the heroin they smuggled was not detected. If most of it had been detected, and the smugglers caught, the ring would not have been in operation. So the total amount that this ring smuggled has got to be in the billions of dollars.

This would make this heroin smuggling operation one of the, if not the, biggest operations of all time. The author has not run into anything like it in many years of researching drug smuggling. We need to also keep in mind that this operation almost totally involved the US military. This was heroin that was moved by military people, in uniform, on military orders, and on military aircraft. Consistently, we have military spokespersons stating, over and over again, that there was no military involvement. This is simply preposterous. Why the consistent denial? Why were there not investigations except those done by other federal agencies, agencies that have a very difficult time catching and prosecuting this criminal military enterprise?

Although it should have been evident that retired and active-duty military personnel were involved in this, there were no courts-martial nor were there any full-scale military investigations. Significant is the fact that retired and reserve personnel are not civilians, and they can be recalled to active duty and court-martialed. The author has seen this happen many times. Even with vast military resources having been misused, killed-in-action bodies having allegedly been defiled, and even a military physician jailed for life over crimes he most likely did not commit, we apparently have no action from the military. One would have expected a storm of investigations, courts-martials, jail sentences, dishonorable discharges, and ad infinitum. Instead, what we saw were repeated denials and cover-ups. Certainly, the army and air force were concerned about their reputations, but this author believes that there was and is a much bigger picture.

We will see in the following chapters that CIA case officers and operatives played a major role in developing the Southeast Asian drug trade, and also starting the Vietnam war. Many of these CIA officers wore US military uniforms and had influential positions in the military. Fletcher Prouty's book, *The Secret Team*, goes into this in detail and explains how these high-ranking commissioned officers used their positions to promote CIA objectives, objectives that are not necessarily in the best interest of the people of the United States. Examples of this are Generals Edward Lansdale and Richard Secord. These two and others will be discussed later in this book. Both played key roles in using their positions to promote war and the drug trade, and there are many more examples that we will see in later chapters. Certainly, these CIA operatives disguised in military uniform would not want their nefarious undertakings exposed. They also would be in positions to make it appear that military drug smuggling be seen as not connected to the military. Further, they would have the CIA training and experience to carry this out.

Conclusions

The above information leads one to believe that the CIA, FBI, and State Department are at least complicit in the international drug trade. It is also clear that pathological personalities have risen to very influential positions in the United States. Further, that Jeffrey MacDonald is an innocent man who has been incarcerated to hide the involvement of influential people that are involved in the narcotics trade. I would add also that the international drug trade has corrupted the judicial branch of government, which is no longer fulfilling its constitutional role of checking and balancing the other two branches of government. Finally, the international drug trade has also corrupted the major media, and as a result, it also is not fulfilling its constitutional role of holding the government accountable to the people. In chapter 3, we will take a closer look at pathological personalities and how, throughout history, they have risen to power.

Chapter Three

Who Are We?

The inspiration for the title of this chapter came from Michael Moore's documentary, *Sicko*. There was a scene where major hospitals and university medical centers were taking patients whose insurance had run out down to skid row and kicking them out onto the street. Some were delirious and all had hospital tags removed so no one could tell what facility they came from. Some even had IV's still sticking out of their veins. Michael Moore ominously asked the question, "Who are we?" and I am asking the question, "Who is running corporate America, the government, the media, and the rest of what we call the country?"

Who would create systems that would destroy whole countries and kill millions of people? Who would throw defenseless sick people out in the street? Who would stuff heroin in the bodies of our young people killed in wars? And the biggest question of all, Why do we let them do these things? Not only do we let them, but we help them! We fight wars for them and even die for them. Why?

Before we go on to the connections the body bag case leads to, we need to explore these subjects. Otherwise, much of what we are going to be looking at, and where we will be going, would just be too unbelievable.

Although I did not major in psychology, I have had a fair number of college courses in this area. I also had some formal training in the air force, mostly in the area of recognizing personality disorders. So I feel comfortable in identifying the kinds of behaviors described in the first chapter as not only abnormal but also in the area of what is referred to as psychopathology. This sort of behavior, and the people that exhibit it, is characterized by a complete lack of guilt or remorse. The more I look around me, the more I wonder if people in this category aren't actually running things. It would explain a lot.

It would explain how all the evidence in the body bag case and also the evidence in the Captain Jeffrey MacDonald case disappeared. Moreover, it would explain how two branches of government could lock up an innocent man for life. If "they" could do that, "they" also would knowingly execute innocent people. Could "they" also start a war on false pretenses, and outright lies, killing hundreds of thousands, perhaps millions, of innocent people? How about the Vietnam War? Was it really a mistake? There sure were a lot of people and corporations that did pretty well during that fiasco.

Did Brown and Root, the predecessor to Halliburton, think they lost out in Vietnam? How about Lockheed, Northrop, and all the rest, did they lose out? And how about Monsanto? Did any of their executives lose any sleep over dumping thousands of tons of Agent Orange all over the Vietnamese and also their fellow Americans? Agent Orange, Agent Violet, and the rest all contained dioxin, one of the most toxic substances known to man. "They" all made millions and billions of dollars while city and farm kids ended up with their guts hanging off a barbed wire fence or unnecessarily dying of disease. Or maybe even have their bodies stuffed with heroin while they're on their way to back to their grief-stricken families. I could go on with depleted uranium and all the rest, but I think you get the picture. So the question remains, who are we?

My search began on how to explain all this. Above, I was only speaking about a very short segment of history. It seems that war, the scourge of humanity, not only has cast its dark shadow over the entire twentieth century, but also has a good start on the twenty-first century as well. Why do we keep allowing this? I have come to the conclusion, increasingly, that the United States has been taken over by psychopaths.

The Science of Evil

I began researching evil in politics and did not find very much at first. Then I found the book, *Political Ponerology: A Science on the Nature of Evil Adjusted for Political Purposes,* by Andrew M.

Lobaczewski. The author was one of several scientists that took part in researching and writing this book. Of the original group, Lobaczewski is the only one left alive. The book was written in secret in Communist Poland. Lobaczewski and the other scientists that worked on the book were victims of one of the most repressive regimes in existence. He describes the history of the how the manuscript came to be, or almost not came to be, below.

> The original manuscript of this book went into the furnace minutes before a secret police raid in Communist Poland. The second copy, painfully reassembled by scientists working under impossible conditions of violence and repression, was sent via courier to the Vatican. Its receipt was never acknowledged—the manuscript and all valuable data lost. In 1984, the third and final copy was written from memory by the last survivor of the original researchers: Andrew Lobaczewski. After half a century of repression, this book is finally available.

Evil is usually treated as a moral issue with religious and philosophical undertones. Lobaczewski, a clinical psychologist, approaches the subject from the direction of the social sciences. This is refreshing. I do not think that lecturers given by clergy would get us very far considering we are talking about evil being conducted at very high levels of power. So first, let's take a look at the question: What exactly is evil?

Psychopaths at the Helm

Lobaczewski's conclusions are that much of what we consider as evil in the world is the result of people who are emotionally abnormal. It is more common than one could imagine for evil people to rise to power in societies, most notably in politics, and start a process of placing pathological individuals around them who, in turn, do the same. This ripple effect permeates the whole society, resulting in what can be described as a pathocracy. In fact, this process has happened throughout history, time and again resulting in incalculable suffering. Lobaczewski's research also led him to conclude that, by a long shot, not all psychopaths run afoul of the law and end up in jail. He states that psychopaths and other personality disorders can be very successful and are actually overrepresented in many social, business, and political settings. Surprisingly, they are overrepresented in prison systems, politics, law enforcement agencies, law firms, and in the media.

Let's take a quick look at what a psychopath is. Although the American Psychiatric Association (APA) no longer uses this term, much of the rest of the world does. The APA has incorporated the term psychopath and sociopath within a broader definition designated as antisocial personality disorder. Even within the APA, there is wide disagreement as to what these terms actually mean.

The most recent *Diagnostic and Statistical Manual of Mental Disorders* (*DSM-IV-TR*) is an American handbook for mental health professionals. It lists different categories of mental disorders and the criteria for diagnosing them, according to the publishing organization, the American Psychiatric Association. The APA defines antisocial personality disorder, which would include Lobaczewski's psychopathic personality disorder, as a pervasive pattern of disregard for the violation of the rights of others occurring since age fifteen years, as indicated by three or more of the following:

1. Failure to conform to social norms with respect to lawful behaviors as indicated by repeatedly performing acts that are grounds for arrest.
2. Deceitfulness, as indicated by repeated lying, use of aliases, or conning others for personal profit or pleasure.
3. Impulsivity or failure to plan ahead.
4. Aggressiveness, as indicated by repeated physical fights or assaults.
5. Reckless disregard for the safety of self or others.
6. Consistent irresponsibility.
7. Lack of remorse, as indicated by being indifferent to or rationalizing having hurt, mistreated, or stolen from another.

When using the term *psychopath*, lack of remorse described in number seven would be essential. Antisocial personality types are capable of feeling remorse, although oftentimes somewhat diminished; however, psychopaths are incapable of feeling guilt or remorse for their actions. This is the overarching identifying mark of a psychopath.

The stereotypical model of a psychopath is personified by the character Hannibal Lecter in the movie *Silence of the Lambs*. Hannibal Lecter did indeed have no conscience or remorse. He did, however, have some other characteristics that are not typical of psychopaths. Although the character Hannibal Lecter was highly intelligent and competent as a physician, Lobaczewski's research indicates that psychopaths are not particularly intelligent, scoring below average on IQ tests. Their inability to empathize with fellow humans makes it impossible for them to fully use their cognitive skills to solve problems. This adversely affects their IQ.

They are, however, extremely manipulative and cunning. They know that they are not normal, but they feel that they are superior to the normal human beings, not being encumbered by normal human emotions. They also are very adept at identifying other psychopaths and networking with them. Further, they spent much time and effort studying normal human beings so that they are able to imitate normal human behavior. They are so accomplished at this that they are oftentimes able to fool professionals. We will be expanding on these concepts later, but for now, please keep in mind that pathological personalities are definitely capable of taking over governments, large corporations, and other large institutions. In fact, they have done so over and over again throughout history.

Critical to our understanding of psychopaths is the realization that they do not always end up in jail. Especially if born of privilege, they are quite capable of being extremely successful. With the right support system, they can, and do, rise to the highest levels of society. Noteworthy is the fact that the percentage of successful psychopaths is higher in competitive societies such as free enterprise and capitalist systems. They do quite well in democracies such as our own.

A psychopath's greatest fear is that of being discovered or found out. They feel threatened by information systems, education, and knowledge. Lobaczewski wrote *Ponerology* in 1984. This was before the advent of the Internet so, of course, he did not mention the Internet in his book. Being an unedited, uncensored medium, you can rest assured that the Internet will be the subject of intensive efforts to control the information on it. It is, however, this author's belief that the information genie is out of the bottle, and that these attempts to control the Internet will fail. Even if psychopaths in the media, government, and the corporate sector succeed at censoring and controlling the Internet, other forms of uncontrolled media will take its place.

Also, throughout history, there has been constant friction between pathological personalities and the highly creative members among all societies. The highly creative among us always find routes around the pathological. Eventually, the creators win, but in the process, pathological personalities cause enormous damage and have done so for hundreds, perhaps thousands, of years.

Civilizations have gone through what Lobaczewski terms "the hysteroidal cycle" throughout history. Mankind has always strived to satisfy its most basic needs so that we, as individuals, can become truly creative. Those familiar with Maslow's hierarchy of needs will recognize this process. We have to have our most basic needs satisfied such as food, water, shelter, and safety before we can let our imaginations wander to create sculptures, works of art, write poetry, dig in the ground for artifacts, or restore a '57 Chevy. Unfortunately, in the process of satisfying our basic needs, we invariably end up exploiting others. This was as true of the Romans as it is of Western civilization today.

We first started with animals using them for food and other items such as tools and clothing. We also exploited them to do our hard work for us. We then found it necessary to exploit our fellow human beings in the form of slavery. It was animal and human muscle that resulted in the glory of Rome. A few of the privileged class benefited from the suffering of many. The Romans found that exploiting other human beings allowed them the dubious luxury of having the time and resources to be creative and also have fun at the expense of others.

This is an inconvenient truth that most societies have found it necessary to avoid. So instead of exploiting defenseless people, we replace the cold hard facts with lofty ideals. From the Romans to the British, militarily weaker peoples were not being exploited but were "being civilized." And of course now, North Americans are "instilling democracy" into societies that are incapable of developing these higher concepts on their own, like Iraq. Never mind that Mesopotamia was the wellspring from whence all western civilization has sprung. The "cradle of civilization" is the term I recall from my studies at a very early age in school.

I also find it noteworthy that the last time I looked at a high school world history book, I found a page and a half about the region that is now Iraq and most of that was a picture of a stone horse. Gone is anything about the cradle of civilization, Hammurabi's code, Babylon, Persia, or much of anything about the region that is roughly what we now call Iraq. Perhaps it is easier to kill people that we think of as having no history and do not understand complex society or government. I have even heard Americans state that they, meaning Iraqis, are "ungrateful" to America for having tried to show them what "democracy and civilization" are all about. It would appear that it is much easier to kill them if you do not know that we came from them.

Back to psychopaths and other pathological personalities. These pathological personalities tend to rise to power when societies are evolving and developing. When it comes to subjugating and exploiting other human beings, psychopaths are masters. They tend to be able to convince people that those "bad" or "inferior" other people are not worthy of basic human rights. Once one group is subjugated and exploited, these pathological personalities select another group to subjugate. Generally, the society goes along with this because the "they" that psychopaths are persecuting and exploiting is not them, and the members of society not being persecuted tend to perceive that they benefit from this. We all, normal people that is, end up to be victimized. Nobody gains except a small cabal of emotional deviants, for a while that is.

This part of the hysteroidal process by which pathological personalities take over a society is best illustrated by a poem attributed to Pastor Martin Niemoller. It is generally referred to as "First they came . . ." It is about the inactivity of German people, especially intellectuals, following the Nazi's rise to power and the purging of their chosen targets, group after group.

> When the Nazis came for the communists,
> I remained silent;
> I was not a communist.
> When they locked up the social Democrats,
> I remained silent;
> I was not a social democrat.
> When they came for the trade unionists,
> I did not speak out;
> I was not a trade unionist.
> When they came for the Jews,

I remained silent;
I wasn't a Jew.
When they came for me,
there was no one left to speak out.

Not speaking out about injustice for fear of persecution is a common human reaction that is fairly well-known, at least as far as the Nazi regime was concerned. Lobaczewski's clinical studies go much further than this. They identify other much more complex factors. He explains that during the good times, and invariably times do become good, truth becomes uncomfortable because it reveals inconvenient facts. People tend to unconsciously ignore inconvenient truths when things are going fine. After a while this becomes the norm and accepted by the majority of society. At this point, even normal people are thinking abnormally. Problems develop when a society such as this has to make complex decisions. They become incapable of making these decisions because they are dealing with distorted and sometimes completely faulty information. Simply put, they become unable to change. They are unwilling to jeopardize the good times for truth or justice.

To further complicate things, the pathological personalities in charge tend to "negatively select" their assistants and lieutenants. Remember that psychopaths are experts at recognizing each other, and so they choose their own kind to assist them. They also select other pathological personalities in specific areas to suit their purposes. So what we end up with is a society that is run and managed by a disproportionate number of abnormal personalities.

This negative selection process permeates all areas of society. Government, industry, and the media all fall under the management and tutelage of networks of pathological personalities. Lobaczewski terms this a "pathocracy." These pathological individuals become extremely difficult to dislodge for several reasons. The first of which is that a large number of society's normal people will tolerate them because of reasons previously stated. They also have the advantage of having most, if not all, of the tools of power and influence, or at least they are perceived as having them.

Because psychopathological individuals have below-average intelligence, they inevitably mismanage the societies they take over. They are incapable of foreseeing the disastrous consequences of their inadequate decision-making processes. They loot the national treasury to enrich themselves and their cronies on fruitless and shortsighted ventures. They start unnecessary wars that slaughter millions of innocent people. They imprison and torture their so-called enemies. They cause untold destruction and mayhem not only within their society but oftentimes throughout the world. This can go on for generations, each generation in turn becoming dysfunctional.

Those times referred to as "the good old days" provide fertile ground for ever-increasing tragedy because of the moral, intellectual, and character decay from within. Abnormal becomes normal, and normal becomes abnormal. Lobaczewski sees this "hysteroidal cycle" happening over and over again throughout history. The phrase "hysteroidal cycle" refers to the hysterical reaction of society to the political manifestation of evil. Hysteria is characterized by acute anxiety and impaired decision-making processes.

Ponerology in Recent History

Lobaczewski uses the relatively recent example of German Emperor Wilhelm II to illustrate this process. He points out that Kaiser Wilhelm was subjected to brain trauma at birth. This fact was hidden from the German people although it had a profound effect not only in the German people but the world at large. This brain damage in Wilhelm resulted in a head of state with a "characteropathic personality," and this played a major role in the sequence of events that led to the disaster we know as World War I.

There is historical record of Wilhelm's symptoms. The upper left portion of his body was impaired. He had difficulty learning grammar, geometry, and drawing, which are typical of the academic difficulties caused by minor brain lesions. His personality was infantile in nature, and he had difficulty controlling his emotions. Further, he was somewhat paranoid and tended to sidestep important issues and dodge problems. He and his family hid his feelings of inferiority with general's uniforms and portraits in which he struck fancy poses. When he came to power, he replaced the political "old guard" with persons of inferior abilities. Negative selection took place. Psychopathological propaganda became commonplace. Slogans replaced arguments, and inconvenient truths were replaced by expedient misconceptions.

Kaiser Wilhelm came to power during a time when what is described by Lobaczewski as a "wave of hysteria" was spreading throughout Europe. Then, Archduke Ferdinand was assassinated in Sarajevo, and the European powers reacted inappropriately. Armies took the battlefield according to war plans that did not fit the situation. Kaiser Wilhelm and others were faced with problems that were way beyond their abilities, and hence we had the absolute disaster that was World War I.

Lobaczewski then delineates how forces came into play that resulted in pathological individuals laying the groundwork for the takeover of Germany by an outright psychopath. Hence, we had Adolf Hitler in World War II. Generally, Hitler is thought of today as having been a very charismatic and persuasive individual. However, to an objective observer watching films of his speeches, it is almost inconceivable that the German people could have chosen for their leader such a ridiculous human being. Lobaczewski explains that this can only happen when a society is in the grips of evil promulgated by pathological individuals that constitute, at most, six percent of the population.

The Ponerological Process

By no means was Nazi Germany the only example of this ponerological process. Lobaczewski explains that this process has taken place over and over again throughout history. He describes how a series of pathological personalities, each laying the groundwork for the next, causes a cascade of events and circumstances that ultimately result in what he describes as a pathocracy.

This process begins with the utopian dreamers who are often times schizoid. Karl Marx would be a good example. Schizoids are usually socially withdrawn and do not have successful intimate relationships. They do, however, seem to have very active imaginations in which they contrive elaborate and creative social systems. They tend to create worldviews that would be appropriate for their own behavior patterns. In other words, an imaginary world in which they would fit. A contemporary example would be the Neoconservative philosopher Leo Strauss. According to some critics, Strauss displayed typical schizoidal characteristics.

Let's look a little closer at Leo Strauss. Nicholas Xenos, professor of political science at the University of Massachusetts, argues that Strauss fulfilled the role of the mastermind behind today's Neoconservative ideologies. In his article "Leo Strauss and the Rhetoric of the War on Terror" published in *Logos Journal*, spring 2004, Xenos states that Strauss "was not an anti-liberal in the sense in which we commonly mean 'anti-liberal' today, but an anti-democrat in a fundamental sense, a true reactionary. Strauss was somebody who wanted to go back to a previous, pre-liberal, pre-bourgeois era of blood and guts, of imperial domination, of authoritarian rule, of pure fascism." As evidence, Xenos cites Strauss's attempt in 1933 to gain favor with Charles Maurras, the leader of the right-wing reactionary group, *Action Francaise*. He also references a letter Strauss wrote to his friend Karl Löwith in 1933 in which he defended the politics of the extreme right against the Nazis. Strauss wrote that "just because Germany has turned to the right and has expelled us (Jews), it simply does not follow that the principles of the right are therefore to be rejected. To the contrary, only on the basis of principles of the right—fascist, authoritarian, imperial—is it possible in a dignified manner, without the ridiculous and pitiful appeal to 'the inalienable rights of man' to protest against the mean nonentity (Nazism)."

There has been a great deal of controversy surrounding Strauss and his perceived role as the "father of the neocons." Some of it supports Lobeczewski's point that the original vision of people who get tagged as the fathers of movements gets corrupted by opportunists who change the meaning of the key concepts and terminology of the so-called "fathers" to suit their own purposes.

Lobaczewski goes even further in diagnosing these opportunists that come after the founders as characteropaths. He explains that this is the next step in the development of a full-blown pathocracy. Just as Marx would have been flabbergasted to see his ideas used for the foundation of what became the pathological system known as Soviet Communism, it is likely that Strauss would have been equally shocked to see his ideas become the political philosophy known as neoconservativism.

The process by which political evil is created is not like a committee of pathological personalities that get together and decide what they are going to do. They do not decide ahead of time that they will first start out with the schizoids; and when they have done their part, the characteropaths are going to take over, who in turn will hand things over to the psychopaths to complete the process. Each group of pathological personalities becomes aware of the opportunity to do the only thing that they know how to do well, and that would be to exercise control over others, each in their own way and when the time is right.

So after the founders of a movement start losing control, the characteropaths seize the opportunity to take over for their own purposes. A great deal of what they do is to change the meaning of terminology to suit their purposes. This is where terms such as "civilizing," supposedly uncivilized peoples, have been used over and over again to mask the characteropaths' true intentions. Of course, "liberating" people sounds better that conquering defenseless people and stealing their natural resources. I once heard a human rights advocate talk about how there were virtually no literary works that came out of Germany after World War II. She explained that the German language had become so corrupted by this process that the words in the language itself did not have clear meaning. The symbols of language no longer represented understandable ideas and concepts, and hence they had a virtual vacuum of expressed thought.

We need to keep in mind the motives of the pathological personalities that were the subject of Lobeczewski's research. First of all, they do what they do because they are not very good at anything else. They are of below-average intelligence and lacking in skills and abilities other than manipulating and controlling other human beings. At this, they are very adept. Also, Lobaczewski mentioned that they seem to derive pleasure from causing suffering and enjoy wielding power and influence over others.

He further explains that the one fear these pathological personalities have is of being discovered for what they are and henceforth losing power. Again, Lobaczewski simply explains that they are most afraid of this because they cannot just choose to do something else. They are only good at controlling and manipulating people and social systems. If they lose power in politics and business, they are out of luck. They have no talent and no ability.

Ponerology Comes to the United States

The above is why these pathological personalities put so much energy into deception and control. This is why they are so adept at word crafting and using the classical fallacies of logic to mask their true intentions. We have only to look at some very recent examples of this process. Anyone who reads the documents that came out of the so-called neoconservative think tank, the Project for a New American Century (PNAC), will recognize many of the points we are talking about here. The best known document produced by this "think tank" is the policy document "Rebuilding America's Defenses." This document openly advocates for total global military domination. It is obvious to this author, and many others, that the only remaining superpower probably does not need to rebuild the country's defenses. If one was planning on how to increase the power of the United States in the twenty-first century, one would start by developing other forms of power other than military, such as political and economic power. One might notice that the United States is not doing so well in these areas lately. Further, the transformation of the United States from a super-power to a hyper-power runs the risk of bankrupting the country. It also appears that this country is not too far from doing this either.

It is obvious that the authors of this document are not altogether very bright. Further, if we consider the findings of Andrew Lobaczewski and compare them to the ideas expressed by the authors of "Rebuilding America's Defenses," we can conclude that these people are also lacking in character. In fact, many of them clearly fit the description of the characteropath. Most of them were put into office with the advent of the Bush administration, and they have run the Pentagon, the Department of Defense, and the White House during most of the administration.

Although they are good at usurping power and control, they are not good at doing anything else. This explains why, with all of the Bush administration's grand ideas and rationalizations, they have failed at everything they have set out to do. Simply put, they have no talent other than taking over, so they have no clue what to do once they have achieved this. The failures and demonstrations of poor judgment will send ripples around the world for many years to come. American prestige has become an oxymoron. Our infrastructure is falling apart, public education is in a tailspin, the dollar is plummeting, and the stock market is in freefall. People in Spain now live longer than Americans, and Cuba has a lower infant mortality rate than the United States. Of the three major categories of national power, we are waning in two, diplomatic and economic, and we are left with using the only form of power we have remaining—military. Hence we have Venezuela's Hugo Chavez giving us the "bird" almost daily and forming economic, military, and political alliances on a global scale, and what is our response? We reactivate the fourth fleet to send to South and Central America to send a "wake-up" message to Chavez and anyone else that dares to defy us. This display of gunboat diplomacy and excessive use of force is a desperate act of a dying empire trying to use fear and intimidation to make up for the lack of ability to lead the world.

Hugo Chavez is a classic example of a world leader who is actually using the resources of the country to benefit his people. This sort of unruly behavior is always characterized by the United States as "Marxism," "left leaning," or "socialism." Mr. Chavez's cardinal sin was, and is, that he did not allow the United States to excessively profit from the country's vast oil resources.

Another example of this would be Saddam Hussein. Although he certainly had the ability to be incredibly brutal, this had nothing to do with the U.S. invasion and occupation of Iraq. Saddam Hussein committed two unforgivable sins. He nationalized the production of oil and used the profits to provide free medical care for the Iraqi people and also free education. Before the Gulf Wars, Iraq had state-of-the-art medical universities attended by students of which over half were women. The next cardinal sin he committed was trading Iraqi oil in Euro dollars. With the American dollar almost in freefall, this prospect looks extremely attractive to many US trading partners including Saudi Arabia. If Saddam Hussein could pull this off, the rest of the world might try it also. This would mean the end of the US dollar as the world standard of exchange and the end of the US global financial system as we know it. Of course, the United States could not tolerate this. These were the two hidden sins that got Saddam Hussein hung high. It was not that he slaughtered his own people to keep his country together, which he did do. But then again, Abraham Lincoln did precisely the same thing, and he is our national hero of all time.

Pathological Personalities, Let's Start at the Top

While reading Lobaczewski's *Ponerology*, I could not help but have contemporary names and faces pop into my head. Although he wrote it over twenty years ago, it is as if he was predicting the future. Even before George W. Bush took office, there were disturbing reports about him, although not front page. A childhood playmate reported that George abused animals when they were children.

Further, in the year following the execution of Karla Faye Tucker, one of the many condemned prisoners put to death during the Bush governorship, conservative commentator Tucker Carlson questioned Governor Bush about how the Board of Pardons and Parole had arrived at the determination on her clemency plea. Carlson alleged that Bush, eluding to a televised interview which Karla Faye Tucker had given to talk show host Larry King, smirked and spoke mockingly about her:[12]

> In the weeks before the execution, Bush says, "A number of protesters came to Austin to demand clemency for Karla Faye Tucker." "Did you meet with any of them?" I ask. Bush whips around and stares at me. "No, I didn't meet with any of them," he snaps, as though I've just asked the dumbest, most offensive question ever posed. "I didn't meet with Larry King either when he came down for it. I watched his interview with Tucker, though. He asked her real difficult questions like, 'What would you say to Governor Bush?'" "What was her answer?" I wonder. "'Please,'" Bush whimpers, his lips pursed in mock desperation, "'don't kill me.'" I must have looked shocked—ridiculing the pleas of a condemned prisoner who has since been executed seems odd and cruel—because he immediately stops smirking.

Apparently, journalist Carlson followed up on Bush's remark by reviewing a videotape of the interview on Larry King's show. Carlson found that Tucker had in fact not uttered the entreaty, "Please don't kill me" or words to that effect.[13]

The above, along with George W. Bush's early appointments, caused this author grave concerns. Further, many of his appointments were troubling. Names such as Cheney, Rumsfeld, Wolfowitz, Faith, Pearle, and other neocons that came up with the documents created by the "Project for a New American Century" sent a chill down my spine. Although this was well before I ran into the works of Andrew Lobaczewski, you could tell that this was a collection of personalities

---

12. Tucker Carlson, Talk Magazine, September 1999, p. 106.
13. Tim Noah, "Bush's Tookie," *Slate Magazine*, 2 Dec 2005.

that are not in the normal range. I noted this at the time and recalled it later when researching evil in politics.

The Bushes

Lobaczewski also went into another area that caught my attention. That was that pathological personalities can run in families. He said that these abnormal personalities could be inherited, and if this was true, the Bush clan would be an excellent subject for research. One of the most prominent critics of the Bush family is John Loftus, a former federal prosecutor and past president of the Florida Holocaust Museum in St. Peter's Petersburg. Loftus co-authored a book in 1994 with Mark Aarons entitled *The Secret War Against the Jews: How Western Espionage Betrayed the Jewish People*. The book alleges various misdeeds by George W. Bush's father, George H. W. Bush, his grandfather, Prescott Bush, and his great-grandfather, George Herbert Walker. Probably the most serious charges were against Prescott Bush.

One of the charges against Prescott Bush is a matter of record. In 1942, Under the Trading with the Enemy Act, Franklin Delano Roosevelt seized several companies in which he had an interest. At that time, Prescott Bush was an investment banker with Brown Brothers Harriman, which had funneled US capital into Germany during the 1920s and '30s. One of these seized companies was the Union Banking Corporation of New York, which was controlled by German industrialists Fritz Thyssen. Thyssen had provided financial support for the Nazi party in its infancy, which was a major factor in its early growth and development. In fact, he wrote a book about it entitled, *I Paid Hitler*. Defenders of Prescott Bush assert that he did not know about these transactions and that he was being unfairly vilified. It is noteworthy, however, that these companies were seized in 1942, well after World War II had begun, and it is also hard to believe that a corporate executive at Bush's level in several organizations was unaware of these facts.

There is also the charge that the value of German industrial assets in which Bush and friends invested increased during World War II, in part due to Nazi slave labor, and that Bush benefited from this increase when the assets were returned after the war. Supposedly, he got $1.5 million when Union Banking Corporation was liquidated. It might be a stretch to conclude that Prescott Bush directly benefited from Nazi slave labor. However, the extent to which Prescott Bush and the rest of American business collaborated with the Nazis is a sad tale.

Possibly the most serious charge against Prescott Bush is the long-lingering claim that he orchestrated a plan to launch a fascist coup in the 1930s. It is a matter of record that marine corps Major General Smedley Butler testified to Congress that a secretive group of industrialists and bankers, including Prescott Bush, were planning a coup. Recent documents released by the national archives seem to support this allegation. Naomi Wolf, author of the essay "Fascist America, in 10 easy steps," best summarized these allegations, and their far-reaching implications, in an interview she gave on *The Alex Jones Show*, November 28, 2007:

> There was a scheme in the 30's and Prescott Bush was one of the leaders of this scheme, an industrialist who admired fascism and thought that was a good idea—to have a coup in the United States along the lines of the coup they saw taking place in Italy and Germany," said Wolf, referring to the testimony of Marine Corps Maj.-Gen. Smedley Butler, who was approached by a wealthy and secretive group of industrialists and bankers, including Prescott Bush—the current President's grandfather, who asked him to command a 500,000 strong rogue army of veterans that would help stage a coup to topple then President Franklin Delano Roosevelt . . .
>
> Smedley Butler had been involved with violent regime change throughout his career, but he was approached by these conspirators, including Prescott Bush, and he outed them and he testified to Congress that they were planning a coup in the United States—it's in the Congressional record," said Wolf, adding that the coup was being bankrolled by German industrialist and one of Hitler's chief financiers Fritz Thyssen . . .
>
> What is amazing to me and resonant to me is that when the Nuremberg trials were finally put in place, these Nazi industrialists, some of whom had colluded with Americans including IBM, were about to be brought to trial and sent to prison—there was a moment at which they were going to look into turning the spotlight on their American partners . . .

> Laws such as the Military Commissions Act of 2006 were consciously designed to protect current President Bush and his co-conspirators from being indicted for war crimes, harking back to Prescott Bush's history...
>
> The family history is that you can make so much money uniting corporate interests with a fascist state that violently represses people, that's why when I saw the recycling of so much Nazi language, Nazi tactics, Nazi strategies, Nazi imagery in the Bush White House and then finally belatedly people brought to me this history of Prescott Bush's attempted coup and Smedley Butler's revelations—it gives me absolute chills.

In the same interview, Wolf said that she was first alerted to begin researching America's slide into fascism when her friend, a daughter of a Holocaust survivor, warned her that the same events that laid the foundations for the rise of the third Reich in the early 1930s Germany, when it was still a parliamentarian democracy, were being mirrored in modern-day America.

This mirrors exactly Andrew Lobaczewski's experience when coming to the United States for the first time in the 1980s. Lobaczewski explained in his book, *Ponerology*, that older Europeans in the United States had told him that they see the same conditions coming into play in this country that were present in Europe and resulted in the coming to power of the Nazi regime in Germany.

Another member of the Bush clan whose character development is questionable is Barbara Bush. Never known to be the friendly, generous sort, she outdid herself with her comments made about the evacuees from New Orleans after hurricane Katrina. On a tour of hurricane relief centers in the Houston area, Barbara Bush said, referring to the poor who had lost everything back home and evacuated, "This is working very well for them." The former first lady's remarks were aired September 5, 2005, on American public media's "Marketplace" program.[14] She was part of a group in Houston that day at the

---

14. Editor and Publisher Staff, "Barbara Bush: Things Working Out 'Very Well' For Poor Evacuees from New Orleans," *Editor and Publisher Magazine*, September 5, 2005, 7:25 P.M. ET updated 8:00 P.M.

Astrodome that included her husband, former president George H. W. Bush, former President Bill Clinton, who was chosen by George W. Bush, to head fund-raising efforts for the recovery. At the beginning of the program (the subject of which was the surge of evacuees to the Texas City), Barbara Bush also said, "Almost everyone I've talked to says we're going to move to Houston." She also added, "What I'm hearing, which is sort of scary, is they all want to stay in Texas. Everyone is so overwhelmed by the hospitality . . . And so many of the people in the arena here, you know, were underprivileged anyway, so this—this (*she chuckles slightly*) is working very well for them."

That a person born of privilege such as Barbara Bush would make these comments is shocking. These people had been severely traumatized, lost everything, and were struggling for their very existence. These insensitive comments, with racist undertones, indicate an individual that is incapable of empathy. Further proof of this is the fact that she would make these comments in public, thus indicating that she is incapable of understanding the implications of what she was saying. Barbara Bush's comments during Hurricane Katrina and its aftermath together with the almost total lack of response from the Bush administration indicated a shocking disregard for human life and suffering.

These examples illustrate an entire family that is morally and ethically damaged and off course. Over and over again, the callous disregard and insensitivity for people along with the displayed ineptitude at any endeavor other than usurping power, deceiving, and exploiting people indicate a family in which pathological processes are inherent. Nowhere in the Bush family do you see reverence for democratic institutions. To the contrary, there appears to be an attraction toward fascist dictatorships, repeatedly and over several generations.

Alberto R. Gonzales, US Attorney General

Another face that popped into my head was that of Alberto R. Gonzales, the first Hispanic US attorney in US history. This is a sad case of an incompetent and morally flawed individual who could not live up to the expectations of this position, nor could he possibly set a positive example for other Hispanics to follow. Gonzales was Bush's legal adviser when Bush was governor of Texas. He advised him on key matters such as stays of execution for death row inmates. With Gonzales's advice and recommendations, Bush set all-time records for executing prisoners.

In his six years as governor of Texas, the state executed 152 prisoners. This is far more than any other state. The only stay of execution that Bush granted was in a case where the DNA evidence irrefutably cleared the death row inmate, and the execution would have been stopped anyway. The *Chicago Tribune* investigated the first 131 of the death cases during Governor Bush's time. The results of this investigation are startling.

In one-third of the cases, the lawyer who represented the death penalty defendant on trial or on appeal had been or was later disbarred or otherwise sanctioned. In forty cases, the lawyers presented no evidence at all or only one witness at the sentencing phase of the trial. In twenty-nine cases, the prosecution used testimony from a psychologist who, based on a hypothetical question about the defendant's past, predicted he would commit future violence. Most of those psychiatrists testified without having examined the defendant. Other witnesses included one who is temporarily released from a psychiatric ward, a pathologist who admitted faking autopsies, and a judge who had been reprimanded for lying about his credentials. When asked about this, Governor Bush said, "We've adequately answered innocence or guilt" in all of these cases. It is obvious that on the matter of life and death, neither Alberto R. Gonzales nor George W. Bush care very much, if at all. Human life has little or no value to them, the hallmark stamp of a psychopath.

A closer look at the mechanics of these life and death decisions indicates a callousness and total lack of concern on the part of Alberto R. Gonzales. Gonzales is a Harvard educated lawyer who went on to become the Texas Secretary of State and a justice on the Texas Supreme Court. He also served Bush as White House counsel and of course United States Attorney General. Gonzales prepared the first fifty-seven summaries in these death row cases. Although he never intended the summaries to be made public, they were determined by a later Texas attorney general to be not exempt from the disclosure requirements of the public information act and subsequently obtained by the media.

These summaries were Bush's primary source of information in deciding whether someone would live or die. The summaries were extremely brief, amounting to from three to seven pages.[15] They consisted of a short description of the crime, a few paragraphs on the defendant's personal background, and a condensed legal history. They generally did not make a recommendation for or against execution, but they all appeared to imply that if an appeals court had rejected a defendant's claims, there was no reason for the governor to second-guess that claim. This ignores the basic rationale for clemency in the first place. Clemency exists because the justice system does make mistakes. It is one more check to ensure that innocent people are not punished under the law. The fact that a Harvard educated lawyer, with much experience, does not seem to understand this is chilling. Further review of these documents discloses that Gonzales frequently failed to appraise the governor of crucial legal issues such as incompetent counsel, conflicts of interest, and even outright evidence of innocence.

While serving as US attorney general, Gonzales's inability to grasp the fundamental legal concepts was illustrated with his assertion that the US Constitution does not grant the right, or writ, of habeas corpus. The writ of habeas corpus is the recourse a person has to challenge unlawful detention. It does not determine innocence or guilt but ensures that due process takes place before somebody is imprisoned. Although the US Constitution does not define habeas corpus as a right, it states that "the privilege of the Writ of Habeas Corpus shall not be suspended, unless when in Cases of Rebellion or Invasion the public Safety may require it (Article 1, Section 9)." It does not take a lawyer to understand that the writ of habeas corpus was provided for by the Magna Carta over six hundred years ago. Further, the US Constitution does not grant rights, it only defines them. The Declaration of Independence is the document that establishes where rights come from, and it simply states that "all men are created equal, that they are endowed by their Creator with certain unalienable rights . . ." This idea came from John Locke, and others, and is embodied in the concept of "natural law." It is shocking that a US attorney general does not understand this. How unfortunate that the first Hispanic US attorney general did not understand the fundamental concepts of the law and foundations of the rights of the people.

---

15. Alen Berlow, "The Texas Clemency Memos," *The Atlantic*, July/August, 2003, http://www.theatlantic.com/doc/200307/berlow

Two Lackluster Secretaries of State

Other faces that came to mind were those of Colin Powell and Condoleezza Rice. Lobaczewski explained that in a pathocracy, the top leaders surround themselves with pathological individuals according to how their psychopathology fits the leader's needs. In government, however, even pathological leaders understand that to conduct foreign affairs, they need to be represented by people that at least have the appearance of being normal. So for these positions, they tend to appoint relatively bright and competent individuals with the exception that they will do exactly what they are told to do regardless of whether it is right or wrong, good or bad, moral or immoral. Pathological leaders tend to appoint individuals with a warped sense of loyalty that enables them to do whatever the leader chooses them to do without complaint.

Colin Powell has a long history of this that goes back as far as the My Lai Massacre in Vietnam. Major Powell, assigned to the Americal Division, has been implicated in the cover-up of this infamous event. Most Vietnam veterans remember the My Lai Massacre as a horrific event where troops of the American old division went into the village of My Lai, spent four hours rounding up villagers, mostly old men, women, and children. They tied them up, put them in ditches, and shot 347 civilians including babies. They even took a lunch break in the middle of these activities.

This incident was reported by young specialist fourth class named Tom Glen who had served in an Americal Division mortar platoon. In a letter to General Creighton Abrams, the commander of US forces in Vietnam, Glen accused the division of routine brutality against civilians, including the My Lai Massacre. The letter landed on Major Powell's desk. After his superficial investigation in which Powell did not even interview Glenn, Powell not only admitted to no wrongdoing by the division but stated that Glenn had not been close enough to the front lines to know what he was writing about. Further, he faulted Glenn for not complaining earlier and for failing to be more specific in his letter. Powell's findings were a collection of distortions and misrepresentations.

It would take an infantryman named Ron Ridenhour to put together the truth about the atrocity at My Lai after completing his tour in Vietnam. Ridenhour interviewed Americal Division members who had participated in the massacre and forwarded a shocking report to the army inspector general. After a thorough investigation, courts-martial were held against the army personnel implicated in the murder of the My Lai civilians, no thanks to Colin Powell.

In his best-selling book, *My American Journey*, Powell made no mention of his handling of Tom Glenn's complaint. He did, however, justify killing unarmed civilians. After mentioning the My Lai massacre in his book, Powell put forth a justification of the Americal Division's brutality.[16]

> I recall a phrase we used in the field, MAM, for military age male . . . . If a Hilo spotted a peasant in black pajamas who looked remotely suspicious, a possible MAM, the pilot would circle and fire in front of him. If he moved, his movement was judged evidence of hostile intent, and the next burst was not in front, but at him. Brutal? Maybe so. But an able battalion commander with whom I had served at Gelnhausen, Lt. Colonel Walter Pritchard, was killed by enemy sniper fire while observing MAMs from a helicopter. And Prichard was only one of many. The kill-or-be-killed nature of combat tends to dull fine perceptions of right and wrong.

We are not talking about "fine perceptions of right and wrong" here. We are talking about war crimes and the senseless slaughter of defenseless civilians. I might add that these civilians were supposedly our allies and for whom we were supposedly fighting so that they could supposedly be free. The fact that a field-grade officer who rose to the position of chairman of the Joint Chiefs of Staff would hold such opinions has ominous implications.

Many years later, Colin Powell would again show us insight into his true character. During Desert Storm, there were mounting concerns about Iraqi civilian casualties. When asked about the growing number of Iraqi civilians killed by US forces, General Powell stated that "that is a figure I'm not particularly interested in." This coming from an

---

[16.] Colin L. Powell and Joseph Persico, *My American Journey*, Ballantine Books, (New York, 1995), 140.

individual of his rank and position is shocking. Further, as Powell well knew, the senseless slaughter of thousands of defenseless Iraqi civilians was a war crime of major proportions, as was the targeting of the Iraqi infrastructure. The almost total destruction of power production and water treatment facilities not only qualified as war crimes but also genocide.

All US military personnel are required, by law, to be trained in the Law of Armed Conflict. They are trained in what it is and how it came about. This body of law directly resulted from the untold millions of civilians senselessly mass murdered during many conflicts and wars, especially WW I and WWII. The wholesale destruction of entire cities and slaughter of millions of civilians shocked the world into realizing that something had to be done. From this incalculable destruction came our present-day tools to manage disagreements and minimize the effects of conflict on defenseless civilians. The civilian world knows these tools roughly as the Geneva conventions, and the military recognizes them as the Law of Armed Conflict. Fundamental among these codes is the law of proportionality. Simply stated, this means that an armed force cannot deliberately target civilians or hit a target that is mostly civilians. The armed force must only select military targets and does everything reasonable to minimize civilian casualties. General Powell could cite chapter and verse about this, but from My Lai to Iraq, with many years in between, it appears that Powell has no moral qualms about killing defenseless civilians and deliberately destroying an entire civilization. He justifies much of this in his book, but I put it in the category of rationalization.

General Powell also participated in some of the most egregious policy decisions made by the George W. Bush administration concerning the use of torture. This was widely reported even in the mainstream media. In an ABC article "Bush Aware of Advisers' Interrogation Talks," reporters Greenburg, Rosenberg, and de Vogue clearly identified specific members of the Bush administration, including Colin Powell, that were members of the National Security Council's Principals Committee.[17] This committee approved very

---

[17]. Jan Crawford Greenburg, Howard L. Rosenberg, and Arian de Vogue, "Bush Aware of Advisers' Interrogation Talks," http://abcnews.go.com/TheLaw/LawPolitics/Story?id=4635175, *ABC News*, April 11, 2008.

specific "enhanced interrogation methods" that have been widely accepted as torture by international and US law. These methods included water boarding, which has been classified as torture for many years.

The War Crimes Act of 1996, a federal statute set forth at Title 18 of the US code § 2441, makes it a federal crime for any US national to violate the Geneva Conventions. This law makes it a crime to not only carry out prohibited acts but also applies to those that order it or even know about it and fail to take steps to stop it. Further, this federal law does not have a statute of limitations, and punishment for violations includes life in prison. If even one prisoner dies due to torture, which has happened a number of times, the punishment can be death.

Of course, Colin Powell knows this, and he would have only approved these outrageous acts if he thought he could get away with it. In fact, George W. Bush freely admitted to the process in which these decisions were made. Probably because he does not possess the critical thinking skills needed to foresee the disastrous ramifications of his decisions. He probably believed Alberto Gonzalez's memos telling him he is exempt from the law because he is the "unitary executive," and therefore whatever he does is legal because he is the president. On the other hand, Colin Powell was not nearly as forthcoming. When contacted by ABC News, he stated through an assistant that there were "hundreds of [Principals] meetings" on a wide variety of topics and that he was "not at liberty to discuss private meetings." Colin Powell knows that his hide could be in jeopardy and just as he did in the My Lai Massacre, he is crafting a web of deceit so that he comes out on top of the dung heap.

Condoleezza Rice chaired the above committee as National Security Advisor and, along with Powell, knows the possible consequences of her participation in this dark undertaking. One notices that she is very adept at dodging tough questions and responsibility. When criticized by California Democratic Senator Barbara Boxer in relation to the war in Iraq: "I personally believe, this is my personal view, that your loyalty to the mission you were given, to sell the war, overwhelmed your respect for the truth . . ." Senator Boxer went on to clarify that who pays the price for the Bush administration's war adventurism are not the families of Senator Boxer or Condoleezza Rice, but the American military and their families. Rice threw out the red herring that Senator Boxer was making some sort of negative comment about Rice not being married and not having children, which of course had nothing to do with the point Boxer was making.

I have also seen Rice just brush aside pertinent questions about the 9/11 attacks. When asked legitimate questions by the press, she simply states that "I hadn't heard that" and just goes on to the next question. She is very good at that. Perhaps good enough that she can be involved in international war crimes and get away with it. It does appear that dodging responsibility is one of the few things she is good at.

For all of fanfare on her behalf, this author cannot think of anything Condoleezza Rice has been successful at since joining the Bush administration. Apparently, she is a gifted athlete, pianist, and university professor; but her record of giving exactly the wrong advice and doing exactly the wrong thing as National Security Advisor and Secretary of State are unprecedented in modern history, with the exception of Colin Powell. Not only wrong but outright immoral and illegal.

The Iraq war is arguably the most disastrous decision this country has ever made, and Condoleezza Rice was instrumental in promoting this policy. With a doctorate degree in political science, she had to have been aware that Iraq was absolutely no threat to the United States security. This was an illegal war from the very beginning. It amounted to waging aggressive warfare against a virtually defenseless nation. Not only a defenseless nation but a war against the civilian population. Condoleezza Rice used effective metaphors to conjure up images of nuclear mushroom clouds that were very effective in scaring the American people into this disastrous undertaking. She had to know what she was doing, and unlike George Bush, she had to have known the disastrous consequences of this ill-advised endeavor. But she did it anyway. She did it because she, along with Colin Powell, is an unprincipled opportunist.

The Rest of the Pathocracy Players

In fact, the principals committee included most of the players in the most disastrous US administration in modern history and possibly for all time. The principals committee included Vice President Dick Cheney, former national security adviser Condoleezza Rice, Defense Secretary Donald Rumsfeld, Secretary of State Colin Powell, as well as CIA Director George Tenet, and Attorney General John Ashcroft.

To say that this is a group of unprincipled opportunists would be generous. This group easily fits Lobaczewski's description of, in the final stages, the pathological personalities that a psychopathic head of state would surround himself with.

Examples of their behavior fit Lobaczewski's mold exactly. One only has to recall Defense Secretary Donald Rumsfeld using a machine to put his signature on the death notification letters going to the next of kin of US troops killed in Iraq and Afghanistan. CIA Director George tenet has been identified by former agents of the CIA as much too willing to politicize his intelligence estimates and forecasts. Vice President Dick Cheney has been identified by several prominent politicians as causing more damage to the Constitution than any individual in US history. In a recent interview of Vice President Cheney, he was asked the question about how he felt about the unpopularity of the Bush administration with the American people. His response was, "So?" As a group, Lobaczewski would probably put the above individuals in the category of characteropaths. These are individuals that have little regard for what is right or wrong. Their only interest is in what they perceive as best for them. Interesting comparisons could be made of these pathological personalities to those of Adolf Hitler's henchmen.

Conclusions

The United States has become a pathocracy and is run for and by an elite group of pathological personalities. This group is putting the final touches on looting the National Treasury, destroying the middle class, destroying the Constitution and also all forms of international law. They use these esoteric terms such as "globalization" to mask their intentions. Globalization is nothing more than a fancy term for mercantilism. These pathological personalities want cheap labor to turn resources into products that nobody really needs and then dump the toxic byproducts on defenseless people and societies.

They find the middle class extremely inconvenient. They do not want the average American to be educated and prosperous because that equates to political power. They do not want average Americans deciding the future of the country. They believe that is their job. This is why union membership has gone from over 40 percent of the workforce to about 17 percent now.

They especially do not want minorities obtaining political power. As long as the ruling elite can keep minorities powerless, they can also control the white middle class. Even though the white middle class is losing ground economically, they can at least feel that they are doing better than minorities. The middle class has been losing ground economically for many years. They do not realize this partly because of credit. Even though their purchasing power has declined, they do not realize this because they can still buy a bunch of junk that they do not need on credit. The white middle class has the illusion of being prosperous and superior to minorities. If minorities become prosperous and join the middle class, the ruling elite will have a real problem with the white middle class. The white middle class is being played like a fiddle, and by the time they figure it out, it will be too late.

Another form of social control that the ruling elite uses is the American drug trade. This very lucrative business roughly amounts to about $300 billion a year. A great deal of this money comes from minority communities in our urban cities and thus plays a key role in keeping minority communities impoverished. Further, the profits from this illegal drug trade are tax-free. If one believes that Crips, Bloods, Mafia, or any other well-known criminal organization is reaping the profits from this extremely lucrative business, they need to read the next chapter.

Chapter Four

How We Got Here—a Short History of the International Drug Trade

In the first two chapters, we saw that there is US government involvement in the international drug trade, and that this is managed by obviously pathological personalities. In this chapter, we explore how the drug trade part of this equation came about.

The international drug trade has a documented history that you probably will not find in the history books. You might find some vague references to "Opium Wars" and so forth, but you will find little about the cause-and-effect issues or what the consequences of these events are to us today. For example, who is aware of the fact that the major reason the French were in Indochina, now Southeast Asia, was to control the opium and heroin trade out of the "Golden Triangle?" And who would have guessed that America would have inherited control of this drug trade from the French in the form of the Vietnam War?

The fact is that drugs are, and have been, an extremely valuable resource and one of the key financial factors in every empire in the last thousand years or so. In fact, drugs have been so valuable that if this resource had been taken away, these empires could very well have not existed at all, at least not in the forms that they took. The most authoritative research in this area was done by Alfred McCoy in his book *The Politics of Heroin*.[18] Much of the rationale that follows as far as how nations use drugs for economic and political gain has been summarized from McCoy.

Let us think about this for a minute. What is more valuable than drugs? One pure ounce of heroin, or cocaine, is literally worth more than its weight in gold, easy to transport, and the customers will do anything to get the money to buy it. Further, there is no need to pay taxes as such. The only "duty" that has to be paid is to bribe officials and law enforcement. There is no better product in any market that can come close to the wild profits, ease of creating distribution networks, and consumers that have a lifetime "devotion" to the product. It is a foregone conclusion that any economic and or military power would want to take control of the international drug trade. This is exactly what has happened for many hundreds, perhaps thousands, of years.

Anthropologists recently found in the bodies of Egyptian mummies traces of cocaine. This is perhaps earliest evidence of what would amount to an international drug trade. Coca leaves grow exclusively in the Andes region of South America, nowhere else. For the ancient Egyptians to have used cocaine there had to have been trade routes connecting the Andes region to ancient Egypt.

Of all the drugs in the world, the two most profitable are opium and cocaine. These two drugs are also the most tightly controlled presumably because of their addictive nature. However, the other reason they are so tightly controlled is to maximize illegal profits.

Let's first take a look at opium and its derivatives. Opium is derived from the poppy, and the history of its cultivation goes way back. The earliest documented use of opium appeared in Greek medical documents during the fifth century BC. Records of Chinese's use of opium occurred during the eighth century AD. It was used to treat conditions such as nausea. Its cultivation apparently spread along the southern rim of Asia in medieval times. Sometime during the fifteenth century, it became a regular item in Asian trade to supply Persians and Indians who used it for recreational purposes. Under the reign of Akbar, the Mongol state of northern India relied on opium as a significant source of revenue.

---

[18] McCoy, Alfred, *The Politics of Heroin: C. I. A. Complicity in the Global Drug Trade*, 2nd Ed., New York, NY, Lawrence Hill Books, 1972.

The Portuguese

Long-distance drug trading did not become well developed until late in the fifteenth century. The Portuguese were the first to take advantage of this lucrative trade. Coincidentally, this period is known as Europe's age of discovery, which coincided with Asia's modern opium trade. The Portuguese first established strategic ports in Malacca, on the Malay Peninsula, Macao, and in the spice islands of Indonesia. The Portuguese discovered that spices, textiles, and porcelains of Asia commanded high prices in Europe, but they were at a loss as to what European goods could be sold in Asia. They needed to find something to trade with Asia so as not to exhaust their supply of gold and silver.

It was not long before they discovered the trading potential of opium. From western India, the Portuguese began exporting opium to China, which they traded for Chinese commodities such as silk. They also began importing tobacco from her Brazilian colony as another commodity to trade with the Chinese. What eventually came to pass was Indian opium mixed with Brazilian tobacco was pleasing to the Chinese. This mixture became wildly popular with the Chinese, and the practice spread far and wide. One region the Chinese brought this practice to was Southeast Asia.

The Dutch

About a century after the Portuguese, the Dutch took control of the region's opium trade. In 1640, the Dutch East India Company began trading the opium of western India for spices in the Indies. By 1699, the Dutch imported eighty-seven tons of Indian opium for distribution to Java and the Indies. Opium was no longer a luxury or medical item. It had become an economic tool of empire.

The British

Next it was Great Britain's turn. The British East India Company developed ports at Calcutta in 1656 and in Bombay in 1661, although they did *not* enter the opium trade for another fifty years. During this period, there was open competition between the Dutch, British, and French merchants; and Bengal opium became highly prized. From its port in Calcutta, the British conquered Bengal in 1764 and reaped the financial benefit of India's richest opium zone. Over the next 130 years, Britain exported Indian opium to China in violation of Chinese drug laws and fought two wars to open China's opium market to British merchants. Great Britain played a key role in making China a vast drug market. By 1900, China had 13.5 million opium addicts consuming thirty-nine thousand tons of opium.

Without the opium trade, there could not have been a British Empire. During the nineteenth century, the British developed an enormous triangular exchange. Trade figures for the 1820s showed that £22 million of Indian opium and cotton went to China, £20 million in Chinese tea went to Britain, and £24 million of British textiles and machinery went back to India. This triangular trade was an extremely efficient way of making a lot of money. If you take opium out of the equation, you cannot buy the Chinese tea to take back to Britain; and without tea, you have nothing to buy the British textiles machinery that went back to India. The British made money on each of the three legs of the journey. If you kicked one of the legs out from under this economic "table," the British Empire would have fallen. The sun would set on the British Empire.

Interestingly, Yankee traders were involved in this trade from the very beginning. Although often at odds with each other, England and the colonies had an interesting balance between collaboration and competition that actually served both well. Shipbuilding expertise in the colonies obviously came from England and was further developed by the Americans. Yankee traders openly competed with the British in the opium trade. They loaded their first cargoes of Turkish opium in 1805 and sailed them around the tip of Africa to China. American merchants, such as John Jacob Astor, made their fortunes in the opium trade with China. Thirty percent of all American cargoes that reached China were opium.

American shipping even played a role in improving the British merchant fleets. In 1829, Capt. William Clifton, a retired Royal Navy officer, made an offer to the governor of Calcutta to build a new kind of ship that could tack into the monsoon winds between India and China. The plans for this ship were based on an American privateer captured in the war of 1812. Clifton christened the ship the *Red River*, the first of the "opium clippers," and in 1829, he set sail for China with eight hundred chests of opium. He made the trip to China and back in eighty-six days, a record in those days. During the next few years, many of these new ships joined the opium fleets including three fast slave ships seized by the Royal Navy between Africa and America. With the advent of these new ships, China's opium imports increased from 270 tons in 1820 to 2,555 tons twenty years later.

The British also introduced another novel concept in the control and marketing of drugs. That is the use of military force to enhance its marketing power. The British not only used military force to control the opium growing areas in southern Asia but fought two opium wars between 1839 and 1858 to force China to allow Great Britain to sell thousands of tons of opium to the Chinese. The drug trade generated enough revenue to pay the staggering cost of operating a huge colonial empire. For example, opium provided from 6 to 15 percent of British India's tax revenues during the nineteenth century. As we shall see, these lessons were *not* lost on the rest of the world, including the French and also United States of America.

The French

The Southeast Asia opium trade was solely a product of European colonialism that the French played a key role in. Initially, the French were not interested in the cultivation of opium in Southeast Asia. They were satisfied with the revenue they were getting in the opium dens from imported opium. Many of the customers were expatriate Chinese that had left China taking their opium habit with them. In 1881, a French administration in Saigon created what was called an Opium Regie, a state monopoly that proved to be very efficient and profitable. They actually were able to market this as a drug control measure.

After World War II, the French had a problem maintaining their colonial empire in Southeast Asia. They had insurrections and a lengthy war of liberation going on with the Viet Minh, the predecessors of the Viet Cong. This was a bitter nine-year struggle that lasted from 1946 to 1954. During most of this time, the French military used conventional tactics and strategies. Their objective was to win battles and control territory.

Their adversaries, the Viet Minh, had very different ideas. Their commander, Gen. Vo Nguyen Giap, was a military genius who defeated both the French and the Americans. Gen. Giap's philosophy was that "political activities were more important than military activities, and fighting less important than propaganda; armed activities was used to safeguard, consolidate, and develop political bases."[19] By 1951, the French understood that they could not fight a war of liberation, or nationalism, with a lot of outside arms and soldiers. You have to gain support from within the country or the region by whatever means necessary. So from that point on, the French tried to use the hill tribes, bandits, and religious minorities as tools to hold strategic territories and block Viet Minh infiltration.

These counterinsurgency activities were plagued by a lack of money. Add to this that this war was becoming increasingly unpopular with the French people. The funds to support these activities were continually being reduced. The solution to this problem became what the French intelligence community referred to as Operation X. This was a highly classified operation that only a few, even in the intelligence community, were aware of.

Basically, operation X transferred profits from the distribution and sale of opium from French government to French intelligence. Operation X produced a cast of Corsican narcotics syndicates, and corrupt French intelligence officers became key players in the international drug trade. The results of this were that the French government lost opium revenue and faced serious budgetary problems, and the French intelligence community had solved their financial problems.

Although French intelligence had found a way to pay for their counterinsurgency activities, the disastrous loss at Dien Bien Phu prompted the French to throw in the towel. In 1954, at Geneva, Switzerland, a peace settlement was arrived at. An armistice was declared, and the war was over.

Here Comes the Americans-Vietnam Was First

As we discussed before, American clippers and traders were involved in the drug trade even before there was a United States of America. It wasn't until after World War II that the United States became heavily involved in one of the trappings of the empire, drugs. When the French Expeditionary Corps withdrew from Indochina

---

[19.] Gen. Vo Nguyen Giap, *People's War People's Army*; Hanoi, Foreign Languages Publishing House, 1961, p.79.

in 1955, French intelligence officers approached American military personnel and offered to turn over their entire paramilitary apparatus. The Department of Defense turned down this offer presumably because they did not want to be involved in any French program.

The United States, however, was already involved. US intelligence operatives were already collaborating with the French. Also, there were several divisions of the Nationalist Chinese that ended up mostly in Laos. These Kuomintang troops were being supported by General Claire Chennault's Civil Air Transport (CAT) service. These Nationalist Chinese troops supported themselves by raising and selling opium. They used opium money to buy weapons, food, and other subsistence items. CAT aircraft transported these items to these troops in Laos.

Facing bankruptcy, Gen. Chennault sold his civil air transport service to the CIA in 1950. The CIA renamed it Air America, and hence we have the groundwork for the Central Intelligence Agency's direct involvement in transporting opium and heroin in Southeast Asia. Although the airline's name changed, this is the framework for the CIA's counterinsurgency efforts. Weapons, food, and subsistence items are transported in, and drugs come out. Of course, the weapons are used to support so-called "counterinsurgents" that are "friendly" to the United States.

This is how the United States became involved in what came to be known as the Vietnam War. This was a war that involved all of Southeast Asia, and it has to be looked at that way to understand it. Although the official war was mostly fought with United States and South Vietnamese soldiers in Vietnam, the secret war was fought in the surrounding countries: Laos, Cambodia, Thailand, and Burma. The secret war was not fought with US soldiers. It was fought with paramilitary troops from these mountain tribes, for example the Hmong in Laos. In all these countries, the formula was almost identical for the mountain tribes involved. Weapons and basic needs come in on CIA aircraft and opium goes out. Additionally, the young men from these mountain tribes are required to fight the CIA's secret war.

This formula was ultimately what failed in Southeast Asia. Although the opium trade was extremely profitable and generated considerable revenue, it was no match against nationalism. Nationalism is free. Soldiers fighting for a cause will keep fighting even without pay. They will continue to fight even when they are wounded. They will fight even if they are starving. During my second tour in Vietnam,

I heard tales of a severely wounded Viet Cong troop who tied a rag around his abdomen to keep his intestines in and keep fighting for three days. The Korean Tiger Division troops told me this and said they came across him when he was dying, and the only thing he wanted was a drink of water. Money cannot buy this kind of dedication.

The entire war effort in Southeast Asia was based on corruption and drug money. Promotions in the Army of the Republic of Vietnam (ARVN) were payoffs that had nothing to do with performance. South Vietnam's entire intelligence apparatus was based on bribes from drug money. Drug revenue is the only thing that kept the South Vietnamese government afloat. Without it, South Vietnam collapses, and this is exactly what happened.

The CIA took so many young men out of the mountain villages to fight the secret war that the whole system began to break down. The vast majority of the young man did not come back to the villages. They got killed. Because the young men were mostly involved in the cultivation of opium, production began to decline. Further, the village leaders began to encounter resistance from their people. So many of their young men were not returning that "the deal" was beginning to look like genocide. The CIA and United States forces even went so far as to bomb these villages that were not cooperating, thus driving the villagers into the surrounding forest. These were our allies. The entire system broke down without the opium production and the revenue that it generated.

We have discussed the essence of the Vietnam War, and a lot has been left out. Vietnam was a turning point from whence we may never return. A foundation was laid that is going to be difficult, if not impossible to undo. Agencies of our government have obtained enormous power using one of the most destructive substances known. This power will not be given up easily; it never has been.

It is difficult to separate the Vietnam War from the Southeast Asia drug trade. They were conjoined twins. One could not exist without the other. Further, this dirty "big" secret could hide under the cover of secrecy. The CIA could use its power to hide "state secrets" from the American people, Congress, the judicial system, and even the commander in chief. Of course, they could not hide it from everyone but from enough people that even those courageous few that did report this dirty secret were largely not believed. In many cases when these true patriots did expose the truth, as we shall see later, not good things happened to them.

In the secret war in Southeast Asia, we see a dangerous concept taking shape, and that is that some functions of government, mostly the CIA, were conducting operations with no oversight. Most of the crucial issues about clandestine drug operations, secret wars, and the like have been hidden from the American people and also from any oversight function whatsoever representing the people. It has been over forty years, and the American people still do not know what that war was about.

What makes matters worse is the fact that unchecked, unsupervised, unaccountable power will always spiral out of control, especially when a few influential people benefit from it. This was and still is the case with the CIA. Pathological personalities will always fill a vacuum. Anywhere they can find a way to abuse power, intimidate people for gain, misuse public funds, usurp resources, undermine the Constitution, ad infinitum, they will do it.

Vietnam was open season for these pathological people, and this was as true of the CIA's involvement in the global drug trade as it was with US-based corporations that jumped on the death for profit bandwagon. Case in point would be Monsanto's Agent Orange. Monsanto knew that the defoliants it made, of which Agent Orange was only one of many, contained one of the most toxic substances known to man, dioxin. Dioxin is not only highly toxic but is also very persistent, which simply means it does not degrade. It stays in the environment for a very long time. The use of Agent Orange started out on a small scale, limited use defoliation operations; but when Monsanto started to make money on the deal, things got a little crazy. Eventually, thousands of tons of this toxic substance were dropped on our troops, I was one of them, and allies. This apparently was done in an attempt to defoliate vast areas of Southeast Asia so that the enemy could not hide in the vegetation.

Not a good idea to try and defoliate an entire region to get a better shot at the enemy. This is like a hunter cutting down the entire forest so he can get a better shot at the deer. Obviously, without the forest, there will be no deer. Further, to deliberately poison your own troops and your allies and say that you are doing this to win the war just doesn't make sense. But then again, winning the war was never the objective in Vietnam. The objective was to keep the war going so that the elite power structure could make obscene profits. That is why the defoliation program was never questioned nor challenged in any serious fashion. Nobody was watching the store.

Neither was anyone watching the Southeast Asia drug trade, which was hidden under this veil of secrecy that exists in war. You can't search that plane because it is classified. We cannot brief you, Mr. Congressman, on that program because it is too sensitive. That evidence cannot be used in court, Your Honor, because it will disclose "state secrets." Nobody was told about these things because they were not supposed to be happening in the first place. You have denial after denial even in the face of overwhelming evidence, to this day. Exposure as to what the CIA is really up to and how it operates would send the citizenry howling for reform. And so we had in Southeast Asia an entire region involved in a lengthy war in which much of the fighting was done outside the realm of public disclosure or scrutiny. The citizenry were virtually left out of the decision-making process and denied any oversight that is a fundamental concept of our Constitution. Not only did we have no accountability, but when college campuses began massive protests and resistance to the war, the National Guard was sent on campuses such as Kent State where they actually shot unarmed students. How could this happen in a democracy?

Chapter Five

The CIA, War, and Drugs in Southeast Asia

The key to understanding how this could happen in a democracy goes back to the National Security Act of 1947. Many believe that the seeds for a global American empire were planted in this controversial act that established the National Security Council and the Central Intelligence Agency. Within one year, the National Security Council's Office of Special Projects issued a directive, NSC 10/2, which gave the CIA the mandate to carry out covert operations. Covert means that the US government denies responsibility for these actions. In other words, they were given a mandate to lie to the world and the American people. Then in 1949, Central Intelligence Agency act, public Law 81—110, authorized the Central Intelligence Agency to keep confidential fiscal and administrative procedures. This act also exempted the agency from most of the usual limitations on the use of federal money. Also exempted was any requirement for the CIA to disclose any information about who worked for the agency, salaries, and so forth. These acts, directives, and laws provide for an agency that has virtually no accountability, a Frankenstein monster.

The framers of the Central Intelligence Agency, in their attempt to give the agency a free hand with which to supposedly combat Communism and other "evils," violated a key principle on which the United States government was based. That principle is that power needs to have checks and balances. The framers of the Constitution did this because of the long history of the abuse of unchecked power. In fact throughout history, that is exactly what has happened every time any person, agency, or government has obtained power without accountability. In so doing, the persons that formed the CIA inadvertently planted the seeds of destruction of the American Republic as we know it. The United States of America has been transformed from a republic into a pathocracy, largely as a result of this one agency, which was deliberately constructed to sidestep democratic processes. We can ill afford to have any instrument of government that is not accountable to the people. The Central Intelligence Agency's involvement in drugs and war came from these ill-advised laws, acts, and programs.

To be fair, we need to keep in mind that the framers of the national security act of 1947 and the legislation and policies that ensued did not give the Central Intelligence Agency the power that it wields today. In fact they were careful to specifically state that the agency was a coordinating agency and not an intelligence-gathering agency. It was to make sense out of many intelligence-gathering agencies' findings. The authority to conduct clandestine secret operations was not specifically stated. The CIA was originally designed to interpret and make sense out of intelligence that came from many sources, analyze the information, and brief the president. One of the first directors of the CIA, Allen Dulles, did more than anyone to find loopholes and expand even vague terminology to suit his means. His objectives were clearly to establish a secret operations role for the CIA.

For example, the duties of the CIA were set forth by Congress in the National Security Act of 1947 as follows:

1. To advise the National Security Council in matters concerning such intelligence activities of the government departments and agencies as relate to national security.
2. To make recommendations to the NSC for the coordination of such intelligence activities.
3. To correlate and evaluate intelligence relating to the national security and provide for the appropriate dissemination of such intelligence within the government . . . Provided that the agency shall have no police, subpoena, law enforcement powers, or internal security functions.
4. To perform, for the benefit of the existing intelligence agencies, such additional services of common concern as

the NSC determines to be more efficiently accomplished centrally.
5. To perform such other functions and duties related to intelligence affecting the national security as the NSC may from time to time direct.

Nowhere in here does it say anything about secret operations or clandestine activities. These activities began and were allowed to continue based on the mechanizations and manipulations of Allen Dulles and others. The reference to "other functions and duties related to intelligence . . . as the NSC may from time to time direct" does not even begin to imply that the CIA has the authority to overthrow governments, assassinate leaders, and become involved in the drug trade. All of which and more the CIA has taken upon itself to do since the national security act of 1947 was enacted.

Further, Central Intelligence Agency's involvement in much of the drug trade that has wrecked havoc throughout the United States has also had a "Trojan horse" effect. Once in the United States, these drugs have corrupted our legal system, law enforcement, Congress, the prison system, media, ad infinitum. To make things worse, the government has used the agency's exemptions under public Law 81—110 to hide other ill-conceived programs and operations from public scrutiny. This is not what is supposed to be: our premier intelligence agency seems to be involved in everything but intelligence work.

An example of this would be the US Agency for International Development (USAID). On the surface, this agency appears to be a tool for Third World economic development. In reality, it is a known CIA front whose hidden agenda is to undermine the economies of nations the United States considers to be "unfriendly" to the United States and its allies. John Perkins, in his book, *The Secret History of the American Empire*, goes into detail on USAID's activities in foreign countries. This agency even went so far in Mali as to undermine indigenous farmers in order to clear the path for Monsanto to market its genetically modified (GMO) seeds.[20]

[20.] John Perkins, *A Secret History of the American Empire*, 1st Ed., (New York, NY: Penguin Group, USA, Inc., 375 Hudson St., New York, NY, 10014, USA, 2007), Locations 3798-3811, Amazon Kindle.

The seeds of destruction planted in the National Security Act of 1947 began to sprout and take root in Vietnam. Drug logistics routes became established using airplanes instead of donkeys. Government agencies and the corporatocracy began collaborating with drug dealers, organized crime, and the media, each playing their own unique role in complicity with regard to the drug trade. In Vietnam, all this was hidden beneath the fog of war and the veil of national security. Could this have been what Dwight David Eisenhower was talking about in his farewell address when he warned of the undue influence of the military-industrial complex? Could he have foreseen this rather nebulous conglomeration of corporations with the power to influence national and international financial, economic, political, and military policies and create a permanent war economy? Could the obscene profits gained from drugs be the financial underpinning necessary to feed this beast?

We will explore these issues in the following chapters. Before we do so, however, I want to introduce some influential players in Vietnam who will play important roles in other issues we will discuss. In researching the material for this book, I was astounded to see the same names associated with the drug trade also implicated or otherwise involved in assassinations and overthrowing governments.

We have already seen the drug smugglers at "Jack's place" involved in both the "Fatal Vision" body bag drug smuggling scheme in 1970 and also the "Body Bag" case I investigated in 1972. Although Helena Stoeckley, a key witness that could have cleared Captain Jeffery MacDonald, was ruled "unreliable" for testimony, I find it most incriminating that she remembered the same names in the MacDonald case that came up in other cases around the world. One name Stoeckley came up with was Leslie "Ike" Atkinson who was the same individual portrayed in *American Gangster*. If she was delusional, how could she come up with real names for real people involved in real crimes elsewhere?

Witness Number 1: DEA Agent Mike Levine

We also have Mike Levine, author of *Deep Cover* and several other books exposing drug smuggling and CIA complicity, whose information dovetails with my knowledge and that exposed by Alex Constantine in his book *Psychic Dictatorship in the USA*. Further, all this is in complete agreement with Professor Alfred McCoy and his exhaustively researched book, *The Politics of Heroin*. None of these people knew each other or collaborated in any way. How is it possible for all of them to come up with the same names and describe the same methods of operation?

Another common thread is that anyone who has exposed, knowingly or unknowingly, where these roads lead to has been systematically discredited, harassed, and sometimes met an early demise. If they were "whacko conspiracy theorists" as portrayed, then why are they such a threat? Why would anyone go to all the trouble to single them out for persecution? My belief is that they have to be onto something. These people threaten powerful forces that will do anything to hide from public disclosure.

Witness Number 2: Captain Jeffery MacDonald

Vietnam era Green Beret captain and physician Jeffery MacDonald is an excellent example of this. By trying to investigate a drug epidemic around him, he fell down a portal into the center of the American heart of darkness. Although it was accidental, he saw it. In fact, he stared it right in the face. It doesn't matter what the evidence showed. Evidence comes and goes as the "powers that be" see fit. I found that out in the case I was involved with. If Captain MacDonald could be believed, then the entire beast is exposed. That cannot be allowed to happen.

As Alex Constantine covered in detail, Captain MacDonald's entire family was murdered on February 17, 1970. During this incident, MacDonald sustained seventeen stab wounds, one of which punctured his lung. The investigation was done by Army CID. As in the case I was involved in evidence that disappeared or was "lost," was crucial to the case. It could not be a coincidence that everything lost was evidence that could have cleared MacDonald. Also, evidence that was not in his favor somehow "appeared." Later, prosecutors would claim that MacDonald inflicted his wounds upon himself, wounds that nearly killed him. They said that he was able to do this because he was a physician so that he knew where to stab without killing himself.

Initially, charges were dropped by the army for lack of evidence, and the military court determined that the charges against MacDonald were "not true." Almost five years later, MacDonald was indicted by a grand jury in North Carolina, and his lawyers appealed based on the constitutional right to a speedy trial. The Fourth Circuit Court of Appeals agreed and dismissed the case. The case eventually was reviewed by the Supreme Court, and that court overturned the dismissal so that the trial was allowed to convene. MacDonald was convicted, and he is in jail to this day.

A key witness that never testified was Helena Stoeckley. She refused to testify because she was not given immunity from being charged for crimes associated with her testimony. Helena Stoeckley had told investigators that she was present when the murders happened and substantiated virtually everything that MacDonald had stated as to how and who committed the murders. Without Stoeckley's testimony and given the fact that evidence appeared and disappeared in the case, MacDonald was convicted.

If he had been released, then maybe what he said was true. What he said was that heroin was being smuggled into the Fayetteville, North Carolina, area through military channels. As long as he is in jail, he is automatically discredited. The media routinely vilified him, portraying him as "narcissistic" and worse. So an honorable man who has had his entire family murdered is put in jail for life. What evil did he see? Most people do not want to know, but we shall see a lot more than this in the next chapters.

Witness Number 3: Dois "Chip" Tatum

Another Vietnam era veteran who fell through a portal into the American heart of darkness was Chip Tatum, sometimes known as Gene Tatum. His given name was, however, Dois Tatum. Chip Tatum, now apparently deceased, fully documented his activities in Operation Red Rock and many other clandestine operations in an explosive document made available online. He called this document *The Chip Tatum Chronicles*; he subtitled it *Testimony of Government Drug Running*. He further documented his activities in extensive interviews conducted and videotaped by Ted L. Gunderson, retired FBI senior special agent in Charge, Los Angeles, office of the Federal Bureau of Investigation. These videos are available online at Google Videos. Having done two tours in Vietnam, I found no inconsistencies in anything that Chip Tatum wrote or stated. Further, he backed up much of what he said with copies of official orders and documents that corroborate everything he states. Chip Tatum had a lot to say.

He joined the air force to become an air traffic controller, and he got that and much more. He not only became an air traffic controller but also a combat controller, which put him in the category of special operations. In Vietnam, this put him under the operational control of the CIA. Chip was selected for a mission, Operation Red Rock, which was a team of special forces tasked to infiltrate Laos. Disguised as North Vietnamese sappers, this team attacked the commercial airport at Phenom Phenn, Laos. Their objective was to cause as much damage as possible and create the impression that the airport had been attacked by North Vietnamese. This was intended to persuade the government of Laos to come on board on the American side of the conflict. Chip found out later that this was a "one-way" mission. That is, that there were to be no survivors. Chip reported, years later, that when Richard Nixon was briefed on Operation Red Rock, he stated that "no one must ever know." This is code for directing that there are to be no survivors returning from this mission. Dead men tell no tales.

The team was successful in attacking the airport and apparently suffered no casualties. They were supposed to rendezvous with a paramilitary group that was supposed to take them out of Laos. Apparently, Chip's platoon sergeant sensed that all was not well and that their supposed rescuers had other intentions. This platoon sergeant flipped a grenade in the middle of them but did not pull the pin. In the ensuing chaos, team Red Rock gained the upper hand and escaped. The team tried to make it out of Laos on their own, but they were captured by North Vietnamese and held for ninety-two days. The entire team was tortured to death with the exception of Chip and his platoon sergeant. They were rescued by a recon patrol of US Marines, and Chip was severely wounded during the rescue.

He ended up in the air force hospital at Clark Air Force Base, Philippines. Within a few days, Chip was debriefed by William J. Colby who later would become director of the CIA. Colby explained to Chip that the events which team Red Rock participated in had been classified by President Nixon for a period of twenty-five years. Due to the sensitive nature of the mission, the president required that Chip be "held close" because of national security. On June 6, 1971, Chip was advised that he was under the operational control of the CIA and that his code name was Pegasus. What Chip Tatum documented as a CIA operative clearly connects the CIA to drug running and political assassinations. We will be seeing him in later chapters.

Actor in the Heart of Darkness Play: L. Fletcher Prouty

Col. Leroy Fletcher Prouty Jr. (January 24, 1917-June 5, 2001) was a leading critic of US foreign policy.[21] He served in WWII as a transport pilot in the North African Theater. From 1955 to 1964, he developed an air force-wide system for military support of clandestine CIA operations. From 1962 to 1963, he created a similar system as the chief of special operations for the Joint Chiefs of Staff.

He was an insider, but one of the few who has spoken out about how the CIA has systematically subverted the national interests of the United States of America. His book, *The Secret Team*, goes into much detail on how, after WWII, a small group of insiders has been able to shape the entire direction of the country. He had much insight into the causes and conduct of the Vietnam War and also the JFK assassination. His second book says it all, *JFK: The CIA, Vietnam, and the Plot to Assassinate John F. Kennedy*. He was also a consultant to Oliver Stone's movie *JFK*.

The subject he virtually does not mention is the CIA's connections to the drug trade and also drug connections to the JFK assassination. When asked about this, he usually would state, "That is another story that I could write about a hundred more books about" or words to that effect. By no means did he side-step the issue. He just did not go into it on his own. Perhaps he just wanted to keep his focus straight and narrow, or maybe he felt a little regretful, like many of us, that we played a part in it, albeit unknowingly. The exchange below between one of his readers and him is interesting. It illustrates that Col. Prouty knew a lot about the drug trade, but it also brings forth perhaps the very beginning of the connections between the US conduct of war and drugs.[22]

---

21. Photo and summarized information courtesy of The L. Fletcher Prouty Reference Site, http://www.prouty.org/
22. Letter of the Month, October 1996, question and answer courtesy of The L. Fletcher Prouty Reference Site, http://www.prouty.org/

Letter of the Month October 1996

From Burt Wilson

Hitler's SS was a self-sustaining organization, getting its funds from running the dope cartel in Europe and also brothels, gambling, etc.

As you state in your JFK book, we collected many German agents after WWII and took them back to become CIA operatives. Did they influence the CIA to get into the drug business to create its own income?

I would like to hear your take on this.

Best wishes,
Burt Wilson

Reply from Col. Prouty

Putting Hitler's SS deep into the drug business—at least during the war—is not the big drug story. After all, look at the geography. Hitler did over-run a good bit of Europe; but he did not get drug producing territory. We were in Turkey more than he was.

But there is a big story about drugs and the war. When we were joined by the British and Chinese to drive against the Japanese through Burma, it was our responsibility to pay the troops. I was with the Air Transport Command in Cairo then. We sent a transport plane every month with the Finance Officers to Burma so they could physically pay the troops with cash.

These men had "foot-lockers" full of cash: American for the Americans, British for the British and foot-lockers packed with small white envelopes of heroin to pay the Chinese. That was the customary Chinese "pay."

We knew where the American and British currency came from; but we did not know, positively, where the heroin came from. But the Army finance men did, ok and they never gave up the contacts. Since we were in Egypt we believed that it came from Turkey where we had easy access at the time. I flew people to Turkey many times.

As the Burmese campaign progressed and drove the Japanese easterly to the Pacific, and the end of the war came along, these Army Finance officers continued paying the Chinese with heroin. But by that time Gen Li Mi of the Chinese had moved to the north and controlled northern Thailand and northern Burma and their drug supply.

As you know the war against Japan ended Sept 2, 1945 and our support of the Indochinese, Ho Chi Minh then, began on that same date. There never was a time when our troops weren't there and when the Army finance officers did not need plenty of heroin. They moved their drug contacts right into the warfare of Vietnam. Did you ever hear about the Nugan-Hand Billion dollar Bank? Mike Hand was a CIA man and Frank Nugan was Australian.

As the Chinese were withdrawn from Indochina and Americans began to come in we continued to get heroin from Ben Li Mi's resources and heroin became plentiful in Vietnam. This continued to be an enormous business through to the end of the warfare in 1975.

By that time the drug trade was big business and continues to be supported by the military and the CIA with their drug importing allies.

The German story was about GOLD, not drugs. The Hitler SS troops ransacked Europe for gold and set up an ingenious smuggling line from Germany, through the Balkans, into Turkey and from there into the hands of American team-mates in Egypt and North Africa. That stolen European gold was shipped, as aircraft parts, etc. from Cairo to Dakar via our own Air Force, Air Transport Command, and from Dakar to Natal, Brazil. There the Germans had set up a connection to Argentina. It was an enormous gold ring.

One day while I was in Cairo, I received orders to visit our commanding general. He told me about the Gold Ring and of a chance to break it. He directed me to report to the Army Counter Intelligence folks. I had a regular passport for Turkey. They told me to fly to Adana, Turkey and visit restaurants and others gathering places there to see if by some hance I recognized some Americans.

I did that, and one night as I was having dinner with my crewmen, we saw a man we knew well who was the ATC Operations Officer from Tunis. We slipped out quietly and flew right back to Cairo and I made my report to the General. A few days later an ATC Colonel asked me to meet him on the large street level veranda of the famous Shepherd's Hotel. When I got ther he said the place was loaded with American undercover agents. He told me to watch the taxis that unloaded to see if I recognized that Operations officer from Tunis. If I did I was to do nothing more than to pick up my coffee cup and hold it higher than usual.

Shortly, a taxi stopped and I saw that same man. As I raised my cup the veranda exploded. There were at least ten agents there and they had their man right away. He was charged with the crime and convicted. Because of the war he was kept in Africa and transferred to the isolated, air base we used at Atar in the desert, just north of Dakar. He was held ther until the end of the war. Then I lost track of him as I was transferred to the Pacific.

This man who was the key cog in one of the world's greatest gold smuggling operations was none other than the Hollywood actor, Errol Flynn's best friend and an actor himself: Bruce Cabot.

The Drug flow continues and that is another story.

Fletch,

The following letter was sent from Prouty to Jim Garrison, March 6, 1990.[23] It is an excellent thumbnail overview of the CIA's role in the Vietnam War, the Southeast Asian drug trade, and an insider's take on the JFK assassination. Lots of interesting information in this little letter! Also interesting is Col. Prouty's comment that Gen. Lansdale bragged about how much fun it was to throw Vietnamese civilians out of helicopters. Is there any doubt that this CIA case officer, wearing the uniform of an US Army officer, fits the profile of a psychopath? The odious CIA operations that we see around the world today, such as GITMO, so-called extraordinary renditions, and Abu Graib just did not come out of nowhere. The question, "Why do they hate us?" is really not that hard to answer. Col. Prouty's typing errors have not been corrected. They illustrate that his grasp of the subject areas flowed from his head, through his fingertips, to print.

> Dear Jim,
>
> It is amazing how things work, I am at home recuperating from a major back operation (to regain my ability to walk); so I was tossing around in bed last night . . . not too comfortable . . . and I began to think of Garrison. I thought, "I have got to write Jim a letter detailing how I believe the whole job was done."
>
> By another coincidence I had received a fine set of twenty photos from the Sprague collection in Springfield, Mass. As the odds would have it, he is now living just around the corner here in Alexandria. Why not? Lansdale lived here, Fensterwald lives here, Ford used to live here. Quite a community.
>
> I was studying those photos. One of them is the "Tramps" picture that appears in your book. It is glossy and clear. Lansdale is so clearly identifiable. Why, Lansdale in Dallas? The others don't matter, they are nothing but actors and not gunmen but they are interesting. Others who knew

---

[23.] Prouty to Garrison letter courtesy of The Col. L. Fletcher Prouty Reference Site, http://www.prouty.org.

Lansdale as well as I did, have said the same thing, "That's him and what's he doing there?"

As I was reading the paper the Federal Express man came with a book from Jim, that unusual "Lansdale" book. A terrible biography. There could be a great biography about Lansdale. He's no angel; but he is worth a good biography. Currey, a paid hack, did the job. His employers ought to have let him do it right.

I had known Ed since 1952 in the Philippines. I used to fly there regularly with my MATS Heavy Transport Squadron. As a matter of fact, in those days we used to fly wounded men, who were recuperating, from hospitals in Japan to Saigon for R&R on the beaches of Cap St Jacque. That was 1952-1953. Saigon was the Paris of the Orient. And Lansdale was "King Maker" of the Philippines. We always went by way of Manila. I met his team.

He had arrived in Manila in Sept 1945, after the war was over, for a while. He had been sent back there in 1950 by the CIA(OPC) to create a new leader of the Philippines and to get rid of Querino. Sort of like the Marcos deal, or the Noriega operation. Lansdale did it better. I have overthrown a government but I didn't splash it all around like Reagan and Bush have done. Now, who sent him there?

Who sent him there in 1950 (Truman era) to do a job that was not done until 1953 (Ike era)? From 1950 to Feb. 1953 the Director of Central Intelligence was Eisenhower's old Chief of Staff, Gen Walter Bedell Smith. Smith had been Ambassador to Moscow from 1946 to 1949. The lesser guys in the CIA at the time were Allen Dulles, who was Deputy Director Central Intelligence from Aug. 1951 to Feb. 1953. Frank Wisner became the Deputy Director, Plans (Clandestine Activities) when Dulles became DDCI. Lansdale had to have received his orders from among these four men: Truman, Smith, Dulles, and Wisner. Of course the Sec State could have had some input . . . i.e. Acheson. Who wanted Querino out, that badly? Who wanted HUKS there?

In Jan 1953 Eisenhower arrived. John Foster Dulles was at State and Gen Smith his Deputy. Allen Dulles was the DCI and General Cabel his deputy. None of them changed

Lansdale's prior orders to "get" Querino. Lansdale operated with abandon in the Philippines. The Ambassador and the CIA Station Chief, George Aurell, did not know what he was doing. They believed he was some sort of kook Air Force Officer there . . . a role Lansdale played to the hilt. Magsaysay became President, Dec 30, 1953.

With all of this on the record, and a lot more, this guy Currey comes out of the blue with this purported "Biography." I knew Ed well enough and long enough to know that he was a classic chameleon. He would tell the truth sparingly and he would fabricate a lot. Still, I cannot believe that he told Currey the things Currey writes. Why would Lansdale want Currey to perpetuate such out and out bullshit about him? Can't be. This is a terribly fabricated book. It's not even true about me. I believe that this book was ordered and delineated by the CIA.

At least I know the truth about myself and about Gen. Krulak. Currey libels us terribly. In fact it may be Krulak who caused the book to be taken off the shelves. Krulak and his Copley Press cohorts have the power to get that done, and I encouraged them to do just that when it first came out. Krulak was mad!

Ed told me many a time how he operated in the Philippines. He said, "All I had was a blank checkbook signed by the U.S. government." He made friends with many influential Filipinos. I have met Johnny Orendain and Col Valeriano, among others, in Manila with Lansdale. He became acquainted with the wealthiest Filipino of them all, Soriano. Currey never even mentions him. Soriano set up Philippine Airlines and owned the big San Miguel beer company, among other things. Key man in Asia.

Lansdale's greatest strategy was to create the "HUKS" as the enemy and to make Magsaysay the "Huk Killer." He would take Magsaysay's battalion out into a "Huk" infested area. He would use movies and "battlefield" sound systems, i.e. fireworks to scare the poor natives. Then one-half of Magsaysay's battalion, dressed as natives, would "attack" the village at night. They'd fire into the air and burn some shacks. In the morning the other half, in uniform, would attack and "capture" the "Huks." They would bind them up in front of the natives who crept back from the forests, and even have a "firing" squad "kill" some of them. Then they would have Magsaysay make a big speech to the people and the whole battalion would roll down the road to have breakfast together somewhere . . . ready for the next "show."

Ed would always see that someone had arranged to have newsmen and camera men there and Magsaysay soon became a national hero. This was a tough game and Ed bragged that a lot of people were killed; but in the end Magsaysay became the "elected" President and Querino was ousted "legally."

This formula endeared Ed to Allen Dulles. In 1954 Dulles established the Saigon Military Mission in Vietnam . . . counter to Eisenhower's orders. He had the French accept Lansdale as its chief. This mission was not in Saigon. It was not military, and its job was subversion in Vietnam. Its biggest job was that it got more than 1,100,000 northern Vietnamese to move south. 660,000 by U.S.Navy ships and the rest by CIA airline planes. These 1,100,000 north Vietnamese became the "subversive" element in South Vietnam and the principal cause of the warmaking. Lansdale and his cronies (Bohanon, Arundel, Phillips, Hand, Conein and many others) did all that using the same check book. I was with them many times during 1954. All Malthuseanism.

I have heard him brag about capturing random Vietnamese and putting them in a Helicopter. Then they would work on them to make them "confess" to being Viet Minh. When they would not, they would toss them out of the chopper, one after the other, until the last ones talked. This was Ed's idea of fun . . . as related to me many times. Then Dulles, Adm. Radford and Cardinal Spellman set up Ngo Dinh Diem. He and his brother, Nhu, became Lansdale overnme.

At about 1957 Lansdale was brought back to Washington and assigned to Air Force Headquarters in a Plans office near mine. He was a fish out of water. He didn't know Air Force people and Air Force ways. After about six months of that, Dulles got the Office of Special Operations under General Erskine to ask for Lansdale to work for the Secretary of Defense. Erskine was man enough to control him.

By 1960 Erskine had me head the Air Force shop there. He had an Army shop and a Navy shop and we were responsible for all CIA relationships as well as for the National Security Agency. Ed was still out of his element because he did not know the services; but the CIA sent work his way.

Then in the Fall of 1960 something happened that fired him up. Kennedy was elected over Nixon. Right away Lansdale figured out what he was going to do with the new President. Overnight he left for Saigon to see Diem and to set up a deal that would make him, Lansdale, Ambassador to Vietnam. He had me buy a "Father of his Country" gift for Diem . . . $700.00.

I can't repeat all of this but you should get a copy of the Gravel edition, 5 Vol.'s, of the Pentagon Papers and read it. The Lansdale accounts are quite good and reasonably accurate.

Ed came back just before the Inauguration and was brought into the White House for a long presentation to Kennedy about Vietnam. Kennedy was taken by it and promised he would have Lansdale back in Vietnam "in a high office." Ed told us in OSO he had the Ambassadorship sewed up. He lived for that job.

He had not reckoned with some of JFK's inner staff, George Ball, etc. Finally the whole thing turned around and month by month Lansdale's star sank over the horizon. Erskine retired and his whole shop was scattered. The Navy men went back to the navy as did the Army folks. Gen Wheeler in the JCS asked to have me assigned to the Joint Staff. This wiped out the whole Erskine (Office of Special Operations) office. It was comical. There was Lansdale up there all by himself with no office and no one else. He boiled and he blamed it on Kennedy for not giving him the "promised" Ambassadorship to let him "save" Vietnam.

Then with the failure of the Bay of Pigs, caused by that phone call to cancel the air strikes by McGeorge Bundy, the military was given the job of reconstituting some sort of Anti-Castro operation. It was headed by an Army Colonel; but somehow Lansdale (most likely CIA influence) got put into the plans for Operation Mongoose . . . to get Castro . . . ostensibly.

The U.S. Army has a think-tank at American University. It was called "Operation Camelot." This is where the "Camelot" concept came from. It was anti-JFK's Vietnam strategy. The men running it were Lansdale types, Special Forces background. "Camelot" was King Arthur and Knights of the Round Table: not JFK . . . then.

Through 1962 and 1963 Mongoose and "Camelot" became strong and silent organizations dedicated to countering JFK. Mongoose had access to the CIA's best "hit men" in the business and a lot of "strike" capability. Lansdale had many old friends in the media business such as Joe Alsop, Henry Luce among others. With this background and with his poisoned motivation I am positive that he got collateral orders to manage the Dallas event under the guise of "getting" Castro. It is so simple at that level. A nod from the right place, source immaterial, and the job's done.

The "hit" is the easy part. The "escape" must be quick and professional. The cover-up and the scenario are the big jobs. They more than anything else prove the Lansdale mastery.

Lansdale was a master writer and planner. He was a great "scenario" guy. I still have a lot of his personally typed material in my files. I am certain that he was behind the elaborate plan and mostly the intricate and enduring cover-up. Given a little help from friends at PEPSICO he could easily have gotten Nixon into Dallas, for "orientation": and LBJ in the cavalcade at the same time, contrary to Secret Service policy.

He knew the "Protection" units and the "Secret Service," who was needed and who wasn't. Those were routine calls for him, and they would have believed him. Cabell could handle the police.

The "hit men" were from CIA overseas sources, for instance, from the "Camp near Athena, Greece. They are trained, stateless, and ready to go at any time. They ask no questions: speak to no one. They are simply told what to do, when and where. Then they are told how they will be removed and protected. After all, they work for the U.S. Government. The "Tramps" were actors doing the job of cover-up. The hit men are just pros. They do the job for the

CIA anywhere. They are impersonal. They get paid. They get protected, and they have enough experience to "blackmail" anyone, if anyone ever turns on them . . . just like Drug agents. The job was clean, quick and neat. No ripples.

The whole story of the POWER of the Cover-up comes down to a few points. There has never been a Grand Jury and trial in Texas. Without a trial there can be nothing. Without a trial it does no good for researchers to dig up data. It has no place to go and what the researchers reveal just helps make the cover-up tighter, or they eliminate that evidence and the researcher.

The first man LBJ met with on Nov 29th, after he had cleared the foreign dignitaries out of Washington was Waggoner Carr, Atty Gen'l, Texas to tell him, "No trial in Texas . . . ever."

The next man he met, also on Nov 29th, was J. Edgar Hoover. The first question LBJ asked his old "19 year" neighbor in DC was "Were THEY shooting at me?" LBJ thought that THEY had been shooting at him also as they shot at his friend John Connally. Note that he asked, "Were THEY shooting at me?" LBJ knew there were several hitmen. That's the ultimate clue . . . THEY.

The Connallys said the same thing . . . THEY. Not Oswald.

Then came the heavily loaded press releases about Oswald all written before the deal and released actually before LHO had ever been charged with the crime. I bought the first newspaper EXTRA on the streets of Christchurch, New Zealand with the whole LHO story in that first news . . . photos and columns of it before the police in Dallas had yet to charge him with that crime. All this canned material about LHO was flashed around the world.

Lansdale and his Time-Life and other media friends, with Valenti in Hollywood, have been doing that cover-up since Nov 1963. Even the deMorenschildt story enhances all of this. In deM's personal telephone/address notebook he had the name of an Air Force Colonel friend of mine, Howard Burrus. Burrus was always deep in intelligence. He had been in one of the most sensitive Attaché spots in

Europe . . . Switzerland. He was a close friend of another Air Force Colonel and Attache, Godfrey McHugh, who used to date Jackie Bouvier. DeM had Burrus listed under a DC telephone number and on that same telephone number he had "L.B.Johnson, Congressman." Quite a connection. Why . . . from the Fifties yet.?

Godfrey McHugh was the Air Force Attache in Paris. Another most important job. I knew him well, and I transferred his former Ass't Attache to my office in the Pentagon. This gave me access to a lot of information I wanted in the Fifties. This is how I learned that McHugh's long-time special "date" was the fair Jacqueline . . . yes, the same Jackie Bouvier. Sen. Kennedy met Jackie in Paris when he was on a trip. At that time JFK was dating a beautiful SAS Airline Stewardess who was the date of that Ass't Attache who came to my office. JFK dumped her and stole Jackie away from McHugh. Leaves McHugh happy????

At the JFK Inaugural Ball who should be there but the SAS stewardess, Jackie—of course, and Col Godfrey McHugh. JFK made McHugh a General and made him his "Military Advisor" in the White House where he was near Jackie while JFK was doing all that official travelling connected with his office AND other special interests. Who recommended McHugh for the job?

General McHugh was in Dallas and was on Air Force One, with Jackie, on the flight back to Washington . . . as was Jack Valenti. Why was LBJ's old cohort there at that time and why was he on Air Force One? He is now the Movie Czar. Why in Dallas?

See how carefully all of this is interwoven. Burrus is now a very wealthy man in Washington. I have lost track of McHugh. And Jackie is doing well. All in the Lansdale—deM shadows.

One of Lansdale's special "black" intelligence associates in the Pentagon was Dorothy Matlack of U.S. Army Intelligence. How does it happen that when deM. Flew from Haiti to testify, he was met at the National Airport by Dorothy?

The Lansdale story is endless. What people do not do is study the entire environment of his strange career. For example: the most important part of my book, "The Secret Team," is not something that I wrote. It is Appendix III under the title, "Training Under The Mutual Security Program." This is a most important bit of material. It tells more about the period 1963 to 1990 than anything. I fought to have it included verbatim in the book. This material was the work of Lansdale and his crony General Dick Stillwell. Anyone interested in the "JFK Coup d'Etat" ought to know it by heart.

I believe this document tells why the Coup took place. It was to reverse the sudden JFK re-orientation of the U.S. Government from Asia to Europe, in keeping with plans made in 1943 at Cairo and Teheran by T.V. Soong and his Asian masterminds. Lansdale and Stillwell were long-time "Asia hands" as were Gen Erskine, Adm Radford, Cardinal Spellman, Henry Luce and so many others.

In October 1963, JFK had just overnme this reversal, to Europe, when he published National Security Action Memorandum #263 saying . . . among other things . . . that he was taking 1000 troops home from Vietnam by Christmas 1963 and ALL AMERICANS out of Vietnam by the end of 1965. That cost him his life.

JFK came to that "Pro-Europe" conclusion in the Summer of 1963 and sent Gen Krulak to Vietnam for advance work. Kurlak and I (with others) wrote that long "Taylor-McNamara" Report of their "Visit to Vietnam" (obviously they did not write, illustrate and bind it as they traveled). Krulak got his information daily in the White House. We simply wrote it. That led to NSAM #263. This same Trip Report is Document #142 and appears on page 751 to 766 of Vol. II of the Gravel Edition of the Pentagon Papers. NSAM #263 appears on pages 769-770 (It makes the Report official). This major Report and NSAM indicated an enormous shift in the orientation of U.S. Foreign Policy from Asia back to Europe. JFK was much more Europe-oriented, as was his father, than pro-Asia. This position was anathema to the Asia-born Luces, etc.

There is the story from an insider. I sat in the same office with Lansdale, (OSO of OSD) for years. I listened to him in Manila and read his flurry of notes from 1952 to 1964. I know all this stuff, and much more. I could write ten books. I send this to you because I believe you are one of the most sincere of the "true researchers." You may do with it as you please. I know you will do it right. I may give copies of this to certain other people of our persuasion. (Years ago I told this to Mae Brussell on the promise she would hold it. She did.)

Now you can see why I have always said that identification of the "Tramps" was unnecessary, i.e. they are actors. The first time I saw that picture I saw the man I knew and I realized why he was there. He caused the political world to spin on its axis. Now, back to recuperating.

L. Fletcher Prouty

Incredible! Col. Prouty, in two short letters, just connected the CIA, the drug trade, the JFK assassination, and the FBI, all of which this author later found much more evidence to substantiate this. No wonder that no one in power will allow anyone to delve deeply into any of these areas. Like hidden passages, if you go into one you will see all the others; these are portals into the American heart of darkness. Add to this the incredible video interviews that Col. Prouty did before he passed away. One titled *Drug Trade* is available at: http://www.youtube.com/watch?v=ear75Mo02uU, which the author accessed March 3, 2013. At about three minutes and 45 seconds into it, Prouty talked about his knowledge of the use of caskets to transport drugs from Southern China to Southeast Asia using military aircraft. This may have been the beginnings of activities of this sort.

Many years ago, when the author started this investigation, the same names kept cropping up in all of these areas. The same names that were reported by many, many investigators and authors that did not necessarily agree with each other. Not only did they not agree with each other but, in some cases, did not know each other. Liberals, conservatives, moderates, and those that were indifferent to political persuasion, it did not matter; the same names kept coming up, over and over and over again.

The above topics are, in turn, connected to control of the media, the Bay of Pigs invasion, Iran-Contra, ad-infinitum. No wonder Senator Fulbright once commented that (a thorough investigation into) the Bay of Pigs invasion and the JFK assassination would open up an "endless can of worms." Perhaps the senator's comment was an understatement. As we shall see, the endless connections would incriminate virtually the entire government (all three branches): corporate America, the media, a surprising number of "academics," and the list goes on. Further, as we shall see, the whole hidden dirty truth logically explains virtually all major news stories that have not been truthfully reported since WWII. All wars have had a drug component. What's more, as we shall see, at least most US political assassinations are related to wars and/or drugs. Add to this that many assassinations and coups throughout the world are also related to these topics. Yes, an endless can of worms.

Below are but a few Americans with deep intelligence ties that will also show up in later chapters and my next book when we discuss assassinations, wars, and other drug-running programs. Many times, they all are involved together and also in more than one incident. There are many more people we could discuss; however, the connections are endless, and the culpability is also almost endless.

The most recent figures on the number of incarcerated Americans were roughly 2.4 million. Not only is that too many, but they are also the wrong people. If Americans that have actually committed the most serious crimes were to be prosecuted, the US government would have to be shut down. We are talking about those that have taken us into illegal wars, committed war crimes, the real culprits in the illegal drug trade, the real assassinations, and so forth; were they to be criminally prosecuted, the number would easily go into tens of thousands and maybe much more. Much of the government would be in jail and of them more than a few millionaires and billionaires. One would presume that there would not be a lack of white faces in this crowd.

Let us take a look at some of the CIA operatives, most of which wore uniforms, that not only played a role in the drug trade in Southeast Asia but also were actively involved in one or more clandestine operations such as the Bay of Pigs invasion, the plot to assassinate Castro, the JFK assassination, the RFK assassination, the Martin Luther King assassination, the capture and murder of Che Guevara, the overthrow and murder of Salvador Allende, the murder of Omar Trujillo of Panama, and many more.

Actor in the Heart of Darkness Play: Paul Lional Edward Helliwell[24]

Paul Lional Edward Helliwell was born in 1915. He was a lawyer before he joined the United States Army during the Second World War. Later he was transferred to the Office of Strategic Services (OSS) where he served under William Donovan.

In 1943, Colonel Paul Helliwell became head of the Secret Intelligence Branch of the OSS in Europe. Helliwell was replaced in this post by William Casey in 1945.

Helliwell became chief of the Far East Division of the War Department's Strategic Service Unit, an interim intelligence organization formed after OSS was closed down.

In 1947, Helliwell joined the Central Intelligence Agency. In May 1949, General Claire Chennault had a meeting with Harry S. Truman and advocated an increase in funds for Chiang Kai-shek and his Kuomintang Army (KMT) in his war in China. Truman dismissed the idea as impractical. However, Frank Wisner (CIA) was more sympathetic; and when Mao Zedong took power in China in 1950, he sent Helliwell to Taiwan.

Helliwell's main job was to help Chiang Kai-shek to prepare for a future invasion of Communist China. The CIA created a pair of front companies to supply and finance the surviving forces of Chiang's KMT. Paul Helliwell was put in charge of this operation. This included establishing Civil Air Transport (CAT), a Taiwan-based airline, and the Sea Supply Corporation, a shipping company in Bangkok.

It was Helliwell's idea to use these CIA-fronted companies to raise money to help support Chiang Kai-shek. According to Joseph Trento

---

[24.] Photo source: Spartacus Educational, http://www.spartacus.schoolnet.co.uk/JFKhelliwell.htm

(*Prelude to Terror*), "Through Sea Supply, Helliwell imported large amounts of arms for the KMT soldiers to keep the Burmese military from throwing them out of the country. The arms were ferried into Burma on CAT airplanes. CAT then used the "empty" planes to fly Helliwell along with Edward Lansdale and others, married the CIA to drugs and war, which has resulted in the destruction of the republic as it once was. In the relatively short time from after World War II to the present, the United States of America has been transformed from a young, powerful, and optimistic democracy to a criminal empire that now has only a thin veneer of democratic processes it once had.

This incredible change was done by only a few hundred bloodthirsty, greedy, murderous, conscienceless unconvicted felons. This is the basis of what has been described as the shadow government, secret government, parallel government, and so forth. To understand the totality of these expressions and concepts, the origins of the pathocracy need to be conceptualized. Simply put, this group of pathological personalities have created and nurtured virtually every armed conflict throughout the world in recent times. Further, they have financed the conflict with drug money and US tax dollars that should be financing education, health care, housing, infrastructure, and other helpful things to society.

To accomplish this, they had to create what is sometimes called "deep politics," or that part of the political system that is hidden from its citizenry. A good example of this is the government's involvement in the international drug trade, which has been well hidden from the people largely by the use of, or abuse of, classification and other national security laws, rules, and regulations. Obviously, hiding criminal activity by government agencies is the reason for this and not protecting national security. To hide deep politics from the American people required more and more control of the very freedoms the country purports to be founded on. The enormous energy put into this inevitably impossible endeavor has corrupted not only every government agency but also the US media, corporate America, and to a large degree, the education system.

Rodney Stich, author of *Drugging America, a Trojan Horse*, goes into much detail and provides numerous examples of how the US government's complicity in the drug trade has been a "Trojan horse" that has corrupted American institutions to the point that the United States can no longer be looked at as a free country. Our next actor was instrumental in corrupting American institutions.

Actor in the Heart of Darkness Play: Major General Edward Geary Lansdale[25]

Edward Geary Lansdale started his intelligence career as a US Army lieutenant with the Office of Strategic Services during WWII. In 1945, he became chief of the Intelligence Division, Headquarters Air Forces Western Pacific Region.

Lansdale was an excellent example of a CIA case officer that wore a military uniform but whose first loyalty was to the CIA. He was in Indochina as early as 1953, advising the French forces on special counter-guerrilla operations. He was well aware of opium and heroin trade conducted by the French, code-named Operation X, and the key player in the United States' assumption and management of the Southeast Asian drug trade.

Col. Prouty has drawn an excellent thumbnail sketch of Gen. Lansdale and his machinations in the Vietnam War and also in the Southeast Asian drug trade. It is interesting to note that Gen. Lansdale had much experience at fabricating both a thesis and also an opposing antithesis from which conflict is inevitable. He would then feed each side of the conflict and escalate it until it resulted in a full-scale war. Gen. Lansdale created this model perfectly both in the Philippines and also the Vietnam War.

This strategy is an example of what some would call an application of the "Hegelian Dialectic," albeit couched in the narrow context of profit derived from militarism. Some have said that this model is the method by which the very top of the world's elite ruling class derive profit from contrived world conflict. The logic of this is that the ruling class can contrive a thesis, for example, capitalism, and also the

---

25. Photo source: Wikipedia, http://en.wikipedia.org/wiki/File:Major-general-lansdale.jpg.

antithesis to this, such as communism. From this would inevitably come conflict, which the ruling elite can then sell arms to both sides and inevitably derive obscene profits.

A model of this would appear as such: Thesis-antithesis-armed conflict-profit. It has been further theorized that not only is this a method that the wealth of nations can be transferred to the very rich, but that by taking this excess wealth away from the people the ruling elite can thus control the rest of the world population, namely the middle and lower class. The removal of wealth from the people ensures that it is not used for education, health, housing, infrastructure, and other services that benefit the society. Further, this process can be viewed as a method to generate fear, despair, and hopelessness to ensure there is no resistance to this process.

Not only can this application of the Hegelian dialectic be used to explain virtually every armed conflict for about the last thousand years, but it fits perfectly when one is trying to understand what Gen. Lansdale and Alan Dulles were doing, according to Col. Prouty, when they moved 1,100,000 North Vietnamese south to become the "subversive" element in South Vietnam. There is no other plausible explanation other than they were deliberately creating conflict and systematically escalating it. Add to this, Col Prouty's comment that these actions were "counter to Eisenhower's orders," and we see that the CIA was formulating US policy that was not only directly opposed to that of the president of the United States but also clearly not in the interest of the citizenry.

Add to this the fact that a large part of this CIA-contrived conflict was financed by the international drug trade, especially those operations that the CIA wanted to hide from Congress and the American people. We now have criminality being conducted on a major scale and people, arguably with psychopathic personalities, that have the motive, means, and opportunity to not only advance this monstrous crime but also to commit other horrific crimes to hide those already committed. Major General Edward Lansdale has been implicated in all of the above and more, as we shall see.

Actor in the Heart of Darkness Play: Theodore Shackley[26]

Born in 1927, Ted Shackley was the son of a Polish immigrant mother. He grew up in West Palm Beach and learned Polish mostly from his Polish grandmother. Shackley joined the US Army in 1945, and his first assignment was to Germany as part of the Allied occupation force. His knowledge of the Polish language led to his recruitment into Army Intelligence. He was sent to the University of Maryland to study after which he was commissioned a second lieutenant and returned to Germany where he was also recruited by the CIA to recruit new Polish agents.

Shackley, whose nickname was the "Blond Ghost," presumably because he avoided being photographed, became involved in CIA counterintelligence operations directed at removing foreign leaders from power. The program known as Executive Action overthrew or assassinated foreign leaders that were "not friendly to the United States." Almost always, this phrase means leaders that use the resources of their country for the benefit of their people, and do not "play ball" with the United States. Executive Action operations included a coup that overthrew the Guatemalan government of Jacobo Arbenz in 1954. Arbenz had committed the unpardonable sins of introducing land reforms and nationalizing the United Fruit Company.

Shackley was also deeply involved in the Bay of Pigs invasion of Cuba. He and Edward Lansdale were also key players in operations to overthrow Castro after the failure of this seriously flawed invasion. The program was code-named Operation Mongoose. We will go into more depth of these operations in later chapters.

In 1966, Shackley was put in charge of the secret war in Laos that involved using mountain tribes to fight the Southeast Asian war.

---

26. Photo source Wikipedia: http://en.wikipedia.org/wiki/File:Ted_Shackley.jpg.

As discussed before, the deal was they offer up their young men to fight for the CIA. Air America flew in rice and weapons and flew out opium. Over many years, Shackley has vehemently denied this, but the evidence is overwhelming. According to Alfred W. McCoy, in his meticulous and thoroughly referenced book, *The Politics of Heroin: CIA Complicity in the Global Drug Trade*, Shackley and his assistant Thomas Clines managed the entire operation. Further, Professor McCoy documents that Shackley and Clines arranged a meeting between Santo Trafficante Jr. and opium lord Vang Pao in Saigon in 1968 to establish a heroin smuggling route from Southeast Asia to the United States. There is no doubt that Shackley was being deceptive, which is what he was noted for, when he stated that neither he nor the CIA had any dealing with the drug trade in Southeast Asia. Other CIA operatives that Shackley took with him to assist in the secret war in Laos were Carl E. Jenkins, David Morales, Raphael Quintero, Felix Rodriguez, and Edwin Wilson. These names will come up in later chapters and my next book. It is interesting to note that Shackley and many, if not most, of the CIA case officers, agents, and operatives involved in the Bay of Pigs, Operation Mongoose, and other anti-Castro operations have also been implicated in the Vietnam war, the Southeast Asian drug trade, the JFK assassination (and/or other political assassinations), Iran-Contra drug and arms dealing, drug and arms dealing in Afghanistan, ad infinitum. Is it possible that hundreds of witnesses made up all of this information on all of these so-called public servants? We shall see.

One of the most odious undertakings that Shackley managed was the program code-named Operation Phoenix. This program involved the killing of tens of thousands of South Vietnamese civilians supposedly suspected of collaborating with the National Liberation Front. However, most Vietnam veterans will remember this program as one that was totally out of control. For example, if one Vietnamese had borrowed a sum of money from another but did not want to pay it back, all the borrower had to do was to report the loaner as a communist agent, and an assassination team would come in the middle of the night and kill the person accused, loan nullified. Not a good way to do business.

Much of Shackley's activities in Southeast Asia are delineated in the following lawsuit filed by Daniel P. Sheehan on behalf of the Christic Institute. Although Judge James L. King ruled on June 23,

1988, that Sheehan's allegations were "based on unsubstantiated rumor and speculation" and dismissed the case, this author was able to find voluminous data to support most, if not all, of the Christic Institute's claims. The claims submitted were far from unsubstantiated rumor. Judge King not only dismissed the case, but in February 1989, he ruled that the suit was frivolous and ordered the Christic Institute to pay the defendants $955,000 in fines. This sanction was one of the highest imposed in history and amounted to roughly four times the total assets of the Christic Institute. By use of this extraordinary sanction, this judge bankrupted the institute and, in effect, shut it down. This is the sort of thing that happens any time anyone shines a light into the heart of darkness.

Below is Sheehan's lawsuit on behalf of the Christic Institute. It is extremely revealing as to the connections between war, drugs, and the CIA. Also revealing are the names connected to these undertakings. The whole affidavit is available at: http://www.spartacus.schoolnet.co.uk/JFKsheehan.htm#source.

Daniel P. Sheehan, Affidavit (12th December, 1986)

1. I am a duly licensed attorney at law, admitted to practice before the State and Federal Courts of the State of New York in both the Northern and Southern Districts of New York . . .
2. While serving as a legal Associate at the Wall Street law firm of Cahill, Gordon, Sonnett, Rheindle and Ohio under partner Theodore Shackley and Thomas Clines directed the Phoenix Project in Vietnam, in 1974 and 1975, which carried out the secret mission of assassinating members of the economic and political bureaucracy inside Vietnam to cripple the ability of that nation to function after the total US withdrawal from Vietnam. This Phoenix Project, during its history, carried out the political assassination, in Vietnam, of some 60,000 village mayors, treasurers, school teachers and other non) Viet Cong administrators. Theodore Shackley and Thomas Clines financed a highly intensified phase of the Phoenix project, in 1974 and 1975, by causing an intense flow of Vang

Pao opium money to be secretly brought into Vietnam for this purpose. This Vang Pao opium money was administered for Theodore Shackley and Thomas Clines by a US Navy official based in Saigon's US office of Naval Operations by the name of Richard Armitage. However, because Theodore Shackley, Thomas Clines and Richard Armitage knew that their secret anti-communist extermination program was going to be shut down in Vietnam, Laos, Cambodia, and Thailand in the very near future, they, in 1973, began a highly secret non-CIA authorized program. Thus, from late 1973 until April of 1975, Theodore Shackley, Thomas Clines and Richard Armitage disbursed, from the secret, Laotian-based, Vang Pao opium fund, vastly more money than was required to finance even the highly intensified Phoenix Project in Vietnam. The money in excess of that used in Vietnam was secretly smuggled out of Vietnam in large suitcases, by Richard Secord and Thomas Clines and carried into Australia, where it was deposited in a secret, personal bank account (privately accessible to Theodore Shackley, Thomas Clines and Richard Secord). During this same period of time between 1973 and 1975, Theodore Shackley and Thomas Clines caused thousands of tons of US weapons, ammunition, and explosives to be secretly taken from Vietnam and stored at a secret "cache" hidden inside Thailand.

The "liaison officer" to Shackley and Clines and the Phoenix Project in Vietnam, during this 1973 to 1975 period, from the "40 Committee" in the Nixon White House was one Eric Von Arbod, an Assistant Secretary of State for Far Eastern Affairs. Von Arbod shared his information about the Phoenix Project directly with his supervisor Henry Kissinger.

Saigon fell to the Vietnamese in April of 1975. The Vietnam War was over. Immediately upon the conclusion of the evacuation of U.S. personnel from Vietnam, Richard Armitage was dispatched, by Theodore Shackley and

Thomas Clines, from Vietnam to Tehran, Iran. In Iran, Armitage, the "bursar" for the Vang Pao opium money for Shackley and Clines' planned "Secret Team" covert operations program, between May and August of 1975, set up a secret "financial conduit" inside Iran, into which secret Vang Pao drug funds could be deposited from Southeast Asia. The purpose of this conduit was to serve as the vehicle for secret funding by Shackley's "Secret Team," of a private, non-CIA authorized "Black" operations inside Iran, disposed to seek out, identify, and assassinate socialist and communist sympathizers, who were viewed by Shackley and his "Secret Team" members to be "potential terrorists" against the Shah of Iran's government in Iran. In late 1975 and early 1976, Theodore Shackley and Thomas Clines retained Edwin Wilson to travel to Tehran, Iran to head up the "Secret Team" covert "anti terrorist" assassination program in Iran. This was not a U.S. government authorized operation. This was a private operations supervised, directed and participated in by Shackley, Clines, Secord and Armitage in their purely private capacities.

At the end of 1975, Richard Armitage took the post of a "Special Consultant" to the U.S. Department of Defense regarding American military personnel Missing In Action (MIAs) in Southeast Asia. In this capacity, Armitage was posted in the U.S. Embassy in Bangkok, Thailand. There Armitage had top responsibility for locating and retrieving American MIA's in Southeast Asia. He worked at the Embassy with an associate, one Jerry O. Daniels. From 1975 to 1977, Armitage held this post in Thailand. However, he did not perform the duties of this office. Instead, Armitage continued to function as the "bursar" for Theodore Shackley's "Secret Team," seeing to it that secret Vang Pao opium funds were conducted from Laos, through Armitage in Thailand to both Tehran and the secret Shackley bank account in Australia at the Nugen-Hand Bank. The monies conducted by Armitage to Tehran were to fund Edwin Wilson's secret anti-terrorist "seek and destroy" operation on behalf of Theodore Shackely. Armitage also devoted a portion of his time between 1975 and 1977, in Bangkok, facilitating the escape from Laos, Cambodia and Thailand and the relocation elsewhere in the world, of numbers of the secret Meo tribesmen group which had carried out the covert political assassination program for Theodore Shackley in Southeast Asia between 1966 and 1975. Assisting Richard Armitage in this operation was Jerry O. Daniels. Indeed, Jerry O. Daniels was a "bag-man" for Richard Armitage, assisting Armitage by physically transporting out of Thailand millions of dollars of Vang Pao's secret opium money to finance the relocation of Theodore Shackley's Meo tribesmen and to supply funds to Theodore Shackley's "Secret Team" operations. At the U.S. Embassy in Bangkok, Richard Armitage also supervised the removal of arms, ammunition and explosives from the secret Shackley/Clines cache of munitions hidden inside Thailand between 1973 and 1975, for use by Shackley's "Secret Team." Assisting Armitage in this latter operations was one Daniel Arnold, the CIA Chief of Station in Thailand, who joined Shackley's "Secret Team" in his purely private capacity.

One of the officers in the U.S. Embassy in Thailand, one Abranowitz came to know of Armitage's involvement in the secret handling of Vang Pao opium funds and caused to be initiated an internal State Department heroin smuggling investigations directed against Richard Armitage. Armitage was the target of Embassy personnel complaints to the effect that he was utterly failing to perform his duties on behalf of American MIAs, and he reluctantly resigned as the D.O.D. Special Consultant on MIA's at the end of 1977.

From 1977 until 1979, Armitage remained in Bangkok opening and operating a business named The Far East Trading Company. This company had offices only in Bangkok and in Washington, D.C. This company was, in fact, from 1977 to 1979, merely a "front" for Armitage's secret operations conducting Vang Pao opium money out of Southeast Asia to Tehran and the Nugen-Hand Bank in Australia to fund the ultra right-wing, private anti-communist "anti-terrorist" assassination program and "unconventional warfare" operation of Theodore Shackley's and Thomas Cline's "Secret Team." During this period, between 1975 and 1979, in Bangkok, Richard Armitage lived in the home of Hynnie Aderholdt, the former Air Wing Commander of Shackley's "Special Operations Group" in Laos, who, between 1966 and 1968, had served as the immediate superior to Richard Secord, the Deputy Air Wing Commander of MAG SOG. Secord, in 1975, was transferred from Vietnam to Tehran, Iran.

In 1976, Richard Secord moved to Tehran, Iran and became the Deputy Assistant Secretary of defense in Iran, in charge of the Middle Eastern Division of the Defense Security Assistance Administration. In this capacity, Secord functioned as the chief operations officer for the U.S. Defense Department in the Middle East in charge of foreign military sales of U.S. aircraft, weapons and military equipment to Middle Eastern nations allied to the U.S. Secord's immediate superior was Eric Van Marbad, the former 40 Committee liaison officer to Theodore Shackley's Phoenix program in Vietnam from 1973 to 1975.

From 1976 to 1979, in Iran, Richard Secord supervised the sale of U.S. military aircraft and weapons to Middle Eastern nations. However, Richard Secord did not authorize direct nation-to-nation sales of such equipment directly from the U.S. government to said Middle Eastern governments. Instead, Richard Secord conducted such sales through a "middle-man", one Albert Hakim. By the use of middle-man Albert Hakim, Deputy Assistant Secretary of Defense Richard Secord purchased U.S. military aircraft and weapons from the U.S. government at the low "manufacturer's cost" but sold these U.S. aircraft and weapons to the client Middle Eastern nations at the much higher "replacement cost." Secord then caused to be paid to the U.S. government, out of the actual sale price obtained, only the lower amount equal to the lower manufacturer's cost. The difference, was secreted from the U.S. government and Secord and Albert Hakim secretly transferred these millions of dollars into Shackley's "Secret Team" operations inside Iran and into Shackley's secret Nugen-Hand bank account in Australia. Thus, by 1976, Defendant Albert Hakim had become a partner with Thomas Clines, Richard Secord and Richard Armitage in Theodore Shackley's "Secret Team."

Between 1976 and 1979, Shackley, Clines, Secord, Hakim, Wilson, and Armitage set up several corporations and subsidiaries around the world through which to conceal the operations of the "Secret Team." Many of these corporations were set up in Switzerland. Some of these were: (1) Lake Resources, Inc.; (2) The Stanford Technology Trading Group, Inc.; and (3) Companie de Services Fiduciaria. Other companies were set up in Central America, such as: (4) CSF Investments, Ltd. And (5) Udall research Corporation. Some were set up inside the United States by Edwin Wilson. Some of these were: (6) Orca Supply Company in Florida and (7) Consultants International in Washington, D.C. Through these corporations, members of Theodore Shackley's "Secret Team" laundered hundreds of millions of dollars of secret Vang Pao opium money, pilfered Foreign Military Sales proceeds between 1976 and 1979. Named in this federal civil suit to be placed under oath and asked about their participation in the criminal "enterprise" alleged in this Complaint is probative of the criminal guilt of the Defendants of some of the crimes charged in this Complaint.

Plaintiffs and Plaintiffs' Counsel, The Christic Institute, possess evidence constituting "probable cause" that each of the Defendants named in this Complaint are guilty of the conduct charged . . .

As stated above, when Saigon fell in April 1975, Shackley dispatched Richard L. Armitage and Air Force Major General Richard Secord to Tehran. There they set up a financial conduit where hundreds of millions of drug dollars were transferred to Iran to be used in several illegal operations. Of course, these names will come up again.

Actor in the Heart of Darkness Play: Richard L. Armitage[27]

Born April 26, 1945, Richard Armitage graduated from the US Naval Academy in 1967. He received a commission in the U.S. Navy, and his first assignment was on a destroyer stationed in Vietnam. Later he became an advisor to Vietnamese naval forces.

In 1973, he joined the office of the US Defense Attaché in Saigon and became involved with Ted Shackley, the CIA chief in South Vietnam. According to Joel Bainerman, author of *The Crimes of a President*, Shackley and his secret team became involved in the entire Southeast Asian drug trade while in Laos. They did this in alliance with General Vang Pao, the leader of the anti-Communist forces in Laos. Eventually Vang Pao, with the assistance of Shackley's secret team, took control of the entire heroin trade in Laos.

As previously stated by Daniel Sheehan, Shackley, Thomas Clines, and Armitage disbursed enormous amounts of cash from an opium fund, presumably to finance Operation Phoenix in Vietnam. Even though this program had become highly intensified, the funds transferred far exceeded the requirements. The excess is reported to have run into hundreds of millions of US dollars and was reported to have been secretly smuggled out of Vietnam to Australia. There it was, deposited into the Nugan Hand Bank in Sydney. This bank was founded by Michael Hand, a CIA operative in Laos, and Frank Nugan, an Australian Businessman.

When Saigon fell in April 1975, Armitage went to Washington as a consultant for the Department of Defense. He was soon sent to Iran where he set up a special account into which he transferred much of the Vang

---

27. Photo source Wikipedia at: http://en.wikipedia.org/wiki/Richard_Armitage_(politician).

Pao drug money from Southeast Asia. This money was used to finance "black" operations inside Iran that were strikingly similar to Operation Phoenix in SEA, the details of which will be covered in my next book. It is interesting to note that Armitage is one name, of many, that seems to crop up over and over again wherever there are wars, assassinations, drugs, et cetera. Almost never do the mainstream media connect these horrendous undertakings. Perhaps it is a coincidence that all US wars seem to happen where there are drugs worth hundreds of billions of dollars.

Secretary of State Collin Powell often referred to Richard Armitage as his "white son," a curious phrase from someone who is only eight years the latter's senior. A little too young for the JFK assassination, several who knew him in Southeast Asia described him as one who enjoyed killing people and talking about it. This author has been around his fair share of killing, and I have never met anyone that enjoyed it, not one. What do you suppose a psychiatrist would say if this individual came in for analysis? And again, we will be seeing more of this person later.

Actor in the Heart of Darkness Play: David Sanchez Morales[28]

Another CIA operative suspected of being involved in political assassinations that operated in Southeast Asia was David Morales. Born in August 1925, Morales grew up with his best friend Ruben Carbajal, who later provided much information about Morales and some of the CIA's darkest operations.

Morales went to college at Arizona State University and later attended University of Southern California. He joined the army in 1946 and went to Germany as part

---

28. Photo source Mary Ferrell Foundation at: http://www.maryferrell.org/wiki/index.php/David_Morales_-_We_Took_Care_of_That_SOB.

of the Allied occupation force. Officially he was a member of the Eighty-second Airborne Division, but Carbajal has stated that he was actually a member of Army Intelligence.

He joined the Central Intelligence Agency in 1951, and as with many in the agency, he retained his army cover. Morales became involved in the CIA's black operations in 1953. He started with a program that would become known as Executive Action, a program to remove so-called unfriendly foreign leaders from power and replace them with leaders "friendly to the United States." This phrase is code for depriving their citizens of the benefit of the resources of the country for the enrichment of the United States. The Executive Action program resulted in the overthrow of the Guatemalan president, Jacobo Arbenz, in 1954 after he introduced land reforms and nationalized the United Fruit Company. During the late 1950s, Morales became known as the CIA's top assassin in Latin America. Some associates of Morales have described him as a stone-cold killer.

Morales moved to Cuba in 1958 in support of the Batista government. In 1961, Morales was posted to the CIA station in Miami, code-named JM/WAVE. There he was involved in operations to destabilize the Castro government and reported to Ted Shackley, who was the CIA's Miami Bureau chief. He was also involved in a plot to assassinate Fidel Castro and reportedly worked for David Atlee Phillips, Tracy Barnes, William Pawley, Johnny Roselli, and John Martino. Researchers such as Gaeton Fonzi, Larry Hancock, Noel Twyman, James Richards, and John Simkin assert that Morales was involved in the JFK assassination. Others reported to have been also involved include Carl E. Jenkins, Rafael Quintero, William Pawley, Roy Hargraves, Edwin Collins, Steve Wilson, Herminio Diaz Garcia, Tony Cuesta, Eugenio Martinez, Virgilio Gonzalez, Felipe Vidal Santiago, Theodore Shackley, Grayston Lynch, Felix Rodriguez, Thomas Clines, Gordon Cambell, Tony Sforza, and William Robertson.

CIA agent Tom Clines identified Morales as having helped Felix Rodriquez capture Che Guevara in 1965. In 1966, Ted Shackley was in charge of the CIA's secret war in Laos. He brought in Morales to take charge of black operations at Pakse, a political paramilitary base in Laos. This base was used for operations against the Ho Chi Minh Trail. As with the others described above, we will see Morales again in coming chapters.

Actor in the Heart of Darkness Play: Richard V. Secord[29]

Born in La Rue, Ohio, in 1932, Richard Secord graduated from West Point in 1955. His first assignment was as a single-engine instructor pilot at Laredo Air Force Base, Texas. His next position was at Tinker Air Force Base, Oklahoma. He joined a special tactical volunteer organization in Florida in 1962 and then was assigned to the government of South Vietnam as an advisor. Within a few months, he had flown over two hundred combat missions. After Vietnam, he served as an advisor to the Iranian Air Force. He was assigned to the first air commando wing in 1965, and he returned to South Vietnam as an air operations officer in Saigon.

Secord transferred to Udorn Royal Thai Air Force Base, Thailand in 1966. That year, Ted Shackley was put in charge of the CIA's secret war in Laos. He took with him Carl E. Jenkins, David Sanchez Morales, Rafael Quintero, Felix I. Rodriquez, and Edwin Wilson. Shackley worked closely with Secord, who directed tactical bombing raids against the Pathet Lao. Joel Bainerman states in his book, *Crimes of a President: New Revelations on the Conspiracy and Cover-Up in the Bush and Reagan Administrations*, that it was at this time that Shackley and his "secret team" became involved in the drug trade. They actively supported General Vang Pao who along with being the leader of the anti-Communist forces in Laos also gained control of the heroin trade. To help him, Shackley and company sabotaged his competitors and obtained financing for the general to obtain his own airline, Xieng Khouang Air Transport company. Vang Pao used this airline to transport opium and heroin between Long Tieng and Vientiane. Eventually, Vang Pao had a monopoly over the heroin trade in Laos; and in 1968, according to Alfred W. McCoy, author of *The Politics*

---

[29]. Photo source Wikipedia at: http://en.wikipedia.org/wiki/File:Richard_V_Secord.jpg.

of Heroin: CIA Complicity in the Global Drug Trade, Ted Shackley arranged a meeting in Saigon between Santo Trafficante Jr. and Vang Pao to establish heroin smuggling routes and operations, including major routes from Southeast Asia to the United States. Just one of many darling folks that we shall see again in later chapters.

Conclusions and Reflections

From Lansdale on, these are the CIA case officers that carry out the CIA's strategic plans. They are not, by any stretch of the imagination, the top strategic planners of the CIA, nor has the author mentioned all of them. These barely human pathological personalities were selected and trained to accomplish whatever assignment they were given, by any means necessary. They do not even think about morality or ethics. It is not a concern to them. Besides, they really do not understand what a code of ethical behavior is. Most of them are not particularly bright, and they are lacking the critical thinking skills necessary to consider the ramifications of their actions.

The reader might notice that all, or most, of them are also commissioned officers in the US military and, as such, have taken an oath to "support and defend the Constitution of the United States against all enemies, foreign and domestic; that I will bear true faith and allegiance to the same . . ." Powerful words! Words that have no meaning to the likes of Edward Lansdale who apparently thought it was fun to throw innocent people out of helicopters, run drugs, and so forth. He and those of his ilk were either unwilling or unable to understand what the US Constitution stands for, much less how to defend it.

We have also seen someone that took the above oath seriously. Fletcher Prouty's outstanding book, *The Secret Team*, paints a picture of an intelligence agency, the CIA, the size and power of which is almost beyond imagination. The looming question is, again, what else would they do? Blow the head off a US president, inches from his wife, and in plain view of the world? Would it bother them to perform such an act? Or how about dump tons of the most powerful and addictive drugs known to man in the middle of minority communities? We shall see.

Chapter Six

The JFK Assassination

Of course the looming question is, "Why would any government agency have an interest in the assassination of the president of the United States?" It is not this author's contention that the CIA, FBI, or any other government agency as a whole, "pulled the trigger." It is conceivable, even confirmed, that they failed to protect the president as it is every member of the government's duty, and especially the executive branch's, obligation to do. There are indications that the CIA and the FBI had specific knowledge, beforehand, of not only the successful assassination in Dealey Plaza but also previous plans that were aborted. Add to this the overwhelming evidence that several agencies of the Executive Branch of the US government used extreme means to cover up the assassination, and we have undisputable evidence of a "palace coup." There were also several CIA operators who later stated that they had been offered large sums of money to assassinate JFK, but that they had refused to do it. They refused to do it, but they also did not report it either, which was their duty to do.

One example of this would be Gerry Hemming, a CIA asset who has openly stated that he knew of many groups that put "money on the table" to have JFK killed. Neither Hemming nor several others reported these offers to their chain of command. These agencies simply did not act on this information, and this failure appears to be deliberate. When the CIA makes it known that it no longer supports a leader, including our own, something will come out of the shadows to eliminate the "persona non-gratis." This was likely how the Vietnamese ruler Ngo Dinh Diem was murdered in a coup in November 1963.

It is widely believed that the CIA withdrew support on Diem and set up the conditions that resulted in his assassination. This could always be denied because the agency did not "pull the trigger." They simply caused it to happen by what they *did not* do.

It is clear, however, that individuals in these government agencies were involved in the plot. This does not mean that the entire agency was involved in it. It is also clear that agencies of the government were actively involved in the cover-up, and the evidence is overwhelming. For example, Noel H. Twyman, author of *Bloody Treason: The Assassination of John F. Kennedy*, and also Donald T. Phillips, author of *A Deeper Darker Truth: Tom Wilson's Journey into the Assassination of John F. Kennedy*, separately provided irrefutable evidence that the Zapruder film was extensively altered, the JFK autopsy X-rays and photos were forgeries, other photos used to "prove" the "lone assassin" theory were altered and forged, and a myriad of other evidence tampered with or withheld. By definition, this makes these agencies, or at least some of these agencies' representatives, guilty of the assassination. Knowingly withholding evidence or lying about a murder makes those individuals accessories to the murder and just as guilty as those who planned, organized, and carried out the assassination itself. There is no question that the directors of both the FBI and the CIA did this. Both of them, and others, should have been tried for murder. There was more than enough evidence for this to happen.

There is no question that America was never the same again after the JFK assassination. It was a, if not the, pivotal event in American history. Some say that November 22, 1963, was the "day the music died." It is not a stretch to state that it was the day that the vast majority of Americans stopped believing their government and possibly stopped believing *in* their government. There have been surveys that indicate that as high as 88 percent of Americans believe they have been lied to, by their own government, about the JFK assassination.

JFK's Plans to Withdraw from Southeast Asia

There has been much disinformation put forth about what JFK was involved in and supported. For example, it is widely believed that Kennedy escalated the Vietnam War. Although it is true that so-called advisors had increased substantially during his administration, there were strong indicators that he was planning a full withdrawal early in his second term. In fact he had started the process of withdrawing forces shortly before his assassination. He signed National Security Action Memorandum (NSAM) 263, dated October 11, 1963, which ordered withdrawal of one thousand military personnel by the end of 1963. His defense secretary, Robert McNamara, and also his vice president, Lyndon Johnson, both corroborated that it was their understanding that Kennedy intended on withdrawing all forces from Vietnam early in his second administration, and it was almost a certainty that Kennedy would have been reelected.

Those that knew him well believed that he was going to withdraw totally, not only from Vietnam, but from Southeast Asia altogether. Many cited the experience and knowledge JFK gained observing the dilemma that the French got into in Algeria, and the likelihood that the United States would suffer the same fate in Southeast Asia. The French were just barely holding on to Algeria, but the cost was beyond what the nation could sustain. Not only the cost in terms of money, but the humanistic and moral cost was beyond what the French people were willing to expend. France's brutal occupation had become extremely barbaric. Torture, mass murder, and inhumane treatment of civilians weighed heavily on the conscience of the country. The French population chose to not continue down this path and made the decision to let go of this valuable possession for humanistic reasons. This made a strong impression on the young congressman from Massachusetts, an impression that he often communicated publicly and privately. He frequently made comparisons between the French in Algeria and the United States' involvement in Vietnam.

The War and Drugs

Back to the question of why the assassination? Simply put, JFK was a threat to the CIA's war in Vietnam and also the opium and heroin trade in Southeast Asia and the United States. Both of these were CIA creations that went hand in hand, one could not exist without the other. Without the war, it would have been impossible to keep the heroin production and distribution going. Without the drugs, the Vietnam War effort folds. Ultimately, this is exactly what happened anyway.

As Professor Alfred McCoy explains in detail in his book, *The Politics of Heroin*, the mountain tribes that grew the opium poppies eventually became exhausted to the point that they no longer could grow the crop. Part of the deal with the tribes was that they sent their young men to fight in what is sometimes called the "secret war" that encompassed all of Southeast Asia. The young men were also needed to plant the poppies, and had been virtually annihilated by the war. When the opium crop failed, the money used by the South Vietnam government to carry on the war also failed. The South Vietnamese military, police, intelligence, and government operated on payoffs and graft. This worked as long as the money was there, but without drug money, the whole system collapsed. Simply put, we were fighting nationalism with a system fueled by corrupt drug money. The drug money stopped, we lost. We will be discussing in later chapters how much the Southeast Asian heroin trade was actually worth. You will be surprised, but for now, we will mention that the entire US drug trade is many hundreds of billions of dollars per year. This is a lot of money, much of which gets laundered through the US stock market and the entire Western banking system, both of which would collapse if this money does not flow through them.

Add to this the money spent on the so-called War on Drugs and also the money that flows to what President Eisenhower called the military-industrial complex, and we see that we are talking about several trillion dollars per year. We also see that anything that threatens both war and drugs, then and now, simply cannot be tolerated by the people and institutions that control the US economy. We are not talking about politicians. We are talking about the people and institutions that put politicians in office. John F. Kennedy threatened this entire economic system and therefore had to be removed. He could not be removed by softer methods such as withdrawing financial support. The Kennedy family had the financial means to back his political campaigns and many others to boot. John F. Kennedy was going to win the upcoming election. Had this happened, the Kennedy family would have stood to dominate US politics well into the twenty-first century without the support of the wealthy, powerful elite that control the US economy.

John Fitzgerald Kennedy's Place in World History

John F. Kennedy stood at a pivotal point in history, a crossroads and quite possibly the last opportunity that America had to fulfill its stated destiny of spreading democracy and freedom throughout the world. His administration could very well have been the last opportunity the American Republic had to share with the rest of the world the cherished gifts of education, health care, decent housing, and clean water. It could have been the beginning of leading America and the rest of the world into the twenty-first century.

This is not to say that JFK did not have his faults. Although it is almost a certainty that his sexual exploits have been exaggerated, it has been documented that he carried on affairs that could only be described as reckless, although most if not all of these incidents occurred before he was president. Seymour Hersh, author of *The Dark Side of Camelot*, went into some detail about JFK's escapades. Other authors that checked his sources, however, found clear evidence of forged documents and false testimony used to create the persona of a totally out of control sex maniac. When some authors and researchers dug into who was behind this concerted effort to destroy the JFK legend and his legacy they found links to the intelligence community, namely the CIA. They also found links to known CIA lap-dogs in the US media.

Even if one wishes to dispute the above, the author does believe that JFK intended on running the country for the interest of the American people. As with his predecessor, Dwight David Eisenhower, he fell through a portal into the American heart of darkness, and it scared him. Eisenhower was introduced to it when he and Nikita Khrushchev, the Soviet Union premier, planned to have a disarmament summit on May 16, 1960. Both were old warriors that had been sickened by what they experienced in World War II. Add to this the fact that these two war veterans and superpower leaders liked and respected each other. Both saw the futility of spending trillions of dollars to make real "weapons of mass destruction," and had indicated that they were committed to ridding the world of these horrendous instruments of annihilation. The conference never happened.

Although Eisenhower had ordered the U-2 photo reconnaissance (espionage) flights that regularly flew over the Soviet Union to stop until the conference, Frances Gary Powers piloted a U-2 flight out of Pakistan that was downed on May 1, 1960. Khrushchev was outraged, and the incident was deeply humiliating to Eisenhower who at first claimed that Powers had accidentally violated USSR airspace but later had to announce that he had approved the flight. What was not known at the time, until Fletcher Prouty reported in *The Secret Team*, was that the plane was deliberately shorted on a critical component of the propulsion system that caused it to flame out at high altitude over the Soviet Union. Prouty presented evidence in his book that this was a deliberate act by the CIA to outrage Khrushchev, embarrass Eisenhower, and keep the Cold War going. The incident succeeded on all counts. The conference was scuttled, and what could have been a turning point for world peace just flew away like dust in the wind.

Why would the CIA deliberately down one of its own airplanes with one of its best pilots? Prouty explains that the CIA, although conceived of to serve the president, actually owes its allegiance to what he terms the "high cabal," which he explains roughly as the military-industrial complex and the elite banking system along with other very powerful influences that thrive on war and conflict. These powerful entities put politicians in office that kept the American public scared of, at the time, Communism. The only way to divert most of America's excess wealth toward "defense" rather than medical care, education, and so forth, is to keep them afraid, very afraid, of the Communist boogeyman. These people will do anything to carry on this charade. They will disrupt peace summits, kill people, cause disasters, and yes, even assassinate heads of state, even their own. Why would they go to such extremes? As psychologist Andrew Lobaczewski explained, they only know exploitation, fear, intimidation, and manipulation to achieve their ends. They cannot do anything else because they have no talent or ability. They only know how to use others and will lie, steal, cheat, and murder to get what they want. They are psychopaths, and they have taken over the American Republic as they have done elsewhere over and over again throughout history.

The author thought it odd that Frances Gary Powers' U-2 was shot down, and Oswald worked on the U-2. Could there be a connection? Could it have been that Oswald was in the Soviet Union when the U-2 was shot down? The answer is yes! Was this a coincidence? No! How could Oswald possibly have worked on one of the United States' most classified projects, with a top secret crypto clearance, and just up and decided to go to the USSR on a whim, within days of his "hardship discharge" from the Marine Corps? Not only that but his visa and all other travel arrangements were acquired and approved at the speed of light! Not only did Oswald work on the U-2 project, but it turns out that he had crucial information as to where every one of them was stationed, secret coding, and radar jamming information. Oswald had enough information for the Soviets to use to take a U-2 down. In fact this is exactly what Francis Gary Powers thought happened. He said that when he crossed the border to the USSR, he had the feeling that "they knew I was coming." He also thought it was strange that the state-of-the-art camera, highly classified in its own right, had been removed and replaced with an older model.

The Cover-up Primer

It has been nearly fifty years since John Fitzgerald Kennedy was brutally assassinated in the Dealey Plaza, Dallas, Texas. Despite obvious cover-ups, major media propaganda, tampering with evidence, the untimely death of many key witnesses, persecution and harassment of all investigators that did not come to the same conclusions as the Warren commission, ad infinitum, the vast majority of the American people believe that Lee Harvey Oswald either did not shoot JFK or that he was part of a much larger conspiracy.

Add to this the many official commissions and committees that have supposedly investigated this assassination. They came up with some but not very much additional information. Altogether, we have indications of a massive cover-up. A key indicator of this is the fact that there has been only one trial associated with one of the most egregious crimes in the history of the United States. This one trial was the trial of Clay Shaw in New Orleans, Louisiana, in which District Attorney Jim Garrison did an excellent job in the investigation and prosecution of this case. Although Clay Shaw was not convicted, the jury all agreed that there was a conspiracy to assassinate JFK that went beyond Oswald.

Garrison accomplished this against extreme opposition from several government agencies and also the major news media. He was portrayed as a narcissistic attention getter that was trying to further his career at innocent people's expense. One only has to read his book, *On the Trail of Assassins*, to realize how far this was from the truth. As much trouble as this trial caused Jim Garrison, it would be hard to believe that anyone would bring this upon himself for selfish reasons.

The reason there has been so much resistance to trials in this case is that only in a trial can you compel people to divulge information that they normally would not be forthright in providing. Not only is the specter of being charged with perjury compelling, but anyone that conceals evidence can be charged as an accessory to the crime. There is also the "let's make deal" scenario that can be played out with people that have committed lesser crimes associated with the more serious crime, in this case, murder. This fact is common knowledge. Anyone who has ever been on a jury can usually recall witnesses that were granted immunity from prosecution for their testimony. The bottom line is that prosecutors can solve crimes through the prosecutorial process, and this is why we only saw one prosecution and that one was not supported by any federal agency. In fact it was strongly resisted. We doubtlessly will not see another prosecution in the JFK assassination. The reason being is that this is a solvable crime that the powerful elite do not want solved. As a US senator once famously stated about solving the JFK assassination, "It would open up an endless can of worms." Let us open that can.

Anyone handy with a rifle would question the conclusions of the Warren Commission and also several other inquiries into the JFK assassination. We will go into more details concerning the facts, but first let us take a broad view of the assassination. It is widely accepted that JFK was about 265 feet, or about 88 yards, from the Texas School Book Depository, TSBD, when he was shot in the head. The speed that the limousine was traveling was about 11 mph. Now, we are to believe that Oswald hit, at the very most, a nine-inch target two out of three shots? Further, he does this with one of the worst weapons that he could have possibly used, and on top of that the rifle had a badly misaligned scope? I know the Marine Corps is very good at teaching marksmanship, but not that good.

Many facts surrounding the assassination just do not add up. For example, the rifle Oswald supposedly used, the 6.5 mm Mannlicher-Carcano, had one of the worst reputations in history. The importer of this almost-worthless weapon took it off the market because of its tendency to blow up. It also was famous for jamming. The supposition that Oswald would have selected this rifle out of a catalog that also advertised some of the best military surplus weapons in the world—Springfield .30-06s, British Enfield .303s, and so forth—is incomprehensible. Add to this the fact that they were all roughly the same price, and you wonder why a marine trained "sharpshooter" would have selected arguably the worst weapon he could have chosen.

Other unmistakable indications that the JFK assassination was way beyond Oswald's capabilities, and his sorry excuse for a rifle, is the number of witnesses that reported gunfire from the "grassy knoll," a phrase coined by witness Jean Hill. Jean and several witnesses were pictured running up the grassy knoll after the assassination. Many of these witnesses also reported the unmistakable odor of gun smoke that could not have come from the book depository. These witnesses were on the south side of the street about a hundred yards from the book depository, and the wind was blowing from north to south. The gun smoke had to have come from the grassy knoll area. Some also saw muzzle flashes and gun smoke.

It is remarkable that none of these witnesses testified to the Warren Commission. Some of the people on the south side of the street also took pictures that were confiscated. Not only did they not testify, but the information they provided to law enforcement and the media was discredited at every turn. Jean Hill and many others were put under surveillance, threatened, and subjected to other forms of harassment. At least one witness that took a picture that had the book depository in the background found the building obliterated on the negative that was returned to her by the developer. Very little of the still and motion photos survived, especially photos of the grassy knoll taken from the south side of the street. One exception is a photo that was taken by Mary Moorman that was returned many years later and in very bad condition. We will be discussing this photo later in this chapter.

We will not dwell too much on the details of the assassination. This author does, however, want to communicate the suspicious nature of this crime that is apparent without much research. Also, we want to look at this as a crime. As such, the obvious questions are, Who had the motive, means, and opportunity? Another obvious question is, *Qui bono?* Or who benefits? This approach is what any investigator uses to solve a crime. And let us make no mistake about it; the JFK assassination was, and is now, a solvable crime. It seems that there were and are powerful forces that do not want this crime solved.

Who Had the Motive?

Although John F. Kennedy had his human frailties, in researching this case, it has come to this author's attention that Kennedy was a threat to what may be referred to as the deep economic and political structure of the United States. In challenging the CIA's actions in the Bay of Pigs invasion of Cuba, the CIA-instigated Vietnam War, and the

CIA's Southeast Asian drug trade, we have a lot of power and influence threatened by one man, or perhaps one family: the Kennedys.

Add to this the threat to organized crime presented by the all-out frontal assault against several well-known crime figures by JFK and especially his US attorney general brother, Robert F. Kennedy, and we have even more power threatened. On top of this, we add what the previous US president Dwight David Eisenhower termed "the military-industrial complex" in position to make hundreds of billions, perhaps trillions, of dollars off the Vietnam War, and we have strong motivation to get rid of Kennedy and the rest of his family's political influence.

The one factor that is linked to all of the above was, and still is, the drug trade. Cuba was a main conduit for the "French Connection" heroin trade. The Golden Triangle in Southeast Asia produced over 90 percent of the heroin in the world. Of course, organized crime could not operate without the drug trade. Even corporate America benefits from it. Profit from the global drug trade, controlled by American interests, easily amounts to several hundred billion dollars per year, most of which goes through Wall Street. Remove this money and see what happens to corporate America, or what Eisenhower sometimes called the military-industrial complex.

Eisenhower's warning was not just a passing comment that he put forth in his last farewell address. The term he coined, "military-industrial complex," was intended to mean much more than just the industrial production of arms and military equipment. It appears to many that he meant not only direct military production but also the influence of indirect or seemingly unrelated activities. An example would be Monsanto and their production of what has been termed "Agent Orange." The procurement and overuse of this incredibly toxic and persistent substance without any apparent oversight or constraints boggles the mind. If you multiply the Monsanto example times hundreds of seemingly innocuous corporations and enterprises, you have a lot of influence over national policy.

You also have a lot of motivation for armed conflict. America should have taken more notice of a president's warning that was previously a supreme Allied commander, five-star general, and one of the greatest military leaders in history. Anyone who has watched his farewell address can see that Eisenhower was plainly worried that the power and influence of these corporations was a threat to democracy and the American republic. He turned out to be right.

Threaten the Southeast Asian drug trade, and who else is threatened? A more appropriate question would be, who is not threatened? Hundreds of billions of dollars per year is connected to just about everyone and everything. Along with corporate America, a short list would be organized crime, the entire banking and stock market system, the gargantuan antidrugs law enforcement establishment, the "prison industrial complex," and all of the functions that depend on these "economic engines." We begin to see the scope of the problem. Take drug money out of this system and the US economy crashes. This is what JFK and some believe Robert F. Kennedy threatened.

He and his family threatened the whole enchilada. His brother, Bobby, or RFK, was at least as much a threat to the system as JFK was. His aggressive prosecution of organized crime was also a direct threat to the drug industrial complex. Add to this the fact that JFK was certainly going to be reelected, and it is not too far-fetched to imagine that his brother, RFK, could have succeeded him as president. Further, we know that the Kennedy fortune could have bankrolled many political campaigns.

This meant that none of them had to make deals with anybody for financial support. On top of all of this was the patriarch of the family, Joe Kennedy, who could swing just about any backroom deal imaginable. He had connections to power and influence, including organized crime, which meant the Kennedy family could have been a dynasty that would set the direction of America well into the twenty-first century. What direction would they take? Where were they headed? Although they certainly had their faults, it is apparent that they had issues with a drugs and war economy owned and operated by psychopaths. The Kennedys had to go.

The Trial of Clay Shaw

Although this trial only scratched the surface of what can only be described as a deep conspiracy to assassinate JFK and frame Oswald, Jim Garrison's investigation turned up some startling information. Some of the irrefutable evidence of a vast conspiracy Garrison laid out in detail in his difficult-to-find book but well worth reading, *On the*

Trail of Assassins.[30] The author obtained his, used, from Amazon Books. Below are a few of the inconsistencies that Garrison and his staff uncovered.

- Five days before the assassination, the New Orleans FBI office received a telexed warning that an attempt would be made to assassinate the president in Dallas. Shortly after the assassination, the telex message was removed from the file drawer of the New Orleans office of the Bureau.[31]
- The great majority of witnesses at Dealey Plaza in Dallas heard repeated rifle fire coming from the grassy knoll in front of Kennedy.[32]
- On the day of his arrest, Lee Oswald was given a nitrate test, the results of which showed that he had not fired a rifle in the previous twenty-four hours.
- For more than five years, the film of the assassination taken by eyewitness Abraham Zapruder was concealed from the public and kept locked in a vault by *Life* magazine. This motion picture showed Kennedy being slammed violently backward—clear evidence of his being struck by a rifle shot from the front.[33]
- Approximately an hour before the arrival of Kennedy's motorcade, Jack Ruby, the man who later murdered Oswald, was observed alongside the grassy knoll, unloading a man carrying a rifle in a case. The statement of Julia Ann Mercer, the witness to that event, was altered by the FBI to make it appear that she had been unable to identify Ruby as the man. This fraudulent alteration has never been explained or even denied by the federal government.[34]
- After the president's body was subjected to a military autopsy, his brain disappeared . . . might have shown from what directions the head shots came. Photographs and X-rays of the

---

30. Jim Garrison, *On the Trail Of Assassins* (Warner Books, Inc., 1991)
31. Garrison, xiii
32. Garrison, xiii
33. Garrison, xiii
34. Garrison, xiv

autopsy, which might also have resolved the issue, were never examined by the Warren Commission.³⁵
- The pathologist in charge of Kennedy's autopsy at Bethesda Naval Hospital burned in the fireplace of his home the first draft of the autopsy report.³⁶
- The FBI had given a copy of it (the Zapruder film) to the Warren Commission, but two critical frames had been mysteriously reversed to create the false impression that a rifle shot to Kennedy's head had been fired from behind.³⁷ (Garrison explains in a footnote, same page) Frame 313 showed the instant of the shot striking Kennedy's head. As photographed by Abraham Zapruder, frames 313 and 315 showed the head falling backward, plainly indicating that the shot had come from the front. Following the FBI's transposition of these two frames, it was made to appear that the president's head was falling forward, indicating a shot from the rear. After a routine examination of the subsequent frames, even the Warren Commission was forced to recognize the transposition of frames 313 and 315 and asked the FBI what happened. Director J. Edgar Hoover explained that an "inadvertent" printing error had occurred.

One of the most suspicious subjects that the Warren Commission ignored was the subject of the parade route. This is one of the clear indicators that a vast conspiracy was involved in the assassination and even more importantly in a methodical cover-up of "the crime of the century." Shortly before Kennedy was assassinated in Dealey Plaza, Dallas, Texas, on November 22, 1963, at approximately 12:30 PM, the president's motorcade route was changed. In fact, the route was changed a few days prior. This change should have been noticed as being highly unusual, because for several reasons, it is a vast departure from the rules and guidelines that govern presidential security.

One of the most important principles in presidential security is to keep the president moving and moving fairly fast. In motorcades, the Secret Service aims for 44 miles per hour, and they get concerned when

---

[35.] Garrison, xiv

[36.] Garrison, xiv

[37.] Garrison, 280

it is necessary to slow down to under 30 miles per hour. The reason for this is that it is much harder to shoot a moving target, and the faster the target is going, the more difficult it is to hit. Any hunter can tell you this. To make the turn in Dealey Plaza from Houston Street to Elm Street, the motorcade had to slow down to under ten miles per hour. If for no other reason, this revised parade route should have set off security alarms because of the fact that the entire motorcade had to slow down to a crawl to make the 120-degree turn.

Another cause for concern is the layout of Dealey Plaza itself. The original presidential parade route went straight down Main Street, and the route did not have any surrounding buildings from which snipers could take advantage of. If the motorcade had gone down Main Street, as originally planned, it would not have been possible to set up an ambush in the Dealey Plaza area. The altered route down Elm Street with two sharp turns, surrounding buildings, the walls and fences on the grassy knoll, and also the railroad overpass was an ideal location to set up an ambush.

Whether an ambush team is civilian or military, when the objective is to make sure that someone is killed, the rules are the same. The team will be looking at what is called triangulation. That is shooting at the target from three directions all set up to hit the target at a predestinated spot, sometimes referred to as the "X." The reader might recall recent congressional testimony about an incident in Iraq. When asked as to why his security personnel had shot up a crowd of unarmed civilians and left the area, Erik Prince, the CEO and owner of Blackwater, testified that his personnel were trying to get what they thought was the target of an assassination attempt "off the X." Over and over again, while providing security for a so-called "high value" target, Blackwater personnel have responded to a real or perceived threat the same way. They shoot the place up and haul out of there. They leave with great speed to get the individual under their care off the X because a fast-moving target is harder to hit. This is how you counter triangulation.

Of course the best way to counter "triangulation" is to not have the person you are protecting on the X. In the case of John F. Kennedy, the parade route was diverted to put him right on the X just two days before JFK's visit to Dallas, and Oswald already had a job in the book depository about a month before anyone knew the route that the motorcade would take—hmmmm! It is obvious when one takes a close look at the route the motorcade took through Dealey Plaza that

President Kennedy was not getting out of there alive. He was vulnerable to gunfire from a variety of locations to include the fences behind the grassy knoll, the Texas School Book Depository, the Dal-Tex building, a storm drain right on the curb just a few feet to the right of the steps that go up to the grassy knoll and very close to the fatal head shot that killed Kennedy. If you were going to set up an ambush, where would you place the snipers, and at what point would you have them shoot?[38]

---

[38]. Dealey Plaza diagram, www.forensicgenealogy.info/images/JFK_dealey-plaza-annotated.jpg. In this view, east is at the top and west is at the bottom. The grassy knoll is on the north side of Elm Street. The grassy knoll is about 300 feet, 100 yards, from the sixth-floor window that is alleged to be the location Oswald was firing from. Photos of the grassy knoll were taken by Mary Moorman and others from the south side of Elm Street.

So, where did the reader place the gunman or gunmen? In the Texas Schoolbook Depository? If so, did the reader have him wait until the target was well down Elm Street to begin firing? Exploring these questions illuminates that the Oswald-as-the-lone-gunman story just does not make sense. Oswald, if he was there, would have had a much easier shot from the so-called Sniper's nest when JFK's limousine was turning into Elm Street. The limo was almost at a standstill, and no one was in the way. It is interesting how the argument has been couched in the framework of "Could Oswald have made the shots that he was reported to have made?" Although the feat has never been duplicated, I suppose anything is possible. One could suppose that Oswald, who made it out of boot camp by the skin of his teeth because of his poor marksmanship record, could have performed this incredible display of marksmanship. But add to this that he supposedly used a mail-ordered rifle that had the worst reputation of any military firearm this author has researched. The Italian troops that used it in World War II would take any rifle off an enemy corps and leave it behind at the first opportunity. They also had a nickname for it. They called it the "humanitarian rifle," a name that calls for no further explanation. The Mannlicher-Carcano was famous for jamming and also blowing up, thus injuring the shooter. On top of all of this, add the fact that the scope was badly misaligned. Further, we have Lee Harvey Oswald hitting a moving target from 175 to 265 feet away and putting two out of three shots within a few inches of dead center of the back of JFK's head. We have now gone beyond improbable to extremely unlikely. Jim Garrison had the same problem with the "Oswald as the lone assassin story."

Possible or Likely?

But the question is not what is possible. Anything is possible. The question is, Is it reasonable to believe that this is what happened in Dealey Plaza on November 22, 1963? Is it reasonable to believe that Oswald had the motive, means, and opportunity to commit this crime? We have already talked about Lee Harvey Oswald's means, which do not amount to much: mediocre marksmanship, inferior weapon, misaligned scope, and so forth. But what about his motives? This author, and many others, could find no animosity harbored by Oswald toward President Kennedy. In fact, several researchers have come to the conclusion that Oswald liked Kennedy. One of these was Lamar Waldron, author of *Legacy of Secrecy: The Long Shadow of the JFK Assassination*, who related that three months before the assassination, a New Orleans police lieutenant had interviewed Oswald and made a note that Oswald "liked the president."

Of course, the easiest way to justify a motive in an assassination is to cast the suspect as a loser and a loner looking for attention. Oswald, however, did not fit this profile. He had relationships that were quite normal. His relationship with his wife was, at times, strained but nothing unusual. He made no threats against the president, nor did he seem to have an ax to grind against anyone. The "Fair Play for Cuba" charade seemed to be out of context with his past, and the whole communist scenario just does not match what many researchers have uncovered about Lee Harvey Oswald. Jim Garrison, in *On the Trail of Assassins*, only found one marine that said that Oswald even mentioned being a Communist, and this guy hardly even knew him. Further, Garrison relates that this marine had CIA affiliations. So what was Oswald up to? He certainly was involved in this horrific act in some way, but in what manner?

Oswald as the "Patsy"

Jim Garrison, the New Orleans district attorney who was the only person whose office prosecuted anyone in connection with the JFK assassination, stated in his book, *On the Trail of Assassins*, that he found indications of Oswald being set up as a patsy in the JFK assassination as far back as 1961. Just a few of the occurrences that led Garrison to the conclusion that Oswald was set up as the patsy are as follows:

- Ruth Paine got Oswald his job at the Texas School Book Depository on or about October 14, 1963, well before JFK's motorcade was scheduled to go past the building. Garrison explains that Ruth Paine was the wife of Michael Paine, an engineering designer who did highly classified work for Bell Helicopter, a major Defense Department contractor. Mrs. Paine was fluent in Russian, and her father had been employed by the United States Agency for International Development, USAID, a known CIA front. Her brother-in-law also worked for USAID.[39] Garrison thought it possible that Ruth Paine had been unknowingly manipulated in the course of obtaining Oswald's job in the book depository.[40]

- The motorcade route was changed literally at the last moment. The change was made so close to November 22, 1963, that the *Dallas Morning News* for that day had a diagram on the front page that showed that the president's parade was supposed to continue on Main Street straight through the center of Dealey Plaza without making any turns. If this had happened, it would have been virtually impossible to have shot JFK on that fateful day. Further, this information was concealed from the Warren Commission. A copy of the front page was sent to the commission, but the diagram of the original routing was blanked out. That is, on five-sixths of the *Dallas Morning News* front page where the diagram was supposed to be was a large square of gray.[41] Anyone looking at that diagram could see that Kennedy was diverted into a fire zone from which he could not survive.
- Who changed the route? No one is or was asking, and no one is telling. One likely candidate was the Dallas City administration headed by the mayor of Dallas at the time, Earle Cabell. Earle Cabell's brother was General Charles Cabell, who was the deputy director of the CIA during the Bay of Pigs fiasco. In fact, he had been in charge of the Bay of Pigs invasion, and while the CIA director, Allen Dulles, was incommunicado at a speaking engagement, General Cabell was on the phone asking John F. Kennedy for air support to save the collapsing invasion. The request was denied, the invasion was a spectacular failure, and both General Cabell and Allen Dulles were relieved of their positions by, you guessed it, John F. Kennedy.[42] To state that neither the general nor Director Dulles was exactly nuts about JFK would be being generous, and Dulles ended up on

---

[39.] Jim Garrison, *On the Trail of Assassins*, (New York, NY: Warner Books, Inc., 1991), 71-72.
[40.] Ibid, 71
[41.] Ibid, 118-119
[42.] Jim Garrison, *On the Trail of Assassins*, (New York, NY: Warner Books, Inc., 1991), 119-121

the Warren Commission, and Cabell's brother was the mayor of Dallas. Both could have played instrumental roles in the JFK assassination and/or the cover-up. Both had the motive, means, and opportunity. One thing for sure is that Oswald could not have known nor influenced any of this. This is how Oswald ended up in the book depository and Kennedy ended up on Elm Street right in front of the same building and not on Main Street. Oswald had nothing to do with this.

- Carlos Marcello, Santo Trafficante Jr., and Johnny Rosselli, suspected by many researchers as playing key roles in planning and organizing the JFK assassination, had learned a long time ago to always have a patsy when planning murders and assassinations. In their book, *Legacy of Secrecy*, Lamar Waldron and Thom Hartman illuminate this important lesson learned by organized crime, including three of the above-mentioned Mafia bosses, during the fifties.[43]

> The mafia assassinations of an Attorney General in 1954 and a president in 1957 had a major impact on how Marcello, Trafficante, and Rosselli assassinated JFK . . . However, in 1954, an anti-corruption Attorney General for the state of Alabama, Albert Patterson, was elected from the town, after he pledged to run the mobsters out of Phoenix City once and for all. The mobsters faced a huge loss of revenue, so the state's new attorney general-elect was assassinated in Phoenix City on June 18, 1954. However, the vice lords had been so used to the lax attitudes toward organized crime by the state of Alabama, J. Edgar Hoover, and the Eisenhower-Nixon administration that they didn't bother to use a patsy to quickly take the heat and divert attention from the real culprits . . .
>
> The error was corrected when the president of Guatemala, Castillo Armas, was assassinated in 1957, at a time when Johnny Rosselli was very active in the country

---

[43.] Lamar Waldron and Tom Hartman, *Legacy of Secrecy: The Long Shadow of the JFK Assassination*, (Counterpoint, www.counterpointpress.com, 2009,) Kindle locations 1089-1109.

and Marcello was developing his extensive ties to Guatemala and to Rosselli . . . A seemingly lone, apparently communist patsy was quickly blamed and soon killed. Like Oswald, the patsy was ex-military, and supposedly an ardent communist who had never bothered to join the Communist Party. The investigation essentially ended with the death of the patsy, who was accepted as the sole assassin by the world press and much of the public . . .

The striking similarities of Oswald to the patsy described above should not go without notice, and let us keep in mind that Oswald certainly was far from the only person missing from the Texas School Book Depository right after JFK was shot. However, right away, authorities started looking for Oswald; and within hours, Oswald was reported to be the lone suspect. These reports went as far as New Zealand about as fast as news could travel in those days. A key indicator of a setup in events such as the JFK assassination is the speed at which the cover story travels. It is important for the conspirators to get one simple big lie out as quickly as possible. Then follow this up with as many "conspiracy theories" as possible; the more, the better. Of course, anyone that questions the one simple lie is cast as paranoid or a conspiracy theorist or even better, conspiracy nut. There is considerable evidence that this is what happened in this assassination that marks the turning point where the American Republic became a pathocracy, owned and controlled by psychopaths.

So Who "Done" It?

This brings us back to motive, means, and opportunity and also what every criminal investigator always keeps in mind, *Qui bono?* or who benefits? As we previously touched on, the CIA's creation of war and drugs in Southeast Asia was worth trillions of dollars a year. The heroin and opium alone generated hundreds of billions of dollars in profit, not to mention the political and economic power associated with these products. Most of this money gets laundered through the US stock market. Stocks can be bought and traded with very little oversight. For example, if you go to the bank and deposit $20,000 in your account, you will have to fill out a form as to where the money came from. However, you could take the same $20,000, or much more, and buy stocks with it, and there will be no questions asked. Trade or sell the stocks and this money is as pure as the new-driven snow. The author does not believe that the design of this "system" was by accident.

Add to this the lucrative arms business and also all the goods and services associated with the war, and we are easily talking about trillions of dollars a year. This money flows through the Western banking system, organized crime operations, the stock market, and the entire "military-industrial complex." All these entities are interrelated, and it is impossible to separate one from the other. This is well understood by many career politicians and the heads of most federal agencies including CIA directors. In fact the majority of CIA directors have come from Wall Street. Their job is to keep this whole system going and hide it from the American people. If the truth was known by the public, it would probably alter our form of government. Many, many Americans who have risked their lives fighting Communism, the so-called War on Drugs, and so forth, would be outraged to find out that what they thought they were fighting and sacrificing for was a big lie and an illusion—a big white lie, the same color as cocaine and heroin. This author believes that the disillusionment would be profound.

We are now looking at very powerful influences that stood to gain at John F. Kennedy's removal from office, and conversely powerful influences that stood to lose a lot if he had stayed in office. The enormity of this was then, and is now, "the elephant in the room." JFK quite conceivably had on his agenda for his second term: drawing down the war in Southeast Asia, dismantling or at least reorganizing the Central Intelligence Agency, aggressively attacking organized crime, decriminalizing illegal drugs, and multilaterally dismantling the world's strategic and nuclear arms. All these issues were publicly spoken to by JFK himself or attested to by those close to him.

These issues are not put forth to cast JFK as a martyr or to idealize him. John F. Kennedy certainly had his faults, and his motives were not always idealistic. For example, he and his brother, Attorney General Robert F. Kennedy, conducted an all-out frontal assault against some of the highest organized crime figures in the country even though these same criminals were reported to have been instrumental in putting him in office. In fact, before the Kennedy administration, there had only been a total of thirty-five convictions of organized crime members in history. In 1963 alone, Robert Kennedy's Department of Justice convicted 288.[44] After the assassination, RFK stayed on as attorney general, and there were none. This author believes it unlikely that the Kennedys' take on top organized crime figures was solely on moralistic grounds. It is more likely that their motivation had to do with control of the Democratic Party in which organized crime had considerable influence in those days, and even now. The possibility also exists that the Kennedys' father, Joseph P. Kennedy, would have advised the brothers to go about things differently had he not had a massive stroke in December 1961. This left him with serious impairment and totally unable to speak. Perhaps the young and inexperienced Kennedy brothers could have used some fatherly advice.

Not only did organized crime help to put him in office, but they also were involved in top secret plans and operations to assassinate the Cuban leader, Fidel Castro. In fact all these endeavors involved the CIA and organized crime collaborating on doing away with Castro. Further, the names of the gangsters that collaborated with the CIA were exactly the same that the Kennedys targeted, and those were Giancana, Trafficante, and Marcello. Although it has been widely reported that the Kennedys knew about the CIA, mob alliance to kill Castro, deep research has uncovered evidence that they did not. This would explain why the Kennedys were after these mobsters at the same time that they were helping the CIA with assassinations. Whatever their reasons, it was most likely not only a bad mistake but also a fatal one to threaten the livelihoods, lifestyles, and freedoms of known sociopathic murderers. Although these organized crime figures had to have had cooperation in the government and at least a nod to go ahead from the very top of the food chain, there is little doubt, corroborated by many credible researchers, that organized crime figures were involved in the JFK assassination. In fact, this is what Bobby Kennedy publicly stated that he believed, and this was substantiated by his aids and others close to him.

There is also little doubt that the CIA was deeply involved in the assassination. Jim Garrison opened this door, and he opened it widely. Although he was unable to convict Clay Shaw, most of the jurors were convinced that there was a conspiracy that accomplished the assassination. They just could not say beyond a reasonable doubt

---

44. Dick Russell, *The Man Who Knew Too Much*, (245 West 17th Street, New York, NY, 10011: Carroll & Graf Publishers, 2003), 336.

that Shaw was involved. Had information come to light at the trial that was available just a few years later, Shaw would have most likely been convicted of murdering JFK. There were key facts that were not available to Jim Garrison in 1967 through 1969 when he prosecuted this case. Even more damning evidence came forth within the next few years compiled by Jim Garrison and also to those that he "passed the torch to."

One of these was Joan Mellen, author of *A Farewell to Justice: Jim Garrison, JFK's Assassination, and the Case that Should Have Changed History*.[45] Joan obtained thousands of documents that were not available to Jim Garrison, and she drew on thousands of interviews. Many of these interviews were people who were speaking out for the first time. Joan Mellen clearly established that Oswald had worked for the FBI, CIA, and also US Customs. She further clearly established the CIA's role in the JFK assassination and also the cover-up that was set into motion well before the assassination. No one with any objectivity toward this subject can read this book and not understand that people in high places in the US government were involved in the JFK assassination and, further, that a conspiracy of the highest order came together to enact an American coup d'état.

The myriad documents destroyed, well over one hundred witnesses that died under suspicious circumstances, evidence tampered with, legitimate investigators harassed and vilified, ad infinitum, are enough to convince this author that not only was someone hiding something, but that people at the highest levels of government agencies, along with organized crime, were involved in the assassination and the cover-up. Neither the CIA, FBI, Secret Service, organized crime, nor the Dallas Police Department could have done it alone. It took elements of all of these, and probably more, to accomplish this infamous deed. For example, organized crime could not have grown and developed Oswald as the "Communist patsy" for years before the assassination. By the same token, the CIA would not have been able to compel Jack Ruby to kill Oswald. However, Carlos Marcello, the undisputed crime boss from Florida to Texas, and James Jesus Angleton, the CIA's director

---

[45]. Joan Mellen, *A Farewell to Justice: Jim Garrison, JFK's Assassination, and the Case that Should Have Changed History*, (Kindle Edition: Potomac Books Inc., October 31, 2005).

of counterintelligence, could have and most likely did collaborate on accomplishing both of these necessary objectives.

Let us take a broad view of this case. If a prominent politician needed to be done away with, who would be the most likely entity to carry out this dark deed? The Census Bureau? The chamber of commerce? No. Who is known for assassinations and murder? Of course it is the CIA and organized crime. I use the term "organized crime" rather than Mafia because the latter implies that the members are Sicilian or Italian when in reality, the top levels of organized crime are considerably more diverse. High-level criminals are usually portrayed as Italian to divert attention away from who they really are. The reader might want to consider that the known cases of murder and assassinations have involved either the CIA or organized crime and very often both. The JFK assassination carries all the earmarks of a professional hit, so who would be the most obvious suspects?

Most of us have also often heard that a conspiracy of this magnitude could not have been covered up; someone would have talked. Well, first of all, someone did talk, which we shall discuss in more detail. Further, we need to keep in mind that there have been very large, in fact huge, operations that have been kept secret for long periods. Just a few examples, the entire Manhattan Project employed hundreds of thousands of Americans, used one-tenth of the electricity produced in the United States, and the vice president of the United States, Harry S. Truman, did not even know about it. Another example is the US Air Force's stealth technology program that was used in the F-117 Fighter and the B-2 Bomber. This program went on for many years and was kept secret the entire time. Most likely, these programs were kept secret because of the repercussions that would be incurred by anyone that talked. Now think about what happened to people, a lot of people, who might have talked "out of school" about the JFK assassination—some were shot in the mouth several times, one had his legs chopped off and was stuffed in an oil drum, many had careers ruined, and we could go on. These were far more dire consequences than talking about a stealth technology program. Not only could the assassination be covered up in this manner, this is undoubtedly what happened.

It is widely known that organized crime figures collaborated with the CIA in attempts to assassinate the Cuban leader, Fidel Castro. So would you say that the CIA or organized crime tried to assassinate Castro? With the JFK assassination, it becomes many times more complex than that. Virtually, all the suspects and players had associations with organized crime, the FBI, the intelligence community, right-wing fanatics, and arms manufacturers. Many had connections to all these entities and more. For example, there is strong evidence that Oswald actually did have associations with all these interests. Jim Garrison proved this beyond a doubt. This is why Oswald's income tax returns have never been made public, because it is very likely that Oswald was paid for many of the incriminating actions he undertook, and this money came from government agencies. Disclosure of these payments would certainly disclose who set him up as a patsy and lead to who was really behind the assassination.

These multiple roles also make it difficult to place any suspect, or suspects, into a specific category. Jack Ruby was an active member of organized crime, and he had done work for the CIA. He also was an FBI informant. Further, he had close ties to the Dallas Police Department. Without a criminal investigation and the information that flows from indictments, plea bargaining, and so forth, it is impossible to uncover the large conspiracy that was certainly behind this deliberate public murder of a president. One of President Johnson's first directives was that there would be no trials in Texas about the assassination. It appears that Johnson and Hoover, along with certain members of the CIA, FBI, Pentagon, Secret Service, and organized crime all had a hand in "the crime of the century." We shall narrow this down a little further.

Who Confessed Involvement, Had Firsthand Knowledge, or "Talked"?

To try to include all of them would be beyond the scope of this work, but there were, in fact, a lot of people that "talked." People generally like to come across to others as "in the know." In short, people like to brag, toot their own horn. Add to this that some people feel guilty and want to "get it off their chests." One way or another, word gets out, and word was getting out that there were powerful forces "gunning" for JFK. In fact there were several attempts to assassinate JFK prior to Dallas. There were plans to assassinate JFK in Miami, Florida; Chicago, Illinois; Los Angeles, California; and Tampa, Florida. All these were aborted; but word of the assassination plot, or plots, was leaking like a sieve. The Secret Service knew about the Chicago plot and cancelled the visit. It was only a matter of time before the whole plot unraveled so Dallas had to be a "green light," and this plot could not fail. We will now take a look at a few of the people that did talk, but strangely, there was no follow-up on what they said. One of these was the fanatical extremist and braggart Joseph Milteer.

Joseph Milteer[46]

Some talked about the assassination in surprising detail before it happened. One of these was Joseph Milteer, an extreme racist, right-wing fanatic to say the least. He was active in the KKK and also was a supporter of the Cuban exile groups long suspected of involvement in the JFK assassination. There is evidence of Milteer's precise prediction in the report of the House Select Committee on Assassinations report. On November 9, 1963, an FBI informant, William Somersett, known as informant 88, made a recording of Milteer clearly stating that Kennedy would be killed by a rifleman from a tall building, and that someone would be picked up within hours after the assassination to throw the public off. Somersett again met with Milteer shortly after the assassination, and Milteer commented that things had gone as he had predicted. Somersett asked him if he had been guessing about the assassination. Milteer replied that he had been certain beforehand that the assassination would take place as he had stated.[47] Milteer added, "Not to worry about the capture of

---

46. Photo courtesy of the Mary Ferrell Foundation, http://www.maryferrell.org/wiki/index.php/Predictions_of_Joseph_Milteer
47. Noel H. Twyman, *Bloody Treason: The Assassination of John F. Kennedy*, Kindle E-Book, First Edition, 2010, Kindle location 15272-15288, citing HSCA Report, 232-233

Oswald, because he doesn't know anything . . . The right wing is in the clear . . . the patriots have outsmarted the Communist group in order that the Communists would carry out the plan without the right wing becoming involved."[48] This information was passed on to the Secret Service that, in turn, passed it on to all of its stations except for Dallas. There has never been an explanation as to how or why the Dallas branch was not notified. Further, the FBI withheld this information from the Warren Commission until two weeks before its work was to be finalized, which made it virtually impossible for the commission to include it in its report.

How did Milteer know all this thirteen days before the assassination? A likely source of information that Milteer could have received might have been through the extreme right-wing organizations to which he belonged. The fanatical racist, anti-Semitic, anti-Castro, anti-Communist, and anti-just-about-anything-you-can-think-of circles that Milteer operated in were the same as General Charles Willoughby who was General Douglas MacArthur's chief of intelligence. With a given name of Adolph Tscheppe-Weidenbach and connections to known Nazis that came to the United States after WWII, Willoughby has been widely suspected of involvement in the JFK assassination. In fact, some consider him to have been the operations officer of the assassination.

When JFK was murdered, Willoughby was oilman H. L. Hunt's right-hand man, and Hunt's views were not too different from either Willoughby or Millteer. H. L. Hunt is another person that is strongly suspected of involvement in the JFK assassination. He had a virulent hatred of the "East Coast establishment," and also JFK had deeply cut into his oil profits by eliminating tax breaks and write-offs in the oil industry. Hunt apparently had many grievances against the Kennedys, real or imagined. Next we have the incredible story of an army cryptographic code operator that opens up more than serious questions about a conspiracy that had to involve the Pentagon and the FBI at the very least.

---

48. Ibid., citing Anthony Summers, *Conspiracy*, 62, 127, citing HSCA Report, Commission documents, and interview with former Miami Police Intelligence Captain Charles Sapp.

Army Private Eugene B. Dinkin

Dinkin was a cryptographic code operator for the US Army stationed in Metz, France, in 1963. In the course of his work, Dinkin decoded information that led him to believe that there was a conspiracy in the making to assassinate JFK. He received information that the assassination involved the US military combined with an ultra right-wing economic group. Dinkin talked about this to the personnel he worked with and heard from his co-workers that he was going to be committed to a psychiatric facility. He went AWOL on November 4, 1963, and took a train to Geneva, Switzerland. There he told his story to the editor of the *Geneva Diplomat*. On November 6, 1963, he appeared in the press room of the UN in Geneva and stated that he was being persecuted. He also added that "they" were plotting against President Kennedy and that "something" would happen in Dallas. After the assassination, one of Dinkin's friends back at his duty station, Dennis De Witt, added that Dinkin had predicted that Kennedy's assassination would occur on November 28, 1963, and later changed it to November 22, 1963. His allegations went to the White House on November 29, 1963, and to the Warren Commission in April, 1964. The FBI was also notified. None of the recipients took any action. Neither Dinkin's name nor his allegations were mentioned in the Warren Commission's 26 Volumes of information. The FBI did not follow up with any interviews of Dinkin, nor did they interview or take statements from his co-workers. No action was taken whatsoever by anyone in an official status, and no documentation was released on this issue until 1976, but Dinkin's name had been deleted.

It was not until 1992 that it became known that a clear record of what Dinkin had alleged was received by the president's Commission on the Assassination of President Kennedy, which is commonly referred to as the Warren Commission. In 1992, a letter from CIA Director Richard Helms, (below) with Dinkin's name included, to the Warren Commission was released by the CIA Historical Review Board.[49] What

---

[49]. NARA Record Number: 1993.06.10.16:04:56:400000, Mary Ferrell Foundation, http://www.maryferrell.org/mffweb/archive/viewer/showDoc.do?docId=96195&relPageId=5

we have here is proof that the CIA, Warren Commission, and the White House knew of Dinkin's prediction about the JFK assassination a matter of days after its occurrence and did nothing about it. Dinkin predicted what would happen, where it would happen, and when it would occur. What are the chances of his having been "mentally ill"? If that was the case, he would be one extremely accurate delusional character. He had to have gotten this information from somewhere.

SECRET

XAAZ-17618

MEMORANDUM FOR: Mr. J. Lee Rankin
General Counsel
President's Commission on the
Assassination of President Kennedy

SUBJECT: Allegations of Pfc. Eugene B. DINKIN,
U.S. Army, Relative to Assassination
Plot Against President Kennedy as transmitted
to Warren Commission

1. Reference is made to paragraph 2 of your memorandum, dated February 12, 1964, requesting that the Commission be furnished copies of disseminations relative to the assassination of President Kennedy that were sent to the Secret Service.

2. Immediately after the assassination the CIA ▇▇▇▇▇ in Geneva, Switzerland, reported allegations concerning a plot to assassinate President Kennedy that were made by Pfc. Eugene B. DINKIN, U.S. Army, serial number RA-76710292, on 6 and 7 November 1963, in Geneva while absent without leave from his unit in Metz, France. Available details of this charge, together with information on its exploitation by Alex des Fontaines, a Time-Life stringer in Geneva, were disseminated as OUT Teletype message No. 85770, on 29 November 1963. This dissemination was sent to the White House, Department of State and Federal Bureau of Investigation, with a copy to the Secret Service.

3. Since the ▇▇▇▇▇ cooperated with the U.S. Military Attache in assembling information on this affair, and the Military Attache reported through his channels, the Commission may have already received information of Pfc. DINKIN's allegations.

APPROVED FOR RELEASE 1992
CIA HISTORICAL REVIEW PROGRAM

WARNING NOTICE
SENSITIVE SOURCES AND
METHODS INVOLVED

201-289248

DATE 19 May 64

SECRET

4. Because sensitive sources and methods were involved, an appropriate sensitivity indicator has been affixed to this memorandum and its attachment.

Richard Helms
Deputy Director for Plans

Attachment - a/s

Distribution:
    Orig & 1 - Addressee
            2 - DDP
            1 - C/CI
            1 - C/CI/SIG
            2 - CI/R&A
            1 - CI/R&A/Hall
            1 - CI/R&A/201

Originated by: CI/R&A/Hall:pm   11 May 1964

201-289248

WARNING NOTICE
SENSITIVE SOURCES AND
METHODS INVOLVED

Of course a confession does not prove that someone did what they said they did, but not many people would confess to assassinating the president of the United States. There have been, however, several credible confessions to this vile deed. In *Legacy of Secrecy: The Long Shadow of the JFK Assassination*, Lamar Waldron and Thom Hartmann found much evidence to substantiate three heads of organized crime that confessed to assassinating JFK. One observation from the book is quoted below.

> Based on conclusive evidence and testimonies that have come to light in recent years, it's now clear that Marcello and Trafficante worked together with Mafia Don Johnny Rosselli to assassinate President John F. Kennedy. All three confessed their involvement to trusted associates shortly before their death, including stunning admissions in FBI files detailed here for the first time.[50]

Recall that Santo Trafficante Jr. set up the major heroin supply channels out of Southeast Asia a few years after the assassination, 1968, and that all three of these men profited enormously from the drug trade following JFK's demise. Let us also keep in mind that the Kennedys were a direct threat to organized crime, not only in terms of the drug trade but also the very vigorous prosecution of all aspects of organized crime. This was especially true of Robert F. Kennedy's justice department that greatly increased prosecutions of the top levels of organized crime. RFK even went so far as to illegally deport Carlos Marcello. There were confirmed conversations between Marcello, Trafficante, and others that they really wanted to get RFK, but then they would have to contend with an enraged JFK with the power of the presidency behind him. The House Select Committee on Assassinations investigated this in some detail. Robert Blakely, chief counsel for the HSCA, summarized a revealing event as follows:[51]

---

50. Lamar Waldron, Thom Hartmann, *Legacy of Secrecy: The Long Shadow of the JFK Assassination*: (Kindle Edition, Counterpoint, November 1, 2009), Kindle locations 1038-1047.
51. Noel H. Twyman, *Bloody Treason: The Assassination of John F. Kennedy*, (Kindle E-Book: First Edition 2010), Location 6826 to 6853. Twyman referenced HSCA Vol. IX, 82-83.

Marcello's anger could have constituted a motive for the assassination. There was a witness, moreover, who said the New Orleans Mafia leader had been quite specific about the manner and method of his revenge, Edward Becker, a former Las Vegas promoter who had lived on the fringe of the underworld, told of a meeting in September 1962 at Churchill Farms at which Marcello became enraged at the mention of Robert Kennedy's name. "Don't worry about that little Bobby son-of-a bitch," Becker reported Marcello said. "He's going to be taken care of." Then he muttered a Sicilian curse: "Livase na petra di la scarpa." ("Take the stone out of my shoe.") Becker said Marcello had even devised a plan: he would use a "nut" to do the job, someone who could be manipulated, for it was important that his own people not be identified as the assassins. Marcello then offered a metaphor. The President was the dog, the Attorney General Kennedy was its tail. If you cut off the tail, the dog will keep biting; but if you chop off the head, the dog will die, tail and all.

Marcello and the other crime bosses could have and probably were involved in the planning and execution of the assassination; however, there is no way they could have covered it up. That would take powerful people in the US government to do that. We need to also keep in mind that Blakely seemed to have the hidden agenda of guiding the HSCA to a conclusion that organized crime was solely responsible for the JFK assassination.

The only person tried in court for the murder of JFK, Clay Shaw, came very close to a confession five years after the trial. Near death from lung cancer, Shaw was visited by a long-time neighbor and friend, George Dureau, and made the following statement:

> As Dureau remembers, Shaw said "You know, I wasn't guilty of what Garrison charged. But Garrison had the right idea. He was almost right. Someone like me, with a background in army intelligence and with post-war intelligence connections, very well might have been asked to meet with someone like Oswald or Ferrie, to give them a package or some money or whatever, and I would have faithfully done it without ever asking what I was doing it for. That "package"

recalls "Donald" P. Norton's testimony that Shaw gave him a suitcase of money to deliver to Oswald in Monterrey.[52]

The above quote is illuminating in lieu of the fact that Clay Shaw denied in court that he was a CIA operative, and he also denied that he even knew Oswald. When Shaw was speaking about doing something without questioning the action, he was referring to what this author was explaining in chapter 1. The CIA and the military operate in like fashion when it comes to sensitive operations. One does not question things. If you are told to do something, you just do it. If you are asked about something, you simply provide it without asking questions. This is one good reason why several of the patsies in assassinations, including Oswald, have been US Marines. They are taught to follow orders without question. Had Clay Shaw not been involved in the assassination, he would not have made the above comment.

Robert Wilfred Easterling[53]

Another credible confession of involvement in the JFK assassination was reported by Michael Benson in his book, *Who's Who in the JFK assassination: An A to Z Encyclopedia*, parts of which are summarized in the next paragraph.

Easterling, Robert Wilfred (a.k.a. Taylor, George; "Hardhat"), possible Oswald witness, possible Ruby witness, confessed assassination conspirator. Easterling was diagnosed ten years after the assassination as a psychotic and schizophrenic. He called author Henry

---

52. Joan Mellen, *A Farewell to Justice: Jim Garrison, JFK's Assassination, and the Case that Should Have Changed History*, (Kindle Edition: Potomac Books Inc., October 31, 2005), Location 4516-4523.
53. Photo courtesy of Spartacus Educational, http://www.spartacus.schoolnet.co.uk/JFKeasterling.htm

Hurt on September 29, 1981, and gave him a detailed confession of his knowledge of, and participation in a plot to kill JFK. He had previously attempted to tell his story to the FBI and the SS (Secret Service) who didn't pay much attention; he said he was confessing because he believed he was dying and wanted to clear his conscience.

Because of his mental state, his confession might be easy to dismiss if it weren't for the key items in his scenario that have been corroborated independently. Here is Easterling's story quoted from Benson:[54]

> Manuel enlisted Easterling in a scheme to kill JFK. Manuel explained that their group wanted JFK dead because they were betrayed at the Bay of Pigs invasion. Easterling says that other members of the conspiratorial group included David Ferrie and Clay Shaw, whom he also saw in the same bar, and a Cuban named Joe who had a deformed hand and who sometimes tended bar . . . . Manuel, who drove a gray Volkswagen, explained that JFK was going to be shot by a 7mm Czech weapon, the design of which he had supervised personally. This weapon fired bullets that disintegrated on impact and left no ballistic evidence. The cover story was going to involve a patsy (Oswald) and fake ballistic evidence. The cover assassination weapon was to be a Mannlicher-Carcano. To create the phony ballistic evidence, Manuel went to a field (behind the trailer park where Easterling lived with his wife) and fired the weapon into a barrel of water. He then collected the shell casings and the fired bullets—which would be planted at the appropriate time to incriminate Oswald . . . .

[54.] Michael Benson, *Who's Who in the JFK Assassination: An A to Z Encyclopedia* (Citadel; 30 Anv. edition, October 1, 2003), Kindle locations 1784-1807. Copyright 1993 by Michael Benson. All rights reserved. No part of this book may be reproduced in any form, except by a newspaper or magazine reviewer who wishes to quote brief passages in connection with a review. Original source: Henry Hurt, *Reasonable Doubt: An Investigation into the Assassination of John F. Kennedy* (Henry Holt & Co. P; 1st Owl Book Ed edition, June 1987).

Later, Easterling claims, he was blindfolded and taken to the group's headquarters. There Manuel showed Easterling a heavy wooden box with a false bottom, in which a rifle could be hidden. The box, Manuel explained, would be placed at the assassination site. After the shooting, the Czech weapon would be hidden in the box's false bottom while the false evidence would be planted. The box would be removed at some later date. Easterling met Oswald, who spoke little, and quickly figured out that Oswald was the patsy. Manuel explained that he had met Oswald in Czechoslovakia, where the weapon had been built. (Oswald was officially in the USSR at that time.)

The above is just one of many incidents that clearly lead one to ask the question, Why have none of these events been presented to the commissions and committees that have investigated the JFK assassination? Of course, the answer is that any number of witnesses that could have easily shed light on how the assassination actually was done would "open up an endless can of worms," as Senator Fulbright famously stated.

Although he had emotional problems, many of the details of Easterling's account have been verified. Further, his account about the actual weapon used fits the results of several investigators. Jim Garrison, who doubted that Oswald even fired at all, came up with the fact that one of the first Dallas Police Department investigators on the scene identified the recovered rifle as a German Mauser, which looks nothing like a Mannlicher Carcano. Also the fact that Oswald's test for gunpowder residue on his face was negative. Add to this the fact that Oswald said that he "was the patsy," and that he was silenced very quickly by a known member of organized crime and a known drug kingpin. We are supposed to believe that Jack Ruby, a tough Chicago gangster, was so worried that a public trial of Oswald would upset his widow, so he felt compelled to shoot Oswald? And what is more, we add to this the fact that Ruby and Oswald not only knew each other, but that they knew each other well. This has been established by several investigators and corroborated by many witnesses. We have to reach the conclusion that the truth has been deliberately hidden from the American people.

Rose Cheramie[55]

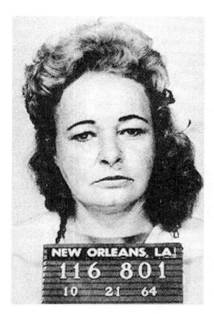

One does not find very many people that are able to state publicly that an assassination is going to happen, and add to that the indisputable fact that Rose also stated exactly how, when, and where it was going to take place. Rose Cheramie did all of these and more. The exact circumstances of this bizarre sequence of events came out of the Garrison investigation and was documented by Joan Mellen in her book, *A Farewell to Justice, Jim Garrison, JFK's Assassination, and the Case that Should Have Changed History*, which is quoted below.[56]

Rose Cheramie was a twenty-eight year old prostitute and drug addict with a long police record and time served at Angola. She had worked for a Basile whorehouse called the Silver Slipper Lounge once owned by Jack Ruby, In 1963, Rose, like others of her trade, plied that strip of Highway 190 extending from Opelousas, birthplace of Jim Bowie, to the Texas border where a gas station more than likely doubled as a brothel. One night in November 1963, Rose had been beaten and tossed form an automobile on this highway. A state trooper booked her as a suspected narcotics addict . . .

"I've got your lady friend here in jail," Fruge said. "She's got something to share with us."

---

55. Photo source: Mary Ferrell Foundation at http://www.maryferrell.org/wiki/index.php/Rose_Cherami.
56. Joan Mellen, *A Farewell to Justice: Jim Garrison, JFK's Assassination, and the Case that Should Have Changed History*, (Kindle Edition: Potomac Books Inc., October 31, 2005), Location 2975-2996.

Three men were traveling from Florida to Texas to kill John F. Kennedy, Rose recounted. "These Cubans are crazy. They're going to Dallas to kill Kennedy in a few days . . ."

On Friday, November 22nd, at twenty minutes before noon, Rose was watching television in the hospital recreation area. Scenes in Dallas flashed on the screen. President Kennedy was on his way.

"Somebody's got to do something!" Rose shouted. "They're going to kill the president!" No one paid any attention. The motorcade pulled into view. "Watch!" Rose cried out. "This is when it's going to happen! They're going to get him! They're going to get him at the underpass!"

"POW!" Rose yelled as the shots rang out.

All that weekend Rose talked. Dr. Weiss heard her say she knew Jack Ruby. She believed Kennedy was assassinated because of narcotics traffic on the Mexican Border. She herself was connected to a drug syndicate. She was not only a stripper for Jack Ruby, Rose confided. She was one of his drug runners. She had seen Lee Harvey Oswald sitting at a table at Ruby's Carousel Club.

That weekend Francis Fruge thought he and Donald White should come forward and "tell what we know." White urged silence, but Fruge telephoned the FBI in Lafayette. "This lady warned us about the assassination," Fruge said.

They've already got their man," the agent said. "Case closed . . ."

Rose Cheramie was found dead on September 4, 1965. It was reported that her head had been run over by a car, and that the death was an accident. Later it was suspected that she had been shot in the head and that the accident was staged to disguise this fact. The driver of the car stated that she was lying in the road and that he swerved to avoid her, but he was unable to avoid her and ran over her head. An investigation into her death did not reveal any relationship between the driver and Rose. The death was ruled an accident, and the case was closed.

Rose's knowledge that Oswald and Ruby knew each other well has been substantiated by several authors and investigators. Also known are the facts that Ruby was deeply involved in the international drug trade, and that Oswald was involved in plots to kill Fidel Castro. Although portrayed as "a low-level organized crime member," it has become evident that Ruby was much more influential than has been reported to the American people. He was well known by most of the Dallas Police Department, and he could have easily provided intelligence as to the department's activities before and during the assassination. Rose, along with many others that had firsthand information, did not testify to any commissions or any other body as to the facts that connect drugs, war, and assassinations. She also, along with many, many others, died under suspicious circumstances.

"Grassy Knoll" Witness Gordon Arnold

If there ever was a witness that ties down the fact that shots came from the grassy knoll, it is Gordon Arnold's recollection of what transpired there on November 22, 1963. Arnold was a twenty-two-year-old army private who was on leave after boot camp. When he learned that John F Kennedy's motorcade was scheduled to go through downtown Dallas, he decided to take movie pictures of the event. He parked his car near a railroad tower, grabbed his movie camera, and walked toward what is referred to as the triple underpass. He told the following story to author Jim Marrs.[57] (comments in brackets from original author)

> I was walking along behind this picket fence when a man in a light colored suit came up to me and said I shouldn't be up there . . . And he showed me a badge and said he was the secret service . . . I said all right in and started walking back along the fence. I could feel that he was following me and we had a few more words. I walked around to the front of the fence and found a little mound of dirt to stand on to see the motorcade . . . Just after the car turned onto Elm and started toward me, a shot went off from over my left shoulder. I felt the bullet, rather than heard it, and it went right past my left

---

[57.] Jim Marrs, *Crossfire: The Plot That killed Kennedy*, (Carrol and Graf Publishers Inc., 19 West 21st Street, New York, NY, 2001), Kindle location 1329-1345.

ear . . . I heard two shots and then there was a blend. For a single bolt action [rifle], he had to have been firing darn good because I don't think anybody could fire that rapid a bolt action . . . The next thing I knew, someone was kicking my butt and telling me to get up. It was a policeman . . . And then this other guy—a policeman—comes up with a gun. And he was crying and that thing was waving back and forth. I felt threatened. One of them asked me if I had taken any film and I said yes. He told me to give him my film, so I tossed him my camera . . .

Many researchers discount Gordon Arnold's story stating that he did not show up in any of the photos taken. That was until Donald T. Phillips wrote, *A Deeper, Darker Truth: Tom Wilson's Journey into the Assassination of John F. Kennedy*.[58] Tom Wilson had spent thirty years with US Steel Corporation. He was an engineer working with and developing systems that could detect flaws in metal products. When he retired, he went into consulting. He had developed image processing and computer analysis systems that could take a photograph and pull out details that the human eye normally cannot see. He discovered that the process could bring out details not visible from any photo source, including still photos and even videotape. A few weeks after he had perfected this process, he saw a JFK assassination documentary on TV. He wondered if his process would bring out details from the assassination's still pictures and video film that no one had seen before.

Beginning in 1988, Tom spent several years analyzing much of the photo evidence available including the Zapruder film and Mary Moorman's seriously degraded Polaroid picture of the grassy knoll almost exactly when the fatal shot hit Kennedy's head. The latter is the picture that some researchers have argued showed a man in the shadows, behind a fence, in a uniform, wearing glasses, pointing a rifle that had a puff of smoke coming out of the barrel, and wearing a badge. In fact, the image is referred to as "badge man." On the other

---

58. Donald T. Phillips, *A Deeper, Darker Truth: Tom Wilson's Journey into the Assassination of John F. Kennedy*, (DTP/Companion Books, Illinois, USA, 2009) Kindle location 1036-1045.

end of the spectrum, we have researchers that believe that "badge man" is only shadows and light playing tricks on over imaginative people. Some go so far as to say that if "badge man" were real, his size would be way out of proportion to the other people in the photo. The photo had been confiscated from Mary Moorman, and when finally returned to her years later, it was in very bad condition. Observing it with the naked eye, one could not say positively what was in the shadows on the grassy knoll.

Tom Wilson's process brought out an image that unarguably shows a shooter wearing what looks like a police uniform firing a rifle. Not only is the badge visible, but Tom also was able to determine that it was shaped like a shield and had an eagle with spread wings in the top area. Tom's process also brought out a large semicircular patch on the shoulder portion of the upper arm. Tom was even able to determine that the shooter had a wart or discolored area on his cheek. The process also brought out an image of man wearing what is referred to as a Garrison cap in the army in exactly the position that Gordon Arnold had said he was standing! Irrefutable evidence that the fatal head shot came from behind the fence on the grassy knoll, and that Arnold was a witness to this. Gordon Arnold was never called to testify what he had witnessed, along with scores of other witnesses.

Not only could Arnold be placed where he was when he said he was there by photographic evidence, but he was also seen there by a US senator. Senator Ralph Yarborough was in Lyndon Baines Johnson's (LBJ's), car in the motorcade. Senator Yarborough saw an "army man" on the grassy knoll who "immediately on the firing of the first shot . . . saw this Army man (Arnold) throw himself on the ground." Senator Yarborough added that he thought to himself, "There's a combat veteran who knows how to act when weapons start firing." We now have photographic evidence that corroborates Arnold's witness statements as to a shot, or shots, coming from the picket fence behind the grassy knoll. We also have a US senator who saw Arnold, in uniform, hit the ground upon hearing a shot whiz by his left ear. Not only was Arnold there, but what he said, happened. At least one shot, the one that blew President Kennedy's head to pieces, came from the picket fence behind the grassy knoll.

Senator Yarborough, along with Texas Governor John Connelly and his wife (both of which were in Kennedy's limousine), and at least another thirty witnesses in the area, all stated that one or more shots were fired from the grassy knoll. This author has found only one of these witnesses to have testified to the Warren Commission and that was Jean Hill. Ms. Hill's testimony was discounted because there were no other witnesses that corroborated her story. Of course not; none of the other more than thirty witnesses that saw, smelled gun smoke, or heard shots that came from the grassy knoll area were called to testify. This includes Senator Yarborough who apparently did not testify to the Warren Commission, or if he did, his testimony was not included in the final report.

Further, both Texas Governor Connolly and his wife have repeatedly stated, over the years, they believed shots came from the grassy knoll. Incredibly, it appears that they were never asked any questions pertaining to this. All the questions asked of them appear to have been couched with the assumption that the only shots came from Oswald on the sixth floor of the Texas School Book Depository. Based on this narrow frame of reference, the Commission then drew the conclusion that this was a fact because they either did not ask the questions or discounted anything that did not fit this scenario. A full analysis of the report is beyond the scope of this book; however, anyone familiar with the facts cannot help but be incredulous as to the methodology of the Warren Commission Report. Just one example is their conclusion that it is conceivable that Governor Connolly was shot through the chest, his right wrist, and the same bullet lodged in his leg, and he did not even realize that he had been hit. Not only this but review of the Zapruder film shows that during this time, he was holding on to his hat and did not let go of it, with having had a bullet from a high-powered military rifle go through his wrist and shatter the bones in it. This is *most* unlikely. The entire report follows suit.

Lyndon Baines Johnson, Scandals, and Confessions

As unlikely as it might seem, Lyndon Baines Johnson was a very troubled man toward the end of his life. Credible researchers and authors have viewed him as a tragic figure in history not unlike Aristotle's classic tragic heroes that all had the same character flaw: arrogant pride or "hubris." Having served the remainder of John F Kennedy's term in office, he won an overwhelming majority of votes against Barry Goldwater in the election of 1964. Many who are old enough to recall the Johnson campaign ads during this election will remember one in particular. This one had Johnson stating that "we must learn to love each other or we must die," while in the background of the TV screen was the mushroom cloud of a nuclear explosion. The intent of this advertisement was to depict Barry Goldwater as a right-wing radical who would plunge the world into nuclear war. The ad was very effective, and Lyndon Baines Johnson was elected to the highest office in the land, president of the United States.

Many who knew him have reported that this most powerful and prestigious office was his overarching goal in life. Johnson's obsession for power has been well documented. Most depict him as a cold, ruthless, overbearing person who would stop at nothing to get what he wanted. There is a frightening record of just how far LBJ would go, and in 1963, Johnson's political career was unraveling. It looked likely that his past was catching up with him, and it was also likely that he would be dropped from the ticket in 1964. This would have not only shattered his dream of the presidency, but the scandals were also likely to land him in jail.

Although a thorough discussion of Johnson's situation just before the assassination is beyond the scope of this book, Phillip Nelson's book, *LBJ: The Mastermind of JFK's Assassination*[59] and others go into plenty of detail about exactly how serious LBJ's problems were during this period. There is a commonality among these authors that LBJ's problems go back to his political career in Texas and also his demonstrated flawed character. One major scandal involved a corrupt Texan named Billie Sol Estes, who had been implicated in a scandal that was reported to be the biggest in Texas history. Among other corrupt dealings, the scandal involved Estes's making millions in federal cotton allotment payments on land that was under water or actually owned by the US government. He also made millions on loans backed up by thousands of nonexistent fertilizer tanks. These scandals were being investigated by a Department of Agriculture official named Henry Marshall who was particularly interested in connections to Johnson.

[59.] Phillip F. Nelson, *LBJ: The Mastermind of JFK's Assassination*, (Xlibris, July 23, 2010).

Marshall was found shot to death while the scandal was still under investigation. It was ruled a suicide, but the facts in the case did not add up. No autopsy was done, but Marshall's wife was able to have the body exhumed and established that Marshall had been murdered. Estes went to jail over the scandal, but he was not charged in the murder. After Estes completed his sentence, he was called before a grand jury inquiring into Henry Marshall's murder. Estes implicated Johnson in this murder, and he stated under oath that Johnson had ordered it because Marshall was going to link him to the Sol Estes scandal. He also stated that Malcolm E. Wallace was the hit man.

Wallace and Johnson had a long and dubious relationship, and it was known that Wallace had done a lot of dirty work for Johnson. Mac Wallace, as he was called, in a jealous rage, murdered a professional golfer who was going out with Johnson's sister, Josefa. Wallace was convicted of first-degree murder, but LBJ's lawyer, John Cofer, was able to get him a five-year suspended sentence! Yes, you read it right, a murder conviction and the sentence was suspended. Mac Wallace spent zero days in jail for first-degree murder.

Wallace was also identified as a shooter on the sixth floor of the Texas School Book Depository by a Native American named Loy Factor. Glen Sample and Mark Collom's book, *The Men on the Sixth Floor*, goes into great detail about who was on the sixth floor of the book depository on November 22, 1963.[60] Mark Collom and Loy Factor were in a hospital together in 1971. This was when Factor confided that he had been involved in the JFK assassination. Over a long period of time, the authors have interviewed Factor, and they have gotten a detailed description of what transpired on the sixth floor of the Texas School Book Depository on November 22, 1963. Factor, an airborne veteran of World War II, was paid, he said, by Mac Wallace; but he did not know that the target was to be the president. Factor stated that there were supposed to be three shooters on the sixth floor, Oswald, Wallace, and Factor himself. He said that he refused to do it, and that he just stood by and watched. He also said that there was a Mexican woman with a radio that was coordinating the gunfire, and that she went by the name Ruth Ann.

---

60. Glen Sample and Mark Collom, *The Men on the Sixth Floor*, (Sample Graphics, Edition 4, digital edition July 4, 2010).

Much of what Factor has stated seemed pretty far-fetched, except that several items have turned out to be factual. Among the incidental items that lead one to believe that he was on the sixth floor was that he stated that there was a table saw there. In fact, it was corroborated by other School Book Depository workers that there was indeed a table saw on the sixth floor. Apparently, the floor was in bad shape, and the workers were sawing plywood to repair it. Factor also gave an accurate description of the layout of the building. This included details of a back dock that was removed shortly after the JFK assassination. It would be most unlikely for Factor to have known these details without having been at the Dallas School Book Depository on or about November 22, 1963.

He also stated that they, the assassins, used a stairway that only accessed the fifth and sixth floors and that only the warehouse workers used this stairway. All other employees, which were office workers, used two elevators that only went to the lower floors. Only fifteen of over forty employees were allowed access to the top floors. This limited access to the top floors must have made it easier for the assassin team to exclude witnesses. How could Factor have known all this without having been there? Of course the possibility exists that Factor could have been there before or shortly thereafter, but it is most unlikely.

Probably the most devastating evidence that came out of the Loy Factor confession is the fact that *Malcolm Wallace's fingerprints were found on a box in the so-called sniper's lair*! Fingerprints were taken just after the assassination, and no match was ever found until over thirty-five years later. The most detailed account of this was in Barr McClellan's, book, *Blood, Money, & Power: How LBJ Killed JFK*, and it is well worth the read.[61] In a nutshell, here is what he and others have reported. The cardboard boxes in the "sniper's lair" were dusted for fingerprints a few hours after the assassination. There were several prints that were Oswald's, but there was one print that did not match Oswald. This print also did not match any of the other TSBD employees.

---

61. Barr McClellan, *Blood, Money and Power: How LBJ Killed JFK*, (Skyhorse Publishing, February 23, 2011).

In 1998, a group of Texas researchers announced that the fingerprint had been matched to Malcolm Wallace. The match was made by a comparison of the unknown fingerprint to the fingerprint card on record that had been accomplished when he was suspected and convicted of the previously mentioned murder in 1951. The match was made by A. Nathan Darby, an expert certified by the International Association of Identifiers. Darby did not know whose print card he was comparing to the print from what had been designated "box A" by investigators. Add to this the fact that Darby had confirmed that he had made a 14-point match that is a positive match in any court in the United States. There was also a positive match done by an expert at INTERPOL. This in itself does not prove that Wallace participated in the assassination of JFK. Nor does it prove that LBJ was involved. It surely is evidence that should be followed up on and joins the rest of myriad evidence that there was a massive conspiracy in the JFK assassination. Also, keep in mind that the House Select Committee on Assassinations did confirm that there was a conspiracy in the JFK assassination.

LBJ's Confession

Lyndon Baines Johnson did not run for a second term of office. The author was at Da Nang Airbase, Vietnam, when President Johnson made the announcement that "I will not seek, nor will I accept the nomination of my party for the office of president of the United States." Surveys had clearly shown that he would not be reelected; the record shows that the war in Vietnam was the issue that would cause him not to be reelected. In fact, the war in Vietnam was the one overriding issue that destroyed his legacy. All that he had accomplished, and he had accomplished a lot, was for naught. He had pushed through more civil rights legislation than any previous president, including John F. Kennedy. His Great Society program was largely a success. However, all of his success as president had been shadowed by the war in Vietnam.

To this day, there is debate about whether it was fair or not that the responsibility for this "conflict" should rest solely, or at least largely, upon LBJ's shoulders. But the fact remains that JFK had only a few thousand "advisers" in Vietnam during his administration, and that he had committed to start withdrawing them. He had also committed to withdrawing all troops by 1965. Of course, no one can be sure that Kennedy would have followed through with his commitments. He had been advised by retired General MacArthur that "any U.S. President that gets involved in a land war in Asia ought to have his head examined." He was also well aware of what the French went through in Algeria. It is likely that JFK would have followed through with these commitments in withdrawing from Vietnam. Lyndon Baines Johnson, however, dramatically escalated the war. Within three years, he had increased troop strength from roughly eight thousand to nearly a half-million troops. The fact remains that American people were fed up with the war and the administration that had promoted it.

Johnson was haunted by the war and the overall record of failure of his presidency as a result. Add to this the specter of the Kennedy assassination upon which he assumed office without the benefit of an election. Some authors go further and state that it was more than a feeling of unworthiness that haunted Johnson. It is evident that Johnson and J. Edgar Hoover were both involved in the cover-up. There is a consistent pattern of cover-up throughout the Executive Branch of the US government indicated by key evidence disappearing, forgeries, alterations, and misrepresentations that had to have been directed by these two individuals. Some authors and investigators state that Johnson probably was not involved in the plot but that he knew it would happen. Some go even further than that and claim that Johnson instigated the assassination itself.

One of these was Barr McClellan. In his previously mentioned book, he not only goes into Mac Wallace's fingerprints, but he goes much further than that. McClellan explains that Johnson had a lawyer, Don Thomas, with whom he confided that he had killed JFK. This was a month before he died, and Johnson was bed-ridden with a failing heart. Johnson also told Thomas that he had told the whole story to his psychiatrist, and that now he could "think straight." Don Thomas states, "Johnson continued, jabbing his right arm. 'You know about the killings. Hell, Don, we had to do it.' Referring to Kennedy, he added, 'That damn Bobby boy. He was stirring everything, and I damn well mean everything . . .'"[62] Thomas states that the exact

---

[62] Ibid., 283.

words such as *murder*, *assassination*, and *killed*, were not used; but the conversation was such that old friends knew exactly what was being talked about. He also went on to explain that Johnson did something that Thomas had never seen him do before, and that was to sob and shake uncontrollably.

McClellan, based on Thomas' testimony, paints a picture of a broken and pathetic dying man who was haunted by Vietnam and the ghost of John F. Kennedy, a failure who had gambled everything, including his soul, and lost. McClellan also identified another of Johnson's attorneys, Edward Clark, as having done most of the dirty work. He further identified Malcolm Wallace and Oswald as the shooters on the sixth floor, and he added that there was another shooter that Wallace had recruited on the grassy knoll. McClellan went on to explain that he was in a law firm with Clark for years, and that among the associate lawyers, it was common knowledge as to what had happened in Dallas, November 22, 1963. He said that the conversations were always cryptic, but there was no doubt about what was being said. Although this writer's opinion is that the planning, organization, and execution of the assassination were far more complex than what Barr McClellan has put forth, the essential elements are conclusive. Lyndon Baines Johnson not only had the motive, means, and opportunity to promulgate the JFK assassination, but there is also credible evidence that he did just that. The fingerprint evidence had been matched by two credible experts. The Department of Justice went on record that the prints were not a match but refused to explain their rational.

It is noteworthy that Loy Factor, without the benefit of this information, stated exactly the same scenario. That was that Malcolm Wallace was a shooter from the sixth floor of the book depository along with Lee Harvey Oswald. He explained that Oswald was shooting from the far left window and that Malcolm Wallace was firing from the far right. Photos taken of the book depository on that date show those two windows had been open. It is not a far reach to assume that many lawyers would be confident in bringing a case such as this to trial. Another person that had an interesting story to tell about events surrounding the JFK assassination is discussed below.

Marita Lorenz and Operation 40[63]

Marita Lorenz was, and is, a most interesting person. Born in 1939 to an American mother and German father, she visited Cuba in 1959 and caught the attention of Fidel Castro. Shortly thereafter, she had an affair with the Cuban leader and claims to have had a child with him. Frank Sturgis, of the CIA and of Watergate notoriety, recruited her to work for the CIA.

In January 1960, she took part in a CIA failed attempt to assassinate Castro. She was supposed to poison him with two capsules that had been given to her by the CIA. According to her, she hid the capsules in a jar of cold cream so that the capsules would not be found going into the country. She says that the capsules dissolved, and that they were useless in the attempt to kill Castro. She also testified that she did not want to poison Castro anyway. She also stated that Frank Sturgis was very upset with her when she told him what had happened.

In 1977, Lorenz stated in an interview with the *New York Daily News* that a group named Operation 40 was involved in plots to assassinate Fidel Castro and John F. Kennedy. She named Lee Harvey Oswald and Frank Sturgis as members of the CIA-affiliated group. This assassination team got its name from the original forty members of the group, many of which have been accused of, by various authors, assassinating both JFK and RFK. They have also been implicated in CIA and organized crime drug operations. Many were also involved in the Bay of Pigs invasion. Further, at least two of the Operation 40 crew, Frank Sturgis and E. Howard Hunt, were members of the

---

[63]. Photo courtesy of Spartacus Educational, http://www.spartacus.schoolnet.co.uk/JFKlorenzM.htm

Watergate Burglars team that caused the scandal that took the Nixon administration down.

In sworn testimony before the House Select Committee on Assassinations, Lorenz stated that Sturgis was one of the gunmen that shot JFK in Dallas. The committee dismissed her testimony. Although her integrity certainly could be questioned, it still was sworn testimony subject to scrutiny and could have provided many leads. Even if she was not totally truthful, it was obvious that she knew a lot. She simply could not have made everything up.

Further, she also testified, in detail, at one of E. Howard Hunt's libel suits. Hunt was known as being "litigious" and was suing the *Searchlight* newspaper for libel. She testified that E. Howard Hunt was a close associate of David Atlee Phillips and that the two were not only involved in the JFK assassination but also in the CIA's successful campaign to overthrow the elected Guatemalan head of state in 1954. They were also involved in the Bay of Pigs invasion in 1961. Hunt was also involved in the Watergate affair that toppled the Nixon administration.

Lorenz also testified that Oswald, Frank Sturgis, and Gerry Patrick Hemming and Cuban exiles Orlando Bosch, Pedro Diaz Lanz, and the Novo brothers, Guillermo and Ignacio, met in 1963 at the Miami home of Bosch and studied street maps of Dallas. She also stated that both she and Sturgis were CIA employees at the time. She testified that they received CIA payments from Hunt under the name "Eduardo." Her testimony went on to state that the above group arrived in Dallas on November 21, 1963, and stayed in a motel that night. The next day, they were joined by Hunt who stayed for about forty-five minutes, and that Hunt handed Sturgis an envelope full of money. She said that about an hour later, Jack Ruby came to the door, and that this was the first time that she had seen Ruby. She again testified that all the people that came in the car with her to Dallas were members of Operation 40, a team formed to carry out high-level assassinations.

Attorney Mark Lane defended *Searchlight* magazine against Howard Hunt, on appeal, and won. The jury determined that there was a conspiracy to assassinate JFK, and that *Searchlight* was not liable for stating that the CIA was responsible. Hunt was not looking good in these proceedings. One of the questions that Mark Lane asked him was that if he had been with his family during the time that Kennedy was shot, "How is it that you are suing for damages because these accusations have caused your family to question whether or not you were in Dallas? Would not your family have known where you were if you were with them?" It has been reported that Hunt had this look of shock on his face, and he could not respond. Besides being litigious, E. Howard Hunt was known to be a prolific liar, but like all liars, he was not as good at it as he thought he was.

Marita Lorenz testified that those involved in the JFK assassination were members of Operation 40, a secret CIA operation that was originally established to assassinate Fidel Castro. Let us take a look at Operation 40.

Operation 40[64]

Alan W. Dulles, director of the Central Intelligence Agency, established Operation 40 in 1959. Operation 40's role was to undermine the communist Castro regime in Cuba. It reportedly got its name from the original forty CIA agents involved in the operation. Later, this number was expanded to seventy agents. As with other CIA organizations, the group was disassociated, sometimes referred to as a "cutout," from the CIA. Funding was obtained from what can be described as far-right financiers and also organized crime's drug profits.

Operation 40 was deeply involved with recruiting for and setting up the Bay of Pigs invasion. Some authors have identified the

---

[64.] Photo courtesy of Spartacus Educational, http://www.spartacus.schoolnet.co.uk/JFKoperation40.htm. Photo was taken in a nightclub in Mexico City on January 22, 1963. Daniel Hopsicker, Author of *Barry and the Boys*, states that the men in the photograph are all members of Operation 40. Hopsicker states that the man closest to the camera on the left is Felix Rodriguez. Next to him is Porter Goss and Barry Seal. He identifies Frank Sturgis as the man on the right attempting to hide his face with his coat.

operation as being assigned the responsibility of assassinating Fidel Castro and starting an insurrection whereby the people overthrow the regime. Many of its members were exiled Cubans from families that were influential in the previous Batista government. These affluent families lost their influence and financial holdings when Castro took over. These exiled Cubans had a passionate hatred for Castro and his regime, and later for JFK whom they blamed for the failure of the Bay of Pigs invasion. Many researchers and authors believe that this was at least part of the motive for the JFK assassination, and that members of the Operation 40 were involved.

Before the Bay of Pigs invasion, the activities of Operation 40 came under the direction of Vice President Richard Nixon in the Eisenhower administration. Everyone in the CIA, the anti-Castro Cubans, and organized crime assumed that then Vice President Nixon would win the upcoming election and assume the presidency on the first of January 1963. He would preside over the invasion of Cuba that would overthrow the Castro regime. CIA Director Allen Dulles, Richard Nixon, members of Operation 40 (author Robert Morrow said that this team was under the direct control of Nixon), organized crime, and others wanted to install a right-wing faction that would run Cuba after the invasion. They intended the new head of state to be Mario Kohly and his cabinet to be comprised of right-wingers that despised any hint of socialism or Communism. This, in effect, would have put Cuba back to its pre-Castro state, which would have included activities such as drug smuggling, gambling, and prostitution. The election of John F. Kennedy, with the assistance of organized crime, threw a big wrench into their plans.

JFK was an unknown, and that would also be true for the rest of the members of his administration. They tended to be young, inexperienced, smart, and somewhat idealistic. They were not from what is referred to in Washington DC as connected "inside the Belt Way." John Kennedy had been a freshman senator from Massachusetts, but he had nowhere near the connections that Richard Nixon had. Nobody knew exactly what to expect from them. Add to this that Eisenhower, and possibly Truman, likely briefed him on some of those overarching obstacles to the initiatives they pursued in their administrations. One of these obstacles was likely the CIA's intransigence toward any peace initiatives. Not knowing how Kennedy would react, Allen Dulles, the director of Central Intelligence Agency, and his deputy, General Charles Cabal, did not go into some of the issues that could be considered controversial. They avoided mentioning that they did not intend on having anyone in the position of power in Cuba whom they considered to be "Marxist," which would also include anyone who had socialist or even progressive tendencies.

Upon taking office, JFK had little choice but to go ahead with the invasion plans. Although Kennedy had serious misgivings about the plan, he had won the election, in part, by his firm stand on not tolerating a Communist regime ninety miles off the Florida coast. He made Richard M. Nixon out to look "soft on Castro and communism" in televised debates mainly because Nixon was hamstrung by the fact that he knew the entire invasion plan. He could not, however, publicly announce any of it or even the fact that it existed. In the debates, Kennedy looked stronger because he was not hampered by the same limitations.

Not comfortable with the CIA's recommendations, he asked his staff to recommend some suitable replacements for the Castro administration. Kennedy did not want Cuba to go back to being led by a corrupt dictator like the pre-Castro Batista regime. He had in mind that a future Cuban leadership would possess liberal views that puts the welfare of the Cuban people first. Kennedy's staff decided to select members of what was known as the Cuban Revolutionary Council. This council was comprised of previous supporters of the Castro revolution that had subsequently become opponents of Castro. Most of them still maintained what could be characterized as socialist ideology.

The CIA had different ideas. Although they did not openly disagree with the Kennedy administration's selections for potential Cuban leaders, the CIA quietly made arrangements for Operation 40 to see to it that all of the potential candidates were assassinated during the inevitable chaos associated with the invasion. In fact, the formal announcements as to the members of the Cuban provisional government in exile were made on Sunday, April 16, 1961, at the Lexington Hotel in New York followed by a lengthy question-and-answer session with the press. Immediately after this session, the Cuban Revolutionary Council, CRC, members of the provisional government were "escorted" under guard out of the hotel and taken to Opa-Locka Naval Air Base in southern Florida where they were put under house arrest. They were to remain there until the overthrow of Castro. They had been promised that they would join the invasion force, but instead they had been held against their will under house arrest. Then they were to be taken by Operation 40 to Cuba where they were all to be shot on the beach. The cover story would have been that it was ruminants of the Castro regime that had killed them. This would be followed by the instillation of the individual whom the CIA wanted as ruler of Cuba, Mario Kohly.

The only thing that saved the so-called "appointees" from the CRC was that they invasion was a total disaster. Obviously, these "provisional government" members could not be slain on the beach as was planned. Add to this that one of them, Tony Verona, managed to escape. Apparently, he jumped out of a back window and managed to evade the guards. He called the White House and got word to Arthur Schlesinger Jr., whose position was Special Assistant to the President, about what had transpired. The Kennedy administration was told by the CIA that this was done for security reasons. Apparently, JFK did not buy this explanation and sent Arthur Schlesinger Jr. to meet with these exile leaders. After a short discussion, Schlesinger had these exile leaders flown on an air force plane to the White House for further consultation. Evidently, they talked with JFK in person, and they had to have figured out what the CIA and Operation 40 had planned for them. It must have been evident to JFK that this was a federal agency that was way out of control. This incident has been substantiated and documented by Dick Russell in his outstanding book, *The Man Who Knew Too Much*,[65] and also by Robert D. Morrow in his equally excellent book, *First Hand Knowledge*.[66] Russell also ran across some intriguing names associated with Operation 40, such as Richard Nixon who had input into the devious plan to use Operation 40 to assassinate the exile leaders that the Kennedy administration would later choose as Castro's successors.

---

65. Dick Russell, *The Man Who Knew Too Much*, (245 West 17th Street, New York, NY, 10011: Carroll & Graf Publishers, 2003), 109-110.
66. Robert D. Morrow, *First Hand Knowledge: How I Participated in the CIA-Mafia Murder of President Kennedy*, (136 West 22nd Street, New York, NY 10011: SPI Books/Shapolsky Publishers, Inc., 1994), 47-48.

This is one of many instances that illuminate the growing mistrust between the CIA and the Kennedy administration. Over and over again, the CIA routinely nodded their heads to JFK and turned around and did exactly what they wanted to do, in effect defying the chief executive of the United States. This is what they did to two previous presidents, Truman and Eisenhower, and they were becoming bolder and more and more defiant as time when on. Something had to be done. JFK reacted by firing the top leadership in the CIA, to include Allen Dulles (who ended up on the Warren Commission), General Charles Cabell (whose brother was the Mayor of Dallas), and William Harvey (the architect of the CIA's assassination team, ZR/RIFLE). All these top CIA executives have been suspected of involvement in JFK's brutal murder. He also put his attorney general brother in charge of the center for all anti-Castro activities known as JM-WAVE. Operation 40 was not disbanded after the Bay of Pigs fiasco but continued on.

Operation 40 members were not only suspected of involvement in some of the most disturbing aspects of the Bay of Pigs invasion and the JFK assassination, but many are suspected of being involved in just about every wicked activity the United States has been involved in since that time. There is no question that at least two members of Operation 40 were involved in the Watergate affair that toppled the Nixon administration. E. Howard Hunt, some researchers say, was the director of Operation 40. Frank Sturgis, attempting to hide his face in the photo, was also a member. Third on the left is Barry Seal, who previously owned the C-123 airplane that was shot down during the Iran-Contra affair. The only survivor of the plane crash was Eugene Hasenfus, who had disobeyed orders and wore a parachute. Hasenfus confessed that this was a CIA operation, which played a key role in exposing the whole affair. First on the left in the photo is Felix Rodriguez, who was involved in the Iran-Contra affair and many other undercover operations. Next to him is reported to be Porter Goss, although he denies that this is him in the picture, who was later the director of the CIA. Not in the photo but also a member of Operation 40 was a man that we have seen before who played a key role in the notorious Vietnam assassination program, Operation Phoenix. David Sanchez Morales's name not only pops up here and in Vietnam but will come up again and again. Other involvement of members of this group in CIA clandestine activities include the Vietnam War (and the

Golden Triangle drug trade associated with it), the Robert F. Kennedy assassination, the Iran-Contra scandal (and the drugs associated with that fiasco), the murder of Che Guevara, the international manhunt for Luis Posada (a member of Operation 40 who blew up a Cuban civilian airliner full of passengers), ad infinitum.

Operation 40 members were the same people that the Church Committee (Senate Select Committee to Study Governmental Operations with Respect to Intelligence Activities) discovered had been involved in several attempts to assassinate Castro. Members of this operation were supported by organized crime figures such as Carlos Marcello. Much of this is well known and some of it came out during the Church Committee hearings and also the House Select Committee on Assassinations hearings.

Cuba and the Drug Trade

Not well known is the fact that Cuba was an important transshipment point in the international drug trade. This connection was lost when Castro gained control of the country. For organized crime and also US agencies involved in the drug trade, for example the CIA, this loss was significant. This was not the only significant loss when Castro took over. Organized crime also lost revenue from gambling and prostitution. American corporations that were nationalized by Castro also lost out. However, the loss of Cuba as a transshipment point for drugs coming out of the golden triangle in Southeast Asia, sometimes called the French Connection, and other drugs from South America amounted to billions of dollars a year, perhaps even more.

Further, previously mentioned Operation 40 also had a large resistance movement inside Cuba that was funded largely by drug money from Carlos Marcello. Twelve days before the Bay of Pigs, Bahía de Cochinos, Robert Kennedy inexplicably deported Carlos Marcello to Guatemala. RFK had him picked up, quite literally, with only the shirt on his back. He had no chance to talk with a lawyer or even call his wife. Actually, RFK's deportation of Marcello was illegal. It also put Marcello in a country in which he had no support. Marcello made it back the United States eventually, but one of the consequences of this action was that Marcello's financial support, largely drug money, was cut off to the Cuban exiles and also the resistance forces inside Cuba. This was obviously at a very critical time. Mario Kohly, the CIA-proposed future leader of Cuba, went to organized crime chiefs Meyer Lansky and Santo Trafficante and received financial support. This support came at a cost; when Kohly assumed the position of president of Cuba, he was obligated to open the doors for US organized crime to operate gambling casinos. Author Robert Morrow wrote that this deal was actually written up by lawyers as a contract.

The Kennedy administration was perceived as an obstacle to war and drugs, the two conjoined twins of the CIA's pathological obsession with destroying Communism. Operation 40 was yet another example of a CIA program without adequate oversight. Whenever this happens, the results are programs that grow wildly out of proportion, which are often headed by psychopaths; and they eventually take in directions that were never intended. This is another example of what is politely referred to as "blowback" or what could be more accurately described as CIA-created Frankenstein monsters.

Many researchers, authors, and those with firsthand experience in the JFK assassination have come to the conclusion that at least some of the Operation 40 members were directly involved in the murder of John F. Kennedy, in Dallas, Texas, on November 22, 1963. It is also a fact that virtually everyone that was scheduled to formally testify to this ended up dying under suspicious circumstances, including members of Operation 40, organized crime, and many other witnesses.

Other Anti-Castro and Assassination Groups

Fidel Castro overthrew the corrupt Batista regime and marched into Havana on January 9, 1959. He immediately began redistributing the resources and wealth of Cuba. This made him wildly popular with the common people but very unpopular with the upper-class wealthy Cubans, many of who left Cuba for the United States. This group of exiled Cubans included landowners, wealthy industrialists, many doctors, and other professionals. They also took their families with them. Many of these upper-class Cuban families did not fare as well in the United States as they did in Cuba. This situation is where the strong anti-Castro sentiments developed into these groups that badly wanted to overthrow Castro.

There were many groups, mostly managed by the CIA, that were formed for the purposes of anti-Castro operations and also assassinations. These groups appeared to have a very loose structure. Also, the CIA clandestine concept of "plausible denial" was always in play. Many of the members of one group were also members of other groups. These were groups that operated in the shadows, so sometimes it is difficult to define exactly who the members of the groups were. Add to this the fact that many used pseudonyms.

In the course of researching the Southeast Asian drug trade, I came across the names of several CIA operatives and also members of organized crime, some of which played key roles in developing the drug trade and also the so-called Vietnam conflict. I began to realize that war and drugs were the products of both the CIA and organized crime, and that the CIA and organized crime collaborated in these endeavors. Further, I wondered if I would see some of the same names associated with political assassinations. Specifically the assassinations of the Kennedy brothers who, I began to realize, stood right in the way of these two organizations' objectives, which increasingly appeared to be developing both armed conflict and the very lucrative drug trade. They not only stood in the way of these two organizations, they were an outright threat to their existence.

There was a very clear track record of Kennedy initiatives to literally destroy organized crime and also dismantle the CIA. Robert Kennedy went after organized crime tooth and nail, and John Kennedy not only fired the top leadership of the Central Intelligence Agency, but he also ordered its force withdrawals from Southeast Asia. He also publicly stated that he would withdraw all troops by 1965. There is also strong evidence that the Kennedys were drawing down hostile actions toward Cuba. This author believes that these actions sealed the fate of both Kennedy brothers.

The following are thumbnail sketches of some of these groups.

Alpha 66 started in Puerto Rico in 1961. Its mission was to fight Communism in Cuba. There were chapters throughout the United States, most of which were in Florida. This was an extremely radical group that planned commando-style raids in Cuba and also carried them out. Many of its members participated in the Bay of Pigs invasion. Several researchers have linked some of the members of Alpha 66 to the JFK assassination. Gerry Patrick Hemming, the owner and operator of Interpen (an acronym that stands for Intercontinental

Penetration Force), has also pointed the finger toward Alpha 66 members as being involved in the Kennedy assassination. Keep in mind that the members of many of these groups moved around in and were associated with other groups. There were no exact borders that defined one group from another. Some individuals were members of more than one group. Add to this that these groups also had splinter groups that went by other names. Further, some of the groups went by different names in different countries.

What defined Alpha 66 was that its members were very volatile and violent. They had their own anti-Castro agenda, and that was to fight and overthrow Castro by any and all means necessary. They would not take orders from any one, including the president of the United States, unless it was an agreement with their plans and philosophy. No one could tell them to hold off or stop what they were doing. They continued raids inside Cuba even after the Kennedy administration had directed the CIA to put the raids to a halt. This added to suspicion that members of Alpha 66 were involved in the Kennedy assassination.

JM WAVE was the CIA's headquarters for anti-Castro activities. The station was located in Florida, south of Miami. The many buildings were supposed to belong to Zenith Technical Enterprises but were used exclusively by the CIA. The head of the station was a person we saw in chapter 4, Ted Shackley, who coordinated a variety of anti-Castro activities. These activities were designed to disrupt the Castro regime with a variety of sabotage, subversion, and also assassination plots against the regime and directly against Castro.

After the Bay of Pigs fiasco, President Kennedy put the anti-Castro initiatives under his brother, Attorney General Robert F. Kennedy. He also fired the CIA director, Allen Dulles, and several other top CIA personnel, including General Charles Cabell who was the deputy director of the CIA. General Cabell's brother was Earle Cabell, who was the mayor of Dallas and, as such, was involved in the planning of JFK's fatal trip to Dallas. Several researchers believe that Earle Cabell was involved in the route change that took JFK through Dealey Plaza, making two sharp turns close to buildings and the grassy knoll. It was no secret that General Charles Cabell hated JFK, and one may assume that Allen Dulles was not exactly fond of him either. Instead of being possible suspects, Dulles was put on the Warren Commission, and neither of the Cabell brothers was called before the Warren

Commission. After the failed Bay of Pigs invasion, JFK was widely despised, and there were many rumors of assassination and death threats.

JFK put his brother in charge of all clandestine activities, essentially making him the CIA director. Among these activities was a committee named the Special Group Augmented or SGA. This committee was in charge of overthrowing Castro's government and was chaired by Robert Kennedy. Included on the committee were John McCone, the new CIA director; McGeorge Bundy, National Security Adviser; Alexis Johnson, State Department; Roswell Gilpatric, Defense Department; General Lyman Lemnitzer, Joint Chiefs of Staff; and General Maxwell Taylor. Secretary of State Dean Rusk and Secretary of Defense Robert NcNamara also attended these meetings.

SGA met on November 4, 1961, and decided to call the operation to overthrow Castro Operation Mongoose, working out of the JM/WAVE station. Robert Kennedy placed a person in charge of Operation Mongoose that we have seen before, air force general Edward Lansdale. The reader will recall that General Lansdale played a key role in the drug trade and also in starting the war in Southeast Asia. One of Lansdale's early decisions was to appoint William Harvey in charge of organizing a variety of activities to bring the Castro government down. This function was designated Task Force W.

In 1962, Harvey was directed to create an assassination team aimed at Castro. This became known as ZR/RIFLE, which we will discuss in more detail later in this chapter. One of the people that Harvey brought into the ZR/RIFLE program was another person whose name keeps popping up: David Sanchez Morales. Morales was also the chief of operations at JM/WAVE. We saw Morales in chapter 4, and we will see him again later. Morales was a known assassination specialist who drank and talked too much. On several occasions, he bragged about killing both Kennedys and many, many more. Powerful people became concerned about his loose tongue. After a trip to Washington DC, he became very ill and eventually died on May 8, 1978. The cause of death was reported as a heart attack. There was no autopsy performed, and at fifty-two years of age, he had no known illnesses. There was strong suspicion that he did not die of natural causes. Several respected researchers have Harvey and Morales way up on their list of suspects in the JFK assassination, along with Shackley and Lansdale. Further, these anti-Castro CIA programs, especially ZR/RIFLE, are strongly suspected of being co-opt for the JFK assassination. Air force Colonel Fletcher Prouty talked about how he suspected that air force General Edward Lansdale played a role in the assassination.

Prouty, who was the focal point between the air force and CIA clandestine activities, said that General Lansdale sent him on a boondoggle mission to the South Pole during the time that JFK was killed. Prouty believed that some of the people in charge of presidential security would have alerted him that there were abnormal happenings associated with the Dallas visit. Prouty also stated that one of his routine duties would have been to arrange additional security in Dallas had he been in Washington, specifically the 112th Intelligence Group. Here is part of what Colonel Prouty had to say in his book, *JFK: The CIA, Vietnam, and the Plot to Assassinate John F. Kennedy*: [67]

> So few of the routine things were done in Dallas. Incredibly, there were no Secret Service men or other protection personnel at all in the area of the Elm Street slowdown zone. How did this happen? It is documented that Secret Service men in Fort Worth were told they would not be needed in Dallas.
>
> The commander of an army unit, specially trained in protection and based in nearby San Antonio, Texas, had been told he and his men would not be needed in Dallas. Another army unit will cover that city," the commander was told.
>
> I have worked with military presidential protection units. I called a member of that army unit later. I was told that the commander "had offered the services of his unit for protection duties for the entire trip through Texas," that he was "point-blank and categorically refused by the Secret Service," and that "there were hot words between the agencies."
>
> I was told that this army unit, the 316th Field Detachment of the 112th Military Intelligence Group at Fort Sam Houston

---

[67]. Fletcher Prouty, *JFK: The CIA, Vietnam, and the Plot to Assassinate John F. Kennedy* (555 Eighth Avenue, Suite 903, New York, NY, 10018: Skyhorse Publishing, 2009), 294.

in the Fourth Army Area, "had records on Lee Harvey Oswald, before November 22." It "knew Dallas was dangerous," the commander told my associate in explaining why he had offered his services, despite a call to "Stand down."

Note how far back the policemen are and how casually they hold their guns

Colonel Prouty also identified Lansdale (arrow) in a picture of the "three tramps" as the person going in the opposite direction.[68] This picture was taken in Dealey Plaza on November 22, 1963. Lt. Gen. Victor Krulak, who knew him well, also identified General Lansdale when he saw the picture and stated, "The haircut, the stoop, the twisted left hand, the large class ring. It's Lansdale."

Sylvia Odio[69]

Several authors have written about and interviewed Sylvia Odio. She is widely considered an intelligent and reliable witness. There have been attempts to discredit her, but the accusations have always turned out to be outright fabrications and distortions. What she saw and heard, also witnessed by her sister, provides compelling evidence of a conspiracy to murder JFK.

Sylvia was born into an influential family in Cuba in 1937. Her father

---

[68]. Photo Courtesy of the L. Fletcher Prouty Reference site, http://www.prouty.org

[69]. Photo source Mary Ferrell Foundation at: http://www.maryferrell.org/wiki/index.php/The_Odio_Incident.

was actively opposed to the Batista regime and later also took issue with the direction of the communist Castro government that replaced it. The family left Cuba and settled in Dallas where Sylvia's father joined the anti-Castro movement.

She had a memorable visit from three men who said they were from New Orleans on September 25, 1953. Two of the men, claiming that their names were Leopoldo and Angelo, stated that they were members of the anti-Castro group "La Junta Revolucionaria." A third man, introduced as Leon, was presented as an American who was willing to participate in an assassination of Castro. They left after Odio told them that she would not get involved in any illegal activities.

The next day, she was called by Leopoldo and told that Leon was a former marine who was an expert marksman. Leopoldo added that Leon had said that "we Cubans (meaning the anti-Castro Cubans in the United States) did not have the guts because we should have assassinated Kennedy after the Bay of Pigs." Odio reported the above to authorities after the assassination, and she testified to the Warren Commission that she was certain the "Leon" was Lee Harvey Oswald. One of the Warren Commission lawyers stated that he had checked out her story and that he was convinced that "Odio is the most significant witness linking Oswald to the anti-Castro Cubans."

Sylvia Odio was likely a reliable witness. There is not much doubt that she saw and heard what she said she did; however, there are more plausible conclusions that can be reached. If Odio had told these uninvited visitors that she did not want to get involved, why would one of them call afterward and add the above details? There is no reason to do this except to establish Oswald as a marine sharpshooter inclined to shoot the president. Further, because Oswald was not privy to this conversation, he would be none the wiser that he was being set up to be the patsy. This is a much more likely scenario that also puts responsibility for the assassination on Cubans, or Communists, and away from any domestic activities. There is also the possibility that this was not the real Lee Harvey Oswald.

More Than One Oswald?

There were several suspicious "Oswald sightings" in the days, weeks, and months prior to the JFK assassination and sometimes in different places at the same time. He was reported to have gone to the Cuban and Soviet embassies in Mexico, on the 27 and 29 of September 1963, but a picture disclosed that this was not the real Oswald. Further, eyewitness accounts describe a person significantly different than Oswald. He was also reported by many witnesses to have been in Clinton, Louisiana, in August to September 1963. Among the witnesses were a State representative, a deputy sheriff, and a registrar of voters. Several of the witnesses were harassed, and one was fired from his job. The witnesses described Oswald to have been in the company of two other men that matched the description of Clay Shaw and David Ferrie, both of whom were strongly suspected of being involved in the assassination.

Not only was he suspected of being involved in the assassination, but Clay Shaw was the only person who has ever been tried in court for it, and David Ferrie had been summoned by the court to testify. Shortly after this was announced, Ferrie "committed suicide" and supposedly left two typewritten unsigned suicide notes, one of which disappeared. When it was announced that David Ferrie would be called as a witness, he also made comments to the effect that he would be killed. Both David Ferrie and Clay Shaw had repeatedly stated that they did not know Oswald even when there was overwhelming evidence that they did.

It is not absolutely clear whether or not the Oswald that was seen in Clinton, Louisiana, was the real Oswald or an impostor; but whoever it was represented himself as Oswald, and his actions were designed to draw attention to himself so that people would remember him as being there. It is also not clear as to why this scenario had been created. Oswald had applied for a job at a mental hospital in Jackson, Mississippi. He was told that he had to be a registered voter to get the job, so he went to Clinton where there was a voting registration initiative going on. It is not clear as to whether or not Oswald did register to vote. He apparently did not take the job in Jackson. It is interesting to note that this same mental hospital was later suspected as being involved in CIA mind-control programs known as MK/ULTRA. There are some researchers that believe Oswald was a mind-control subject.

There were several other documented instances of Oswald being involved in activities that were incriminating. The problem is that on two occasions, there was credible evidence that he was in two places at the same time, obviously impossible. For example, he could not possibly have been at Ruth Paine's house continuously from 8 to 11

November in Irvine, Texas, and also have practiced on a rifle range on 10 November in Dallas. Another instance was when he was reported to have had his scope adjusted in Dallas on 28 September when he was also reported to have been in Mexico City on the same day.

Either one or the other of these instances was in error, or there would have had to have been at least one Oswald impersonator. Although presenting an airtight case for either proposition is beyond the scope of this book, there is overwhelming evidence, presented by several respected researchers and authors, that there was at least one Oswald impersonator involved. There is no doubt that a man representing himself as Oswald was photographed going into the Soviet Embassy, and the photo was clearly not him. This is convincing evidence that someone, or some group, was impersonating Oswald and setting him up as the patsy. For this to have happened is also convincing evidence of a conspiracy, and not only a conspiracy but one that had to have been carried out by persons in an agency, or agencies, of the US government.

The whole idea of Oswald being set up as a patsy, including the doubles of Oswald seen in several places, points directly to the people employed by the CIA. Organized crime and other suspects in the JFK assassination simply could not have pulled this off. Further, the practice of implicating the Soviet Union, Communists, and/or other countries as a backup position (should the assassination plan "blow") is "standard operating procedure" for the CIA. This practice goes back to the very origins of a program that was started in 1959 and designated as ZR/RIFLE.

ZR/RIFLE

This program was a CIA assassination program that is sometimes referred to as "Executive Action," which was created during the Eisenhower administration and, make no bones about it, is still with us today. It was designed to assassinate foreign leaders, and records show that Allen Dulles proposed the program to President Eisenhower in 1959. Eisenhower approved it, and it is this writer's opinion that, in so doing, President Eisenhower opened up the gates of hell, thus allowing psychopathology to become an instrument of US foreign policy. Several authors believe that this program was co-opted by the JFK assassins and used to explode Kennedy's head in front of the world and inches from his wife, in broad daylight, a crystal clear message to the world that "we" can kill *anyone*, and also that "we" are in charge now. This was treasonous murder and, even further, an American coup d'état. Everyone involved in the planning, organizing, and execution of this, by definition, qualifies as a psychopath.

When the CIA creates programs that backfire, they call it "blowback" or "unintended consequences" when the truth of the matter is that the creators of these undertakings are just not bright enough to see the long-term ramifications of their harebrained schemes. As good as these people are at manipulation and intimidation, they are, as psychologist Andrew Lobaczewski categorized them, "psychopaths that are typically of below-average intelligence." In plain English, they are stupid and lack the critical thinking skills needed to foresee the end result, or ramifications, of their plans. They are only able see one-step, immediate results; hence we have programs such as ZR/RIFLE that end up causing many times more problems than they do good. The author also tends to wonder how bright the presidents are that give the nod to such programs. It should be intuitively obvious that a program to murder other heads of state, and especially ones that are staffed by organized crime members, ex-Nazis, CIA psychopaths, and other murders—could be co-opted to blow your head off. Further, would not having a program like this be an open invitation for another head of state to return the "favor?"

Let us now take a look at ZR/RIFLE and some of these possibilities. In 1962, Allen Dulles gave the program to CIA case officer William Harvey to develop. Harvey made handwritten notes of a rough outline of the program that contained the overall operations concepts of the ZR/RIFLE program. Harvey's notes have been released by the National Archives over a period of years, the most recent of which were released on April 25, 1995. Even so, only nine pages have been found of a total of forty-three. Different pages survived in different places in the archives. Some areas were blacked out in one batch, but not the same areas were blacked out in all of the documents. Therefore an almost complete record of Harvey's outline has been synthesized.

Most of this work was done by researcher Anna Marie Kuhns-Walko, who worked for Noel H. Twyman, author of the excellent book, *Bloody Treason: The Assassination of John F. Kennedy*. Twyman published the entire transcript of Harvey's existing notes, which even though not complete, gave a great deal of insight into the construct of this operation. Many of the basic principles, or one could say essential elements, of the ZR/RIFLE program were strikingly similar to the JFK assassination, in fact too similar to be mere coincidence. Below is a summary of the essential elements of Twyman's compilation of these released documents, especially those that were reminiscent of the JFK assassination.[70] (Clarifications in parentheses are Twyman's; emphasis has been added by this author):

[70.] Noel H. Twyman, *Bloody Treason: The Assassination of John F. Kennedy*, (Kindle Edition: Laurel Mystery Books, 2010, Location 10283.

PROJECT ZR/RIFLE
(Harvey's Notes)

Identification: The purpose of Project ZR/RIFLE is to spot, develop, and use agent assets for Division D operations (covert operations).

Agents will be spotted in several areas, including the United States, *but for operational security reasons will probably not be used in their countries of residence*. Present developmental activity is being conducted in the WE (Western Europe) and EE (Eastern Europe) areas, but it is anticipated that this will be extended to other division areas. The project will be operated against third-country installations and personnel.

(Note to reader: The following statement of "objective: was obviously written by Harvey to conceal the true nature of the project. The Church Committee and the inspector general confirm this. There is no doubt that these notes are for Project ZR/RIFLE and for assassinations.)

Objectives: The objective of this project is the procurement of code and cipher materials (read professional assassins) and information concerning such materials, in accordance with requirements levied on the clandestine services, primarily by the National Security Agency (NSA). Since these requirements are subject to frequent revision, *no listing of targets would be valid for the duration of the project*. Specific operations will be mounted on the basis of need and opportunity. The project will be conducted by Division D with assistance from area divisions and stations as needed.

Background: In response to the increasing requirements for the operational procurement of freight code and cipher materials, Division D in 1960 began the spotting of agent assets as a developmental activity. During the same period requirements from NSA became more refined and, in many respects, more sensitive. Because most stations are not equipped to conduct this type of operation and because of the desirability of completely centralized control over this entire effort, it was determined that Division D, which is in closest touch with NSA on procurement requirements, could best conduct the activity. The spotting activity has now advanced far enough to justify removing from the DDA (Deputy Director of Administration) category.

Operational Assets:

Personnel: QJWIN[71] is under written contract as a principal agent, with the primary task of spotting agent candidates. QJWIN was first contacted in 1958 through the Chief of the Luxembourg I.S. by the Chief of Station, Luxembourg, *in connection with an illegal narcotics operation into the United States.* For a period of a year and a half he was contracted sporadically by COS (Chief of Station) Luxembourg, in behalf of the Bureau reflect an excellent performance by QJWIN. In October 1960 . . .

. . . *require most professional, proven operationally competent, ruthless, stable, CE-experienced (counter espionage) OPC officers (few available), able to conduct patient search and w/guts to pull back if instinct or knowledge tells him he should, and w/known high regard for operational security assessments.*

Maximum security:

Kubark (CIA) only . . . *no approach to other government agencies.*

Within Kubark, one focal point for control, search, tracing, case officering etc. DDP authority in this focal point mandatory, DCI (Director of Central Intelligence) officially advised?

. . . *No approach to officials of foreign governments* . . . .

---

71. QJWIN was the code name for the principle assassin recruiter for ZR/RIFLE, and he is strongly suspected to have been in Dallas with a team of shooters, on November 22, 1963. CIA director Richard Helms testified that he "just could not recall" this individuals name, nor has anyone seen this person's name mentioned in association with this code name.

. . . *No use of any agent who has worked for a U.S. government agency.* Tracing?

. . . *no discussion in stations, i.e. no "steam" until ready to go . . .*

No American citizens or (illegible) *or people who have obtained U.S. visas.*

No meeting any candidates in home territory.

. . . *Cover: Planning should include provisions for blaming Soviets or Czechs in case of blow.*

. . . *Should have phony 201 in RF to backstop this, all documents therein forged and backdated. Should look like a CE file.*

. . . *One focal point for search, control, tracing, case-officer and P.A. selection. Complete DDP authority in this focal point mandatory.*

. . . *No American citizens or Corsican nationals for* (illegible); *possibly for approach to—no criminal who is tainted by use of other American agency. Use of case officers who can pass as foreigners—and limited official reference.*

No choice of conversations permitting blackmail.

. . . *Corsicans recommended. Sicilians could lead to Mafia.* (*A possible source for agents*) . . . .

These concept notes have key elements that were also in the JFK hit. There is solid evidence that Corsican contract killers were directly involved in the execution phase of the assassination, most likely behind the "grassy knoll" where there was a wall and a picket fence. At least one, and possibly two, of the teams that were actually trigger pullers were very likely Corsican Mafia, and there are several reasons for this. The first reason is that Corsicans are famous for not talking even when tortured. There has never been a case where a Corsican in custody anywhere in the world has succumbed to threats, intimidation, coercion, or even outright torture. They will, and have, killed themselves first.

Corsican organized crime, usually referred to as "Corsican Mafia," is not like a mirror image of the Sicilian Mafia, the latter of which is organized much like the military. Corsican criminal factions are not organized in a hierarchy where orders come from the top down to the bottom. It is laterally organized by function, and the glue that holds it together is the shared values of the organization. This sounds strange, but all organizations have values; these being simply what are important to the organization individually and collectively. Sicilian and American mafiosi have the code of silence, omertá, which is enforced largely by fear, whereas Corsican counterparts will not talk because of the sense of identity that a Corsican has. That is not to say there would not be consequences for talking, but the value strikes at the heart of what a Corsican is, and this makes them very desirable when deniability is essential.

The second reason is that it would be more difficult to link Corsicans to the CIA, the Secret Service, the FBI, or American organized crime. If Corsicans were captured and would not talk, it would be difficult to link them to anything American. The CIA concept of "plausible deniability" would be maintained.

When Harvey's notes mention that assassins would not be used in their country of origin for security reasons, he is referring to the fact that it is easier to maintain control of a "shooter" if he is not in surroundings that he is familiar with and does not speak the language. The shooter is less likely to run if things do not go as planned because he does not know the surrounding and is not a native speaker of the language. It therefore would be difficult for this individual to try to run and fit in to the surroundings. In a foreign country, the would-be assassin is almost totally dependent on his handlers. Oswald would not be a good choice for an assassin, but he would—and was—perfect as a patsy.

Notice Harvey's reference to QJWIN as having been involved in the illegal importation of narcotics into the United States. In the early 1960s, this would most likely mean that he was affiliated with the "French Connection," which along with the CIA and organized crime, was in control of importing heroin into the United States. Since QJWIN would not have been an American, this would indicate that this person was most likely a Corsican; and we also have another link between the CIA, drugs, and assassinations. Further, the description of an ideal candidate is a thumbnail sketch of a psychopath. The words Harvey used to describe this person, such as competent, ruthless, stable, etc., are descriptive of a psychopath.

Harvey's notes also refer to no use of anyone that has worked for a (US) government agency, no approach to foreign governments and not US citizens, and no approach to (US) government agencies. It is self-evident that Harvey is outlining a deniable assassination program run by the CIA with no oversight, and he pretty much says that in his notes. Nowhere does he even infer that this program is monitored by anyone or any agency including the president. When and if President Eisenhower approved this program, it is highly unlikely that it was presented in this form. How much of this program was JFK briefed on when he took office, or was he even briefed at all? It cannot be ignored that what Harvey is describing is a veritable blueprint for the JFK assassination. Could this out-of-control program run by ethically and morally bankrupt individuals have been used, or parts of it, to assassinate a sitting president?

Was this what Harry S. Truman, thirty-third president of the United States, was talking about in 1961 when he famously stated, "I never would have agreed to the formulation of the Central Intelligence Agency back in forty-seven, if I had known it would become the American gestapo." Truman was president when the National Security Act of 1947 became law. We have already seen where this act only mentioned clandestine activities "from time to time," not constant and concerted efforts to overthrow sovereign governments, assassinate heads of state, and conduct these actions with no oversight. And was this what Eisenhower was also referring to when in his farewell address, he talked at length of uncontrolled power that threatens the foundations of democracy? What an unusual thing for a president to be speaking about in his last formal address to the American people. Why would President Truman talk specifically about the CIA and use such a provocative term as *gestapo*?

Further, what would these two presidents that were in key positions during WWII tell the newly elected president? World War II was probably the most formative period in the history of the new American Republic. The nation that emerged was much different than the one that went into it. The forerunner to the CIA, the OSS, had considerable power with very little oversight, and this is a formula for abuse. Also, this clandestine agency had an end-justifies-the-means-philosophy, which is a formula for certain abuse and future trouble for the young republic. Were these the reasons that President John F. Kennedy virtually came through the White House doors, confronting the awesome power of the CIA, FBI, organized crime, right wing fanatics, and extreme factions in the Pentagon? Was he intent on either reforming or destroying these rogue elephants that had taken on lives of their own? Had a coup already taken place and Kennedy was trying to get the American Republic back on track, or were the Kennedys creating a dynasty that arguably could have lasted over fifty years? Whichever it was, John F. Kennedy walked into a hornet's nest of psychopaths that would do anything to remain in power.

Chapter Seven

A Likely JFK Assassination Scenario

The author is an avid reader and, as such, wants to know who did what to whom when it comes to literature about crimes. In lieu of this, we will explore a likely, or probable, sequence of events concerning the JFK assassination. An in-depth analysis of all the contributing evidence to reach these conclusions would entail, at least, writing a complete book about this subject. Because this criminal act is but one part in this writing, the reader needs to keep in mind that the author has synthesized the following from many sources. There had been hundreds of books on this subject alone. Many of these have been well done, and almost all of them have contributed something to the overall picture. Some of the best have been cited in this writing. Keeping this in mind, the following is presented as the most likely scenario that resulted in "the crime of the century." The author will try to indicate when an issue most probably happened a certain way, and when it has been established beyond a doubt. So let us begin.

The United States emerged from World War II with intelligence agencies that had an "end justifies the means" philosophy. They also tended to see only the immediate objectives and not have the capacity to foresee the long-term consequences of their actions. This tendency was especially prevalent in the CIA. Simply stated, the CIA incorporated and used organized crime and drug dealers to accomplish their immediate objectives. As we have seen in the case of Southeast Asia, the CIA has gone so far as to be directly involved in creating drug trafficking operations to pursue their objectives. At the time of the Kennedy assassination, almost all the heroin coming into the United

States arrived via the "French Connection"; and much of it, prior to the Castro administration, came through Cuba.

Even after the Castro takeover of the Cuban government, a considerable amount of heroin came into the United States through Cuba, and the Bay of Pigs veterans played a major role in this. Operation Eagle, a 1970 federal roundup of 150 drug trafficking suspects, was considered to be the largest of its kind in history. A surprising 70 percent of the suspects were found to have been part of the CIA's Bay of Pigs invasion force. This indicates that the drug trade, along with gambling and prostitution, was a major factor in the CIA and Mafia's motivation in regaining control of Cuba. Also, Castro had nationalized large US businesses in Cuba, and this had enraged the business community. The CIA's use of drug traffickers, drug money, and organized crime figures to attempt to overthrow the Castro regime set the stage for the Kennedy assassination. These actions and related activities set in motion a cascade of events that spun out of control for the CIA, FBI, Pentagon, organized crime, and also the Kennedy administration.

Authors such as Fletcher Prouty and Robert Morrow have thoroughly discussed how it was assumed that Richard M. Nixon would win the election and assume office in 1960. Nixon already headed up secret operations to overthrow the Castro regime. He knew all the players in the entire operation. When John F. Kennedy won the election, with the help of mob boss Sam Giancana and organized labor, no one knew what to expect; but those who helped put JFK in office believed that the Kennedy administration would have some appreciation for their efforts. They did not, and especially in the area of organized crime. Robert F. Kennedy in particular showed no "consideration" for the mob. There were also huge defense contracts up in the air, and the big wild card was a top secret Bay of Pigs invasion. Add to this that Nixon had been very friendly with certain organized crime figures, and the Kennedys not only did not have these relationships, but showed outright contempt for the mob, especially Carlos Marcello.

Not only were the Kennedys' intentions not known, they were largely not trusted. Some of this had to do with Joseph Kennedy Sr.'s ambassadorship to Great Britain prior to World War II. Kennedy was widely perceived as being critical of Great Britain and supportive of Nazi Germany. Whether this perception was real or imagined, it was indeed prevalent. Apparently, Joseph Kennedy Sr. believed that Great Britain had no chance of winning a war against Nazi Germany, and that the United States would do best to stay out of it. This did not go over well with the British leadership, and Ambassador Kennedy was recalled by President Roosevelt. Although the Kennedy family supported the war effort to the maximum extent, this negative perception persisted even after the war.

Along with this was the suspicion that Joseph Kennedy Sr. was trying to create a Kennedy dynasty that would last at least a half century. As author Robert D. Morrow explained very well, if JFK played his cards right, Robert Kennedy would succeed him, after eight years; and after RFK would be Edward "Teddy" Kennedy. Once established, the Kennedy children and grandchildren could continue the "dynasty." This, in fact, is exactly how the Kennedys were perceived by the CIA and the Pentagon. Author and CIA operative Morrow explained in *First Hand Knowledge* that JFK knew since 1960 that the Soviets had put offensive medium—and intermediate-range nuclear missiles into Cuba but did not act on this until just before the midterm elections. Morrow and most of the CIA believed that the Republicans would have gained a majority of seats in the House and also the Senate had Kennedy not pulled off his confrontation with Cuba at the time that he did. Kennedy looked strong in the eyes of the American voter, and they voted for Democrats in these crucial elections.

The Bay of Pigs invasion fiasco brought the conflict between the Kennedy administration and the CIA to a crescendo. The resentment that the anti-Castro Cubans and the CIA felt cannot be understated. Probably because CIA Director Allen Dulles and Deputy Director Charles Cabell did not trust Kennedy and could not predict how he would react, they failed to brief him on crucial facts prior to the invasion. Facts such as the CIA had arranged to murder all of Kennedy's nominations for the proposed top positions in a free Cuban government were not briefed for obvious reasons. Much has been said about JFK's refusal to provide air cover. However, Col. Fletcher Prouty has emphatically stated that both the CIA and JFK knew that they had to take out *all* of the Cuban air force. When that did not happen, Prouty said that JFK was never asked to have US air power take out the few remaining fighters that were still functional. He added that the request went to McGeorge Bundy who did not understand that the invasion would be doomed if even a few Cuban fighters were operational. Bundy refused the request and the invasion failed. Kennedy had also delayed the invasion several times which the Cuban anti-Castro mastermind of the invasion, Mario Kohly, said allowed Castro time to destroy the resistance movement fighters inside Cuba.

On the day of the invasion, Dulles was strangely incommunicado. Apparently, he was at a speaking engagement and out of the loop. When the invasion started to unravel, this left the CIA deputy director, Air Force General Charles Cabell, in the position of having to authorize air support for the faltering invasion. If he had just gone ahead and given the green light, the invasion probably would have succeeded. Not sure of what the Kennedy administration's position was, he called the White House to authorize air support. The answer, from Bundy, was a resounding "no." Cabell later said that he realized that he had really screwed up by asking this question. There is an old military saying that it is far better to "beg for forgiveness than ask for permission" or phrased differently, "if you can't stand the answer, then don't ask the question." Cabell asked the question three more times, in different ways, but the answer came back the same resounding *NO!* It is possible that if Dulles was at the helm, where he should have been, the outcome could have been much different. No one will ever know.

There was plenty of blame to go around in both the Kennedy administration and also the CIA for the hundreds of brave Cuban patriots and CIA personnel killed that day. No matter who was wrong or right, anyone who will get on a ship and land on a beach facing enemy fire for a cause has courage and the author's utmost respect. These brave men and women who fought and died for this cause were also idolized by the entire anti-Castro community that blamed JFK for this dismal failure. This community was beyond angry against the Kennedy administration. Mario Kohly said about JFK when it was clear that tens of thousands of the Cuban resistance had been rounded up, "I say we kill the son of a bitch." Robert Morrow heard him but ignored it given the situation. The free Cuba movement was demoralized and very, very angry. Some of them would be used in the assassination.

The fact that Operation 40 and Mario Kohly's personnel were going to slaughter the CRC cabinet members, handpicked by the Kennedy administration, as soon as they arrived in Cuba threw JFK into a rage. Kennedy famously promised that he would "splinter the CIA into a thousand pieces," and he proceeded to do just that. He gave Secretary of Defense Robert McNamara the job of revoking the CIA's power.[72] JFK also directed that a new intelligence agency be formed in the Defense Department, and that CIA operatives that obtained intelligence about offensive missiles in Cuba be transferred to it. He directed other strong actions to reign in the power of the CIA. Vice President Johnson found out about these actions and documented, in detail, all of the actions President Kennedy was going to take. He then gave this document, with vice presidential letterhead, to the CIA. This alarmed and alerted the agency to exactly what the president had in mind and also put LBJ on the side of those in stark disagreement with the Kennedy administration. LBJ had raised his true colors, and he certainly had no sense of loyalty to his president. The CIA's very survival was being threatened, and this included the careers of all of its top leaders, including Allen Dulles.

LBJ's Role

Another career that was threatened was that of Vice President Lyndon Baines Johnson himself. Not only his career, but his reputation and actual freedom were at stake. The previously mentioned Billy Sol Estes and Bobby Baker scandals that were brewing had the potential to put LBJ in jail and for a long time. As long as he was in office, he could not be prosecuted. However, if he was not on the upcoming "ticket," he was ruined, and he knew it. If he was president of the United States and in control of the executive branch of government, he could squelch any attempt at prosecuting him. It was fairly well known that JFK was going to drop LBJ off the ticket for the next term. In fact, JFK said exactly that to his secretary, Evelyn Lincoln, just prior to departing on the fatal trip to Dallas.[73] It would be the last time they talked.

Evelyn Lincoln had a pretty good idea as to what happened to her boss, and when she was asked about it, she so stated "her take" of the assassination. Author Noel H. Twyman received a copy of a letter from Ms. Lincoln to a schoolteacher, Richard Duncan, at Northside Middle

---

[72.] Robert D. Morrow, *First Hand Knowledge: How I Participated in the CIA-Mafia Murder of President Kennedy*, (136 West 22nd Street, New York, NY 10011: SPI Books/Shapolsky Publishers, Inc., 1994), 76.

[73.] Noel H. Twyman, *Bloody Treason: The Assassination of John F. Kennedy*, (Laurel Publishing; Kindle Edition, January 16, 2010), Location 1167.

School in Roanoke, Virginia, in which she shared her insights into the JFK assassination. The letter has been authenticated, and the following is what she had to say:[74]

> Dear Richard:
>
> It was a pleasure to receive your kind letter concerning your desire to obtain my assessment of President Kennedy's administration and assassination to pass along to your students.
>
> I am sending along to you an article which was written by Muriel Pressman for the "Lady's Circle" October 1964, and was recently reprinted in a current issue of that magazine, which will give you an insight into my impression of the Man.
>
> As for (sic) the assassination is concerned it is my belief that there was a conspiracy because there were those that disliked him and felt the only way to get rid of him was to assassinate him. *These five conspirators, in my opinion, were Lyndon B. Johnson, J. Edgar Hoover, the Mafia, the CIA and the Cubans in Florida* (emphasis added). The House Intelligence Committee investigation, also, came to the conclusion that there was a conspiracy.
>
> My very best wishes to you and your students.
>
> Sincerely,
> [signed] Evelyn Lincoln

This letter was written about October 1994. Mrs. Lincoln died seven months later on May 11, 1995. She was eighty-six years of age. The author believes that she had it about right. She should have been taken more seriously.

As we have seen, Johnson did confess, and there is other evidence that he at least knew about the assassination ahead of time. There is proof beyond a reasonable doubt that he covered up the assassination. This means that there was sufficient evidence to indict Vice President

---

74. Ibid, Location 21076.

Johnson for first-degree murder. Johnson should have been tried for treason as well. No democracy can tolerate this sort of behavior from officials that the people have put their utmost trust in and hope to survive. These wounds cannot heal on their own. The Republic cannot just say that it was unfortunate, but we have to go on. These extreme actions have torn the very soul out of the country, as did the Native American genocide along with slavery and its long shadow. All these are festering wounds that will not heal.

Hoover's Role

Another candidate for indictment should have been FBI director John Edgar Hoover. Hoover created the FBI, and it was literally "his baby." He was coming up on the mandatory retirement age of seventy, and it was widely believed that the age limit would not be extended, by Kennedy, for him to stay as director. Both of the Kennedy brothers despised Hoover and often showed it. Bobby Kennedy was reported to do things like summon Hoover to his office like he was a clerk. Both Kennedy brothers would tell people that complained about Hoover "not to worry about it . . . he will not be around much longer." Things of this sort must have gotten back to Hoover because he was acutely aware that his job was in jeopardy. The only way for him to stay on the job as director was for Johnson to assume the office of president, given the fact that it was an almost certainty that JFK would be reelected and J. Edgar Hoover was going to be out of a job that was his only reason for being. It was his whole life.

Both Johnson and Hoover had connections to organized crime. This has been substantiated by many authors and researchers. As unlikely as it seems, Hoover and top gangster Meyer Lansky regularly met for dinner.[75] Hoover also had trouble even acknowledging that there was even such a thing as organized crime or the Mafia presumably because he did not want to prosecute them. As we have seen, Hoover had to be forced, mostly by Attorney General Bobby Kennedy, to prosecute anything other than cases that did not involve organized crime; and there are several reasons for this. It has been widely written

---

[75.] Michael Collins Piper, *Final Judgment: The Missing Link in the JFK Assassination*, (American Free Press, Sixth Edition, 2004), 81.

that Meyer Lansky, along with the CIA's James Jesus Angleton, had photos of Hoover engaged in homosexual acts with his deputy Clyde Tolson. This is believed to be the reason he did not prosecute organized crime. He stuck to prosecuting those he saw as "anti-American," communist, homosexuals, African Americans, and so forth. He went after those that did not have any compromising pictures of him. Author and retired FBI agent M. Westley Swearingen, who wrote *To Kill a President: Finally—an Ex-FBI Agent Rips Aside the Veil of Secrecy That Killed JFK*, also established that Hoover's biological father was black. This seems counterintuitive that this rabid racist would have African heritage, but this appears to be the case. It is not unheard of for people who do not think very much of themselves to attack those that have similar attributes. Hoover had snakes in his head. He was a very dangerous man especially when one considers that he was a very powerful man and he was about to lose this power. It appears that Hoover cared about the reputation of the FBI more than he did of its effectiveness. His priority was of reputation and appearance only.

There is another reason that Hoover did not go after real crime and real criminals. For law enforcement, it is much easier and safer to prosecute low-level, powerless "street criminals" than to go after real gangsters. It is safer simply because they are less likely to shoot back or fight back. You have a better chance of getting a conviction against powerless people. A professional gangster has access to excellent legal representation. Someone who has been "busted" for selling marijuana generally does not have access to expensive legal counsel. Minor street criminals have virtually no connection to power. An investigator can pull in one person off the street and make him or her think that they are going to do umpteen years in jail if they don't talk. This "game" is sometimes called "roll over Beethoven." It doesn't matter whether the "suspect" is guilty or not, nor is it important that the people named are guilty of anything. The vast majority of these mostly low-level criminals, at best, plea bargain. They do little or no time, the FBI agent gets a good rating based on how many arrests made, the prosecutors establish a good conviction rate, and a lot of minorities get taken off the voting rolls. Everyone in power is happy. This formula would apply to relatively minor drug offenses, so-called Communists, dissident college students, war protestors, and so forth. This is how the FBI and other law enforcement agencies made their name as "crime fighters."

This whole system has been documented by Rodney Stich, author of *Drugging America: A Trojan Horse*.[76] This feeds the "prison industrial complex" to the tune of 2,424,279 Americans in jail in 2008, and this was the average number in jail on any given day, a snapshot if you will. It is not the total in and out over the period of a year. This is the highest incarceration rate in the "developed" world, and a disproportionate number are minorities, most of whom are taken off the voting rolls. We will be discussing this in more detail in my next book. Hoover had a nice little gig until the Kennedys showed up and forced him to go after real gangsters, his buddies. J. Edgar Hoover has been described by most people that knew him as "a man with absolutely no redeeming qualities whatsoever." Hoover was a rabid racist who had no black agents in the bureau. He was a homosexual who hated and persecuted homosexuals. One of the few "friends" he had was Lyndon Johnson, and if he became president, all of Hoover's problems with the Kennedys would evaporate.

Hoover knew JFK was going to be assassinated, and he knew exactly where and when it would take place. He got this from several sources, one of whom was author Dick Russell's *The Man Who Knew Too Much*, Richard Case Nagell.[77] Nagell was a CIA counterespionage double agent who sent a registered letter in September 1963 to Hoover, warning him that "Lee Harvey Oswald" was involved in a conspiracy to" murder the chief executive of the United States, John F. Kennedy." He went into enough detail that anyone would not take this as a crank letter. Hoover and the FBI denied ever receiving the letter. Nagell also formally notified the Warren Commission and the House Select Committee on Assassinations of what he knew, and he knew a lot. He was never called to testify before either of these agencies.

There is proof beyond a reasonable doubt that J. Edgar Hoover covered up the assassination and that he also destroyed and forged evidence of the same. He even ordered his agents to destroy any evidence that reflected unfavorably on the FBI. He intimidated the Warren Commission members by letting them know that he

---

76. Rodney Stich, *Drugging America: A Trojan Horse*, (Kindle Edition: Silverpeak Enterprises, December 8, 2006)
77. Dick Russell, *The Man Who Knew Too Much*, (Carroll & Graf Publishers, 245 West 17th Street, New York, NY, 10011), 9.

had dossiers on each of them of embarrassing information. He also interfered with New Orleans District Attorney Jim Garrison's investigation of the assassination and the trial of Clay Shaw for the murder of JFK. Again, Hoover was guilty of murder in the first degree and treason.

Hoover surrounded himself with bootlickers and toadies, and he got rid of anyone that did not do exactly as he wanted done. It is likely that Hoover directed and controlled most, if not all, of the cover-up operations within the FBI. Of course, there are always those around that know exactly what the boss wants without a word being said. Therefore it is likely that many within the FBI were guilty of criminal behavior in relation to the JFK assassination, but had it not been for J. Edgar Hoover, the FBI would probably not have been a player in the crime of century.

Richard Helms and the CIA

This cannot be said of the CIA. "The company" was in it from very high up to the very bottom. When the assassination happened, the director was John McCone, who had been placed there by the Kennedys. McCone was not well respected and was kept "out of the loop" by the rest of the agency. The person who was actually calling the shots was the deputy director of plans, Richard Helms, who later would be the director of the CIA under Johnson. Helms came from the old Office of Strategic Services or OSS. During World War II, he helped organize guerilla warfare, sabotage, and espionage against the enemies of the United States and its allies. After the war ended, he joined the newly formed CIA, and he worked for Frank Wisner, who was the Directorate of Plans or DPP. DPP was actually a nice sounding title for what is more accurately referred to as clandestine operations or "dirty tricks." This actually means assassinations, overthrowing regimes unpopular with the United States, sabotage, and other activities that the CIA and the United States do not admit to.

Wisner ended up having a mental breakdown and was replaced by Richard Bissell. Helms was his deputy, and together they became responsible for the CIA's black operations. Within these operations came to be a policy later known as Executive Action. Simply put, this was an operation designed to murder heads of state that the United States had decided were too inconvenient to deal with in conventional ways. Sometime in 1960, the operation, or teams, set up to actually do this was code named ZR/RIFLE, designed and managed by a name we have seen before, William Harvey. Bissell and Helms used the resources in Executive Action to overthrow the democratically elected government of Jacobo Arbenz, president of Guatemala, in 1958. His crime was to introduce land reforms, and he nationalized the United Fruit Company. These two acts were considered "not friendly to the United States." The United Fruit Company was also active in the drug traffic that came into the United States through New Orleans. Carlos Marcello's crime syndicate made sure there were no "labor disputes" on the docks to ensure that fresh fruit does not spoil waiting to be unloaded.

Other political leaders deposed by Executive Action included Patrice Lumumba of the Congo, Rafael Trujillo of the Dominican Republic, General Abd al-Karim Kassem of Iraq (replaced by none other than Saddam Hussein), the overthrow of the democratically elected government of Iranian Prime Minister Mohammad Mosaddegh in 1953, and Ngo Dinh Diem who was the premier of South Vietnam. This last coup was done about two weeks before JFK was murdered. These were some busy boys, and we did not cover all the coups that resulted from Executive Action. Of course, the big one that Helms and many others under him were after was Fidel Castro. Helms hid from the Warren Commission the joint Mafia and CIA attempts to assassinate Castro using Operation Mongoose out of the JM/WAVE station. Helms was later called before the Senate Foreign Relations Committee when it began investigating the CIA in 1975. Senator Stuart Symington asked Helms if the agency had been involved in the removal of Chilean President Salvador Allende. Helms lied to the committee and stated an unequivocal "no." He also lied about providing funds to Allende's opponents that resulted in his overthrow and murder. He further lied to and/or hid evidence from the Warren Commission, the CIA's inspector general, the House Select Committee on Assassinations, and the Select Committee on Intelligence Activities (also referred to as the Church Committee).

Richard Helms believed that he and the CIA were above the law. He even commented that he had the authority to assassinate heads of state without informing the president. He said this authority was "inherent in his position." He obviously believed that the "end justifies the means." It is also obvious that this was a man who believed that if someone gets in his way, he will kill them. This was his mode of operation and identical to that of organized crime. Helms killed just about everyone and anyone that got in his way before the JFK murder and afterward, and JFK was in his way. He blamed Kennedy for the Bay of Pigs fiasco and then saw Kennedy methodically go about dismantling the CIA. Having access to assassination teams, top levels of organized crime, fanatic right-wing groups, and control of the enraged anti-Castro movement, and also the US media, all he would had to do was give the green light. These groups and many others had their own grudges against Kennedy. Helms would also have known that Johnson and Hoover would not only also nod, but they could and would cover the assassination up. Helms was convicted of lying to Congress and was given a two-year suspended sentence. In its final report issued in April 1976, the Select Committee on Intelligence Activities concluded, "Domestic intelligence activity has threatened and undermined the Constitutional rights of Americans to free speech, association and privacy. It has done so primarily because the Constitutional system for checking abuse of power has not been applied."

The Media

An important area that Helms had control over was the US media and, as ominous as it sounds, the world media. His control was through a CIA program identified as Operation Mockingbird, and this was critical in covering up the assassination plan. The Church Committee commented extensively on this decidedly undemocratic and unconstitutional threat to a free and independent press. By analyzing CIA documents, Church was able to identify over fifty US journalists who were directly employed by the CIA. The Church Committee also determined that there were many times that number of US journalists that were "being paid regularly for their services, to those who received only occasional gifts and reimbursements from the CIA."[78] This was only the tip of the iceberg. The Church Committee revealed that the CIA virtually controls the major US media and also much of the foreign media.

---

78. Final Report of the Select Committee to Study Governmental Operations with Respect to Intelligence Activities, (April 1976), 195

These were not small-town reporters in small-town newspapers that we are talking about here. One of the most important journalists under the control of Operation Mockingbird was Joseph Alsop, whose articles appeared in over three hundred newspapers. Other journalists that were more than willing to promote the CIA's view of world events were Stewart Alsop (*New York Herald Tribune*), Ben Bradlee (*Newsweek*), James Reston (*New York Times*), C. D. Jackson (*Time* magazine), Walter Pincus (*Washington Post*), William C. Baggs (*Miami News*), Herb Gold (*Miami News*), and Charles Bartlett (*Chattanooga Times*). According to Deborah Davis, author of *Katharine the Great: Katharine Graham and her Washington Post Empire*, the CIA "'owned' respected members of the *New York Times*, *Newsweek*, CBS and other communications vehicles."[79] There is much more to Operation Mockingbird, but for our purposes, it is important to recognize that after the Bay of Pigs invasion, Richard Bissell, the Director of Plans, was forced to retire along with all of the top leadership on the CIA. This left Richard Helms as Director of Plans, which put him in control of the CIA's assassin teams and also control of the media using Operation Mockingbird. Some authors and investigators build a good case for others being the "mastermind" for the assassination, but it is more likely that Richard Helms played a key role in planning, organizing, coordinating, directing, and controlling the crime of the century. He had a lot of powerful help along the way, such as J. Edgar Hoover, LBJ, Carlos Marcello, Santo Trafficante, Sam Giancana, and possibly some even in the Secret Service. Richard Helms may or may not have been the impetus behind this crime, but he certainly put the plan in motion and also the cover-up.

Now we know why all we saw over the last forty-three years was the "lone assassin." The mainstream media had been and probably still is co-opted by the same forces that they are supposed to "check and balance." It is bad enough that many of the founders of the US media were extreme right-wing reactionaries to begin with. An example would be Time Inc. that published both *Time* and *Life* magazines in 1963. This company was founded by Henry and Clare Boothe Luce who were both well known for rather extreme right-wing

---

[79.] Deborah Davis, *Katharine the Great: Katharine Graham and Her Washington Post Empire*, (Sheridan Square Press, 1991), 130.

views. *Life* magazine was widely suspected of playing a role in altering photographic evidence in the JFK assassination. The author vividly recalls *Life* magazine's photo of the fatal shot to JFK's head and the red mist in front of his head. Everyone that saw that photo had to come to the conclusion that JFK was shot from behind. Many years later, we discover that the photo had been "enhanced" presumably to illustrate clearly what had happened. What *Life* magazine had done was, presumably, alter the photo to deceive their readers. Neither magazine published anything that the author recalls that did not support the lone-gunman, "magic bullet" theory. This continues to the present, and the rest of the media is just as guilty. Newspapers and news stations readership and viewership are down, and down so far that many are going out of business. One would think that this situation would cause the media to rethink their fundamental role in society, but no. What they do is rail against those that get their information over the Internet, stating that Americans only want to "see information they agree with." The author does not recall one survey on why people do not read and watch mainstream media anymore. We would be glad to tell them that we just cannot believe anything they say anymore. They are lying to us and expect us to pay them for it. No thanks. Virtually, the entire US media is guilty of complicity and conspiracy to cover up the murder of JFK, and let us not forget all the witnesses that were murdered. "Free and independent," not on your life. They took the bribes and ran. They sold their soul to the devil and gleefully entered the American heart of darkness. It is interesting to note that Andrew Lobaczewski's research disclosed that an elevated number of psychopaths reside in the media. What odds would one give that the money these media prostitutes were paid came from CIA and mob drug profits?

By the end of 1961, the Kennedy administration had forced Allen Dulles to retire as the director of the CIA. He was replaced with John McCone, who was not a CIA career man, and largely bypassed by the high-ranking career people. Richard Bissell, Director of Plans, was removed and replaced with Richard Helms. Tracy Barns was selected by Helms as the head of the new, super secret Domestic Operations Division. Note that the CIA's charter prohibits it from performing domestic intelligence. This is within the purview of the FBI, not the CIA. Domestic Operations Division is also referred to as the division of "dirty tricks." Barns selected E. Howard Hunt as Domestic Operations Division chief of covert activities. Yes, the same Hunt who was also infamous for the Watergate Hotel "break-in" that took down the Nixon administration. Others removed were Charles P. Cabell, deputy director of the CIA, and William Harvey, who created ZR/RIFLE and was a case officer for Johnny Rosselli in Operation Mongoose, the program working to assassinate Castro. There were other CIA personnel removed from office over the Bay of Pigs fiasco, but these are the most dramatic.

Organized Crime

At least by early 1962, evidence starts to come forth of a plan to assassinate JFK. By this time, Carlos Marcello had made threats to kill JFK and the anti-Castro Cubans along with several of the members of the top and middle echelons of the CIA, had to have been seriously thinking about it, if not already planning this act of treason. It is a certainty that a plan had been formulated by October 9, 1962. This was the date that Tracy Barns met with author and CIA operative Robert D. Morrow and briefed him that he (Barns) suspected that a plot was being formulated to assassinate JFK, and that it was out of New Orleans. In fact, the plan that Barns shared with Morrow was almost exactly what Jim Garrison concluded as a result of his investigation into Clay Shaw that resulted in Shaw's trial on January 29, 1969. Shaw was the only one to be tried because almost all the rest of the conspiracy had conveniently committed "suicide," had fatal "accidents," or in the case of Jack Ruby, died of one of the most virulent cases of cancer to be seen in the annals of medicine. Lung cancer can metastasize rapidly, but not very often is someone diagnosed with it and dies in less than a month. Jack Ruby claimed that a mysterious character came into the prison and injected him with something that caused him to get cancer. There is some evidence that CIA contract employees had been working on just such an injection to kill Castro, and this was underway in New Orleans. In fact, there are indications that David Ferrie was involved with this.

Barns had a meeting with Morrow October 9, 1962, the purpose of which was to get Morrow updated on the direction the CIA was going as far as getting rid of Castro. Morrow had been working on forging Cuban currency to destabilize the Cuban economy. Morrow and David Ferrie had flown into Cuba during the Bay of Pigs invasion to determine the status of the Soviet missile program in Cuba, and

Morrow had been involved with several other CIA programs. In the course of their discussion, Barns briefed Morrow about a plan coming together in New Orleans to murder JFK.[80] Barns stated that:

> If our suspicions are correct, *we have a New Orleans-based assassination team, operated with agency sanction under the direction of Clay Shaw and his organization . . . along with mob boss Carlos Marcello* (emphasis added).
>
> Now, about Jack Ruby's activities in Dallas. What I'm getting at is this: we suspect Jack is running an open narcotics business under the protection of the agency (CIA). If in fact he is, he knows we can't stop it without blowing our ZR/RIFLE program. To make matters worse, David Ferrie, who is supposed to be under our direct control is also operating with Marcello and Shaw . . . . Interestingly enough, most of Shaw's Dallas and New Orleans personnel were recruited from the Minute Men.

When Morrow asked Barns about who else could be involved, Barns went on to further explain:

> It could be Shaw's right arm and Ferrie's superior, a man in his forties named Guy Banister, a contract employee about whom I know very little. He's an ex-FBI man, the former Special-Agent in Charge of the Chicago office. In fact, he was Robert Maheu's boss. Maheu, as I'm sure you remember was the man who helped set up the Agency's Castro assassination attempt within the Mafia. You met his two contacts at Mario's place after the Bay of Pigs. Messrs. Rawlston and Gold—or I should say Mr. Johnny Roselli and Mr. Sam Giancana . . .
>
> Bannister also founded an organization called the Friends of Democratic Cuba (FDC) in January of last year. The FDC was originally an arm of the *Cuban Revolutionary*

---

80. Robert D. Morrow, *First Hand Knowledge: How I Participated in the CIA-Mafia Murder of President Kennedy*, (136 West 22nd Street, New York, NY 10011: SPI Books/Shapolsky Publishers, Inc., 1994), 162-175.

Front, which Kohly opposed as being full of former Castro people with the exception of Carlos Prio Socarras and New Orleans based Sergio Arcacha Smith. This was the group that attempted to take control of the Bay of Pigs invasion, afterward being known as the Cuban Revolutionary Council...

And what worries me is that a lot of people we used to count on are getting out of hand because of this new regime... Until now we had assumed that Banister was coordinating Jack's activities. Today, it could also be *Marcello and Shaw* (emphasis added). We're just not sure...

Morrow interjected that "Banister must have quite a crew," to which Barns filled in the details:

To be precise, several dozen; although only a few are in the inner circle. He uses Ferrie now more and more as a personal aide and pilot. There is also a young man named *Hugh Ward* (emphasis added) who is used as both a hatchet and research man, and a pilot by the name of Maurice Gatlin, Sr., who is supposed to be another of the Agency's inside men. Perhaps the most dangerous of all Bannister's men is *Carlos Rigal* (emphasis added), a hit man of French origin, whose Agency code name is *QJ/WIN* (emphasis added). He was spawned from *ZR/RIFLE* (emphasis added). I won't tell you his real name.

The conversation between Barns and Morrow continued. Morrow became convinced that Barns was alluding to an assassination plan coming out of Clay Shaw's group in New Orleans. Barns had also stated that this group was operating, as previously quoted, *with agency sanction!* The author surmises that Barns's boss, by inference, was the one who sanctioned this; and it might have come from as far up as the director at the time, John McCone. It is possible that Allen Dulles was also involved with this. It is a fact that Allen Dulles was a member of the Warren Commission and played a key role in the assassination cover-up. At any rate, it is apparent that Tracy Barns did not, on his own, give the order to allow the CIA operation in New Orleans to proceed with the assassination. Richard Helms was clearly in the operational chain on the assassination and possibly made the decision himself. Of course he would have had to have known that the green light had been given by the power structure. "Executive Action" assassinations came under Helms as Director of Plans, and he had plenty of experience at this in South America and Africa. Helms had control of the ZR/RIFLE assets to include the organizer, William Harvey, and also QJ/WIN, whose real name Helms had trouble recalling when he testified before the House Select Committee on Assassinations. To be sure he knew that name. Instead of invoking classification, sensitivity, state secrets, or some other plausible explanation for not divulging this name, Helms outright lied and stated he did not remember.

Richard Helms was up to his eyeballs in the JFK assassination, and he very likely was the mastermind of this treasonous "crime of the century." He had plenty of help, and he had to have known that that the Department of Defense, CIA, FBI, Secret Service, and all other agencies in the executive department would not go after those that planned and executed the assassination. Helms and the rest had to have known that JFK's successor and next chief of the executive department, Lyndon Baines Johnson, would cover for them, which he did. All of them had to have been also assured that the president's brother, Attorney General Robert F. Kennedy, would also be kept in check. He was slated to be a "toothless tiger" without his brother as the chief executive. This is exactly why the head mobsters—Marcello, Trafficante, and Giancana—were after JFK, although RFK is really the brother they despised most; and all three of them were known to have made statements to that effect.

Along with the mob and virtually the entire executive branch, JFK had the titans of industry and the entire "radical right" in the United States not only against him but wanting to see him dead. It even went further than that. These forces wanted everything that they lumped together as "the Kennedys," that is everything this political family stood for, eradicated by any and every means possible. They all gave an almost imperceptible nod for the assassination players to go ahead. These "nods" probably were conveyed during Georgetown poker games and on the golf courses frequented by the Washington power elite. The Kennedys were not invited to these poker games, nor did they play golf with this crowd. Also, Hoover, Johnson, chief justice of the Supreme Court Earl Warren, Warren Committee member Gerald Ford, and others were Freemasons, and John F. Kennedy was not. This is not to suggest that the assassination was a Masonic conspiracy. It is only to suggest that if JFK was a Freemason, there might have been enough hesitation on the part of the Masonic brothers to not murder him.

There were no memos or telephone conversations that said "kill Kennedy" or words to that effect. No board meetings. All it took were a few subtle phrases, such as "Something needs to be done about Kennedy . . . He is going to wreak the country," were all that was necessary. Recall Chip Tatum's explanation as to all Nixon had to say that made Operation Red Rock into a "one way" mission. All President Nixon said was "No one must ever know . . . ," and the CIA knew that he meant that the military personnel sent on this mission would be killed, a done deal. In the same manner, Barns and all the participants would know that no one in power would kick about it, and that it would be covered up. Of course, what they did not say or insinuate was that all the pawns were going to be "neutralized." Not only the pawns but all the pieces up to the mastermind, or masterminds, were slated to be "taken out." Who had the means to do this? The answer could only be organized crime and the CIA. But let us continue with the likely sequence of events.

At least toward the end of 1962, according to Tracy Barns, plans were being formulated for the assassination. According to Robert Morrow, mob boss Carlos Marcello took out a contract on JFK in April of 1963.[81] Also, the Cuban exile community was at a point that they felt the only way they were going to be able to retake Cuba would be if JFK was out of the way. The Kennedy administration had cut off all funds to the anti-Castro Cubans and other actions convinced them that they no longer had the administration's support. They threw their lot in with the mob. Jack Ruby was running drugs out of Cuba for Carlos Marcello that was financing part of the assassination. Clay Shaw had access to the infamous Permindex corporation. This was a CIA-front company that was used to launder money used for CIA dark projects. Shaw was on the board of directors. Entire books have

---

81. Robert D. Morrow, *First Hand Knowledge: How I Participated in the CIA-Mafia Murder of President Kennedy*, (136 West 22nd Street, New York, NY 10011: SPI Books/Shapolsky Publishers, Inc., 1994), 188.

been written about Permindex, and it has been widely suspected of financially backing the assassination.

Santo Trafficante put together a team that would go into Cuba ostensibly to assassinate Castro. The team was under the impression that they were acting at the behest of the CIA, and they were equipped with the CIA's best weapons and equipment. Trafficante had his lawyer deliberately leak to Castro enough details so that the team would be captured, and as a result of their inevitable torture, they would confess that they were CIA sent by the Kennedy administration. This was to blame Castro for the assassination as it was inevitable that Castro would announce something along the lines that JFK is putting himself in jeopardy by actions such as this because he would be vulnerable to the same sort of assassination schemes, hinting that he, Castro, might reciprocate. Actually, this scheme worked and Castro did make an announcement just as planned.

The whole idea was to get Kennedy out of the way and create a war with Cuba. It was not only the anti-Castro Cubans that wanted a war with Cuba. There were extreme right-wing elements in the Pentagon, organized religion, organized crime, US business, the CIA, the FBI, and also in the media that wanted to invade Cuba. Air force chief of staff Curtis LeMay actually wanted to do a nuclear first strike on the Soviet Union because he believed that there was an open window where the United States had such overwhelming nuclear superiority that the United States could annihilate the Soviet Union and only lose "a few million" Americans. LeMay, and others, believed that that window of opportunity would close in 1964, so according to this extreme ideology, it would be advisable to invade Cuba and do a nuclear first strike on the USSR; and as far as LeMay was concerned, the sooner, the better. This was the ideology that existed at that time in many powerful sectors of the US government and also the civil sector.

Some authors have David Ferrie as the mastermind of the assassination, but this is unlikely due to the fact that Ferrie was murdered as soon as it was announced that he was being investigated. Within hours of Garrison's announcement that Ferrie was also being investigated, he ended up dead, and this could not have been an impulse decision to take him out. The "mastermind" would have been the one that decided who was expendable and who was not. Obviously, this person would not rule himself as one to be done away with. It is, however, certain that Ferrie did much of the planning for the assassination, especially at the local level. Ferrie was the brains behind both Carlos Marcello and Clay Shaw, and as such, he selected Oswald as the patsy. The CIA had "sheep-dipped" Oswald as a Communist fanatic and malcontent for one reason. That reason was to go into the USSR as a counterespionage agent and bring Marina soon-to-be Marina Oswald out. There was a KGB Soviet intelligence colonel that wanted to defect to the United States, and Marina was the only blood relative. The Soviets were known to take unpleasant actions against relatives of defectors and CIA Counterintelligence chief James Jesus Angleton very much wanted what this KGB colonel knew. Lee Harvey Oswald was a counterintelligence operative and a pretty good one at that. He spoke Russian so well that Marina thought he was a native speaker when she first met him. When things went awry in Russia, Oswald went so far as to slash his wrists to convince the Russians that he was unstable, and they let him return, with Marina. Mission accomplished.

Oswald, however, had one fatal flaw. He would do exactly what he was told to do without questioning authority, and this was not altogether unusual for a marine, especially one that had been an orphan. Oswald desperately was trying to fit into the Marine Corps and later as a counterintelligence operative. As a teenager, he was fascinated with a popular TV program at the time, *I Led Three Lives*. This was a series about a double agent, the hero of which was in the United States pretending he was a Soviet spy when he actually was spying on Soviets for the United States. Oswald was active in the Civil Air Patrol (CAP), and actually was in David Ferrie's CAP unit. There are authentic photos of the two at CAP activities. Oswald's problems in the Marine Corps were undoubtedly part of the "sheep-dipping" procedure. He got into a minor fracas while in Japan to make him believable as a malcontent that wanted to defect to the Soviet Union.

David Ferrie recognized that Oswald would make the perfect patsy in the assassination, and he did a first-class job of setting him up as such. Obtaining the Carcano rifle, handing out the "Fair Play for Cuba" pamphlets, the radio debates, and all the rest were all staged. Oswald probably had the understanding that he was infiltrating leftist organizations. In Dick Russell's *The Man Who Knew Too Much*, Richard Case Nagell agreed that Oswald was the patsy but believed that Oswald was in the assassination plot "up to his eyeballs." Nagell believed that Oswald thought that he was going to be spirited out of the country to Cuba where he would be welcomed as a hero. This author believes that the preponderance of evidence is that Oswald thought that a staged assassination plot was going to happen in which Cuba would be implicated, and this would result in a US invasion of Cuba. Oswald most likely thought that his job was to plant evidence in the sixth floor of the Texas School Book Depository to that effect.

William Harvey's Role

Let us move on to another name that we have seen before that had to have played a key role in the assassination, and that would be William King Harvey. The CIA inspector general did a report in 1967 that investigated assassination plots against Castro. In the report was evidence that implicates several people in the CIA, organized crime, and others in the JFK assassination. One key name mentioned was Harvey, who apparently met with some interesting people in 1963. By 1963, Harvey had been relieved of his position as a result of his actions prior to and during the Bay of Pigs invasion. His career was over, and he was assigned to a nominal job in Rome, Italy. The report shows that Harvey had met Johnny Rosselli, a member of the Executive Action ZR/RIFLE team for the Bay of Pigs invasion, in Miami and Los Angeles in February 1963 and also in Washington DC in June 1963. This was long after Harvey had been removed from supervising the ZR/RIFLE program and after Harvey had told organized crime figures that Castro was no longer a target. Harvey also admitted to receiving a phone call from Rosselli in April 1963. What could be the reason these two were seeing each other?

Other documents released from the National Archives of Harvey's expense accounts show that he was in the Florida Keys in April 1963, and add to this that he was at a place long suspected to be an assassination training location. Harvey filed expense accounts with the following header: "Voucher—All Chargeable to OPS Expense QJ/WIN/ZR/RIFLE"[82] QJ/WIN was the code name for the top secret coordinator of the Executive Action assassination program. The above was exactly what Jim Garrison believed had happened in Dallas, and

---

82. Noel H. Twyman, *Bloody Treason: The Assassination of John F. Kennedy*, (Kindle E-Book, First Edition, 2010), Kindle location 11167-11174

that was that a CIA assassination team constructed to kill Castro had been turned against JFK. It is likely that QJ/WIN was in the Florida Keys and met with Harvey and others to plan the JFK assassination. Author Noel Twyman reviewed all of the voucher items and came to the following conclusions:

Harvey stayed at the Plantation Key, Florida, between April 13 and April 21. While staying there, he chartered a boat to go to another island; bought a round-trip airplane ticket from Chicago; paid for a room next to him for an unknown guest whose address was listed as 56510 Wilshire Boulevard, Los Angeles, California, an address that did not exist. He also put on the voucher dinner at the Fontainebleau Hotel and rooms at the Eden Roc Hotel. These were favorite places for known mob members such as Sam Giancana and Johnny Rosselli, both of whom made statements of involvement in the assassination. There was also an expense that referenced "ZR/RIFLE/MI, which would be a military intelligence component of an assassination team.[83] It is pretty clear that Harvey was not on vacation in Florida. In fact, he was very busy with phone calls, hosting several individuals, and making airline reservations that had something to do with assassinations. Further, he was supposed to be in Italy all this time. It looks like he was planning an assassination, and from the timing of it alone, it looks like the final arrangements were being made to kill JFK.

Big business titans, right-wing fanatics, the mob chiefs, Hoover, Lyndon Johnson, and other national politicians all gave the nod to go ahead. No, they probably did not have a meeting and vote on it, but the lackeys that worked for them, as always, were very good at reading the boss. For the plan to go into effect, the players had to have known that they had the approval of the power structure of the United States behind them. This was not done with meetings and no notes were passed or taken. There was no correspondence. There were not telephone calls. Very powerful people softly mentioned, "Something needs to be done about those Kennedy's . . ." and words to that effect. That was all that was needed. Of course, the crime bosses flat out said what they intended on doing, but by no means could they or would they have done it and gotten away with it without the nod from the

---

[83] Ibid, Kindle location 11207-11252.

power structure of the United States. They might have been able to do it, but to cover it up would be a completely different matter.

James Jesus Angleton

Although mentioned before, this person's role in the assassination cannot be overemphasized. Angleton, as counter intelligence chief, had his hands into every aspect of the JFK assassination. Always behind the scenes, Angleton's footprints were all over this operation from planning and execution to the cover-up. Although Angleton vehemently denied that Oswald was a counter intelligence operative sent into the Soviet Union as a spy, his office had a "201 file" on him. The House Select Committee on Assassinations had a difficult time getting Angleton and his people to define exactly what a 201 file was used for. The best that they could gather was that this file was used to either keep track of counter intelligence operatives of the CIA or suspected operatives of other nations.

However, Angleton and his office also denied that Oswald was suspected of being a Soviet operative. Their position was that they knew nothing of Oswald's defection to the Soviet Union, and that that was the FBI's responsibility. If Oswald was not a CIA agent or operator, and he also was not being tracked as a spy for the Soviet Union, why the 201 file? Someone was lying somewhere, and they were lying under oath at that. Many on the House Select Committee on Assassinations (HSCA) strongly suspected that Oswald was under the direction of the CIA when he "defected" to the USSR for this and several other reasons.

Let us recall that Oswald was a radar operator for the U-2 project at Atsugi Air Base, Japan. This was a highly classified CIA project. It is impossible to imagine that the CIA would take no interest in Oswald's defection to the USSR. Another flag goes up when we consider that Oswald entered the Soviet Union through Helsinki, Finland. This channel was only known and used by intelligence operatives and there were no commercial airline flights available at this time. How would Oswald have known how to do this? Add to this that Oswald got a humanitarian discharge from the Marine Corps because a candy box hit his mother in the nose? Try getting a discharge from the marines based on anything like this. And on top of this Oswald gets a passport and visas to defect to a communist country during the height of the Cold War within hours of his discharge? There is considerable evidence that Oswald was one of several ex-military who had been "sheep dipped" by Angleton to spy on the soviets. It is also interesting to note that the Russian friends whom Oswald hunted with considered him a poor shot, and would share some of the game for the day with him because he never was able to shot anything.[84]

As almost unbelievable as it may seem there is considerable evidence that there were actually two Oswalds, one went by Lee and the other by Harvey. There are also indications that these two Oswalds were both the creation of Angleton. They appeared to be almost indentical but there were differences. "Lee" Oswald was 5' 11" and "Harvey" was 5' 9". "Lee" had a front tooth missing, as evidenced in grade school pictures, but the body that was buried as Lee Harvey Oswald was exhumed and was *not* missing a tooth. This likely was "Harvey" who grew up in a Russian speaking community in New York. The whole story is probably far from being known but is a fascinating subject. More than just fascinating, the two Oswalds theory would fill in a lot of gaps, such as how the same person can be seen by credible witnesses in different places at the same time, and also the impossibility of Oswald having become fluent in the Russian language by reading Russian magazines in a barracks. Richard Helms, at the time the Director of the CIA, stated to a *Washington Post* reporter, 8/10/1978, that "No one would ever know who or what Lee Harvey Oswald represented . . ." This implies that he *did* know, and we can presume that Angleton also knew because Lee and Harvey Oswald were a creation of the CIA.

Angleton also had control of the "Executive action" assassination teams formed by William Harvey code named ZR/RIFLE. Recall Harvey's notes on this that the assassins would ideally be Corsicans, widely suspected to have been positioned on the Grassy Knoll, and that triggermen would have a phony 201 file (Let us not forget Oswald's 201 file). These teams were tucked into Angleton's counter intelligence unit and designated "Staff D." Harvey had an excellent working relationship with Angleton and after having been fired by the Kennedys (Harvey) would have had a motive to participate in the "crime of the

---

84. James DiEugenio, author, editor, Lisa Pease, editor, *The Assassinations: Probe Magazine on JFK, MLK, RFK and Malcolm X* (Washington: Feral House, 2003), Kindle Edition. Loc., 4750-56.

century." Angleton was a rabid anticommunist and as such viewed Kennedy as a traitor. This also would explain the deliberate trail created by Angleton to implicate the Cubans and the soviets in the JFK assassination.

Let us not forget the compromising pictures Angleton had of Hoover and his deputy director Clyde Tolson. With Hoover in his back pocket that put the entire FBI at his disposal. There is conclusive evidence that Hoover knew about the assassination well before it happened, but it is possible that he was not directly involved in the planning and execution of it. Angleton's pictures ensured that he would be in control of the FBI investigation and coverup of the assassination even if Hoover did not "do it." Angleton also had a working relationship with organized crime and the "godfather of all godfathers" Meyer Lansky. He was also the CIA liaison to the FBI, and also the liaison to the Israeli Mossad, which is Israel's intelligence service. He had a lot of power and specifically in the areas associated with assassinations.

Lisa Pease found that Angleton headed up the initiative to undermine Jim Garrison's prosecution of Clay Shaw in New Orleans. She even found evidence that Angleton was doing name traces of prospective jurors in the case.[85] Additionally, Angleton had a propensity for showing up when key witnesses were killed or died under suspicious circumstances and "sanitized" their personal effects. When Mexico City CIA station chief Winfield Scott died Angleton caught a plane so fast to Mexico City that he forgot his passport. He took charge of copious files and paperwork. Also when Mary Pinchot Meyer was gunned down while on an exercise run, Angleton was already on the way to her place. He ended up taking charge of her personal effects including her diary. The diary was suspected of having explosive information in it about the JFK assassination. Author Robert D. Morrow, a CIA agent, went into detail on how the CIA murdered Mary Pinchot Meyer and why.

The omnipresence of Angleton can also be seen in every facet of the assassination. Oswald was set up so pretty that he never knew what hit him, until it was too late. Angleton's planning methods were always

---

85. James DiEugenio, author, editor, Lisa Pease, editor, *The Assassinations: Probe Magazine on JFK, MLK, RFK and Malcolm X* (Washington: Feral House, 2003), Kindle Edition. Loc., 1555-60.

meticulously thorough, and he planned for failure or "blow" as well as success. Upon being briefed on the Bay of Pigs invasion, Angleton asked what the plans were in case the invasion failed. Upon not hearing a satisfactory answer he refused to get involved with it. In fact, both he and Richard Helms stayed clear of the Bay of Pigs fiasco and this has been credited to their rise in the CIA. If Angleton had planned the invasion we can be assured that Castro would have been dead before it started.

Another Angleton signature mark was the multiple layers to the plot. Jim Garrison described these layers as akin to peeling an onion. After removing one layer there is another underneath, and another, and another . . . The first layer of the "who done it" onion was Castro, and the next was the soviets, and then we had organized crime, and then right wing militias, oil barrons, rouge elements of the Military, FBI . . . After all of the layers have been peeled we have the CIA that does the bidding of the wealthy elite power structure. And we might add a reactionary Fascist power structure at that. All this elite power structure has to do is nod.

The Assassination Plot Goes Into Action

After the nods, Richard Helms and/or James Jesus Angleton gave the key contact the green light and probably some general instructions. "Don't hit Jackie . . . Don't hit any of the Secret Service . . . Make sure he is dead . . . The plan cannot fail . . . If you miss, there will be hell to pay . . . Make it look like the Cubans and/or Soviets did it . . . Do not tell me what you are doing . . ." Oddly enough, in 1963, it was a federal crime to threaten the president, but not to kill him. It was also a federal crime to shoot or kill a Secret Service agent, but not the president. The crime needed to be under local jurisdiction and/or the FBI. Hoover had total control of the FBI, and local officials could be easily controlled in Dallas, from the autopsy to the investigation, or the lack of one for that matter. That key contact was likely to have been William Harvey. Harvey would have gotten with mob liaison Johnny Roselli (the CIA's link to Marcello, Trafficante, and Giancana), David Sanchez Morales (a top CIA assassin with vast experience), QJ/WIN, David Atlee Phillips (a CIA expert at propaganda and disinformation), and possibly Clay Shaw to coordinate the New Orleans activities along with Marcello.

As previously mentioned, Marcello took out a contract on JFK's life in April of 1963. Shortly thereafter, certain members of the anti-Castro community decided that Kennedy had to go if they were ever going to take Cuba back. The above was according to Robert Morrow and he further relates that: [86]

> The Cuban-Mafia consortium planned to rely on Santos Trafficante's assets: Cuban Mafia mercenaries, Kohly's anti-Castro exiles, inside men on the Dallas police force and an assassination expert who worked on the CIA's official hit squad—John Michael Mertz.
>
> Rolando Masferrer (a Cuban exile leader) would be the financial conduit for Kohly's Miami exile groups and Cuban Mafia Mercenaries. Carlos Marcello would utilize Guy Bannister and David Ferrie for Kohly's exile groups at Lake Pontchatrain, Louisiana. Eladio del Valle was the coordinator and liaison between the two groups. This network had been established at the time of the Bay of Pigs invasion and had remained intact, as Kohly had continued to rely upon Mafia monies to finance his anti-Castro activities.

Much of the planning took place inside Marcello's six-thousand-acre Churchill Farms estate where Marcello hosted Ferrie and Bannister, who designed the assassination plan and coordinated it with many others. As with any sensitive operation, it was heavily compartmentalized. Many who contributed to the murder did not know the whole picture. They were only told what to do, and they only knew their part. Many, in fact almost all, died prematurely under suspicious circumstances. Of course, the shooters and their handlers had to know what they were doing. They were professional assassins that did this for tangible reward, and also the anti-Castro Cubans who had a grudge to bear. All of them got out of Dallas, and Oswald was left to take the heat. Along with planners and organizers, most of the shooters did not live very long. Of the organized crime members

---

[86.] Robert D. Morrow, *First Hand Knowledge: How I Participated in the CIA-Mafia Murder of President Kennedy*, (136 West 22nd Street, New York, NY 10011: SPI Books/Shapolsky Publishers, Inc., 1994), 188.

involved in this, only Carlos Marcello lived past the inquiries into the assassination. Santo Trafficante, Johnny Roselli, Sam Giancana, and others all were murdered; and most were taken out just before they were called to testify at assassination hearings. David Ferrie and Eladio del Valle were killed on the same day, and that was the day after Garrison announced that both of them were under investigation for the murder of JFK.

Ferrie did most of the local planning and coordinating. Also, he without a doubt did the logistics planning, that is getting the teams in and out and collecting all of the needed equipment. Robert D. Morrow wrote that toward the end of June 1963, Tracy Barns told him to buy four 7.35 mm Mannlicher-Carcano rifles.[87] This rifle came in two bore sizes, 7.35 mm and the rifle attributed to Oswald which was 6.5 mm. Barns stated that the former was much more accurate, and he had to make sure that he did not get the latter. Barns added that he wanted the rifles modified so that they could be taken apart, hidden, and reassembled rapidly. The next day, Morrow also wrote that he got a call from Eladio del Valle, an Alpha 66 member, requesting four transceivers that were undetectable by other radio equipment. Del Valle told Morrow that the rifles and the radios were for his Free Cuba Committee, and that David Ferrie would fly to the District of Columbia area to pick them up. Morrow purchased the rifles from Sonny's Supply Store in the Baltimore area, and he had them modified to specifications by July 15, 1963. The transceivers Morrow obtained were made by Motorola for railroad communications equipment and operated at a very low, undetectable frequency. Morrow had the transceivers ready by the first of August and gave them to Ferrie along with the rifles.

Eladio del Valle was most likely the radio communications central coordinator. He was a member of Alpha 66, and has been identified as "Leopoldo" by Cuban intelligence and also a leader of Alpha 66, Tony Cuesta. Cuesta also identified "Angel" as Herminio Diaz Garcia who was also part of one of the assassination teams. These are the same two that visited Sylvia Odio, along with Oswald or an Oswald

---

[87]. Robert D. Morrow, *First Hand Knowledge: How I Participated in the CIA-Mafia Murder of President Kennedy*, (136 West 22nd Street, New York, NY 10011: SPI Books/Shapolsky Publishers, Inc., 1994), 204.

impersonator, and represented themselves as anti-Castro Cubans. Tony Cuesta gave Castro's counterintelligence chief, Fabian Escalante, these names and identities when Cuesta was a prisoner in Cuba. In 1995, author Dick Russell and Escalante were at a Kennedy assassination forum in Nassau, Florida; and Escalante passed this information on to Russell. Escalante also informed Russell that Cuesta, del Valle, and Garcia were all on the assassination teams in Dallas.

The transceivers that del Valle obtained from Morrow have shown up in Dealey Plaza photos. There exist several photos of a man referred to as "the dark complected man" sitting center, carrying, and using a radio. In the photo at left, the radio and the antenna are visible.[88] The bottom two are other photos of the same man apparently putting the radio in a holder on his lower back. The man next to him is the "umbrella man." These are the two men that were pumping their right arms up and down, one had an umbrella, when JFK is seen in the Zapruder film emerging from behind a large sign and holding his throat. This undoubtedly was a signal that JFK had not received a fatal wound and to keep firing. Alpha 66 assassins were most likely in offices of the Dal-Tex building. They could have also been on the roof of the Texas School Book Depository, as there was an empty 30-06 cartridge found there years after the assassination.

The wound on JFK's upper back, about six inches below the collar line, probably came from the Dal-Tex building. Although this information was suppressed, the autopsy team found that this entry wound did not go through and exit out the front of his neck as reported by the Warren Commission. In fact they had determined that the wound went in about a finger length and that the bullet stopped there. The team's observations were that the wound Kennedy

---

[88]. Dark complected man holding radio, light shirt in the middle. Source: *Col. L. Fletcher Prouty Reference Site,*" http://www.prouty.org/photos.html.

received at his Adam's apple was an entry wound and not connected to the back wound, which was about six inches below the front neck wound. Commander James Humes was in charge of the autopsy at Bethesda Naval Hospital. Although all of the above was originally in his notes, he burned them presumably because they did not match what he was directed to state in his formal report. The enlisted medics that assisted with the autopsy were not called to testify, and they were also told that if they "said anything," that there would be extremely dire consequences. They were sworn to secrecy and threatened with imprisonment should they discuss anything about the autopsy. It was not until 1978 that they were released from these restrictions by an act of Congress that they tell their stories. Incredibly, they testified before the House Select Committee on Assassinations in 1978, but their testimony remained buried in the National Archives until released in 1994.

There were at least four teams of shooters in Dealey Plaza and maybe more. It has been well established that there were two teams of French Corsicans behind the picket fence on the grassy knoll. There are photographs in existence of two shooters there and also records of at least two "French Mafia" assassins in Dallas with connections to ZR/RIFLE and US organized crime. The FBI found record that Michael Mertz, who also went by the names Jean Souetre and Michael Roux, was in the United States during the time of the assassination. In fact, the FBI found record of Jean Souetre and also Michael Roux as being in or around Dallas on the day of the assassination. The French professional assassins were known to use other French assassin's names while on a mission. Of course, this would throw any investigator off as they would be likely to chase the assumed person down who would then have an alibi. Mertz was known to do this. He was also known to wear police uniforms, badges, and devices during assassinations; and this, of course, would give someone authority to tell people to leave the area and so forth.

Michael Mertz was involved in the drug trade, intelligence, and assassinations.[89] It is most likely that he was a shooter behind the picket fence on the grassy knoll on November 22, 1963. Jean Souetre had a

---

[89.] Noel H. Twyman, *Bloody Treason: The Assassination of John F. Kennedy*, (Kindle E-Book, First Edition, 2010), Kindle location 10526-10547

similar background to Mertz. Additionally, he met with E. Howard Hunt in Madrid, Spain, in April 1963 and also with General Edwin Walker during the same month in Dallas. Further, he had contact with an anti-Castro group in New Orleans.[90] The FBI identified him as being in Dallas in November 22, 1963. He very well could have been one of the shooters behind the picket fence on the grassy knoll. Another possibility is a man named Lucien Sarti. He was identified by E. Howard Hunt to his son, St. John Hunt, as being a shooter on the grassy knoll. Sarti was also identified by French prisoner Christian David as "one of three" assassins on the grassy knoll on November 22, 1963. David refused to identify the other two, stating that they were still alive and dangerous. Sarti had been killed by police in Mexico City in 1972. Sarti certainly fit the profile. He was a Corsican mobster, "French Connection" drug trafficker, and a known assassin for hire.

The shots that came from the grassy knoll were the first one that hit JFK in the throat from the front and also the last that hit him in the right temple. Additionally, there was one more shot that hit the sign that blocked Abraham Zapruder's movie camera view of the first shot. The shot that hit JFK in the throat was likely a partial misfire due to a manufacturing defect or the projectile portion of the shell was removed and tampered with. A sabot could have been used, which will be explained below, or a mercury-filled projectile put in place of the original projectile. If this was not done right, a partial misfire would be the result, and a low-velocity projectile would be fired without much noise and also not much killing capacity. The last and fatal shot was a full load that functioned as it was designed to do. This shot could have been a lead-and-silver alloy, which would shatter on impact, or it could have had an X cut in the point of the projectile, which would also cause it to fragment. Both scenarios would result in bullet pieces that would not be identifiable with a particular weapon.

It is very likely that there were one or two teams in the Dal-Tex building, and probably two teams in the sixth floor of the Texas School Book Depository. All of the teams, no matter where they were placed, would logically consist of one shooter and at least one other person to pick up shell casings, handle or hide weapons, and get the shooter in and out. The previously mentioned Alpha 66 members were almost

---

[90.] Ibid. Kindle location 10551.

certainly in the Dal-Tex building. It is also likely that Frank Sturgis and E. Howard Hunt were somewhere in Dealey Plaza but probably not members of a shooting team, and we can take David Sanchez Morales's word that he was there also. There is some evidence that General Edward Lansdale was also there as discussed earlier. At least one shot was fired at Kennedy from the Dal-Tex building and one from the book depository. The shot from the Dal-Tex building likely hit Kennedy in the back about six inches below the collar line. This shot did not go through JFK and hit Governor John Connelly as the Warren Commission reported. Connelly was hit with another shot that most likely came from the book depository.

The shot that hit JFK in the back either did not contain a full charge of powder, or it did not fire properly. Any military rifle would have not only gone through Kennedy but would have also gone through anything else in front of him, including the limousine, and JFK would have been mortally wounded. There are two possibilities here. One is that the powder charge was deliberately loaded short of a full charge. This would have been done if a sabot, a plastic projectile casing over a projectile fired from another rifle, was used to make it appear that JFK was shot with a 6.5 mm Mannlicher-Carcano when the actual weapon was another, say for instance a Mauser or a 30-06 Springfield. It could have happened that Robert Easterling's account of assassins firing bullets into a barrel of water and then collecting the bullets and the casings to incriminate Oswald occurred just as Easterling said it did. These bullets from a 6.5 mm Carcano would have the rifling marks of the Carcano. They would have then been placed in plastic casings, or sabots, and fitted in the shell casings of a larger-bore rifle. With underloaded powder charges, the bullets, or bullet, would not go through JFK but would lodge in his back.

The plastic sabot comes off as the bullet leaves the bore so that, for example, a Mauser or a 30-06 could fire a 6.5 mm Carcano round, with the rifle markings of the Carcano, into JFK and no one would be the wiser. The evidence would be that the Carcano was the murder weapon. The other possibility is that the bullet encased in the sabot was not crimped right. If the crimp to the shell casing was not tight enough, the gunpowder would then burn rather than explode, and this would produce a low-velocity bullet that would not go through JFK's body. The shot would have also dropped several inches and hit him in the back instead of the head. There would have not been the sharp crack of a high-powered rifle either. The sound would have been a dull thud instead. Jim Garrison found that there was an entire bullet found in the JFK autopsy that was turned over to the FBI, never to be seen again. This possibly was that very same bullet, and it would have completely negated the entire "lone assassin" cover story. At any rate, JFK and Connelly were shot from behind and hit with separate bullets.

There is conclusive evidence that Malcolm Wallace, LBJ's personal hit man, was in the sixth floor of the Texas School Book Depository. His fingerprints were there, and he was identified by Loy Factor's confession of involvement in the assassination. Factor put forth a detailed account when he was interviewed for the book, *The Men on the Sixth Floor*. It is possible that Lee Harvey Oswald was also there, although it is not likely. His role was that of the patsy, and there is a lot of evidence that he was not there. There is, of course, also evidence that he was there, but the preponderance of evidence is that he was not on the sixth floor at the time of the assassination. Too many witnesses saw him right before the assassination and right after. He was seen calmly drinking a soda on the second floor of the book depository about one and a half minutes after JFK was shot. The paraffin test done on Oswald for evidence of nitrate residue came back negative. This would not have been the case had he fired three rounds, as accused. If Oswald was on the sixth floor, he did not shoot at JFK, and he certainly did not hit him. Oswald was a notoriously bad shot.

Not only is it virtually not possible for Oswald to have shot JFK, but it is equally unlikely that he shot Dallas Police Officer J. D. Tippit. The Warren Commission report states that Oswald used his .38 caliber revolver to kill Officer Tippit, shooting him a total of four times. Any revolver has a revolving chamber that fires one round at a time through the barrel. For the chamber to revolve each time that it is fired there has to be a space between it and the barrel. Each time it is fired, gas escapes from between the cylinder and the barrel. Oswald should have had nitrates all over him, but he did not. There were four spent cartridge shells, or casings, left at the scene. A revolver does not automatically eject shells. They have to be removed by the shooter. Further, the shooter has to swing the cylinder open and manually eject all of the shell casings at once. Most, if not all, .38 revolvers carry six shells, so it does not make sense for there to be four empty shells at the scene. The evidence indicates that Tippit was shot with a .38 caliber semiautomatic handgun that ejects shells one at a time as they are fired.

It is also likely that Tippit was shot by more than one shooter because the four shells left at the scene were from two different manufacturers. It is possible, but not likely, that one shooter used ammo from two different manufacturers. Also, witnesses described two men at the scene of the shooting, and neither matched Oswald's description. Either Tippit was a part of the assassination and was eliminated for some reason, or he stopped someone involved in it and they shot him.

Let us put the above information together so that we have a logical sequence of events of what happened in Dallas in less than ten seconds that changed history. If the reader would refer back to the Dealey Plaza diagram and notice that the motorcade went down Main Street, the motorcade made a 90-degree right turn at Houston Street and then a sharp 120-degree left turn on to Elm Street. The motorcade was headed to the Stemmons Freeway entrance just after the railroad overpass. The Texas School Book Depository is roughly North of Elm Street, and the Dal-Tex building is east of the TSBD. It is about one hundred yards, three hundred feet, from the east end of the TSBD to the walkway that leads from the grassy knoll to Elm Street. Roughly seventy-five feet after making the sharp left turn on Elm Street, JFK is hit in the neck. This is the first shot, and it came from the grassy knoll. The shooter was at the most northerly position, behind a picket fence. This shooter is referred to as "badge man" because he is in a police uniform, and his badge is visible. The shooter next to him, or south of him, fired at the same time. This shot hit the Stemmons Freeway sign on the north side of Elm Street, between Kennedy and the grassy knoll. We will call this the second shot. About one second later, Kennedy is hit in the back about five and one-half inches below his shirt collar. This third shot was a low-velocity shot that did not go through but lodged in Kennedy's back. It was probably fired from the northeast corner of the sixth floor of the TSBD. This is where Oswald is presumed to be. About one and one-half seconds later, Texas Governor John Connelly is hit. This fourth shot probably came from the Dal-Tex building. It went through Connelly's chest, left wrist, and lodged in his left thigh.

At this point, the limousine driver, William Greer, slowed down considerably. Some witnesses said that he stopped completely. The fifth and final shot was fired no more than four seconds later. This shot came from the grassy knoll shooter to the right, which was south of "Badge Man." This was the fatal shot that witnesses say "exploded" Kennedy's head and violently threw him to his left and back. There are several photos of this that match virtually all witness accounts. The shot came from the grassy knoll and hit Kennedy in his temple on his right side. The author recalls reading many media accounts to explain how someone shot in the back of the head ends up thrown backward. It took this author over forty years to figure out that this position that violates the basic laws of physics came from the same powers that both hated JFK and control the media. To this day, *Time* magazine adheres to the position that this last fatal shot came from behind, against mountains of evidence to the contrary. No way could the above scenario, or anything like it, have been done by one person.

We will not get into the aftermath of the assassination. It will suffice to say that Evelyn Lincoln, Jim Garrison, and many others had it right. John F. Kennedy was loved and admired by the people and despised by Washington insiders, power brokers, criminals, the military, right-wing extremists, racists, and Nazis. Also, there was and still is no line of separation between these factions. Some of the players fit into many of the above categories, and many of these people were pathological personalities despite their expensive suits. The top levels of organized crime and the CIA worked together to assassinate the thirty-fifth president of the United States. This was facilitated by Lyndon Johnson, J. Edgar Hoover, and others in the executive branch of government. The above conspirators then covered up the assassination and murdered most of the material witnesses, going so far as to even murder most of each other. That is how it has happened throughout history. Able and dedicated people start a new country; psychopaths take it over and screw things up so badly that the whole thing finally collapses; then we start anew.

John and Robert Kennedy were no match for the Washington power structure that wanted to go in a completely different direction. So what was the direction that the power structure wanted to go? The rest of this work will explore the fundamental values and guiding principles that the nation was founded on. We will not go into what your average high school US history textbook claims these are, but we will look at what they were in reality. To do this, we will need to explore what the founders of the nation actually did more than what they publicly said. Some insights from friends and acquaintances and more private conversations were also revealing. Suffice to say that the journey from the very beginnings of what became the United States of America has actually been well documented, although most of what this author found was largely not known to the American people. The marked disparity between what the country purports to be and what it actually is are at odds with each other, and this disparity has caused the American people much hardship. It has been said that "one can ignore reality, but one cannot ignore the consequences of ignoring reality." It appears that that is what has happened to the American Republic.

Chapter Eight

The JFK Assassination— Democracy to Pathocracy

Let us begin by stating that John F. Kennedy probably had a few defects in his character. Idealized by the nation and the world, he treated the multitudes much better that he did those closest to him. Seymour Hersh's *The Dark Side of Camelot* paints a very ugly picture of JFK, including almost chronic venereal diseases[91] Over time it has been discovered that much of what has been reported about JFK's promiscuity has been, at best, exaggerated. Further, the sources of misinformation tended to be from the intelligence community along with their lapdogs in the media. To accomplish their aims, the power elite had to destroy JFK's legacy along with murdering the man.

JFK and Narcissism

There is some evidence that JFK had a personality trait referred to by social scientists as a "narcissistic personality." Some even go so far as to say that it was pronounced enough in him to qualify as a personality disorder. Either way, he exhibited some behaviors of one with higher-than-average hunger for such things as public approval and adoration. His serial sex encounters in his youth is also typical of

---

[91.] Seymour M. Hersh, *The Dark Side of Camelot*, (Boston, New York, Toronto, London: Little, Brown and Co., 1st ed, 1997) 231.

narcissism. Apparently, when very young children, from birth to about three years, do not get the affection and interaction needed for healthy emotional development, they grow up to crave love, attention, and affection from a distance. They do not know how to handle intimate relationships from those close to them and often think of people around them as extensions of their own ego. They want people around them to behave in ways that serve their needs and no one else's. They can be demanding, controlling, and totally oblivious to the emotional needs of family members and others close to them. Many of them have multiple and serial sex partners with whom they have shallow relationships. Narcissists are also usually insincere.[92]

All of us have some narcissism in us, and actually experts, in human behavior tell us that we need this. This is why we do not mind looking like a slob, or worse, in front of our family, but when we go out, we get all dressed up. We do this even when the people we will see are unknown to us and might not ever see us again. Logically, one would think it would be the other way around. The author would not be writing this book if he did not want to impress people he does not even know, and that would be you, the reader. The social scientists call this "healthy narcissism." That is why it is so hilarious when we see these "Wal-Mart shoppers" pictures in our e-mail. These are people who literally "let it all hang out" and could care less. Now how many of us look a lot like that around the house, but when the door bell rings, the mad scramble begins?

Apparently, the desirable trait we call charisma can be just a little too much narcissism, which seems to be a common element in many famous people. The author recalls a series on the History Channel in which experts analyzed famous people from history. One of those was Cleopatra, a historical character whom most people in the world are familiar with even today. The name automatically conjures up images of beauty, grandeur, and intrigue. The History Channel experts had her as narcissistic and explained how her servants would wrap her in a carpet, sneak her unnoticed through the city, and unroll her in front of Mark Antony in grandiose fashion. Even in death, she exhibited grandiosity by being found all decked out in her finest, and the asp-bite

---

[92] A more complete analysis of JFK and narcissism can be found in: Nigel Hamilton, *JFK: Reckless Youth*. (New York: Random House, 1992).

scenario was Hollywood all the way. Thousands of years before there even was a Hollywood, production crews, and so forth, she put on a show for all time.

It is interesting that narcissism is considered to be a desirable trait in today's leaders in politics and also business. This author came across something, perhaps in a written piece related to business, that top executive recruiters actually seek out this trait when looking for top business executives. Add to this that writers and researchers in this area have identified this personality variable in several modern presidents. Franklin D. Roosevelt, Lyndon Johnson, Richard Nixon, and Ronald Reagan all have been mentioned although the author would be more inclined to believe that Lyndon Johnson was more in the realm of selfish, obnoxious, greedy, and most likely psychopathic. Perhaps malignant narcissism would fit the bill; more about him in book 2. Strange that we seem to gravitate toward someone who was left in a crib all alone as a baby to lead our country. Another fact we might want to keep in mind is that leaderless groups are often taken over by narcissists.

Probably what the executive recruiters are looking for in their prospects would be more in the positive side on narcissism. Recognized traits of people who might be just "a little bit full of themselves" are optimism, friendliness, enthusiasm, charming, attractive, excellent platform speakers, good at politics, good at talking others into doing things . . . you get the picture. Overused, the person can become manipulative, insincere, exploitive, grandstanding, and has to win at all costs. Often one will get a "pull push" feeling when you get to know them. They come on as open and inviting, but the closer you get to them, the more you get the feeling of being pushed away. They are uncomfortable with intimacy, but they want to be admired and even loved, at a distance. The author believes that the true record shows that JFK was in the healthy narcissism realm. As a good looking and charming young man from a wealthy family, JFK probably did what many of us would have done in his place. As president, what has been portrayed as grandstanding probably was more in line with the courage to stand up for what was right. He displayed the courage and lived his life in the same manner that he wrote about in his book *Profiles in Courage*.

Reflections on Greatness

Let us consider a concept which was well stated by five-star Fleet Admiral William (Bull) Halsey.[93] He commanded all forces in the South Pacific during WW II, and one only has to glance at his photo to come to the conclusion that this man was not one to be trifled with. His courage was then, and is now, legendary. He was clearly one of the greatest military leaders of all time. Here is what he had to say about greatness:

There are no extraordinary men . . . just extraordinary circumstances that ordinary men are forced to deal with.

John F. Kennedy was president during a period that was nothing less than extraordinary. Having been one of the most intelligent and insightful presidents, he was well aware of the position he was in. As discussed before, he saw France struggle to maintain its imperial holdings in Algeria and Vietnam, and the lessons were not lost on him. He had to have seen the famous photo of the tall French general at Dien Bien Phu surrendering to the opposition Vietnamese commander who was about a foot shorter than he was. The French general has a swagger stick tucked under his left arm, and his opponent appeared to have none of the accoutrements of power. Slim, small, unassuming, and wearing a pith helmet, the contrast was memorable. The powerful surrendering to the weak. Probably this very same contrast occurred to JFK who must have seen this picture about fourteen years prior to the author. JFK's congressional addresses and communications indicate that he was acutely aware of the predicament France was in with its brutal occupation of Algeria. The more brutal the French army got, the more resistance they encountered. Torture and mass murder had spiraled out of control,

---

[93]. Fleet Admiral William Halsey Jr. photo source: *Wikipedia*, http://en.wikipedia.org/wiki/William_Halsey,_Jr.

and the French people were increasingly disgusted with the cost and the brutality. These are clear indications that JFK was not too anxious to have an American Algeria or a Dien Bien Phu. In fact, he said so.[94]

Although Admiral Halsey died before JFK took office, there was another military man who wore five stars and gave JFK an interesting piece of advice about committing troops to Southeast Asia. That was General Douglas MacArthur, and this is what he had to say this about it: "Anyone wanting to commit American forces to the mainland of Asia should have his head examined."[95] The "anyone" MacArthur was talking about obviously included JFK, for whom the comment was directed. These lessons were not lost on the young president, nor did the advice go unheard or unheeded. When we consider what was on JFK's table, we have to be somewhat taken aback. The Cold War and all it entailed—Vietnam, the Bay of Pigs, the Cuban Missile Crisis, and Berlin—were all difficult challenges. Each of these could have started WW III and the end of the world as we know it. Add to this, there was much more than meets the eye in each case. For example, his refusal to invade Cuba for a second time brought forth outright rage in many powerful arenas. Castro had kicked out big US businesses and organized crime, both of which had run wild in Cuba. In so doing, he had shut down Cuba as a vital link in the distribution network for the enormously profitable drug trade. All of this had put much of the Cuban upper middle class and upper class out of power and influence, and most of these disenfranchised Cubans left for the United States. So now we have powerful corporations, Mafia dons, and thousands of influential Cubans howling mad at JFK.

Add to this the fact that JFK was going to withdraw from Vietnam by 1965, as so stated. It was front page news in many papers including the *Stars and Stripes*.[96] JFK followed this up by signing National Security Action Memorandum 263 that directed withdrawal in stages,

---

[94.] Arthur M. Schlesinger Jr., *A Thousand Days: John F. Kennedy in the White House* (Mariner Books: 1st Ed., June 3, 2002) 339.

[95.] Ibid.

[96.] Front page headlines in the *Stars and Stripes*, an authorized publication of the Armed Forces in the Far East, read as follows: U.S. TROOPS SEEN OUT OF VIET BY '65, Vol. 19, No. 276, Friday, Oct. 4, 1963.

resulting in virtually all troops out by 1965. As discussed in the previous chapter, the date of this document was October 11, 1963. Of course, JFK was to die in a little over a month from this major commitment that was publicly stated and officially documented. To state, as some have, that Kennedy would have reversed this had he lived flies in the face of logical thought processes. Secretary of Defense, for both Kennedy and Lyndon Johnson, Robert McNamara, was all over the map on this issue. Author Noel H. Twyman interviewed him in 1994 and asked him about the contention that Lyndon Baines Johnson had reversed JFK's plan to withdraw from Vietnam, and that he had signed National Security Action Memorandum number 273 countermanding JFK's above directive within three days of assuming the presidency. McNamara stated emphatically that Johnson had only carried on with Kennedy's plans. Reading the entire interview was an exercise in head shaking and consternation for this author because of McNamara's seemingly naiveté and lack of command of major facts and details. Twyman also stated as much in his book, *Bloody Treason: The Assassination of John F. Kennedy*.

Kennedy's proposed withdrawal probably would have resulted in a total stand down of the entire Southeast Asian war and easily turned around expenditures in excess of over one-half of a trillion dollars, which was a lot of money then and now. Hughes Aircraft, Brown and Root (now Halliburton), Monsanto, Lockheed, and all the rest would all have had a serious "cash flow problem." Add to this the problems caused by disrupting over 90 percent of the world's opium produced in the Golden Triangle. Much of the money from this was floating through American banking, the U.S. Stock Market, and organized crime, thus adding to the number of howling mad faces in powerful positions. We now have organized crime even angrier and add to that the "military-industrial complex" and the Pentagon. Through this, once again we see that the people loved him, but the power structure hated the ground he walked on.

Operation Northwoods

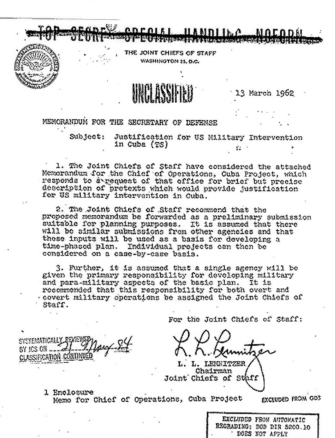

The Joint Chiefs of Staff actually proposed Operation Northwoods to Secretary of Defense McNamara and JFK. This was a "false flag" operation that would have entailed CIA and military hijackings and bombings within the United States that would be blamed on Cuba. The objective was to enrage the American people enough to foster an all-out invasion of Cuba and, if Air Force Chief of Staff General Curtis LeMay got his way, a nuclear war with the Soviet Union. LeMay had calculated that war with the USSR was inevitable and that the United States would have a better chance of winning it the earlier it happened. He figured that in a few years, the USSR would have increased their nuclear capability such that much heavier damage and casualties would be suffered by our side by waiting.[97] So why not get it on now? He actually believed this and verbalized it, and what he was proposing would have killed many millions of people. LeMay was another legend in his own time, especially among US Air Force personnel. He was, however, a very dangerous man as JFK was well aware. There has been testimony that there was a four-star general present at the JFK autopsy who was issuing orders as to what should or should not be done. Some, including New Orleans district attorney Jim Garrison, suspected that it was LeMay; but this has never been proven. Just about everyone knows that there are only a handful of military that wear four stars, and this should not have been too difficult to narrow down. Several key witnesses and participants to the autopsy have died under suspicious circumstances, and some who lived a normal life span were scared out of their wits. LeMay stated that he was on a fishing or hunting trip at the time of the assassination.

Domestic Achievements and More Enemies

JFK was enraging not only the Pentagon, organized crime, the military-industrial complex, and the rest of corporate America and Wall Street, but his domestic policies were also making powerful enemies. Today, the myth is that JFK was charismatic and popular, but that he was not able to get such things as civil rights legislation passed and programs implemented. Further, the myth goes on that it took Lyndon Baines Johnson's administrative skills to implement Kennedy's ideas; otherwise, none of these would have happened. That is not how it happened, and the record shows that.

He was making big changes in the direction of the United States that have been quietly forgotten over the years. He was not just talking about integration, health care, and education; he was doing something about it. He had introduced record numbers of bills and legislation in Congress that had never been seen before. There also was legislation

---

[97.] Source: *Wikipedia* article titled "Operation Northwoods," http://en.wikipedia.org/wiki/File:NorthwoodsMemorandum.jpg. This is the cover sheet for the operation. Links to the entire declassified document can be accessed on this page.

to tax US corporations that had not been paying taxes on off-shore operations and subsidiaries, and this included very big, very profitable, and very powerful US oil corporations. Add to this the oil-depletion allowances that his administration was marshaling, and we had an all-out frontal assault upon the most powerful corporations in the world. Any one of Standard Oil's "Seven Sisters" had more power than many nations in the world, and together they arguably had more power than all of them, including the United States. If you steer the ship of state, you own it. Even today Exxon Mobil, derived from Standard Oil, sees itself as a sovereign entity. That is to say not beholding to any country, including the USA. They keep a very low profile but are thought to have been in Vice President Richard "Dick" Chaney's office, carving up Iraq on a map before the 9/11 attacks. Did it happen that way? No one is talking, especially not Chaney.

These allowances were not chicken feed. We are not talking about millions or billions but hundreds of billions of dollars a year that would have been torn from these corporations' "bottom line." What did Kennedy have in mind for this money? He said he was going to use it for the American people, that is for education, health care and wellness programs, roads and bridges, housing—well, you know, sort of like the things that taxes are supposed to be used for in the first place, such as provide for the common good and do the things that we cannot do individually. People just do not go out and build thirty feet of freeway in front of their house and expect their neighbors to do the same. Obviously, it just does not work that way.

"Free enterprise" and "capitalism" do not take too kindly to paying taxes for the common good of the American people. It is their nature to maximize profit and keep it for their own purposes. Not only is it their nature, but this concept is infused in our business heritage and even into law. There have been lawsuits over these issues. No corporate president, director, or chief executive officer can go to a board of directors' or shareholders' meeting and say that he or she just thought it would be good for the country if the business payed more taxes. Civic duty and so forth is in the company brochures and news advertisements, but no one in their right mind would advocate such a thing.

He was also forcing integration and equal employment opportunity. The JFK administration was using its control over hiring government contractors to insist that every business entity was employing a reasonable number of minorities. If minorities were not well represented in the company, a government contract was not going to happen. The federal government was hiring record numbers of minorities,[98] and in the north especially, minorities were flocking to the big cities to get these jobs. These were mostly African Americans, and they were also flocking from the south to the north. These were large shifts on population, and this was not a small thing. Some people did not like this one bit, and some racist organizations were, along with the previously mentioned areas of power, howling mad.

The JFK administration was goring every pet ox in the country, and it was taking the United States to a place that very powerful people and institutions did not want to go, and they would not stand for it. This is probably one reason that there were so many JFK assassination theories around. Virtually, the entire power structure wanted to get back on course, and that course was to use resources that belonged to the people to control and dominate the world's resources, the same as every empire before it. To do this, it is necessary to usurp the wealth of the common people and direct it to conquest. That is, money or taxes that presumably were collected to go toward education, housing, health care, and infrastructure were increasingly being diverted to the military. The word *triumph* came from ancient Rome. Its meaning was a parade or a display by the army of all of the newly acquired gold, silver, loot, and booty that the Roman army had "acquired" from far-off places. The problems that arise from this system are always the same. More and more resources have to be directed from internal development to having to go out farther and farther to acquire wealth. Add to this that this acquired wealth does not end up benefiting the common people. More and more force is directed farther and farther out until the entire system collapses on its own weight.

The best example of this was Rome. When Caesar crossed the Rubicon, it was a pivotal event that had nothing to do with the size of

---

[98]. Figures for fiscal year 1962 show that although African Americans were only 10.5% of the population, they accounted for 17% of the 62,633 civil service jobs. The percentage was as high as 25% in the Veterans Administration and 20% in the Post Office Department. Source: James Hepburn, *Farewell America* (Vaduz [Liechtenstein]) printed in Canada and Belgium: Frontiers Co., 1968) 73.

the river. In fact, the Rubicon was a small stream. In Ohio, you would call it a creek. No problem crossing it. The significance of crossing the Rubicon was that it was a border of the city of Rome, and to take an army across this border was considered an act of treason. It was too easy to do. Take a legion across the Rubicon into Rome and take the city, and you now take the empire. Julius Caesar took his army into Rome in a military coup, and he knew exactly what he was doing. When he did this, Rome went from a republic to an empire and was never the same there after.

Just as Rome turned from a democratic republic into an empire when Caesar crossed the Rubicon, so the United States of America was transformed from a republic to a pathocracy when John F. Kennedy's head exploded at 12:30 PM, November 22, 1963. It was not a change in direction as much as a course correction. The ship of state had been heading toward being run by a democratically elected dictator from early on. The seeds had been planted at Jamestown and nurtured for hundreds of years, which we will explore further in the next chapter. It was, however, not an outright pathocracy before JFK was shot. At times it came close, but somehow, the American people were able to pull it back. That all changed in Dealey Plaza on that fateful day in 1963 when a group of thugs wearing fancy suits and having official titles carried off a coup. Further, they did this in plain view of the world, "broad daylight," so to speak. After seizing power, the assassins put the ship back on the course of inevitable self-destruction. They then tried to cover the whole thing up.

Supreme Court Justice Earl Warren, robes and all, was propped up as a distinguished-looking figurehead who did not run the "President's Commission on the Assassination of President Kennedy." Who ran it was Allen Dulles, who should have been a prime suspect. He was assisted by John Jay McCloy, who was implicated by one of LBJ's mistresses as having been in at a secret meeting in Dallas the day before the assassination. Some of McCloy's "not-worthy" accomplishments included refusing to bomb the railroad tracks going to Auschwitz, commuting and pardoning the sentences of many war criminals at Nuremberg, and refusing to compensate Japanese Americans imprisoned during WW II. Dulles had been fired by JFK over the Bay of Pigs fiasco.

Definition of Pathocracy

It is this author's contention that the American republic transitioned into a pathocracy in Dallas on November 22, 1963. After this date, it was a republic in form only with mere vestiges of representation of the people's interests. The shift had been coming for a long time. As we will discuss in the last chapter, there was a plot to take over the government and install a Fascist dictatorship in the United States during the Franklin Delano Roosevelt administration, prior to WW II, and there were other serious threats. This time it happened. This time the mask was off. This time the message was sent to the American people and the world that "we decide who is president, not you . . . , and we run this country not you . . . , and if you don't like it, we will take care of you too." The message was sent that we have the power to take out the leader of the free world, and no one can stop us. Democracy was ripped away from us, and all three branches of government literally froze. Like zombies, the Warren Commission compiled file upon file of useless data, such as Oswald's grades in the third grade and other superfluous information that had nothing to do with anything. The FBI was like a slow motion or stop-action camera compiling reams and reams of useless data, failing to follow obvious leads, even harassing and intimidating witnesses. Hoover actually issued edicts to his agents in the field that any evidence that contradicted the lone-assassin premise was to be destroyed.[99] Certainly, any investigative agency whose director could say such a thing had to have complete confidence that this was what was expected of him, and that he would be backed without reservation.

The Congress did nothing; it froze. The media did nothing; it froze. The Supreme Court did nothing, it froze. The people demanded action, investigations, inquiries; and what did they get? News pundits droning on and on about the nation coming together and having faith in their leaders, etc.` Checks and balances? There were none. Oversight? There was none. The list of witnesses that the Warren Commission did not call to testify could have convicted a courthouse full of conspirators. Although the institutions were there in form,

---

[99.] Noel Twyman, *Bloody Treason: The Assassination of John F. Kennedy* (E-book edition: Laurel Publishing, January 16, 2010) Kindle loc. 20010-17.

they were frozen; they had no substance. They ceased to function as it was their sworn duty to do. Many were terrified, which is the reason Kennedy's head was vaporized in the first place. "If they could do that to him, what could they do to little old me?" The people did not get suspicious right away; it took a while. But slowly they started to ask questions and demand answers. The media largely went along with the storyboard, and that was that Oswald, the loner, the attention seeker, had pulled off the entire operation all by himself. Preposterous! Those in the media that did not go along with the program did not fare too well. The vestiges of government institutions were left with no power. It had been stolen from them and also the people. Anyone who spoke up was slapped down, or worse. It was the day the music died; no more democracy, no more republic. "We are the deciders, and we will do anything to retain power because that is all that we know how to do" was the message. We report, we decide, end of story.

Let us now take a close look at what a pathocracy is, according to Lobaczewski. Compare for yourself the marked difference between the JFK and LBJ administrations while you read the definition and characteristics below: [100]

> Definition: **pathocracy** (n). A system of government created by a small pathological minority that takes control over a society of normal people (from Political Ponerology: A Science on the Nature of Evil Adjusted for Political Purposes, by Andrew Lobaczewski)
>
> **Pathocracy**
>
> from Greek pathos, "feeling, pain, suffering"; and kratos, "rule"
>
> A totalitarian form of government in which absolute political power is held by a *psychopathic elite* (emphasis added), and their effect on the people is such that the *entire society is ruled and motivated by purely pathological values* (emphasis added).

---

[100]. Source: WordPress.com, http://pathocracy.wordpress.com/definition/, accessed October 12, 2012.

A pathocracy can take many forms and can insinuate itself covertly into any seemingly just system or ideology. As such it can *masquerade under the guise of a democracy* (emphasis added) or theocracy as well as more openly oppressive regimes.

Characteristics

1. Suppression of individualism and creativity.
2. Impoverishment of artistic values.
3. Impoverishment of moral values; a social structure based on self-interest and one-upmanship, rather than altruism.
4. Fanatical ideology; often a corrupted form of a valid viable "trojan" ideology, which is perverted into a pathological form, bearing little resemblance to the substance of the original.
5. Intolerance and suspicion of anyone who is different, or who disagrees with the state.
6. Centralized control.
7. Widespread corruption.
8. Secret activities within government, but surveillance of the general population. (In contrast, a healthy society would have transparent government processes, and respect for privacy of the individual citizen.)
9. Paranoid and reactionary government.
10. Excessive, arbitrary, unfair and inflexible legislation; the power of decision making is reduced/removed from the citizens' everyday lives.
11. An attitude of hypocrisy and contempt demonstrated by the actions of the ruling class, towards the ideals they claim to follow, and towards the citizens they claim to represent.
12. Controlled media, dominated by propaganda.
13. Extreme inequality between the richest and poorest.
14. Endemic use of corrupted psychological reasoning such as paramoralisms, conversive thinking and double-talk.
15. Rule by force and/or fear of force.
16. People are considered as a "resource" to be exploited (hence the term "human resources"), rather than as individuals with intrinsic human worth.

17. Spiritual life is restricted to inflexible and indoctrinare schemes. Anyone attempting to go beyond these boundaries is considered a heretic or insane, and therefore dangerous.
18. Arbitrary divisions in the population (class, ethnicity, creed) are inflamed into conflict with one another.
19. Suppression of free speech—public debate, demonstration, protest.
20. Violation of basic human rights, for example: restriction or denial of basic life necessities such as food, water, shelter; detainment without charge; torture and abuse; slave labour.

Not only did this author see a marked difference between these two administrations, but also a shift even further toward the above characteristics in succeeding administrations. The harassment, vilification, and murder of witnesses to the assassination alone indicates that we are no longer in a healthy government. The number of suspicious deaths and disappearances of witnesses spiked before inquiries into the assassinations of John Kennedy, Martin Luther King, and Robert Kennedy. Recent polls show that roughly 75 percent of Americans believe there was a conspiracy in the JFK assassination. The House Select Committee on Assassinations said they believed there was a conspiracy also. There are piles of evidence to that effect, and yet virtually, all inquiries, investigations, and books into what really happened are portrayed as "looney" or worse. A free country does not persecute its most courageous citizens.

JFK—Cold Warrior to Peace Ambassador

In a very short time, JFK went from a rich, privileged playboy to a visionary world leader. The comparison of what he was like just a few years before taking on the enormous challenges of the presidency to what he was just before the assassination are striking. He exemplified Admiral Halsey's insightful description of greatness. Flawed as he was, he averted global disaster several times, and against overwhelming pressure to do otherwise. Emblematic of his role as a transformational leader was the address he gave at American University on June 10, 1963. Please read this carefully as it is one of the most inspiring and insightful addresses ever given. Not only did it define him as a transformational leader, but we would do well to take Kennedy's words to heart today.

Key Excerpts[101]

> What kind of peace do I mean and what kind of a peace do we seek? Not a Pax Americana enforced on the world by American weapons of war. Not the peace of the grave or the security of the slave. I am talking about genuine peace, the kind of peace that makes life on earth worth living, and the kind that enables men and nations to grow, and to hope, and build a better life for their children—not merely peace for Americans but peace for all men and women, not merely peace in our time but peace in all time.
>
> Today the expenditure of billions of dollars every year on weapons acquired for the purpose of making sure we never need them is essential to the keeping of peace. But surely the acquisition of such idle stockpiles—which can only destroy and never create—is not the only, much less the most efficient, means of assuring peace. I speak of peace, therefore, as the necessary, rational end of rational men. I realize the pursuit of peace is not as dramatic as the pursuit of war, and frequently the words of the pursuers fall on deaf ears. But we have no more urgent task.
>
> First examine our attitude towards peace itself. Too many of us think it is impossible. Too many think it is unreal. But that is a dangerous, defeatist belief. It leads to the conclusion that war is inevitable, that mankind is doomed, that we are gripped by forces we cannot control. We need not accept that view. Our problems are manmade; therefore, they can be solved by man. And man can be as big as he wants. No problem of human destiny is beyond human beings.
>
> For in the final analysis, our most basic common link is that we all inhabit this small planet. We all breathe the

---

[101]. Source of excerpts: *Wikipedia*, American University Speech, http://en.wikipedia.org/wiki/American_University_speech.

same air. We all cherish our children's futures. And we are all mortal.

It is our hope—and the purpose of allied policies—to convince the Soviet Union that she, too, should let each nation choose its own future, so long as that choice does not interfere with the choices of others. The Communist drive to impose their political and economic system on others is the primary cause of world tension today. For there can be no doubt that, if all nations could refrain from interfering in the self-determination of others, the peace would be much more assured.

I'm taking this opportunity, therefore, to announce two important decisions in this regard. First, Chairman Khrushchev, Prime Minister Macmillan, and I have agreed that high-level discussions will shortly begin in Moscow looking towards early agreement on a comprehensive test ban treaty. Our hope must be tempered—Our hopes must be tempered with the caution of history; but with our hopes go the hopes of all mankind. Second, to make clear our good faith and solemn convictions on this matter, I now declare that the United States does not propose to conduct nuclear tests in the atmosphere so long as other states do not do so. We will not—We will not be the first to resume.

The United States, as the world knows, will never start a war. We do not want a war. We do not now expect a war. This generation of Americans has already had enough—more than enough—of war and hate and oppression.

We shall also do our part to build a world of peace where the weak are safe and the strong are just. We are not helpless before that task or hopeless of its success. Confident and unafraid, we must labor on—not towards a strategy of annihilation but towards a strategy of peace.

Nikita Khrushchev was so inspired by this address that he made it available throughout the Soviet Union. Khrushchev followed up with his enthusiastic support of a nuclear test ban treaty, which went into effect in October 1963. Kennedy and Khrushchev already had back channels, which they were using to communicate directly with one another. The same was true for Castro and Kennedy. Khrushchev encouraged Castro to pursue this opportunity to stand down tensions. Noteworthy is the fact that these private and direct channels enraged the US Department of State.

It is also interesting that it did not get much media attention in the United States. At least not as much attention as it got in the USSR, but look at the established power and money that this address threatened. Every move that Kennedy made toward peace was countered by opposition. His administration was becoming increasingly alone and isolated. Major agencies ignored him, some of whom came directly under him. One example was the CIA, an increasingly out-of-control agency that answered to no one, and Kennedy was determined to "shred the CIA into a thousand pieces." Kennedy's threat along with his firing of Allen Dulles, and others, and his American University speech, and others, sealed his fate.

Jack Kennedy's rise to greatness certainly was in part due to the extraordinary challenges that he faced, but it also took an extraordinary person to meet them. Most of all, he was able to see in his mind's eye the far-reaching consequences of his actions. He could analyze problems and synthesize solutions. It not only takes an intelligent person to do this but also one who has compassion and deep feelings of identification for all of humanity. Perhaps it takes extraordinary problems to bring out in us that which we do not know we are capable of, but when one reaches way down deep inside themselves, there has to be something there to grab a hold of. Mahatma Gandhi, Martin Luther King, Franklin Delano Roosevelt, Nelson Mandela, Archbishop Desmond Tutu, and possibly Robert F. Kennedy were able to rise above their human frailties and show us the power of courage. It is a wondrous thing to see what human beings are capable of doing. These people and many others that do not get noticed are an inspiration for all mankind, for without them, we are totally lost.

How did we get to the point where murders and thugs actually took control of the country? How is it that in striving for "life, liberty, and the pursuit of happiness," we have turned into what we now have? When we look around us today, we see anything but happiness. Where did we go wrong? Or maybe we had problems from the very beginning. Were we ever really on the right course? These questions we will explore in the next two chapters, and frankly, you might be as surprised as the author was to look at some of the unvarnished facts.

Chapter Nine

The Age of Fanaticism: Jamestown to World War I

For not only every democracy, but certainly every republic, bears within itself the seeds of its own destruction.

—Robert Welch

How did America come to the point where anything like the JFK assassination could happen? How in the "land of the free" and the "home of the brave" could a coup of the magnitude that took place in Dallas on November 22, 1963, happen? How could the most powerful criminal elements of society and from within the government itself blow the head off one of the most popular presidents of all time, in broad daylight? Add to this the unbelievable prospect of his replacement, who should have been a suspect, clearly covering the whole thing up. This just cannot happen in America! Or can it? This assassination, and others, just did not come out of nowhere. It is this author's assertion that this was not an anomaly; it was a course correction. America had been on a course that could not be deviated from, and that course was one of a neocolonial empire that would dominate the entire world. Any president that either did not understand this or deviated from this course would be neutralized and, if necessary, neutralized with extreme prejudice. If they could not be dealt with in less extreme ways, they would be publicly executed. A shot to the head is two things. First is that it is almost certain that it would be fatal, and second is that it is the mark of a professional assassin, a contract killer who knows that the powers that be will protect him. It is a message to the rest of the country, as discussed before, that you do not run the country, we do. This was a course correction to get back on track, and that course had been set over three hundred years ago, as we shall see.

First, let us begin with the author's personal observations and recollections of how JFK was perceived by "middle America." These memories are roughly in line with much that has been written about JFK from anyone but the power elite and their minions over the years. We had some criticisms of the man but, by and large, accepted him as our leader who truly had our best interests at heart. We will then regress to the very beginnings of America, all the way back to Jamestown and the first settlements in Massachusetts. We will explore how these first European Americans thought and acted. How did they perceive this new land? What did they value? What were their religious beliefs? What principles and assumptions guided them? We will find that there were three metaphysical themes that reinforced each other in a way that set America on a destructive course that gained momentum as the years, and hundreds of years, went by. These forces came to a head when John F. Kennedy became president. The man was swimming in a pool of sharks. The world-domination course that America was on could not go forward with JFK at the helm. Let us begin first with a few recollections from a high school student.

Regardless of what anyone's opinion was of John F. Kennedy, or the Kennedy family for that matter, there is no question that he stood at a crossroad in history. When he was brutally murdered in front of the whole world, there was this overwhelming sense that things would never be the same again. From that day forward, Americans would not look at their government in the same way, nor would the majority of Americans fully trust their government again. This was the day the music died. This author was sixteen years old at the time and a junior in high school. We were all in shock along with our teachers and parents. The cold reality that this young man with a young family who was the leader of the free world could be gunned down like that was hard to get your mind around. Add to this the soaring optimism that prevailed at this time. Most thought that solutions for the problems of the world were going to finally be solved: racism, war, starvation, you name it, would be in the rearview mirror.

Then the author's history class, along with all the other classes, were called into the auditorium and told the "the president had been shot in the head . . ." and that "it does not look good . . ." as far as his survival. We returned to our rooms, and about a half hour later, the announcement came over the intercom that "the president died . . ." The students were all in shock; many were crying. I remember just feeling stunned, like what was happening could not be real, but it was. This just cannot happen in America. Somehow, everyone knew that same day that America had changed. Where was America headed without this young, dynamic leader? Could Vice President Johnson handle the job? He did not seem as sharp. Kennedy appeared to have a vision for America that mainstream America could sign on to, and he was very popular with the people. The same, however, cannot be said for the power structure that openly despised Kennedy and all he stood for.

Prior to the assassination the author recalls friends telling him that we should go on a fifty-mile hike, which was being organized in the community. He asked, "Why would we want to do that?" The answer was that "President Kennedy says that all Americans should be fit. It will make our nation stronger." Well, if President Kennedy says so, I suppose we should do our part. This was the attitude of most Americans at that time. We memorized parts of his speeches and imitated his accent. Our parents listened to the late Vaughn Meader do his imitation of JFK in the comedy album, *The First Family*. I remember one of the routines was JFK telling Caroline bedtime stories about the steel magistrates, Castro, and other problems of the times. At the end, he says good night, leaves the room, and Caroline says, "These sessions do him so much good." We made jokes about him and laughed at his accent, but we all knew he was a leader, and we felt that America and the world were being led well.

Yes, there was a dark side to "the Kennedys." Old Papa Joe made his money running bootleg liquor; everyone knew that. And being from Chicago, Cook County, Illinois, we all knew that there were a few thousand democratic votes that appeared out of nowhere that got JFK elected. But we figured that is just how things happen in politics. We had no idea, however, that old Joe Kennedy had made a deal with the devil when he promised Chicago organized crime, and that would be Sam Giancana, that his son would take care of mob interests once he got in office. This was in exchange for critical votes, of course. This was a promise that both of Joe Kennedy's sons, John and Robert, welched on, and it played a big role in the assassination. And yes, mostly when he was young, John Kennedy was a womanizer of the first magnitude and also reckless in other personal affairs. He had been carefully taught how to exploit women by the master himself, his father. Add to this the fact that he was receiving steroid treatments for Addison's disease, which it is believed increased his libido considerably.

He was a bad boy, and he had some character flaws, there is no question about that. There were, however, larger, looming issues that America had to face. It appears to this author that John F. Kennedy had the intellectual capacity and also the motivation to face these issues. It could be looked at that he rose above himself to do the right thing no matter what the consequences. The republic had been transforming into a neocolonial empire for some time, and to pretend otherwise was becoming more and more difficult. The CIA, Pentagon, FBI, organized crime, extremist groups, and what can be termed the "religious right" were itching to further expand and consolidate their power as they saw fit. They wanted to invade Cuba and install a despotic regime that would return Cuba to a place where US corporations and organized crime could run wild. The Joint Chiefs of Staff even proposed to Kennedy an operation that was eerily similar to the 9/11 attacks thirty-eight years later. This plan, Operation Northwoods, entailed what are referred to as "false flag" operations and had such outlandish elements as deliberately blowing up American planes and ships and blaming Cuba for it. It also called for shooting Americans in the streets and again making it appear that Cubans had done it. Many of these groups even advocated a war with the USSR, which Air Force Chief of Staff Curtis LeMay thought would be a great idea. He figured that we could annihilate the Soviet Union and only lose about 30 million Americans, and that it would have been "worth it."

Another war, drugs, and corruption hot spot was Vietnam where they wanted to fan the flames of American imperialism. And then we had J. Edgar Hoover who wanted to break the back of the civil rights movement on the presumption that it was a Communist conspiracy and in the process put as many black males in jail as possible. One agency in particular, the CIA, was hell-bent for all of the above and more. They wanted to continue overthrowing regimes in resource-rich countries and installing dictators that would steal from the people and split the profits between themselves and the United States. The list of countries where the CIA had overthrown governments already contained Guatemala, Iran, Iraq, Vietnam, and the Congo; and they had big plans to do the same in many more countries. These groups were run by the most ruthless, brutal, and pathological personalities in the country; and they would not be stopped, especially by a rich, spoiled, playboy from Massachusetts named Kennedy.

What John F. Kennedy's rationale was for opposing these dark forces is subject for debate. One could argue that he opposed them for selfish reasons, but then again, it could be also argued that he did it for altruistic reasons. There is, however, much evidence that he did oppose these forces and the direction that they were taking with everything at his disposal, and still he came up short. Kennedy knew what they were up to, and he made a deliberate decision to stop them. With all of the power of the presidency, and with Bobby at his side, this very bright man and his street fighter brother went against organized crime, racism, and militarism and lost. Anyone may say whatever they want to about the Kennedys, but compared to the psychopaths they were up against, they were saints. It is this author's belief that JFK, the playboy rich kid, rose above himself to become the most dynamic and courageous leader the United States had seen for a hundred years. This ordinary man met the challenge of redirecting the American Republic toward where it should have been headed all along, but it is too early to tell what effect he had.

JFK also knew he probably would not live long. Addison's disease was considered a fatal disease at the time, and this quite conceivably could have entered into his decision to put America back on course. If you do not have much time anyway, why not go for the gusto? Why not make your mark on history, rise above yourself, and be the transformational leader that America sorely needed at that time? Why not lead America to where the founding fathers had told us we should be, even though they did not live up to their own expectations. It can be argued that he decided to ignore the consequences and become that transformational leader. Or one could argue that he was consolidating power and establishing a Kennedy dynasty that would last for at least another fifty years. Either way, it was John F. Kennedy and the Kennedys against real power, and the future direction of the country was at stake. John F. Kennedy was at the crossroads, and he was also in the crosshairs.

Let us ponder something for a minute. Imagine the power the people that murdered Kennedy believed or actually knew that they had. They knew they would be able to blow the president of the United States' head apart, in broad daylight, and not get caught. They knew they could do it, and they knew they would be able to get away with it by covering it up. They knew they had complete control of the government of the United States because that is what it would take to pull this assassination off. If not, they would not have done it. Further, to have the audacity to try and sell the preposterous story that one very young man did this all by himself, with absolutely no help whatsoever and then turn around and intimidate, discredit, and/or murder virtually all of the material witnesses. That takes some hard bark. This was a message to the American people that you do not control your own government, "we" do. And you have no say in what America is or will be; "we" do. You do not have power, "we" do. And "we" do not care if you like it or not as long as you keep your mouth shut; if you do not, we will kill you. This was the message sent to the American people and the world on November 22, 1963. It is sobering to say the least. This was a bloody coup, straight out, plain and simple.

We will next take a look at some of the enormous issues this flawed and vulnerable man who unquestionably had a world-class intellect was facing. There are no clear lines between the following topics. They overlap and weave into each other. They are, however, the core moral and ethical issues that the United States of America had been wrestling with for a long time, some from the very beginning. They are no different from the dilemmas faced by every great nation that has come and gone before. From the glory of Rome to the British Empire, upon which the sun was never supposed to set, there were seeds of destruction that were sown into the very foundations of their power and not too much different from the ones sewn into the USA. The indisputable fact remains that not one of them survived to fulfill what they all believed was their destiny, and sadly, the United States of America will be no exception.

Racism

The first dilemma we will discuss is racism, and this one has been with us from the very beginning. Racism in America has its roots in slavery, and this nightmare goes all the way back to the first permanent

English colony in America. This colony was named Jamestown, and it was founded in Virginia in 1607. This was thirteen years before the Pilgrims landed at Plymouth, Massachusetts. The new colony was sponsored by the Virginia Company of London, a group of English investors who intended to make money. During the first years, the colony barely survived due to a number of factors, one of which was that the first settlers were largely upper-class Englishmen who did not possess the necessary labor skills. Indentured servants were brought in to provide these much-needed skills. Indentured servitude was much like slavery with the exception that it was not permanent. An indentured servant would be required to provide labor for their master for an agreed-upon number of years and then would be free, and this was irrespective of where the indentured servant came from. Even when the servant's contract was lengthy, some were lifelong, the children were born free. Initially, this was the system in Jamestown; that is, until the advent of growing tobacco.

In 1613, colonist John Rolfe introduced tobacco into the colony as a cash crop. Compared to other crops, tobacco required a great deal of land and labor. The land was taken from the Native Americans, and the labor initially came from European indentured servants. There were, however, not enough indentured servants to fill the labor gap, so the colony began receiving Africans captured by England during a war with Portugal. The first Africans were treated as indentured servants, but by midcentury, the practice of owning slaves for the slaves' entire lives became customary. Along with this came a social system whereby the children of Africans were born into slavery. The number of African slaves increased significantly by midcentury and replaced indentured servants as the primary source of labor. This socioeconomic model, slavery, was replicated throughout the South and became established for over a hundred years before the Declaration of Independence was written. In fact, many of the authors of this document that declared that "we hold these truths to be self-evident, that all men are created equal, that they are endowed by their creator with certain unalienable rights, that among these are Life, Liberty, and the Pursuit of happiness," were slave owners. One of these men was Thomas Jefferson, whose motives are questioned to this day. Was he, and those of his ilk, nothing more than hypocrites? Did they believe that they had bigger fish to fry? Did they plan on confronting the dilemma at a later date or perhaps not at all? Surely they knew that their words did not reflect reality. Were they trying to chart a new course for America, or were they simply slave owners that wanted to be free?

The transition from indentured servitude to slavery happened very fast. Perhaps it was not a conscious decision. Perhaps it came out of expediency or convenience. However it came about, it has proven to be the most disastrous "mistake" this country has made. This created a whole new social system whereas America set a course to become an inherently unjust and barbaric nation. Once set, this course could not be changed easily. In fact, it appears that it could not be changed at all. By far, the bloodiest war America ever fought was supposedly over slavery, and even the Civil War did not change the course of injustice for Americans of African descent. This seed of destruction was planted on day-one of the American Republic and grew into a poisoned tree that bears toxic fruit to this day.

One indication of the dilemma the founding fathers faced came from none other than Thomas Jefferson himself, who lived a long time after the Revolution and the ratification of the Constitution. There is on record that a revealing conversation took place between Jefferson and John Holmes at Jefferson's home in Monticello on April 22, 1820. The discussion centered on whether or not the new state of Missouri would enter the union as a slave state or free. In framing the slavery dilemma, Jefferson used an interesting allegory when he stated, "But as it is, we have the wolf by the ear, and we can neither hold him, nor safely let him go. Justice is in one scale, and self-preservation in the other." It is apparent that Jefferson had thought deeply about this dilemma for over forty years but still had not come up with a satisfactory solution. Clearly he believed that this unjust and immoral system could not be abolished without catastrophic economic disruption. It is also apparent that even after fighting the bloodiest of wars, the Civil War, America still had the same wolf by the ear that it can neither hold on to any longer nor let it go.

Did JFK try to let go of the wolf's ear, and did it ferociously turn on him? Equal opportunity initiatives certainly did not begin with Kennedy. For example, from 1932 to 1937, Franklin Delano Roosevelt doubled the number of African Americans employed by the federal government. Also, the military forces were desegregated during the Eisenhower administration. Further, the Supreme Court outlawed segregation in schools in 1954 and in public transportation in 1956. Voting discrimination was also outlawed by Congress in 1957. Of course, passing laws and so forth does not necessarily make things happen. Civil rights and equal opportunity, especially for African Americans, was long overdue; and these initiatives resulted in a lot of friction. Extreme reactionary groups were becoming more violent. There were riots in Tuscaloosa, Alabama, in 1956 and Little Rock, Arkansas, in 1957. So-called "white moderate" groups were saying "give it more time," and Martin Luther King was answering with the question, "How much time is enough?" He was reflecting that it had already been hundreds of years that "Negroes have been waiting for justice," and he stated that he considered the white moderate to be more dangerous than outright professed racists. Time was running out; the wolf was becoming more dangerous. America had to act, one way or the other.

The JFK administration was using its control over hiring government contractors to insist that every business entity was employing a reasonable number of minorities. If minorities were not well represented in the company, a government contract was not going to happen. The federal government was hiring record numbers of minorities, and in the North especially, Southern African Americans were flocking to the big cities to get these jobs. The figures tell a surprising tale. In 1962, African Americans were 10.5 percent of the population but comprised 17 percent of the civil service jobs.[102] In the veterans administration, the figure was 25 percent and 20 percent in the postal service.[103] From 1961 to 1963, the percentage of African Americans in the middle grades of civil service increased by 35.5 percent, and in the upper grades, the increase was an incredible 88.2 percent.[104] During this period, Attorney General Robert Kennedy had appointed forty African-American US attorneys.[105] The Kennedy administration was bringing true justice to America by making civil rights and equal opportunity actually work. The author has seen many arguments to the contrary, but the facts and figures are on record, and

---

[102]. James Hepburn, *The End of America*. (Vaduz, Liechtenstein: Frontiers Publishing Company, 1968), 73.
[103]. Ibid.
[104]. Ibid.
[105]. Ibid.

they paint a clear picture, and that is that JFK was doing what had been paid lip service to for hundreds of years.

This did not sit too well with the titans of industry, one of which we have seen before, Haroldson Lafayette Hunt Jr. whom *Fortune* magazine had placed as the eighth richest person in America. Along with enormous wealth and power, Hunt was also a venomous racist and an extreme right-wing fanatic, and he had ties to many reactionary organizations. Hunt is only one example in corporate America, and although his views were extreme, they were not at all unusual. The above figures did not sit too well in Congress either. Senator Richard B. Russell Jr., senator from Georgia who opposed all civil rights legislation during this time, publicly stated, "To me, the president's legislative proposals (on civil rights) are clearly destructive of the American system and the constitutional rights of American citizens. I shall oppose them with every means and resource at my command." Russell was chosen by LBJ to be on the Warren Commission, presumably because he did not like the Kennedys. As it turned out, Russell ended up having serious misgivings about the findings of the commission and had to be coerced into signing it. He never did feel right about it and so stated many times. He died in 1971 of what probably were natural causes, but many others that were vocal in their opposition to the "lone assassin" story did not live as long as he did.

To this day, there are comments as to how bad or good John F. Kennedy was. Some even say that he was into Satanism, and others make him out to be a saint. The fact remains that the country was at a crossroads when it came to civil rights. America had to either go in one direction or the other. It is also a fact that JFK had his own agenda. He could not be controlled by these radical groups that wanted to push him and the country in the direction of increased oppression and continued denial of civil rights. Some criticisms were, no doubt, valid. I doubt that the private clubs that the Kennedys belonged to had more than token memberships of minorities, if that. That was the big criticism of the Kennedys. "They wanted to tell everyone else how to live by making rules that did not apply to them." The fact remains that the majority of average Americans believed that "Maybe Kennedy is right and we do need to change. Maybe it will be a sacrifice; maybe it will not be easy, but it is the right thing to do, and maybe we will be better off for it." The election was coming up in 1964, and John F. Kennedy was going to win by a landslide. There is no question about that. Surveys showed it, and political experts were forecasting this. Slavery had been abolished, but the fruits of this poisoned tree were still on the table. This issue, although certainly not the only one, resulted in the murder of John F. Kennedy and in the continued legacy of hatred and oppression for the United States. America's inability to live up to the high ideals of the Declaration of Independence, the Constitution, and the Bill of Rights have destroyed these documents and transformed the American Republic into a pathocracy. As Martin Luther King so aptly stated in his Letter from the Birmingham Jail, April 16, 1963, "Injustice anywhere is a threat to justice everywhere." By denying justice for African Americans, everyone in America has lost it for themselves.

Militarism

> *The dangerous patriot . . . is a defender of militarism and its ideals of war and glory.*
>
> —*Colonel James A. Donovan, US Marine Corps*

It is evident that influential people from the CIA, Pentagon, and other areas of US society actually wanted to start a war with Cuba and even a nuclear war with the Soviet Union during the Kennedy administration. These same proponents of militarism also wanted to greatly escalate the so-called Vietnam conflict. This seemingly insane milieu did not come out of nowhere. America has had influential elements that have wanted to start wars for a long time, and it appears that these elements have gained more and more power as time goes on. Since World War II, the United States has been almost constantly at war, and all of them have been undeclared. The United States is now not only constantly at war but is fighting several wars at the same time, and it looks as if the United States is busy looking for more of them at the time of this writing. For example, the State Department recently stated that there were less than one hundred Al Qaeda operatives in Afghanistan, and the United States now has over one hundred thousand troops in that country. That is a ratio of about 1,000 to 1. Add to this that each troop in that country is costing the American taxpayer roughly a million dollars a year. This would figure out to be a billion dollars a year to chase just one "Al Qaeda" operative. Add to this the fact that the United States does not seem to be catching or killing very many of them. How have we gotten to this place where we are at war continuously against a rather abstract foe? War against Al Queda, war against terrorism, war against drugs, ad infinitum; how do you know you have won or lost when the enemy is an abstraction? Maybe that's the point, perhaps the objective is not to win or lose; but as in Vietnam, the game seemed to be to keep the game going.

Let us begin with some framework as to what militarism actually is. The new Oxford Dictionary, 2007, defines *militarism* as the "belief or desire of a government or people that a country should maintain a strong military capability and be prepared to use it aggressively to defend or promote national interests." So what is wrong with that? The problem is that, throughout history, a "strong military capacity" tends to take on a life of its own; it grows and needs to be fed. We may further describe *militarism* as the glorification of war and the promotion of large standing military structures along with support systems that enjoy undue influence in the government. It is the propensity to use military force in the conduct of foreign affairs when other options should be considered. The leaders of militaristic nations are characterized by threats of force and bellicose blustering to intimidate other nations. Throughout history, when a large military force is developed, the nation that owns it ends up making war against somebody. One would be hard-pressed to find an exception.

It has been recognized that the founders of the nation were very concerned that militarism would eventually prevail and destroy the democratic republic; at least that is what they said. The lessons of what militarism had done throughout Europe were fresh in their minds, and they did not want to have the same thing happen to the United States. They were opposed to militarism for good reason, and they carefully built checks and balances into the Constitution to make it very difficult for it to ruin the country. They made the president commander-in-chief of the armed forces so that US military would be under civilian control. They also gave Congress, and only Congress, the authority to declare war. This power could have been given to any one of the three branches of government. As unlikely as it would appear, the Supreme Court could have been given this power. In the writings of the founding fathers, it appears that this power was given to Congress for two reasons. The first of which was that they believed that, of the three branches of government, Congress was the governing body that most represented the will of the American people. The other reason was that they believed that Congress would be the branch that would be least likely to want to get entangled in military adventurism and opportunistic wars. They believed that the president, as head of the executive branch of government and also commander in chief of the armed forces, would be *most* likely to get the nation involved in military adventurism, and wars of opportunity.

George Washington's farewell address was interesting. In paragraph thirteen, he states,

> Hence, likewise, they will avoid the necessity of those overgrown military establishments which, under any form of government, are inauspicious to liberty, and which are to be regarded as particularly hostile to republican liberty. In this sense it is that your union ought to be considered as a main prop of your liberty, and that the love of the one ought to endear to you the preservation of the other.

Although he did not mention militarism, it can be construed that that was what he was talking about when he used the term "overgrown military" that he stated threatens liberty under any form of government. Powerful ideas! One may certainly conclude that the founding fathers were all very bright, educated, and learned. They certainly had their faults, and these faults—it can be argued—became infused in the new republic and caused almost constant problems later on, but these men were courageous, intellectual giants. There is no dispute about that.

Another check and balance in the Constitution that is not talked about very much is delineated in Article 1, Section 9, which states, "No money shall be drawn from the treasury, but in consequence of appropriations made by law; and a regular statement and account of receipts and expenditures of all public money shall be published from time to time." A simple but powerful concept was set forth here, and that is that the US Congress, answerable to the American people, "controls the purse strings." It plainly says that *no* tax money will be spent without Congress appropriating it. It does not state that the CIA and the Pentagon may spend money on so-called "dark projects," "black operations," and "state secrets." This is money that no one knows about, and just screaming to be used in evil ways. No checks, no balances, and no oversight, what is going to happen? If Congress and the American people knew what this money was being spent on, they would be howling for heads to roll. Assassinations, drug running, overthrowing governments, harassing Americans exercising their right to free speech, spying on the American people, blowing up environmental activists' cars,[106] and so forth, are just some of what goes on under the veil of secrecy. A great deal of this "dark money," if not most of it, is spent on militarism, and I doubt if there are vouchers filed to show these expenditures. These are American tax dollars soaked in our own blood, and we are not allowed to know anything about where this money goes nor for what purpose. If article 1, section 9, had been strictly enforced, we would not be in the situation we are in now, and that is literally billions of people all over the world hating our guts and we seem to have no idea why. We let this happen by not knowing the Constitution and not insisting that it be adhered to, plain and simple.

Thomas Jefferson stated repeatedly that he was very much opposed to America having a large standing army and navy. He also said that doing so jeopardized democracy in that military power would challenge the power that should be vested in the people. That is, he believed this until he became president and found it very inconvenient to deal with issues such as the Barbary pirates without the ability to project power far from America's shores. During his administration, Jefferson also, upon the advice of George Washington, started the US Military Academy at West Point. One could look at this as a major step toward militarism in that it created a permanent class of career, professional army officers.

Jefferson also commissioned the Lewis and Clark Expedition ostensibly to find a water route to the West Coast to conduct trade with China. The expedition was led by Meriwether Lewis and William Clark, who were both Virginia-born veterans of Indian wars in the

---

[106.] Judi Bari, director of Earth First!, was severely injured when her car was bombed in 1990. She was arrested by the FBI for transporting a bomb in her car. She sued the FBI and the Oakland Police for damages and won a judgment for $4.4 million dollars, although she had died of her injuries before the judgment. This was reported by author and retired FBI agent M. Westley Swearingen in his book, *To Kill a President, Finally—an Ex-FBI Agent Rips Aside the Veil of Secrecy that Killed JFK.* (Lexington, KY: Booksurge Publishing, 2008), 255, 261.

Ohio Valley. They started out in 1804, reached the Pacific Coast in 1805, and returned in 1806 without finding the water route they were looking for. They did, however, demonstrate that commerce between the East and West Coasts was something that could be done. Although not a formally stated goal of the expedition, Jefferson conveyed to Lewis and Clark that he was very interested in declaring US sovereignty over the Native American tribes along the Missouri River and also assessing the resources in the Louisiana Purchase. The Louisiana Purchase also happened during Jefferson's administration, which more than doubled the size of US territory.

When it was brought to Jefferson's attention that the proposed purchase was unconstitutional, he simply had the Constitution changed to allow for it. It is apparent that Thomas Jefferson was laying the groundwork for an American nation that stretched from coast to coast, and he also was thinking in terms that this was destined to happen. This concept would later be developed into what became called "manifest destiny," which was, in a nutshell, that it was God's plan for America to span the North American continent from coast to coast and maybe even a little north and south. It was destined to happen because it was "God's will." Because it was willed by God, this means that whatever the new country did to achieve this was blessed and sanctioned by the Almighty himself. Anyone in the way was impeding this divine destiny. Native Americans were heathens that were squatting on sacred land that they had no right to, and if it took military force to remove or eliminate them, then so be it.

Apparently, the words crafted by Thomas Jefferson in the Declaration of Independence were not exactly what he meant. It appears that when he stated the most famous of words that "all men are created equal," he had a very narrow interpretation of what he meant by "all men." From his other writings and actions, it can be construed that first of all, he did not mean mankind. He meant males and not women. Further, he apparently meant English-speaking, European, white men or something along those lines. It is a certainty that he did not mean Native Americans or anyone of African descent. As we have discussed before, Jefferson owned many slaves, about three hundred at the time he authored the Declaration of Independence. He most certainly did not intend for freedom to extend to them. Jefferson's writings clearly paint a picture of a man of lofty words, but the truth was that he not only did not believe in freedom and equality for anyone that did not share his profile, but he held all of them in unabashed contempt.

This could be certainly stated for Jefferson's attitude toward indigenous peoples. One example was when he instructed his secretary of war that "any Indians who resisted westward expansion must be met with the hatchet."[107] This was not an offhand comment. In consistently stating that the native peoples of America must either get out of the way or be annihilated, Jefferson was invoking the long-held European "Doctrine of Discovery." This was the predecessor of Manifest Destiny and goes back to the right of anyone representing a European sovereign ruler to claim territory simply by laying eyes on it and mumbling some words over it. The people that lived there had no right to the land they were born on. They were not "God's children." They were not even Christians; so therefore they had no right to the land nor did they have the right to live. Non-Christian heathens may be killed, and it is not murder. They have no rights. This mind-set had been around for hundreds of years. It was nothing new, and despite Jefferson's wonderfully crafted talk of "all men are endowed by their creator with unalienable rights," his belief systems were no different from the kings and monarchs he railed against. The only difference being that *he* wanted to be free, and those of his ilk. Everyone else was in the way.

Genocide

Thomas Jefferson's character flaws were emblematic of the flaws in the new republic. He was, however, not exceptional when it came to glaring defects of character. George Washington and many of the rest of the founding fathers had their share also, and then some. In fact, the name the Seneca had for Washington was "Town Destroyer." He regularly ordered his officers to annihilate whole tribes. His orders were to kill all of them, including women and children. Washington killed many more Native Americans than British soldiers by a long shot. Author of *American Holocaust: The Conquest of the New World,* David

---

[107.] David E. Stannard, *American Holocaust: The Conquest of the New World.* (Kindle Edition, Oxford University Press, October 1, 1992), Kindle Location 2802-2822.

E. Stannard, goes into much detail about the genocidal makeup of the founding fathers and Washington in particular: [108]

> George Washington, in 1779, instructed Major General John Sullivan to attack the Iroquois and "lay waste all settlements around . . . that the country may not be overrun but destroyed," urging the general not to listen to any overture of peace before the total ruin of their settlements is effected." Sullivan did as instructed, he reported back, "destroying everything that contributes to their support" and turning "the whole of that beautiful region," wrote one early account, "from the character of a garden to a scene of drear and sickening desolation." The Indians, this writer said, "were hunted like wild beasts" in a "war of extermination," something Washington approved of since, as he was to say in 1783, the Indians, after all, were little different from wolves, "both being beasts of prey, tho' they differ in shape . . ." "For their part, the surviving Indians later referred to Washington by the nickname "Town Destroyer," for it was under his direct orders that at least 28 out of 30 Seneca towns from Lake Erie to the Mohawk River had been totally obliterated in a period of less than five years, as had all the towns and villages of the Mohawk, the Onondaga, and the Cayuga.

The truth be known, the "father of our country" the man who "never told a lie" was a genocidal mass-murderer. There is no question about this. Stannard also reports that Washington's troops, with impunity, did such grotesque activities as to skin the bodies of their victims to make boot tops or leggings for themselves. Stannard goes on to aptly document that American leadership far surpassed the Nazis both in sheer numbers killed, cruelty, and outright barbarism. And they had the audacity to call Native Americans "beasts." Racism was the ideology, and militarism was the tool of the "American holocaust." It is difficult to see these most idealized and revered leaders as serial

---

[108.] David E. Stannard, *American Holocaust: The Conquest of the New World*. (Kindle Edition, Oxford University Press, October 1, 1992), Kindle Location 2809-2829.

mass-murderers, but the record is clear. That is exactly what they were. The die was cast from the very beginning of the republic; this country would go through a ponerization process no different from all those that preceded it. This new age heart of darkness would emanate not from the Thames River in England as did Joseph Conrad's, but from the mouth of the Potomac in the land of the free.

To simplify matters, the below illustration covers US acquisitions from the original colonies to the present.

Source: Wikipedia, U.S. Territorial Acquisitions

We will not cover how these lands were acquired because most Americans have a pretty good idea how this all came about from public education. The exceptions are the roles that racism and militarism played in these so-called "acquisitions." For example, Mexico was opposed to slavery in any form. Despite the romanticized story about the fight for independence, the fight was over Americans wanting to import slaves into Texas, which was illegal so long as the land was a part of Mexico. There was even an initiative to "acquire" all of Mexico. The odd thing about this was that both sides of the "acquire Mexico" debate were racist, considering Mexico as mostly inhabited by Indians whom they saw as inferior to white Americans. One side wanted to take Mexico in to save or "civilize" them, and the other wanted no part of them. Senator John C. Calhoun of South Carolina made his opinion very clear in a speech to Congress on January 4, 1848:

> We have never dreamt of incorporating into our Union any but the Caucasian race—the free white race. To incorporate Mexico, would be the very first instance of the kind, of incorporating an Indian race; for more than half of the Mexicans are Indians, and the other is composed chiefly of mixed tribes. I protest against such a union as that! Ours, sir, is the Government of a white race . . . . We are anxious to force free government on all; and I see that it has been urged . . . that it is the mission of this country to spread civil and religious liberty over all the world, and especially over this continent. It is a great mistake.

Some wanted to "annex" Mexico, advocating that this would ensure peace on the continent. This ideology was perhaps one early example of what has recently been put forth as "preemption," that is to attack a country because it might, some day, be a threat. Actually, a preemptive attack is only such if another nation is massing forces to attack you. It is not preemption to attack another country that might, some day, attack you. The latter is merely an excuse to invade another nation, or rationalization would be another way of describing it. At any rate, it is certain that the proponents of the "annex Mexico" school of thought had in mind to "acquire" it by use of force. It seems no one thought to ask Mexico what it thought of this idea. Although not all of the newly acquired lands were taken by force, the militaristic belligerency was there, backed up by "Manifest Destiny" and also what became known as "American exceptionalism," which simply put means that America is so good and so different that anything the country does is good. The foregoing is not right out of the dictionary, but that is pretty much it. One has to admire the speed in which this all happened. In about seventy years, a lifetime, the continental United States territory went from nonexistence to coast to coast, an incredible feat, albeit murderous. One could look at this as grand and glorious, or one could see it as a nation built by slave labor on stolen land. The author tends toward the latter.

The first act of American militarism was the War of Independence itself, which set the precedent for the American way of resolving conflict. When all is said and done, the American colonies were the British-controlled territories that went to war for independence. Canada and Australia did nothing of the kind and seem to have fared all right. Of course, India won independence, but that was largely based on nonviolent, passive resistance. Mahatma Gandhi led India to independence by simply not abiding by Great Britain's laws, edicts, and directions. As Gandhi told the Indian people, "A few thousand British soldiers cannot force hundreds of millions of people to do what they refuse to do." It worked. Of course, it was not all that simple, and not all of the independence movement was nonviolent. It further could be argued that without the violent factions in the Indian independence movement, Gandhi and the rest of the nonviolent movement would not have had as much traction as they did. It was, however, effective in gaining independence.

This leads us to the almost imponderable rift between what the "founding fathers" said and what they actually were and did. Slave owners that wanted to be free? And all of these exalted ideas about rights and freedom and then they turn around and put into motion a genocidal, mass-murdering, and militaristic machine that takes the native population from roughly eighteen million people to only a few thousand? What was going on?

Actually, the killing machine had been in motion for about two hundred years. Estimates of pre-Columbian population figures once were accepted as only a few million in all of the Americas. As time goes on, the figures keep growing and growing. Independent studies from around the world have been coming up with startling figures since the midsixties. One research group out of University of California, Berkley, led by anthropologist Henry F. Dobyns, now has the peak population for the Americas as having been about 145,000,000.[109] This was much more than Europe and Russia combined. North of Mexico, the team

---

[109.] David E. Stannard, *American Holocaust: The Conquest of the New World*. (Kindle Edition, Oxford University Press, October 1, 1992), Kindle Location 6138-6157.

estimates that there were about 18,000,000[110] inhabitants with very sophisticated food production methods and highly developed cultures.

So why the Revolutionary War, and why did the European Americans find it necessary to exterminate the Native Americans? Further, why were the "founding fathers" stated intensions diametrically opposed to what they actually believed and did? After the Seven Years' War, or what is sometimes called the French and Indian War, the English treasury was almost exhausted, and England also wanted to find ways to avoid warfare in the New World. Although portrayed as something akin to a high-functioning moron in American public schools, King George III actually instituted measures that made perfect sense from an English perspective. He imposed new taxes that we all know were very unpopular with the colonists. He did this for very logical reasons. He was trying to "balance the budget," so to speak, and pay for a very costly war with France that was fought on behalf of the New World colonists. He also imposed the concept of preemption that was part of the Doctrine of Discovery. This was not related to the term "preemption" as in a "preemptive strike" but meant that when land was claimed by a European sovereign ruler, that ruler has absolute jurisdiction over the sale and transfer of that land. The French and Indian War largely was caused by the chaos in the lands between the Allegheny and Appalachian mountains and the Mississippi River as far as who could sell land to whom. Between the Native Americans, French, British, and the colonists, there was much bickering and fighting over this issue. King George III was asserting his authority under the Doctrine of Discovery to control these issues, and bring some sense of order to these territories. George III also gave some legitimacy for the presence of Native Americans in these lands. Although he claimed them, he invoked another element of the right of first discovery in that he stated that the Native American governments, having settled this land, were caretakers of it. In essence he gave them the right to be there. He also issued a proclamation in October of 1763 that forbade his subjects to cross over the Alleghany and Appalachia mountains and settle on this land.[111] The king had just defined Indian

---

[110.] Ibid.

[111.] Robert J. Miller, *Native America, Discovered and Conquered: Thomas Jefferson, Lewis and Clark, and Manifest Destiny*, (Praeger, September 30,

territory as having been all lands between the above-mentioned mountains to the Mississippi. He also included in this declaration that Great Britain would control all commercial activity in this region. These attempts to assert his sovereignty over this land were very unpopular in the colonies and ended up being included in the grievances outlined in the Declaration of Independence. It is noteworthy that many of the founding fathers, including George Washington and Benjamin Franklin, had purchased extensive lands in this region and stood to lose a lot of money because the king had declared all such prior transactions to be "null and void."[112] "Our boys" did not care for that too much. In fact, they disliked the whole arrangement so much they decided to fight about it.

This author learned more about history helping his kids and grandkids with their homework. Last year, my granddaughter was in the sixth grade, and she was writing a paper on the Revolution. She and I were going over what she had found out. Several of the facts she had included in her paper were revealing. She had discovered that the Revolutionary War was not very popular with the American people at that time. Only about one-fourth of the colonists was in favor of it, and about the same number was against it. The other half was indifferent; they did not care one way or the other. So how are you going to fight a war against one of the most powerful countries in the world when only a small minority of the population is strongly in favor of it? Where are the troops, money, arms, and supplies going to come from? It was going to take a committed and unified population to fight this war, and even then the results would be questionable. As in any war, the people had to be literally "up in arms" about emotional issues. There had to be an evil, wicked enemy. There had to be a noble, emotional cause. There had to be slogans, speeches, and carefully crafted words and phrases that would incite the common man. There had to be heroes, villains, and traitors . . . We all know the routine. Nothing has changed in this regard for thousands of years. You cannot go and ask a shop owner to take up arms because of an unpopular tax. It has to mean something important. So we now had "no taxation without representation" and so forth.

2006) Kindle Location 639-642.
[112.] Ibid, Kindle Location 661-666.

The master at framing and fleshing out noble causes and rallying people to fight for ideals was Thomas Jefferson, who was considered to be the author of the Declaration of Independence. This is how we ended up with a slave owner, who fully intended on annihilating the Native Americans and turning America into an empire, proselytizing about "all men are created equal . . . endowed by their creator with certain unalienable rights, that among these are life, liberty, and the pursuit of happiness." Now we have something worth fighting for, especially when you have this evil, brutish, and oppressive King George III denying these "unalienable rights." Jefferson's grievances against George III were written in parallel style to magnify and hammer home the idea that this was the worst ruler that ever lived. Each paragraph a sentence that started with the exact same words, "He has" followed by an action verb, or "for" also followed by an action verb, such as refused, obstructed, deprived, and so forth. Very effective! This parallel style was so effective that Martin Luther King Jr. also used it to his advantage in his famous Letter from the Birmingham Jail in which he hammered, over and over again, his grievances toward "white moderates."

It is too bad that the founding fathers apparently did not believe their own words. These grand ideas and inspirational phrases evidently were only to incite their fellow countrymen to war. If ever there was a golden opportunity to abolish slavery and include First Nation Americans as equal citizens, this was the time to do it. Although not an easy task, this was doable and could not have been as difficult as the nation having to endure all of the heartache of slavery, genocide, war, and everything else that went along with the disastrous course the country ended up taking. If the founding fathers had the courage to fight a global superpower, why could they not have had the courage to be true to their own words?

Once the decision was made to go to war, they could not have taken half measures. They had to go all the way, and the Declaration of Independence was carefully crafted to do this. A cause worth fighting for, and let us keep in mind that if the revolution had failed, Jefferson, Washington, Franklin, and all the rest would have been hung for treason. There is no question about that. In fact, just before signing the Declaration of Independence, Benjamin Franklin was reported to have addressed the Continental Congress with the following advice: "We must, indeed, all hang together, or most assuredly we shall all hang separately." Sobering words indeed! Failure was not an option.

The founding fathers had to inspire and incite their fellow countrymen to use military force as a tool for a violent, bloody revolution; and in so doing, they laid the foundation for the direction the United States would take from 1776 to the present. Any disagreement, anyone, or anything in our way, and we fight. This is as true today as it was then. This frame of reference was one of racism and militarism that would entail genocide on a scale never seen before, and one which is still going on. Tens of thousands of indigenous Guatemalans have been slaughtered in the last few years, and many of the perpetrators of this were trained at the so-called "School of the Americas" at Fort Benning, Georgia. Another example is that Israel is, today, committing genocide against the Palestinians, and this is funded and supported almost entirely by the United States. The rationale used for this act of international criminality is strikingly similar to that used by the founding fathers in their quest to annihilate the Native Americans. "God gave this land to me . . . They weren't doing anything with it (the land) anyway . . . Their religious beliefs are not the same as ours." And we have the same mentality in that people do not own the land they are born on, and we have the same extreme rationalizations that, somehow, foreigners have more right to the land than the people born there. Because God willed it . . . and on and on. It is clear that the United States is still using the Doctrine of Discovery in the holy lands and elsewhere in the world also.

Essential to the run-up of the invasion of Iraq was the modern version of the British rationalization of "civilizing savages." We were not taking control of oil. We were "instilling democracy," because Iraqis do not know how to govern themselves. Never mind that Saddam Hussein was a CIA asset who basically fell into disfavor with the United States over two issues. One of which was the nationalization of Iraq's oil and the other was trading oil in Euro-dollars, both of which the United States strongly disapproved of. One could say that he had "left the reservation," so to speak. The United States had to make an example of him such that no other oil-producing country would dare to even consider these two "cardinal sins." Invasion and a public hanging of the infidel who dared to defy the master would set the proper example for any other Persian Gulf heathen who even so much as entertains such acts of disobedience. This very same region that the United States had to "free" and "reeducate" in ancient times was called "Mesopotamia," which means "between the rivers." This happens to be the very same land that we studied in public school as the "cradle of civilization" where agriculture came from along with Hammurabi's Code, the first written set of laws with the concept that punishment should be commensurate with the gravity of the crime. We were taught that Western civilization came from there, thousands of years ago. The last time this author checked a high school world history textbook, there were less than two pages about Mesopotamia, and most of that was a picture of a stone horse. This is not the same history we were taught fifty years ago. If the United States has a country or a region in its crosshairs, there is no reason to teach the American people to appreciate the people and the culture, much less the contributions to American culture.

The Presidents

Let us return to the founding fathers and briefly discuss the first three presidents' attitudes toward racism, genocide, and militarism. These men set the course for the United States that is still followed today, and they generally were in agreement on the major issues although they were, at times, ferocious political enemies. George Washington owned and controlled about three hundred slaves. He treated them in the same manner in which most Virginia slave owners treated theirs. They were whipped for disobedience, attempting to run away, and so forth. Washington believed that European Americans were intellectually and morally superior to Africans and Native Americans, and as such were entitled to own land and participate in government. If you were not white, Caucasian in Washington's words, you had no rights. If you could not be exploited you were "in the way" and to be exterminated. Some historians have found evidence that Washington had misgivings about slavery, noting the stark contrast between it and the Constitution. There is no evidence that he did anything whatsoever about these misgivings. Washington held egalitarian views until it was inconvenient to do so. When he felt it was to his advantage, his behavior could be exactly the opposite from his professed beliefs.

After Washington came his vice president, John Adams, who was probably best known for the Alien and Sedition Acts that were signed into law during his administration. These clearly unconstitutional acts were used by Adams mostly to persecute his political opponents.

Oddly enough, some of these laws were not repealed and were used by the United States to intern Japanese Americans during WWII and steal their property. Although Adams assisted Jefferson in writing the Declaration of Independence, it is clear that he did not use it as guide during his presidency. Adams was a one-term president. He lost the election for what would have been his second term to none other than Thomas Jefferson, who was very critical of the Alien and Sedition Acts. A little known fact was that Adams waged an undeclared war against France during his administration, and he increased taxes to pay for it. He also greatly strengthened the army and navy. His record as president also clearly showed that he had the most wonderful of ideas about equality and rights until they got in the way of what he wanted to do. He was capable of using unconstitutional means to persecute his political enemies and did so without hesitation. This did not seem to bother him one bit.

We have already discussed the third president, Thomas Jefferson, at some length. Of all the founders of the nation, no one was more influential and no one typified the stark contrast between what the country formally stated it was and what in reality it actually was. What we were and still are, is a militaristic, genocidal, racist state that formally has on its books the ideals of freedom and equality. Apparently, Jefferson had all of these contradictions in mind from the very beginning. Author Robert J. Miller found evidence that Jefferson wrote President James Madison in 1809 saying of the US Constitution, "No constitution was ever before so well calculated as ours for *extensive empire.*"[113] (Emphasis added.) Miller also documents that Jefferson also wrote Madison, advocating an invasion of Canada and, four years later, "set his eyes on Texas."[114] Jefferson's vision for American Empire was an "empire of liberty," in his words, and one that would not only stretch from coast to coast but also contain virtually all of North America. That is, it would include all of Canada and most, if not all, of Mexico.

---

[113] Robert J. Miller, *Native America, Discovered and Conquered: Thomas Jefferson, Lewis and Clark, and Manifest Destiny*, (Praeger, September 30, 2006) Kindle Location 43-46.

[114] Ibid.

As knowledgeable and learned as Jefferson was, one would think that he would have come across the idea that empire and liberty are incompatible. There had been a few empires to study in Jefferson's time, Rome coming to mind immediately, that could not pull this off. A nation never has, and arguably cannot be, both. The word *empire* itself comes from the Latin word *imperium* that literally means "power." Romans used this word to denote the power of the state over the individual, which is the opposite of democracy. In a democracy, the people are supposed to have power over the state. When Julius Caesar crossed the Rubicon, an act of treason in those times, that was the end of the Roman Republic, and he knew exactly what he was doing. Democracy is too unwieldy a form of government for an empire. Empires are constantly at war, stealing land and resources, and they have to go farther and farther out to keep the whole process going. A state cannot have debates, referendums, votes, and so forth every time it is deemed necessary to attack someone. An empire is like a worm. The more it eats, the bigger it gets, which means it has to eat even more. Empires always find it necessary to conquer. Eventually, they have to go farther and farther out and expend more and more resources in the process. They have to deprive their citizens of health care, education, and set human rights aside so as to direct more and more resources to militarism. Eventually, they collapse of their own weight, and not just sometimes but always. After Caesar, Rome still had some vestiges of democratic processes, but they were "rubber stamp" affairs that only looked like democracy. Sort of sounds familiar, doesn't it? Recall the so-called "Patriot Act" that most, if not all, of Congress did not even bother to read? And although the United States has been almost constantly at war since WWII, Congress has not exercised its constitutional role in declaring war since that time. They have rubber-stamped every military action initiated by the executive branch. Jefferson had to have known full well what happened to Rome. What on earth was he thinking?

After the first three US presidents, things did not improve, especially in the area of racism. Carefully hidden in most US history books and courses is the fact that twelve of the first eighteen US presidents owned slaves during their lifetimes, up to and including Ulysses S. Grant. Added to this is the fact that even those presidents that did not own slaves catered to the demands of racism and slavery.

Historian David Brion Davis, author of *The Problem of Slavery in Western Culture*, summarized his findings on the disastrous effects that the institution of slavery has had on American Democracy:[115]

> Even most history books fail to convey the extent that the American government was dominated by slaveholders and proslavery interests between the inaugurations of Presidents Washington and Lincoln. Partly because of the clause in the Constitution that gave the South added political representation for three-fifths of its slave population, Southern slaveholding presidents governed the nation for roughly 50 of those 72 years. And four of the six Northern presidents in that span catered to Southern proslavery policies. For example, Martin Van Buren, who came from a New York slaveholding family, sought to undermine the nation's judicial process and send the captives from the slave ship Amistad back to Cuba—and certain death. Millard Fillmore, also from New York, signed the Fugitive Slave Law of 1850, which enforced return of escaped slaves even from free states.
>
> From the start, America's foreign policy favored slaveholding interests, and administrations refused to cooperate with efforts by Britain to suppress the international slave trade, even though the United States had defined the African slave trade in 1820 as piracy, a capital crime. The one exception to this proslavery stand was the support John Adams's administration gave to Toussaint L'Ouverture during the Haitian Revolution—both to help the slaves gain freedom and to expel the French.

Davis goes on to support his premise that the South actually won the Civil War. Not the battles of course, but that the South prevailed politically by being in control of race issues, Jim Crow legislation and so forth, to present times. Much of our form of government was designed to accommodate slavery. One example is the Electoral College that selects the president every four years. This came about to

---

[115.] Source: http://www.racematters.org/legacyofsouthscivilwarwin.htm

accommodate the slave states to allow for representation of slaves that were not allowed to vote. The three-fifths rule again. Slaves counted as three-fifths of a human being. It could be argued that there are present-day forms of slavery. One issue being the 2.4 million prisoners incarcerated in the United States as of this writing, among whom African Americans are vastly over represented. This is the highest incarceration rate of all of the so-called "developed" countries. This in itself is startling, but the story gets even worse when you discover that this figure is no accident. Journalists Mike Elk and Bob Slone have disclosed that a virtually unknown lobby, known as the American Legislative Exchange Council (ALEC), has influenced legislation to cause this extremely high incarceration rate.[116] This "council" represents corporations that profit by employing cheap prison labor and has not only influenced legislation, but in some cases has actually written it. Many of the extremely long mandatory drug sentences were a product of ALEC initiatives. ALEC was also able to change laws that prevented the use of prisoners as unfair competition in the private sector. Making license plates is one thing, but in Florida, prison labor is used for one of the largest printing corporations in the state. This cheap source of labor has a significant impact on many small local printers that just cannot compete.

The fact that there are disproportionately high numbers of African Americans in jail is also not an accident. For example, federal sentencing laws require a mandatory prison term of five years for possession of as little as five grams of crack cocaine. However, one could have as much as 500 grams of powder cocaine to get the same sentence.[117] What is the difference between "crack cocaine" and "powdered cocaine?" There really is none; cocaine is cocaine. Crack cocaine is mixed with baking soda and "cooked" to form lumps or "rocks," and powdered cocaine is "cut" with some other powder, such as sugar. That is pretty much it. There is, however, one big difference, and that is that whites tend to "snort lines" of coke, that is powder

---

[116.] Mike Elk and Bob Sloan, "The Hidden History of ALEC and Prison Labor," *The Nation*, 2011-08-01 13-13.

[117.] Rodney Stich, *Drugging America: A Trojan Horse*, 2nd Ed., Kindle, (Silverpeak Enterprises, Nevada, Dec. 8, 2006), Kindle location 13684-13721.

cocaine, whereas African Americans tend to smoke crack cocaine in a pipe.

Add to this the "profiling" that law enforcement does, which means that black males get pulled over and searched a whole lot more frequently than do whites. Also, if you are a drug investigator and you need a certain number of arrests per month, what would be the easiest way to get that number? Go after a powerful organized crime or government figure, or just pick someone off the street that can't really defend himself. Now you have this "suspect" who gets a court-appointed attorney who tells him that his only option is to plea-bargain. It does not matter if the accused is guilty or not. Part of the plea bargaining is for the accused to "drop some names" in exchange for a lighter sentence, and it does not matter if these people are guilty or not. The investigator calls these people in and goes through the same scenario with them. Before long, you have hundreds, thousands, and even more than a million people in jail, many of who have done nothing at all. These are defenseless people whose only "crime" is to be virtually powerless. This happens much more frequently to African Americans than it does to whites and it especially happens a lot to black males. On top of this, consider that in most states, a felony conviction makes the person ineligible to vote. This is present-day neocolonial slavery, a subject we will be discussing in more detail in my next book.

American Holocaust

Along with empire, militarism, racism, and slavery came the Native American genocide. As mentioned earlier, all these subjects are related and intertwined, and it is not possible to separate them. This is the most horrible and shameful story that has ever happened in human history, far exceeding anything the Nazis ever came up with. It is not a pretty story, to say the least, and it is beyond the scope of this writing to document that which cannot begin to be fully covered in entire works covering this subject. It is, however, fundamental to understanding the Anglo-European ideology that is the foundation of the United States of America. That foundation was built on what can only be termed as genocide on a grand scale.

As previously mentioned, pre-Columbian North America population estimates are now around eighteen million, and some estimates go as high as thirty million. Also there is growing evidence that humans have inhabited the Americas for much longer than previously thought. For a long time, scholars put the number at about six thousand years that humans were in the "New World," and as the story went, these first peoples crossed over a "land bridge" between Asia and the Americas. More recent research indicates that the land bridge was about one thousand miles wide and more resembled a continent than it did a land bridge. There is even is a name for it, "Berengia." When the glaciers melted after the last Ice Age, almost all of this land ended up underwater. There is now compelling archeological evidence that humans were in Chile at least by 32,000 BC and in North America at about 40,000 BC. There are even some highly respected scholars that put the figure at about 70,000 BC for first entry into the hemisphere.[118] Imagine that: many more people in the Americas and much earlier than anything like what developed in Europe.

The first Europeans, including Columbus, were in awe of the advanced civilizations they encountered. Columbus and his men wrote about the huge populations, enormous cities, advanced food production, food storage, and food-distribution systems. They were amazed at the cleanliness, lack of disease, and order. Let us keep in mind that these early conquerors, so-called explorers, and early settlers came from starving and diseased populations that were also extremely violent. Although these Europeans somehow believed they were superior, they certainly were not. They were convinced that they were God's chosen people and that Christianity alone put them above the native peoples. Nothing could be farther from the truth. On his return to Spain after his first encounter with the New World, Columbus passed through the Azores. He described his discovery of what he thought was the Indian Sea and its many islands and people. One of the first major islands he landed on was Cuba, which he called "Juana." Columbus stated that the island "was so long that I thought it must be the mainland, the province of [Cathay]."[119] He also landed on the

---

[118.] Richard S. MacNeish, "Early Man in the New World," *American Scientist*, 63 (1976), 316-27.

[119.] David E. Stannard, *American Holocaust: The Conquest of the New World*. (Kindle Edition, Oxford University Press, October 1, 1992), Kindle Location 1528-1523.

island known today as Hispaniola, which now contains the nations of Haiti and the Dominican Republic. Columbus called this island "La Spanola." Let us take a look at what Christopher Columbus said about the land and people that he first came in contact with.

> As Juana, so all the other [islands] are very fertile to an excessive degree, and this one especially. In it there are many harbors on the sea coast, beyond comparison with others which I know in Christendom, and numerous rivers, good and large which is marvelous. Its lands are lofty and in it there are many sierras and very high mountains, to which the island Tenerife is not comparable. All are most beautiful, of a thousand shapes, and all accessible, and filled with trees of a thousand kinds and tall, and they seem to touch the sky; and I am told that they never lose their foliage, which I can believe, for I saw them as green and beautiful as they are in Spain in May, and some of them were flowering, some with fruit . . . Upcountry there are many mines of metals, and the population is innumerable. La Spanola is marvelous, the sierras and the mountains and the plains and the meadows and the lands are so beautiful and rich for planting and sowing, and for livestock of every sort, and for building towns and villages. The harbors of the sea here are such as you could not believe it without seeing them, and good streams, the most of which bear gold.[120]

His description of the people was also interesting:

> The people of this island and of all the other islands which I have found and seen, or have not seen, all go naked, men and women, as their mothers bore them, except that some women cover one place only with the leaf of a plant or with a net of cotton which they make for that purpose. They have no iron or steel or weapons, nor are they capable of using them, although they are well-built people of handsome stature, because they are wondrous timid . . . . [T]hey are

---

[120.] Ibid, 1533-1546.

so artless and free with all they possess, that no one would believe it without having seen it. Of anything they have, if you ask them for it, they never say no; rather they invite the person to share it, and show as much love as if they were giving their hearts; and whether the thing be of value or of small price, at once they are content with whatever little thing of whatever kind may be given to them.[121]

Columbus's observations were not unusual. Virtually, all of the first Europeans found very similar environments and cultures. One of the most famous of the Conquistadores was Hernando Cortez, probably best known for his conquest of the Aztecs. He had a chronicler with him by the name of Bernal Diaz del Castillo, who documented much of the expedition's travels and discoveries. On the way to the Aztec capitol city, Tenochtitlan, the party came in contact with several smaller cities. Diaz wrote in some detail of the party's observations of one of these cities:

When we entered the city of Iztapalapa, the appearance of the palaces in which they housed us! How spacious and well built they were, of beautiful stone work and cedar wood, and the wood of other sweet scented trees, with great rooms and courts, wonderful to behold, covered with awnings of cotton cloth, When we had looked well at all of this, we went to the orchard and garden, which was such a wonderful thing to see and walk in that I was never tired of looking at the diversity of the trees, and noting the scent which each one had, and the paths full of roses and flowers, and the native fruit trees and native roses, and the pond of fresh water. There was another thing to observe, that great canoes were able to pass into the garden from the lake through an opening that had been made so that there was no need for their occupants to land. And all was cemented and very splendid with many kinds of stone [monuments] with pictures on them, which gave much to think about. Then the birds of many kinds and breeds which came into

---

[121.] Ibid, 1546-1555

the pond. I say again that I stood looking at it and thought that never in the world would there be discovered lands such as these.[122]

Upon reaching the main city of Tenochtitlan, Cortez beheld a sight that was almost beyond belief. In fact his soldiers repeatedly asked one another if they were dreaming. They found a city that reminded them of Venice, except much larger, and one that had floating gardens which the Spaniards had never seen before. Aqueduct systems that provided the city with pure, clean water the likes of which the Spaniards had never seen. Cortez and his men also noted the personal cleanliness and hygiene of the well-dressed populace and their use of soaps, deodorants, and breath sweeteners.[123] Cortez was most impressed with the markets that were in the city. He describes what he called "the great market" on the northern end of the city:

> More than sixty thousand people come each day to buy and sell, and where every kind of merchandise produced in these lands is found; provisions, as well as ornaments of gold and silver, lead, brass, copper, tin, stones, shells, bones, and feathers . . . areas where timber and tiles and other building supplies are sold . . . earthenware braziers and mats of various kinds like mattresses for beds, and other, finer ones, for seats and for covering rooms and hallways . . . Each kind of merchandise is sold in its own street without any mixture whatever . . . They were very particular in this . . . There were streets where herbalists plied their trade, areas for apothecary shops, and shops like barbers' where they have their hair washed and shaved, and shops where they sell food and drink . . . as well as green grocer streets where one could buy every sort of vegetable, especially onions, leeks, garlic, common cress and watercress, borage, sorrel, teasels and artichokes; and there are many sorts of fruit, among which are cherries and plums like those in Spain . . . There were

---

[122.] Ibid, 210-224
[123.] Bernard R. Oriz de Montellano, *Aztec Medicine, Health, and Nutrition*, (New Brunswick: Rutgers University Press, 1990), 127-28.

stores in streets that specialized in game and birds of every species found in this land: chickens, partridges and quails, wild ducks, fly-catchers, widgeons, turtledoves, pigeons, cane birds, parrots, eagles and eagle owls, falcons, sparrow hawks and kestrels [as well as] rabbits and hares, and stags and small gelded dogs which they breed for eating.[124]

Cortez goes on to state that he saw so many wondrous things in this mercantile center that he could not begin to describe all of it in detail. He also mentioned that the entire center was "overseen by officials who enforced laws of fairness regarding weights and measures and the quality of goods purveyed." Bernal Diaz corroborated this and wrote, "We were astounded at the number of people and the quantity of merchandise that it contained, and at the good order and control that it contained, for we had never seen such a thing before."[125]

It is obvious, by the Conquistadors' own accounts that they had come to a land rich in resources on which very sophisticated peoples did an excellent job of managing resources and activities. They had advanced sanitation methods along with food production and water management. They had advanced medical treatment. The first Europeans in North America also testified to the advanced cultures that they first encountered. It is also noteworthy that they were not nearly as violent and greedy as the Europeans were. They did have conflicts and rivalries, but apparently, they were able to solve these problems in much more reasonable ways than the Europeans. They had armies and sometimes wars, but it does not appear that they even had the concept of genocide. Their goal was not annihilation of their enemies. Their purpose in fighting was more in the arena of demonstrating courage and addressing transgressions. It was considered unthinkable in all of the Americas to kill women and children. It also appears that the sacrificing of captured combatants was grossly exaggerated by the Spaniards. This is not to say that the killing of women and children and so forth never happened, but it was by far the exception.

[124.] David E. Stannard, *American Holocaust: The Conquest of the New World*. (Kindle Edition, Oxford University Press, October 1, 1992), Kindle Location 258-274.

[125.] Ibid, 271-276.

It is also clear that by all accounts of the first so-called explorers and settlers that they had an appreciation of the advanced civilizations they encountered, at least at first. It is also evident by all accounts that none of the Europeans, that landed in the Americas, from north to south, would have survived without the generous hospitality of the native peoples they first encountered. The native peoples had no concept of what the consequences of their generosity would be. They had no idea of the diseases, outright mass-murder, torture, slavery, theft of land, and so on that would be brought upon them from these infinitely cruel, greedy, and murderous peoples. They had no concept of people who could take religion and turn it upside down such that burning people alive was somehow honoring God, and stealing people's land was "God's will." They had never experienced anyone that could take the murder of millions upon millions of people and rationalize it as "fulfilling God's plan." Never could they even imagine that countless cultures, languages, knowledge, and wisdom would be annihilated in a very short time. All told, probably a hundred million Amerindians would die of disease, starvation, or outright slaughter; and virtually, all of their knowledge and wisdom would be lost. This was the crime of the ages. Nothing in the history of the world can possibly compare to the savagery and injustice imposed on the native peoples of the Americas, absolutely nothing.

We tend to look at the United States as having begun at the time of the Declaration of Independence, but we must keep in mind that the colonies already had a history of over 150 years. This time was unfortunately grounded in racism, mass murder, and destruction toward the native peoples of the Americas. Add to this the hundreds of years of the same having been pursued by the European nations from which the colonists came. Spain's goals in the Americas were simple. They wanted to enslave the native people to extract and refine gold and silver. As brutal as they were, their objective was not to annihilate the native people. If they had done that, there would not be anyone to do this work. They considered the supply of people—slaves—to be virtually infinite so that they did not have to be concerned with feeding the workers enough, mistreatment, working conditions, and the like. They figured that it was easier to work the people to death and replace them. To force them to work under these conditions, they simply used terror and brute force. They cut people's hands off, burned them alive, and things of that nature. Although genocide was not the goal, they murdered and tortured by the millions, so much so that there are records that the Spanish rulers were concerned that these operations would collapse for lack of natives to work the mines.

Although not their intention, the Spaniards' murderous onslaught clearly met the present-day definition of genocide. Oftentimes we think of genocide as killing every member, or virtually every member of a race, religion, national or ethical group. However, consideration is also given to intent; and under international law, even complicity in genocide is a punishable act. Of course, Spain did what they did in the Americas many hundreds of years ago, but by gauging contemporary views on genocide, we get a picture of the gravity of what was done.

Let us take a look at what the 1948 Genocide Convention of the United Nations adopted unanimously and without abstentions:

Article II

In the present Convention, genocide means any of the following acts committed with intent to destroy, in whole or in part, a national, ethnical, racial, or religious group, as such:

(a) Killing members of the group;
(b) Causing serious bodily or mental harm to members of the group;
(c) Deliberately inflicting on the group conditions of life calculated to bring about its physical destruction in whole or in part;
(d) Imposing measures intended to prevent births within the group;
(e) Forcibly transferring children of the group to another group.

Article III

The following acts shall be punishable:

(a) Genocide;
(b) Conspiracy to commit genocide;
(c) Direct and public incitement to commit genocide;
(d) Complicity in genocide.

There have been arguments that the above is too broad and also arguments that it is too narrow, but it appears to be the most universal definition of genocide, simply stated, and carries with it the force of international law. In comparing this contemporary standard to the actions of Spain in the Americas, it is evident that Spain not only met and exceeded any example but met and exceeded *every* example. It could be argued that Spain's intentions were not to destroy the native peoples of the Americas, but if it was not their intention, they sure did a good job of it.

Although Spain did not set out to annihilate the native people of the Americas, the same cannot be said for the British and the colonists. They clearly wanted to remove the native people from the land for several reasons. The first of these reasons was that from the beginning, the British wanted to replace the native peoples with immigrants. The British solution to poverty was to kick them out. If the poor were in the cities, they were kicked out to the country. If they were in the country, they were kicked out of the country, literally. Getting kicked out of the country meant to be put on a ship and sent on a one-way trip to somewhere else (the Americas, Australia, New Zealand, and other places). The same solution was in store for criminals (many of whom were simply in debt), political prisoners, and other "undesirables." The British attitude was that although these people were undesirables, they were Christians whose souls could be redeemed in the New World. They were not considered "heathen savages" as the native peoples were, which put the natives as expendable or even worse. The attitude was that these people had better get way out of the way or be killed. When it became evident that the native peoples would resist leaving their land and would not adapt to Western ways, the die was cast—kill them all.

These were our ancestors, and almost all of them got here on a boat that was not exactly "The Love Boat" for those that remember that TV program. They were in it for keeps and not only that there was a good chance that they were not too happy about the process that got them on the boat in the first place. These were tough, determined people that certainly had the capacity to be cruel, sometimes exceedingly so.

Some of the most abused and toughest American immigrants were the Scotch-Irish from Northern Ireland. These people sometimes called the "Ulster Irish," and until very recently, one could hear them involved in violence in Northern Ireland. Most of the Scotch-Irish originally came from the Highlands of Scotland where the British "lost their patience" with them and literally depopulated the entire region. Many of these people, those that were not killed anyway, got kicked out of the highlands to Northern Ireland. The Irish and these new arrivals had a lot in common with each other, but they did not seem to think so. They apparently only paid attention to what was different. The Highlanders were Protestants, and the Irish were Catholics. There were disputes over land, political rivalries, and other fractious issues. In fact, they did exactly what the British wanted them to do, and that was to fight with each other. The more they fought with each other, the easier it was for the British to control them. Many of the Scotch-Irish ended up in North America, and one of them even became president. His name was Andrew Jackson, and if you are Native American, you might not hold this president in high esteem.

Both of Andrew Jackson's parents, along with his two older brothers, were born in Northern Ireland. The family came to the Camden area of South Carolina where Jackson was born on March 14, 1767. He never knew his father who died shortly before his birth. Andrew and his two older brothers decided to fight the British when he was thirteen. One brother died of heat stroke, and Andrew and his other brother were captured by the British. Andrew refused to shine a British soldier's boots, and the soldier slashed him across the face with a sword. This is the famous scare that Jackson had that was depicted in many of his portraits. He and his brother contracted small pox, and their mother arranged for their release. His older brother died while Jackson slowly recovered. His mother then went off to help nurse wounded and sick Continental soldiers, contracted cholera, and died, leaving Andrew an orphan—his entire family gone—at the age of sixteen. He finished his education, taught high school for a while, and decided to become a lawyer at seventeen. This was not a weak man, by any means.

Andrew Jackson, our seventh president, also signed the Indian Removal Act in 1830. This act ostensibly was to exchange frontier land west of the Mississippi for prime eastern Indian land, mostly in the south. This repulsive undertaking took land from over forty-six thousand Native Americans and resulted in the deaths of between four thousand to eight thousand Cherokees on what became known as the Trail of Tears.[126] To their credit, Jackson's descendants, along with the various foundations and committees that manage the presidential library of Andrew Jackson, have done an excellent job of documenting this dark chapter in American history. They have even gone as far as to teach an excellent course on a subject that is too often hidden from the American people. For example, the "Trail of Tears" lesson plan has, in its introduction, "This program will make students wonder who were the settlers, and who were the savages."[127] Also included is a quote from a Georgia militiaman regarding the removal process: "I fought through the Civil War and have seen men shot to pieces and slaughtered by thousands, but the Cherokee removal was the cruelest I ever saw."[128]

Andrew Jackson's stated purpose was contained in his second message to Congress in 1830. He said that the purpose in the Indian Removal Act was to

> [E]nd conflict between state/federal government . . . provide a place for the 'dense and civilized' population to expand . . . strengthen the southwestern frontiers . . . relieve Mississippi and Alabama of Indian occupancy . . . separate Indians from immediate contact with whites . . . free the Indians from the power of the States . . . help them preserve their heritage and traditions.

Although his racist attitude toward the native peoples was evident, these were almost noble-sounding intentions, on the surface that is. It should have been obvious that you do not steal someone's land and then force them to walk over a thousand miles (including women, children, the old, and infirm), shoot the ones that cannot keep up, and

---

[126.] The Jackson Presidential Library is located at Jackson's home, the Hermitage, in Nashville, Tennessee. They offer an excellent course on the "Trail of Tears" story that is very frank, factual, and informative. The downloadable lesson plan is at the following website: http://www.thehermitage.com/visit/school-programs/sm_files/Trailunit.pdf.
[127.] Ibid.
[128.] Ibid.

then dump them in land completely foreign to them to "preserve their heritage." Add to this, Jackson's often-stated contempt toward native people and you have what we have seen with Thomas Jefferson, a lot of lofty talk followed by criminal behavior. When one is president of the United States and his words do not match his behavior, he is not called a hypocrite or a liar; he is referred to as "complex." Both Jackson and Jefferson were referred to in this manner along with many other prominent Americans in history.

The Civil War

Nowhere do the three elements of the American Empire—racism, genocide, and militarism—come together resulting in the most tragic event in US history than the Civil War. Although the causes of this disaster are being debated to this day, there is no question that racism was at the core of it. We also had militarism as the method of choice used by both sides to attempt to resolve it. The factor that is not quite as plain as the other two is genocide, and we will need to take a close look at cause and effect to clarify the picture.

Of course, the unresolved issue of slavery was a key factor in the war, but there certainly were others. One of the most prominent of these was the looming questions of what sphere of power was going to run the United States, slave South or free North? These two economic and political centers had been jockeying for dominance for a long time. Open conflict was intensifying. Added to this was the fact that many states were coming into the Union from the territories. Each one was a battle for power between the North and the South. This friction was becoming more and more of a problem, and the whole thing was coming to a head. Abraham Lincoln was at least as interested in preserving the Union as he was getting rid of slavery. These issues have been argued in other works, so we will not get into the nuts and bolts of what caused the Civil War and details of battles and so forth.

Suffice to say that the North "won" on paper anyway. One overriding factor in this war was the manufacturing capacity of the North that far exceeded that of the South. Cavalry charges against cannons loaded with Grape-shot do not work very well, no matter how brave the cavalrymen are. There was another factor that arguably shortened the war and also was used effectively against the Western

Plains Indians afterward. This was the strategy of "total warfare" embraced by William Tecumseh Sherman. Simply put, this strategy amounts to not only attacking military targets but destroying the infrastructure of the enemy for the purpose of destroying the enemy's will and means to resist. Food, transportation, housing, manufacturing, and everything else that supports the war-making capability of the military forces is destroyed. Sherman did this very well and explained this strategy such as that war is so horrible that it is best to win it as quickly as possible. It is interesting that Sherman did not use the term "total warfare" and even denied that he was doing that. Sherman used the term "hard war" to characterize this strategy, perhaps because this was on the edge of what was considered to be war crimes even at that time. Although history has placed ownership of "Total Warfare" with Sherman, both Lincoln and Grant supported this philosophy, and many Northern generals, such as Sheridan, followed suit. Sherman "gets the credit," but it goes at least as far back in American history as to George Washington himself. As discussed earlier in this chapter, Washington issued clear orders to his commanders that were instructions to exterminate and annihilate whole tribes of Native Americans, which included burning crops and stores of food, burning houses, and destroying all means of sustenance and support necessary to a society. One could go back even further to Jamestown in 1636 where Captain John Underhill spent his days "in burning and spoiling" Block Island in one of the many Native American extermination projects conducted by America's first permanent settlement.[129] In these cases and many more, the intent was the same: the destruction and extermination of the societies, cultures, and peoples of Native America; to literally wipe them off the face of the earth along with their languages, culture, and way of life.

Robert E. Lee surrendered to Ulysses S. Grant at Appomattox on April 9, 1865, and the nation quickly set about the process of "securing" the rest of the country known as "Indian territory," and the South feverishly set about revising social and political systems to deny the newly freed slaves basic constitutional rights. It can be argued that the Civil War was fought to decide what sphere of influence was

---

[129.] Richard Drinnon, *Facing West: The Metaphysics of Indian-Hating and Empire-Building*, (University of Oklahoma Press Norman, 1997), 332.

going to run the country and then take control of the rest of the land between the states that had already come into the Union and the West Coast. This was the final chapter in the annihilation of the remaining Indian Nations. Let us first briefly summarize how the freed slaves were kept virtually powerless.

The North had won, at least on paper anyway. During the so-called "Reconstruction period," the South slowly gained traction in regaining political power and keeping the newly freed slaves "in their place." African Americans now counted as a whole person as far as representation in Congress but, through a variety of methods, were denied the right to vote. There were "literacy tests" and the like that de-facto denied African Americans the right to vote. This system of "legal" disempowerment became known as "Jim Crow" legislation. No one knows what would have happened had Lincoln not been murdered, but there is record that he intended on doing everything that he could to make the country whole again. Reconstruction of the South might have been very different had he survived for another term. The Lincoln assassination was presented to the American people as the first of many "lone assassin" events to include JFK, Martin Luther King, and RFK even when there was solid evidence that there was more to it. Ask anyone, "Who killed Lincoln?" and you will immediately hear, "John Wilkes Booth." Never mentioned or remembered is the fact that Lincoln's successor, Andrew Johnson, was suspected of involvement in the assassination and, as Lincoln's successor, pardoned others that were involved. The whole affair was eerily reminiscent of the JFK assassination. This was arguably the first time that the United States had a president that could have steered the country away from racism, genocide, and militarism. It is not a "slam dunk" that either of these two men could have accomplished this, but they might have, and this might have just sealed both their fates.

Both had the potential to become transformational leaders, and both were shot in the head in public. Both had successors that methodically covered up these two outrages against the country and the American people. Of course, no one can ever know what Lincoln or Kennedy would have accomplished had they not been murdered. It is, however, a fact that the possibility existed that the strikingly similar issues they both faced could have turned out much differently had they not been both "eliminated." Would Lincoln have allowed the Jim Crow South and the "final solution" of the Native Americans to have taken place? Of course, we will never know the answer to this question, but we do know that Andrew Johnson was a very different person than Lincoln was, and he had a very different attitude toward these two pivotal questions. Maybe that is why he ended up in the White House.

We will not delve into this matter any further, as it is not the intent of this writing, and others have gone into this subject in great detail. The intent of this work is to explore where all this came from. In other words, are we able to understand the metaphysics of where racism and its two conjoined twins, militarism and genocide, all came together to cause slavery, the extermination of the Native Americans, almost continuous warfare, and assassinations of the only leaders that could have taken us in a different direction? These are not exceptional moments; they are a continuum of catastrophic events that show that America is "locked in" to dysfunctional responses. Although there certainly is much disinformation about slavery, most Americans have an understanding that it was wrong. In contrast, not much is known about the extermination of the Native Americans, and that what is thought to be known is mostly pure fantasy and misinformation. For example, Native Americans were not nomadic and this includes the plains Indians. Some had summer and winter homes that they went back and forth to, but all of them had permanent residences. Ask most Americans about this, and they will argue and argue with you about it, although they have nothing to base their "knowledge" on. Why is this fallacy so ingrained in our belief system? Because it is part of the rationalization process to justify genocide. "They were just wandering nomads that were not making good use of the land . . ." The misconceptions are almost endless, such as "They really were not here that long . . . They were war-like and brutal . . . They were hunter-foragers . . . There were only a few million of them, and the land was virtually uninhabited . . . They had no religion . . ." And you could go on and on. All of the above, and more, has been proven to be false; but the belief system still exists, even today. But why?

William Tecumseh Sherman[130]

As Jefferson's beliefs were emblematic of the colonists, William Tecumseh Sherman's beliefs embodied those of America during and after the Civil War, and the two belief systems had striking similarities. As in the case of Jefferson, the author asked the question earlier, "What was he thinking?" Let us take a look at what Sherman was thinking because it was what America was thinking from its very beginnings at the first settlements at Jamestown and Plymouth to the present. It is ironic that a man whose middle name was "Tecumseh" would write the final chapter in the destruction of the native peoples.

Actually, there is record that Sherman's first name had been Tecumseh, the name coming from his father's admiration for the Shawnee chief who was known to be philosophical. The first name "William" came along later in his childhood when he was raised by foster parents. How did a man named after a great Indian chief end up to have almost total contempt for the native peoples?

He, along with most of the Civil War generals on both sides, was a graduate of West Point. He was known by his classmates as very bright, studious, diligent in academic matters, and so forth. He did have one "shortcoming," if you could call it that, in that he had a marked indifference to orders, regimentation, and minor rules. He was known as a prankster, and he noted in his memoirs that he averaged about 150 demerits per year. He also noted that this moved him down from fourth in his class to sixth upon graduation. This indifference to rules might have actually been a strength. This particular trait has been observed in many great military leaders. It could even be a sign of

---

[130] Photo source Wikipedia at: http://en.wikipedia.org/wiki/William_Tecumseh_Sherman.

person who can make their own decisions without worrying too much about how these decisions would be looked at by superiors. Overly cautious military leaders do just fine in peacetime, but perhaps not so well in war. The Northern commander, General George B. McClellan, would be a good example.

First, let us briefly take a look at what he did believe. It has been widely suspected that after the Civil War, Generals Sherman, Sheridan, and others turned their "total warfare" strategy against the Plains Indians by destroying their food source, namely the buffalo. The author once had a college professor who was Native American and mentioned to our class that the European Americans had slaughtered "many, many, millions of buffalo and left them rotting in the fields as an *act of genocide* against the native people." She went on to explain that her ancestors were incredulous that "anyone would do such a thing." Some say that it was "greedy buffalo hunters" that had virtually wiped the buffalo clear from the American Plains, and that this was not a deliberate act by the State. In fact, this was exactly what this author was taught in public school. This debate continues to this day when all one has to do is to read Sherman's memoirs where, in his own words, he explains exactly what happened and why. No, he did not say that "we deliberately slaughtered all of the buffalo to starve the Indians," but he does frame this sordid account in enough detail that one is able to conclude that the eradication of the buffalo was a deliberate act of genocide, and it is a certainty that he had nothing but contempt for First Nation peoples. Almost at the end of his memoirs, Sherman "tipped his hand," so to speak, that he knew full well what the relationship was between the buffalo and the Plains Indians. This is what he had to say:

> I am sure that without the courage and activity of the department commanders with the small bodies of regular troops on the plains during the years 1866-69, the Pacific Railroads could not have been built; but once built and in full operation the *fate of the buffalo and Indian was settled* for all time to come.[131] (Emphasis added)

[131.] William T. Sherman, *Memoirs of William Tecumseh Sherman*, (MacMay, 2nd Edition, December 25, 2007), Kindle location 15212-15218.

Not much further, he also indicated exactly what he thought of the Native Americans. Notice that he considers cattle as a superior form of food, and also the entire lifestyle of the descendants of Europeans he considers far superior to Native Americans. He offers no rationale to this conclusion and presents it as obvious. This was the attitude of white America from its inception. Despite all of the disease, squalor, hatred, violence, and racism that the European settlers took with them to America, they considered themselves far superior, as noted below.

> They (his troops after the war) naturally looked for new homes to the great West, to the new Territories and States as far as the Pacific coast, and we realize to-day that the vigorous men who control Kansas, Nebraska, Dakota, Montana, Colorado, etc., etc., were soldiers of the civil war. These men flocked to the plains, and were rather stimulated than retarded by the danger of an Indian war. This was another potent agency in producing the result we enjoy to-day, in having in so short a time replaced the wild buffaloes by more numerous herds of tame cattle, and by substituting for the *useless Indians* the intelligent owners of productive farms and cattle-ranches.[132] (Emphasis added)

In his final reference to the fate of the buffalo and Native American being intertwined, he indicates that he fully understood the relationship between destroying a people's food source and genocide. Of note is the fact that he almost eulogizes the Native Americans and now refers to them as "brave" instead of "useless."

> Still, the Indian Peace Commission of 1867-'68 did prepare the way for the great Pacific Railroad, which for better or worse, have settled the fate of the buffalo and Indian forever. There have been wars and conflicts since with these Indians up to a recent period too numerous and complicated in their detail for me to unravel and record, but they have been the dying struggles of a singular race of brave men fighting against destiny, each less and less violent, till

---

[132.] Ibid, 15226-15233.

> now the wild game is gone, the whites too numerous and powerful; so that the Indian question has become one of sentiment and charity, but not of war.[133]

There are other examples of Sherman's understanding of what he and the Civil War generals were doing. He mentioned it many times in his lectures after retirement and also in personal conversations. Of course he did not say "point-blank" that one purpose of putting the railroads in was to exterminate the food source (buffalo) of the remaining Indians for the purpose of annihilating them. That could have been considered to be a war crime, even in those days. Add to this the fact that deliberately starving women and children was considered "unchivalrous" at best. He did, however, most certainly know what was being done and was at least complicit in it. It is noteworthy that the last remaining Native Americans living free were in the Western Plains, and that Civil War generals, such as Sherman and Sheridan, were in charge of these regions. Also, the commander of the Union army, Ulysses S. Grant, was president. All these generals espoused to the doctrine of "total warfare." That is they knew how to, and were experienced at not only killing soldiers but also destroying the support structure, sustenance, and the will to resist of the opposing force's society. It certainly cannot be a coincidence that all these factors came into play at that time to destroy the people in the way of "Manifest Destiny."

Not only did Sherman allude to the final sequence of events that destroyed the Native Americans, but General Phil Sheridan was considerably more forthright about the whole thing. Author S. C. Gwynne explained this sordid chapter that has virtually been left out of the history books in his excellent work, *Empire of the Summer Moon*, as noted below.

> Surprisingly, only a few voices cried out against the slaughter of the buffalo, which had no precedent in human history. Mostly people didn't trouble themselves about the consequences. It was simply capitalism working itself out, the exploitation of another natural resource. There

---

[133]. Ibid, 15697-15701

was another, better, explanation for the lack of protest, articulated best by General Phil Sheridan, the commander of the military division of the Missouri. "These men [hunters] have done in the last two years . . . more to settle the vexed Indian question than the entire regular army has done in the last thirty years," he said, "They are destroying the Indians' commissary . . . . For the sake of a lasting peace, let them kill skin and sell until the buffaloes are exterminated. Then your prairies can be covered with speckled cattle and the festive cowboy." Killing the Indians' food was not just an accident of commerce; it was a deliberate political act.[134]

So the question remains as to how the seemingly intelligent, well-educated, and articulate people can so despise a native population that had helped them settle in the new world? And further, we have common elements of extreme fear and hatred that goes back to well over two hundred years. Forests that the native people saw as their friend were viewed by these new settlers as dark and evil along with everything in it. This would include wolves, bears, and everything else that resided there, including the people. These new settlers needed to tame and/or destroy all this wild, uncontrolled evil. Consistently, over hundreds of years, we have a clear record of metaphors and analogies such as George Washington's comments equating Indians with wolves as being wild and dangerous. We had the Civil War generals that wanted to replace the wild buffalo with domesticated cattle along with replacing the "wild" Indians with "useful" people such as farmers and blacksmiths and so forth. You had the "Pilgrims" at Plymouth who would whip the flesh off and cut the ears off and banish anyone that challenged this ideology of these evil heathens that lived in the dark, foreboding forest with sinister animals such as wolves. Where did this fear and hatred come from that has driven these European Americans on a consistent course of racism, militarism, and genocide?

[134.] S. C. Gwynne, *Empire of the Summer Moon*, (New York, NY: Scribner, 2010), Kindle Edition, Loc. 4906-5006.

Calvinism and Puritanism

Author Richard Drinnon, in his excellent book, *Facing West: the Metaphysics of Indian-Hating and Empire-Building*, traces these pathological fears and manifest hatred back to the very foundations of these Europeans' belief systems. Although they thought of themselves as devout Christians, it is hard to see anything in their belief systems and behavior that had anything to do with the ministry of Christ. This author does not recall anything in the teachings of Christ that advocated racism, militarism, and genocide resulting from extreme fear and hatred. One would venture to say that such beliefs and behavior are, in fact, antithetical to the teachings of Jesus. One could look at Christianity as having been founded by a leader who had transcended the belief systems at the time only to have later "followers" corrupt virtually everything he stood for. These so-called "followers" would fit Andrew Lobaczewski's description of "characteropaths" that manipulate the founder's teachings to serve their own malevolent self-interests. Add to this the final stage of Lobaczewski's ponerization process whereby outright sociopaths gain control of the system, and we now have what has become of much of Christianity in the Americas. One has only to turn on the news to see such aberrations as self-proclaimed "evangelists" advocating such things as "taking care of" heads of state that do not suit their likings. Pat Robertson did exactly that a few years back when the democratically elected head of Venezuela, Hugo Chavez, did or said something that was not to the "right Reverend" Robertson's liking. This author does not believe that Jesus would be humored by such actions in his name. Further, one would be hard-pressed to even imagine that Jesus would be impressed that the first "Christians" in the Americas would undertake the wholesale slaughter of millions of "heathen savages," witch trials, burning people alive, hanging natives in groups of thirteen to honor Jesus Christ and the twelve apostles (the Spaniards did this), and so forth. One would think that Jesus would be disgusted by these criminal actions.

The settlers in North America had some interesting belief systems that were infused in their religious beliefs. Although interesting, these beliefs were very destructive and actually persist to this day. One common thread, for example, is Calvinism of which one essential element is that anything that is not turned into a commodity and marketed is "useless": forests need to be cut down and the wood "harvested." It is "worthless" when just left to grow. The native peoples did not cut the forests down to harvest the wood, plant crops, and so forth. They therefore were considered worthless people that needed to either change or be done away with. They were not doing anything useful with the land. Never mind that these people raised plenty of food by working with the land rather than against it and had been nurturing themselves quite well for many thousands of years. It is hard to find facts on the native people's health, life span, medicine, and quality of life. However, the records from the native peoples themselves and even the descriptions from Westerners, including the Spanish and the English, paint a picture of a people that had advanced medicine, were much healthier than the Europeans, probably lived longer, and were clearly happier than the Europeans. There have been several European sources that also stated that when Europeans lived with the Indians, they did not come back. They voluntarily stayed when they had the option. This apparently was always the case as there was not even one case documented during colonial times of Europeans that voluntarily returned. If there were any cases to the contrary, this writer missed them; and the reverse was not the case either. This writer found no instances where Native Americans voluntarily stayed with the colonists when given the option. It appears that the Indians were having a good time and that the colonists were not.

It also appears that this relative misery of the colonists was largely self-imposed, and this apparently manifested itself into a real problem for the Indians. Having a good time, pleasurable experiences (especially when physical pleasure was involved), laughing, joking, playing cards, dancing were considered by the Puritans mostly to be sinful, against God, and therefore evil. Of course, anything evil had to be dealt with in very severe terms. It had to be stopped at all cost. So between Calvinism and Puritanism, you had the perception of useless, evil, godless, and sinful savages that clung to their ways and would adopt neither Christianity nor a "civilized" life style. The outcome is clear, these people and their way of life had to go; and the quicker, the better. This conclusion had been arrived at almost four hundred ago along with the methods of accomplishing this. These powerful forces were in play throughout American history and are just as much a player today as they were then.

Even today, the Native Americans are losing treaty rights, land, and resources. From the early sixteen hundreds on, there has been continuous warfare against Native Americans, and that warfare has consisted of the use of all means of destruction and extermination. Not only military force was used but also social, political, cultural, economic, and legal policies were employed to destroy the native peoples. The media played an instrumental role in what can easily be described as a North American holocaust. Anyone the author's age is able to recall the *Cowboys and Indians* scenarios in the movie theaters where brutal, bloodthirsty Indians attacked wagon trains of virtuous settlers scalping women and murdering children until the brave US cavalry came to the rescue. Apparently, this was the theme from the very beginning to the end. This entire process went on until extermination, which could be marked as early in the twentieth century when the native population was down to roughly two hundred thousand people. This was an insignificant number. The native population had been exterminated. This was something that had never been done in history, but an act that rippled across the Atlantic Ocean.

Author and lecturer Noam Chomsky, linguistics professor emeritus, Massachusetts Institute of Technology, makes the connection that "all of Europe was watching this." He also points out that the methods and propaganda techniques used were not lost when the Nazis began to formulate their own programs of annihilation against the European Jews, Roma, and others. One has only to watch the Nazi propaganda films from the WWII era to notice the similarities. Visual parallels and analogies to vermin and inferences of nonhuman status were evident in both. Concentration camps were not much different from reservations where inhumane conditions, including starvation, where prevalent. Chomsky goes into interesting details on how the Nazis were keenly interested on the American ability to control public opinion on a variety of fronts.

Chomsky explains why propaganda is much more sophisticated in democracies, and that is because these systems need to deceive the people in order to control them. He provides the example of American President Woodrow Wilson's ability to win an election based on what appeared to be a pacifist, noninterventionist approach to WWI raging in Europe. Once elected, Wilson was able to turn the American public into a "German-hating machine" that propelled America into the war in a matter of a few months. According to Chomsky, the lessons and methods of the Wilson administration were not lost on Hitler's propaganda minister, Joseph Goebbels, who methodically employed the very same methods in his campaign against the Jews and others in WWII. These connections have been conveniently left out of the history of the United States along with many, many not-so-convenient facts and connections.

Manifest Destiny Past Western Shores

Back to continuous warfare, there is no question that there was constant warfare against the native peoples to the point of extermination. This war only stopped when there were no more Indians to kill, and this is an undeniable fact. There were, however, other lands to conquer and other "Indians" to kill. War and conquest went literally from coast to coast with a Civil War along the way to decide who was going to run the empire. Once that was decided, the Indians were totally annihilated; and right away, the United States started to devour what were the remnants of the Spanish Empire. Most of this territory was referred to as the Spanish East Indies, which consisted of the Philippine Islands, Guam, the Mariana Islands, the Caroline Islands, parts of Formosa, Sabah, and the Moluccas. Following the Spanish-American War in 1898, most of the above territory was acquired by the United States. Cuba's War of Independence against Spain also greatly increased United States' control and influence in that country. The Philippines also had a war of independence against Spain. The United States, however, decided that the Filipinos were unfit to govern themselves. This apparently obligated the United States to kill or otherwise cause the death of about one million Filipinos so that they would not have the opportunity to mismanage their own affairs. The United States had already purchased Alaska in 1867, acquired Midway Atoll also in 1867 and Samoa in 1899, had its eye on the Virgin Islands and the area where the Panama Canal was eventually built. The United States also formulated what became known as the "Open Door Policy" toward China in 1899, which meant that imperial powers had free access to China without any of them in control of the country. Add to this the acquisitions of Puerto Rico, Hawaii, and others, and we now have more and more the appearance of a colonial empire.

From the very beginning, the empire had spread west and south in a continuous march, and water did not stop the onslaught. By any means and any rationalizations necessary, land and control of sea lanes was acquired, always west. Open talk of empire became a part of discussions at high levels. Also at high levels, racist and derogatory terms were used toward the "new Indians," and rationalizations that were markedly similar to those used in the past. Just as Spain was blamed in Florida for having allowed chaos and mismanagement to flourish, which somehow threatened American security and required Andrew Jackson to "restore law and order," the same arguments were used to justify the United States' "pacification" of Cuba. Yes, the same exact word was used, *pacification*, to describe an armed invasion. And yes, we would hear this word used again in Vietnam. Also, more and more, the British and the United States were collaborating and supporting each other. Political cartoons of the era depicted Uncle Sam and John Bull, the British version of the former, in supportive roles. The cartoon on the left depicted Uncle Sam acquiring some of the above-mentioned lands represented by demeaning stereotypes. It also contained a legend that had an admiring John Bull stating, "It's really most extraordinary what training will do. Why, only the other day I thought that man unable to support himself." We also see the beginnings of Anglo-American alliances against Germany.

Source: *Philadelphia Inquirer*, 1898

In the broad view, the American Revolution may be viewed as a relatively minor family squabble. Although Americans thought of themselves as different from the British, there was a shared ideology. They were much more alike than different. Calvinism and Puritanism formed the metaphysical foundations of this ideology that manifested itself in the form of racism and militarism. Although the British had no problem with killing thousands of anyone that resisted them, they did not come close to the outright genocide that clearly happened in the Americas. At the beginning, the British had every intention of displacing and replacing the Native Americans, but it fell within the purview of the Americans to carry this out. This resulted in future Americans incorporating genocide into empire building and using racism along with militarism as the tools of the trade. Both were methodically building and developing empires, or perhaps one Anglo-American global empire that would be ruled by the English-speaking peoples of the world. America was expanding westward, and Briton was moving eastward. Had not a few setbacks occurred such as in India, Vietnam, and such, the empire owned and controlled by English-speaking whites might have been completed some time ago.

Philippine Casualties
Source: http://cdn.theatlantic.com

Wounded Knee Casualties,
Source: http://www.websters-online-dictionary.org

Let us return to 1899 and revisit one example of America's westward grasp for power and empire. The Philippine War of Independence was brutally put down by the United States, and it can be argued that it was deadly enough to qualify as an act of genocide. Although casualty rates vary widely, it can be deduced that at the minimum over two hundred thousand Philippine civilians and military lost their lives. Philippine historian E. San Juan Jr. compared the population of the Philippines before the war, which was estimated at nine million, to after the war, which was less than eight million. He came up with the figure of 1.4 million casualties that the United States was responsible for, and asserted that this was an act of genocide.[135] Descriptions of the United States' conduct of this war are familiar to this author, who is also a Vietnam veteran. Forages into the

---

[135.] E. San Juan, Jr. (March 22, 2005). "U.S. Genocide in the Philippines: A Case of Guilt, Shame, or Amnesia?" Archived from the original on 2009-06-22. http://replay.waybackmachine.org/20090622095234/http://www.selvesandothers.org/article9315.html. Retrieved October 3, 2007.

countryside were often scorched earth affairs whereby entire villages were burned to the ground. The author recalls a US commander who said that his men had to "burn the village to save it." Some tactics were also familiar to Native Americans such as herding civilians into concentration camps termed "protection zones" where many if not most died of disease. Any that tried to escape had to go through "free fire zones," which meant that they would probably be shot. Native Americans familiar with the slaughter at Wounded Knee noticed the similarity between Wounded Knee and photos of slaughtered Filipinos, as noted in the above photos.

Source: http://waterboarding.org

Waterboarding, a subject debated today, was even then known as torture. The practice was widespread in the Philippines as men in the camps were routinely tortured and executed. Huge piles of dead Filipinos were everywhere. The author recently heard a member of Congress advocating the practice of waterboarding to suspects for information as a part of the so-called "war on terror." His advocacy was along the lines that if we can get information from a suspected "terrorist" that using "a little water" in the process should not be a problem. This author wonders whether or not this same congressman would have the same opinion if he was the suspect. One must keep in mind that what is done to "those bad people" today will be done to Americans tomorrow. In fact, at the time of this writing, Americans are being tortured and executed by the US government without due process. We will go further into this in my next book.

Most of the above took place during the first administration of President William McKinley, from 1897 to 1901. During the election campaign of 1900, the issue of the United States' increasingly colonial posture became a central issue. The Democratic Party headed by their candidate William Jennings Bryan was increasingly critical of what they perceived was a rapidly expanding American colonial empire that they saw as a threat to the Constitution. McKinley and the Republicans won. McKinley was ostensibly a reluctant participant in the territories gained during his first administration, but he had no problem taking credit for it. McKinley was shot at the Pan-American Exposition in

Buffalo, New York, on September 6, 1901. He died eight days later, which put Theodore (Teddy) Roosevelt into office.

Source: http://en.wikipedia.org/wiki/Big_Stick_ideology

There was nothing reluctant about Teddy Roosevelt. He had campaigned, as McKinley's vice president, in favor of acquiring the Philippines for their "stability" and also to enhance American prestige. As president, he promoted what became known as his "big stick" policy toward the Caribbean, Central, and South America which amounted to a very robust interpretation of the Monroe Doctrine. In short, the Monroe Doctrine was that the United States of America took precedence over the entire region and that no other power had the right to interfere with the affairs of the entire region. President Roosevelt's policy was also known as "gunboat" diplomacy, whereas Roosevelt would send an entire naval fleet complete with a few thousand marines to a "trouble" spot, which usually meant any country that was deviating from US interests. The concept came from a saying that Roosevelt used, "Speak softly and carry a big stick; you will go far." This practice served him well, and he used it to advantage in Cuba, Panama, and Nicaragua. There is little doubt that Teddy Roosevelt had imperial ambitions far beyond America's shores. He was a confident, forceful leader, and it was not wise to try to get the best of him. He had no qualms about keeping corporate power in check, resulting in another nickname, the "Trust Buster."

However, as with almost all American leaders, he had a dark side that just did not seem to get into the history books we studied in school. His wholehearted support for racist genocide in the Philippines and the same in the continental United States against the American Indians just has not been very well publicized. One particular incident, beyond any doubt, that clearly showed this dark side of him was the repulsively sickening slaughter of unarmed Cheyenne and Arapaho at Sand Creek in the territory of Colorado in 1864. This senseless and barbaric slaughter of mostly women and children was perpetrated by US Army Colonel John Chivington, who ordered about seven hundred Colorado militia to attack a peaceful encampment of a few hundred unarmed natives that assumed they were under US Army protection. Most of the men were away on a Buffalo hunt when Chivington ordered his attack. It was such an atrocity that two of his commanders refused to order their men into action. The entire affair resulted in a congressional investigation of which there was undisputed evidence of some of the most disgusting behavior of uniformed American soldiers that can be imagined. The congressional testimony of one witness, John S. Smith, follows:

> I saw the bodies of those lying there cut all to pieces, worse mutilated than any I ever saw before; the women cut all to pieces . . . With knives; scalped; their brains knocked out; children two or three months old; all ages lying there, from sucking infants up to warriors . . . By whom were they mutilated? By the United States troops.[136]

Another witness was Stan Hoig who had this to say:

> Fingers and ears were cut off the bodies for the jewelry they carried. The body of White Antelope, lying solitarily in the creek bed, was a prime target. Besides scalping him the soldiers cut off his nose, ears, and testicles-the last for a tobacco pouch . . .[137]

Other accounts described soldiers cutting female genitalia off and displaying them on their hats. Here is what famous frontiersman Kit Carson had to say of the whole affair:

> Jis to think of that dog Chivington and his dirty hounds, up thar at Sand Creek. His men shot down squaws, and blew the brains out of little innocent children. You call

---

[136.] PBS has documented this incident and many others. This quote is from an article originally reported by the *Rocky Mountain News*, 1864, and is available at: http://www.pbs.org/weta/thewest/resources/archives/four/sandcrk.htm#smith.

[137.] Stan Hoig, *The Sand Creek Massacre* (Norman: University of Oklahoma Press), 153.

sich soldiers Christians, do ye? And Indians savages? What der yer 'spose our Heavenly Father, who made both them and us, thinks of these things? I tell you what, I don't like a hostile red skin any more than you do. And when they are hostile, I've fought 'em, hard as any man. But I never yet drew a bead on a squaw or papoose, and I despise the man who would.[138]

Years later, here is what President Roosevelt said about the Sand Creek Massacre: "As righteous and beneficial a deed as ever took place on the frontier."[139] It is not as if Roosevelt did not know what had happened at Sand Creek; he did. The fact is that Theodore Roosevelt was as much a genocidal racist as most of the US presidents before him. Further, he used militarism to promote these vicious pursuits toward a colonial empire that the world had seen many, many times before.

The difference is that this time, the empire of the day would be global in the sense that it would control the world economy to include banking and the world's resources. Also included would be oil, drugs, water, and precious metals. As always, the true ambitions of empire would be largely unexposed. They would be carefully masked in the same genre as the British code words such as *civilizing savages* and so forth. The new empire-speak would entail veiled references such as *spreading democracy, self-determination,* and a variety of terms that contained nice sounding words such as *liberty* and *freedom*. One of these terms, *pacification*, was used extensively in Vietnam and actually goes back at least to Andrew Jackson's war against the Seminoles and the Creeks. Jackson actually used this term to describe what amounted to extermination. These terms and the obfuscations of true intentions were becoming more and more sophisticated to the point that America was becoming one country with two governments. One government would be the one discussed in the media, political campaigns, and in the schoolbooks. The other was the one of deep politics or that which the American people are

---

[138.] Hampton Sides, *Blood and Thunder: An Epic of the American West* (New York: Doubleday, 2006), 379.

[139.] Thomas G. Dyer, *Theodore Roosevelt and the Idea of Race*, (Baton Rouge: Louisiana State University Press, 1960), 79.

unaware of. It was the same elected leaders in both instances at the helm, but what they said they were doing and what they were really up to were two completely different things.

As discussed previously, Thomas Jefferson was an absolute master of deceit and deception, and he probably set the course for this practice to the present. As MIT professor of linguistics Noam Chomsky so aptly points out in his lectures and writings, only in a democracy is it necessary to use very sophisticated forms of propaganda. In a dictatorship, it is not necessary because the dictator does not need to fool the people. They just do whatever they think is best without concern for how popular their decisions are. They do not have to win elections, nor do they need to answer to the people. In a democracy, however, if you want to control the people you have to trick them. This is done by using very advanced forms of propaganda.

Woodrow Wilson

Under the Wilson administration, which took office in March 1913, propaganda took a quantum leap, and all of Europe was watching. Actually, European colonial powers had already been taking note. As previously mentioned, the extermination methods used against the Native Americans, and the rationalizations were closely observed. One who took particular notice, albeit a few years later, was Joseph Goebbels who became Adolf Hitler's Third Reich minister of public enlightenment and propaganda during WWII. From an early age, he was fascinated with the idea of shaping thought, and he particularly noticed and studied the United States' use of propaganda against Germany in WWI. Goebbels consistently mentioned how the "enemies" of Germany were much more adept at the use of propaganda, and he clearly attributed Germany's defeat as having resulted from this.[140] He also studied Woodrow Wilson and his incredible ability to say one thing and do another. For instance, while campaigning for president, Wilson told the nation that he did not want America to get involved in foreign wars. Storm clouds were brewing in Europe, and it seemed likely that there was going to be a major war

---

[140.] Joseph Goebbels, *Goebbels on the Power of Propaganda*, (Kindle Edition: Shamrock Eden Publishing, May) 31,2009)

involving Germany. Wilson repeatedly stated that he would keep the United States out of this. Once in office, he literally turned the United States into a German-hating machine in a matter of only a few months. Some Americans did notice, but he mostly got away with this.[141] This 180-degree turn caught the attention of both Goebbels and Hitler, and they used Wilson's techniques to their advantage years later.

Woodrow Wilson was a piece of work. History books mostly portray him as this kindly fellow who was reluctantly dragged, along with the country, into WWI. Afterward, he was so appalled at the death and destruction that he worked to create the League of Nations, a world body that would work for world peace. Nothing could be farther from the truth. Wilson won the presidential election of 1912 only because Teddy Roosevelt had split the Republican vote when he ran as a progressive for the Bull Moose Party. Wilson only got 6.3 million votes and 42 percent of the electorate. His presidency was characterized by racism, foreign intervention on a scale that surpassed even Teddy Roosevelt's administration, and an all-out frontal assault on civil liberties. Neither before nor since the administration of Woodrow Wilson has America come closer to a police state run by a dictatorship.

For example, Wilson pushed the Espionage Act of 1917 in June through Congress, which rivaled Adams's Alien and Sedition Acts of 1798. He even tried to strengthen the Espionage Act with a provision that would give broad censorship powers directly to the president.[142] Wilson also had his postmaster general suppress all mail that was socialist, anti-British, pro-Irish, or anything else that Wilson determined threatened the war effort. He even put a movie producer, Robert Goldstein, in jail for ten years for producing *The Spirit of '76*, which was about the Revolutionary War that gave an unfavorable

---

[141.] Professor Noam Chomsky is a linguistics expert and professor emeritus from MIT University. He often uses this as an example of the extreme manipulation of information that is prevalent today in democracies. Most Americans, including this author, would have never made this connection that is noticeably not in our history books.

[142.] James W. Loewen, *Lies My Teacher Told Me: Everything Your American History Textbook Got Wrong*, (New Press, Kindle Edition, April 8, 2008), Locations 632-637.

representation of Britain, according to Wilson.[143] Some attribute Wilson's suppression of free speech to pressures of fighting WWI; however, some of Wilson's most egregious actions happened after WWI. Wilson refused to pardon Eugene V. Debs, who was in jail for giving a speech attributing WWI to economic interests and also criticizing the Espionage Act. It is interesting to note that this was after WWI was over.[144]

Wilson intervened in Latin America more often than even Teddy Roosevelt. He put troops into Mexico in 1914, 1916 (and nine more times during his administration), Haiti in 1915, the Dominican Republic in 1916, Cuba in 1917, and Panama in 1918.[145] He also maintained troops in Nicaragua, forcing his will in elections and the administration of that country. He actually blockaded Russia and invaded three Russian towns in attempts to thwart the Russian Revolution.[146] These interventions had far-reaching ramifications that set the stage for much animosity many years later. During the Cold War, the Soviet Union made several references to them and even claimed damages. In Cuba, the Dominican Republic, Haiti, and Nicaragua, Wilson's interventions resulted in brutal dictators coming to power in each of these nations. These oppressive dictators were, in turn, overthrown by leaders whose popularity was defined by how anti-American they appeared to be. To this day, there is strong anti-American sentiment throughout South and Central American and also the Caribbean; and to a great extent, this sentiment can be traced back to the Wilson administration.

As we discussed before, WWI just did not make much sense. Archduke Ferdinand was assassinated in Serbia, and nearly all the armies of Europe were marshaled and commenced to slaughter one another on an unprecedented scale. The casualties quickly numbered

---

[143.] Ibid, 637-642.

[144.] Ibid, 642-646.

[145.] Ibid, 502-507. Original source: Everett M. Dirksen, "Use of U.S. Armed Forces in Foreign Countries," *Congressional Record*, June 23, 1969, 16840-43.

[146.] N. Gordon Levin Jr., *Woodrow Wilson and World Politics: America's Response to War and Revolution*, (New York: Oxford University Press, 1968), 67.

in the millions. Most historians believe that had the actual numbers of casualties not been hidden from the people, in many countries, there would have been civilian insurrections that would have overthrown governments on both sides. France, the British Empire, and the Russian Empire each lost over a million uniformed soldiers. This was a slaughter and mass murder that is offscale. It was irrational, and the fact that several of the key players were pathological personalities, as discussed before, does not fully explain this carnage.

Most of the pathological thought processes have a familiar ring. Germany and England were in a naval arms race; Germany was building an Iraq-to-Baghdad railway that would have given Germany industry access to Iraqi oil and German trade a port in the Persian Gulf; Wilhelm II and his generals considered war with Russia as inevitable, and since Russia was rapidly strengthening its military, they might as well get started as soon as possible; the fact that there were more than two spheres of power and influence, which meant that each had to form alliances with others to protect themselves; and many other reasons. It is noteworthy that all English-speaking peoples were on one side, termed the allies, and this would be true of World War II also. This included India that committed more troops at the beginning of World War I than England did. The British Empire was a sizable force; add to it the United States, and you had a force to be reckoned with. Add to this the reality that virtually all of these English-speaking peoples were convinced that they alone had God on their side and that they would eventually inherit the Earth, and make the world "safe for democracy." A global empire of all English speaking people was beginning to take form.

The Anglo-American Empire

Also noteworthy was the ever-increasing gap between what America said that it stood for and what it did. Both the British and the Americans from the seventeenth to the nineteenth century were "civilizing savages," "Christianizing heathens," and getting rid of "useless" people and societies. Britain and the United States both had their Calvinist mind-set that anything that could not be turned into commercial goods for profit was useless. Both also had the Puritan view that anything they considered wild was evil and a threat to Christianity and God. The Puritan view that God directed everything tended to validate such things as the vulnerability of the Native Americans to

European diseases. Especially that the Americans saw the disastrous effect disease had on the natives as confirmation that these had to be evil people that God was punishing. The reader might take note that even today, these illusionary, self-fulfilling prophesies still come into play. One needs only to watch a news interview with one of today's so-called "televangelists" to hear such nonsense as God is infecting homosexuals with AIDS as punishment for being gay and so forth.

Although both countries had common roots in racism, genocide, and militarism, America became the more extreme, and also the more adept. This was undoubtedly due to slavery and the extermination of the native population. These two egregious endeavors required sophisticated propaganda to mask what was really going on, and at the beginning of the twentieth century, the disconnect between what America was doing and the explanation as to why were at opposite ends of the spectrum. Now we had statements coming from the Wilson administration that America needed to enter the "great war" to make the "world safe for democracy," and invasions of sovereign countries were "liberating" the citizenry. Any head of state that did not conform to US interests was an "oppressive brutal dictator" that had to be removed to "free" the people. Posters were put up depicting Germans as "savage Huns" that would enslave and murder women and children. Of course, all this had no basis in reality. World War I had nothing to do with democracy, and some of Wilson's outlandish acts such as jailing movie producers for casting Great Britain in a bad light and illegally opening mail were more of a threat to democracy than Germany and the other Central powers could ever be. Of course these increasingly irrational justifications could not have had much traction without increasing influence and control of the media. Wilson, a venomous racist who outright persecuted blacks and certainly was not too partial to anyone who was not a white, Anglo-Saxon, or Protestant, used outright intimidation to control and influence the media. The man would flat put you in jail if you said anything that he did not agree with.

We mentioned Joseph Goebbels earlier and his study of British and American propaganda. It is of interest that not only Goebbels but Adolf Hitler also believed that as a direct result of sophisticated propaganda, Germany lost WWI. They studied the methods in depth and determined that the British Ministry of Information had a campaign that targeted American intellectuals whom they had determined were the most likely influential segment of the US population to believe propaganda.[147] Of course the British were also no slouches at the sophisticated use of propaganda, without which they would have sorely lost WWI, and history might have been written much differently today.

Although both countries were becoming more adept at the use of propaganda, the use of it and the effects it had grew by leaps and bounds during WWI, and again, it was the Wilson administration that put it into the "turbo" mode. Also, according to Noam Chomsky, the "huge public relations industry, which is a US invention and a monstrous industry, came out of the First World War."[148] The Wilson administration also set up America's first and only major state propaganda agency in US history, the Committee on Public Information, which was also known as the Creel Commission.[149] This commission's actions had ramifications that affect the world today. One of the members of the commission was Edward Bernays who later wrote the book *Propaganda* in the late 1920s, and he was the architect of the public relations campaign against the democratically elected government of Guatemala. This was the government of Jacobo Árbenz Guzmán, which was overthrown by a US-backed coup in 1954. Even today, when a leader of a country falls into disfavor with the United States, all of a sudden they are referred to as "the dictator" or "strong man." This was done to Manuel Noriega of Panama and many others. Another technique was and is to tell a simple lie and repeat it over and over, using exactly the same words. "We now know for a certainty that Saddam Hussein has weapons of mass destruction . . ." Vice President Cheney and George W. Bush said this over and over again, and apparently, it worked. They offered no proof whatsoever. They simply said virtually the same thing over and over again. Both knew exactly what they were doing, and they had to have been coached by someone sometime in their careers. These things do not come out of nowhere.

Another member of the Creel Commission was Walter Lippmann, a name that many remember even today, who was a key figure in

---

[147.] Russ Kick, Ed., *The Disinformation Guide to Media Distortion, Historical Whitewashes and Cultural Myths*, (New York, NY: Anthology, The Disinformation Co. Ltd., Sep. 2003) 23. From a talk by Noam Chomsky at Z Media Institute, June 1997.

[148.] Ibid.

[149.] Ibid, 24.

American journalism for a half century. One of the concepts he coined when he became an advisor to Woodrow Wilson was the "manufacture of consent."[150] America was becoming more democratic in the run up to WWI. More people were involved in politics, voting, and demanding that the government be responsive to the will of the people and not the other way around. This was overcome by the process of shaping American opinion to conform to the needs of the ruling class. The phrase first used by Lipmann that became emblematic of this was "manufacturing of consent." Both the phrase and the concept are still with us today.

Collaboration of the English-speaking peoples, especially the white ruling elite, was also starting to take shape during the end of the nineteenth and beginning of the twentieth centuries. An elitist control structure began to form in 1870 that is still in operation today. Sometimes this is referred to as the "shadow government," deep politics," "power control group," or "high cabal" when someone is speaking of powerful people and forces that control things from behind the scenes. This is the basis for any number of "conspiracy theories" and "secret societies." It started with John Ruskin who was appointed to a fine arts professorship in 1870 at Oxford University.[151] He told his students that they were the possessors of a superior legacy of education, beauty, rule of law, freedom, fine arts, decency, and self-discipline, and that they would have to give it away to keep it.

His students were virtually all the privileged children of England's ruling elite, and he told them they would have to pass these virtues on to the lower class in England and the non-English masses throughout the world. When Ruskin said "throughout the world," he literally meant all habitable portions of the world. He also cautioned that should they fail in doing this, these virtues would wither away, and they would be gone forever. He introduced these ideas in his inaugural lecture at Oxford, and in the audience was Cecil John Rhodes, the man that the African country Rhodesia was named after. These concepts had a profound effect on Rhodes who had his own grand ideas of British colonialism. Rhodes internalized everything that Ruskin said and brought it back to South Africa with him. He was one of the most

---

[150]. Ibid.
[151]. Carroll Quigley, *Tragedy and Hope: A History of the World in Our Time*, (Angriff Press, June 1975), 130.

incredible individuals in history who imposed his will on much of the world.

He founded the De Beers diamond company, which controlled over 90 percent of the world's diamonds in his rather short, forty-eight years, lifetime. Even today, this company controls about 40 percent of the world diamond trade. Rhodes also had interests in gold and oil. He was financially backed by members of the Rothschild family, which was and is the subject of infinite conspiracy theories. He was also a Mason, a fact that has also fueled a conspiracy theory or two. He used his growing power and influence toward his vision of creating a British Empire in new territories north of South Africa by obtaining mineral concessions from indigenous chieftains. He was an adept politician who was able to use his wealth to cultivate power and influence. His astute ability to invest capital complemented imperial expansion. He sometimes was at odds with British politicians because he believed that British colonies should operate independent of Britain.

Rhodes wanted to expand the British Empire because he believed that Anglo-Saxons were a superior race that was destined to rule the world. In his first will of 1877, he advocated a secret society that would bring about British rule of the entire world. [152] The wording he used follows:

> To and for the establishment, promotion and *development of a Secret Society* (emphasis added), the true aim and object whereof shall be for the extension of British rule throughout the world, the perfecting of a system of emigration from the United Kingdom, and of colonization by British subjects of all lands where the means of livelihood are attainable by energy, labour and enterprise, and especially the occupation by British settlers of the entire *Continent of Africa, the Holy Land, the Valley of the Euphrates* (emphasis added), the Islands of Cyprus and Candia, the whole of South America, the Islands of the Pacific not heretofore possessed by Great Britain, the whole of the Malay Archipelago, the seaboard of China and Japan, *the ultimate recovery of the United States of America as an integral*

[152.] Robert Rotberg, *The Founder: Cecil Rhodes and the Pursuit of Power.* (Oxford University Press: 1990), 101-102.

part of the British Empire (emphasis added), the inauguration of a system of Colonial representation in the Imperial Parliament which may tend to weld together the disjointed members of the Empire and, finally, the *foundation of so great a Power as to render wars impossible* (emphasis added), and promote the best interests of humanity.

The above is mind-boggling. If one is to take into account that when Cecil Rhodes spoke of the "British Empire," he is talking about all English-speaking Anglo-Saxons, including the United States, which he intended on "recovering" for Great Britain. He also had much respect for Germany and he planned on including it in his plans to dominate the entire world. It is possible that Rhodes was actually alluding to a united Europe, led by Great Britain, dominating the entire world. If one is to look at the above, it is apparent that Cecil Rhodes actually did much that he set out to do. America and Great Britain have been virtually inseparable in their strategic plans since WWI and can be looked upon as one entity. Rhodes also did start a secret society that arguably has morphed into several institutions and infused itself into the fabric of many institutions. Also, America's nuclear and military arsenal far exceeds its defense needs and could be looked upon as "so great a power as to render wars impossible." His mention of the "Holy Land" and the "Valley of the Euphrates" tracks fairly well with the conquest of Palestine and Iraq, which can easily be construed to function as Anglo-American-dominated colonies.

The secret society that Rhodes started and its ramifications could be a book unto itself. In fact, Professor Carroll Quigley's *Tragedy and Hope*[153] goes into this subject, and more, in much detail. This book, all 1,359 pages of it, was Professor Quigley's magnum opus in which he says that he was granted access to the files of the world's ruling elite, and that he had a personal relationship with many of them. Quigley, an American, for most of his life had no problem with an international Anglophile network running the world; he just thought that the network did not need to be secret. Later in life, apparently, he changed his mind and became suspicious of them. He became convinced that

---

[153]. Carroll Quigley, *Tragedy and Hope: A History of the World in Our Time*. (NY: Macmillan, 1966). Reprint: (Angriff Press, June, 1975).

the ruling elite were suppressing publication of his book, and he presented a pretty good case on exactly how this was being done. This is not, however, pertinent to our discussion, but it does tend to support the position that there must be something to what he wrote. If not, what would be the purpose in suppressing it?

Quigley traces the power and influence of British merchant bankers back to the British Industrial Revolution, which was roughly from the eighteenth to the nineteenth century. This was the advent of fossil fuels to power steam engines, and it replaced work being done by animal and human muscle. These new methods produced enormous wealth and profit that became concentrated in the hands of a few British merchant bankers. These bankers organized money and credit into integrated systems that were based in London and later developed offshoots in New York and Paris. Control of these international banking systems resulted in family dynasties that wielded great power. Chief among them were the descendants of Mayer Amschel Rothschild in Europe and bankers associated with what became known as J. P. Morgan & Co. in the United States. Both families had their roots in British banking, and both acquired businesses and corporations that are with us today.

For example, Rothschild financed Cecil Rhodes; and J. P. Morgan financed the creation of General Electric, United States Steel, the Chase Manhattan Bank, and many others. Actually, Morgan either organized or underwrote the securities of forty-two major corporations from 1890 to 1913.[154] Many of these, in one form or another, are still with us today. Between these two related and intertwined financial empires, we have most of what today is referred to as the "Western Banking System." Add to this the corporations owned and/or financed by this system and we now have what is termed the "military-industrial complex," which includes much more than just arms, explosives, and so forth. We also have major energy businesses, shipping, railroads, and so forth; and we further have the unmentionable—the world drug trade—woven into the fabric of all these most lucrative and powerful endeavors. We are talking about real power here, in the hands of a few, a formula for world domination with no checks and balances to curb it, nor is there any oversight whatsoever to keep it in check.

[154.] Meyer Weinberg, Ed. *America's Economic Heritage*, (Greenwood Press, Set, Documentary Reference Collections, 1983), 2:350.

The historian and moralist Lord Acton, who was around during this timeframe, expressed in a letter to Bishop Mandell Creighton in 1887 the opinion that "power tends to corrupt, and absolute power corrupts absolutely. Great men are almost always bad men." If Quigley was accurate, we see concentration of power on a scale unlike anything the world had seen before. Even a hundred years ago, these men had more power than the leaders of empires. Strange as it seems, there were international banking and business leaders that told the leaders of powerful nations what to do. They also had the power to install and remove whomever they wanted from the leadership of states. According to Quigley, this power has grown by leaps and bounds since these early days to now. And let us not forget that this enormous wealth came about as a result of the transition from muscle power to fossil fuel power. Steam engines do not get tired, nor do you have to pay them. They also do not strike or revolt. As with the enormous profits generated because of computers in the 1970s, the power elite took the profits for themselves and used the money to solidify their positions. The average working person did not measurably benefit from these increased profits at the end of the nineteenth and twentieth centuries. This is incredible.

Let us track just a few of these pathways of power. In his last will and testament, Rhodes said of the British, "I contend that we are the first race in the world and that the more of the world we inhabit the better it is for the human race.[155] Also in his last will, he created the famous Rhodes Scholarships at Oxford for the purpose of spreading the English ruling class tradition throughout the world. Rhodes did a lot of planning to accomplish this. He went into detail on how he not only wanted these students to attend Oxford University, but he wanted them to interact with the upper crust of English society. He wanted his scholarship students to absorb the values of the elites and share his and their vision for an Anglo-elite-dominated world. He wanted them to return to their homes with this template of empire and world domination implanted in their hearts and souls. One of the most recent American names to have been a Rhodes Scholar was William Jefferson Clinton.

[155.] Cecil J. Rhodes, "Confession of Faith," essay included in *The Last Will and Testament of Cecil John Rhodes,* with elucidatory notes to which are added some chapters describing the political and religious ideas of the testator, ed. WT Stead (London: Review of Reviews Office: 1902).

Between his first and last will, Rhodes developed many followers of his and Professor Ruskin's grand philosophy. Noteworthy among them was Lord Alfred Milner who became Rhodes's right-hand man and carried on Rhodes's grand vision of an Anglo-American empire after Rhodes's death in 1902. Along with the first group formed at Oxford, another like-minded group formed at Cambridge University that included Lord Eshler and Lord Grey. A William T. Stead, says Quigley, brought these two groups together in 1891. Stead was England's most successful journalist and also a social reformer and imperialist. At this time, Rhodes and Stead formed the secret society that Rhodes had been dreaming of for many years. Rhodes was to be the head; and Stead, Esher, and Milner formed the executive committee. Quigley says that the group itself was called the "Circle of Initiates" among whom were Lord Mayer Amschel Rothschild and Lord Arthur Balfour. Rothschild we discussed previously, but Lord Balfour's place in history needs some illuminating.

```
                              Foreign Office,
                            November 2nd, 1917.

Dear Lord Rothschild,
            I have much pleasure in conveying to you, on
behalf of His Majesty's Government, the following
declaration of sympathy with Jewish Zionist aspirations
which has been submitted to, and approved by, the Cabinet

        "His Majesty's Government view with favour the
   establishment in Palestine of a national home for the
   Jewish people, and will use their best endeavours to
   facilitate the achievement of this object, it being
   clearly understood that nothing shall be done which
   may prejudice the civil and religious rights of
   existing non-Jewish communities in Palestine, or the
   rights and political status enjoyed by Jews in any
   other country"

        I should be grateful if you would bring this
declaration to the knowledge of the Zionist Federation.
```

Balfour Declaration of 1917, Source: Wikipedia.

Lord Balfour had a long career as a British diplomat. Many, including Winston Churchill, described him as a very dignified and aloof person who was not inclined to do very much. In fact some said he accomplished absolutely nothing. He did, however, sign the letter on the left that is known to have created the state of Israel. This letter became known as the Balfour Declaration of 1917, and at the time, Lord Balfour was the United Kingdom's foreign secretary. Zionist influences in Great Britain and the rest of Europe had been pushing for a Jewish state in Palestine since Theodor Herzl published *Der Judenstaat* (*The Jewish State*) in 1896. Rothschild and others were able to convince Balfour to sign this declaration in 1917. Let us keep in mind that these two were both members of Cecil Rhodes's secret society that intended to take control of certain strategic locations, one of which was the "Holy Lands," on the way toward an Anglo-American empire that would rule the world.

In his will of 1877, Rhodes did not just come up with the locations to be controlled for sentimental reasons. For example, to control the "whole of the Malay Archipelago" is to control virtually all commerce between the Indian Ocean and the Pacific Ocean, most of which goes through the Strait of Malacca. This strategic "choke point" is about 500 miles wide. Control of this means control of about one-fourth of the entire world's traded goods, including oil, between the major economies of India, China, Japan, and South Korea. It is considered part of Southeast Asia and is a major reason that empires have been and probably will always be interested in having a presence there. Every war planner is aware of this, as was Cecil Rhodes.

By the same token, the Holy Lands were and are valued for their strategic importance. At the turn of the twentieth century, Palestine was part of the Ottoman Empire and an important trading and commerce point between the Middle East, Africa, the Mediterranean, and Asia. The booming oil industry was within proximity as was the critical Suez Canal. Nations do things for their own reasons. They almost never do anything for a "noble cause." There is no evidence that Lord Balfour, Lord Rothschild, or Cecil Rhodes had any burning desire for a Jewish homeland to protect and nurture Jews. They had imperial plans, and they formed a secret society to accomplish these plans.

Quigley goes on to explain how this original secret society was replicated throughout the English-speaking world. These offshoots of the "Circle of Initiates" became known as "Round Table groups" that were set up in Great Britain, the United States, Canada, South Africa, India, and elsewhere. After Rhodes's death, these groups were sometimes referred to as "Milner's Kindergarten," and Quigley says that they still function in eight countries. They founded the Royal Institute of International Affairs in Britain and similar organizations in other English-speaking countries. In the United States, the organization is known as the Council on Foreign Relations. In the British-controlled territories of the Pacific region, it is known as the Institute of Pacific Relations.

Along with major educational institutions, international business, banking, and major media outlets became controlled by this secret society. The *Times*, owned by the Astor family, became a primary mouthpiece for these Round Table groups. In addition to owning the *Times*, Lord and Lady Astor had gatherings at their country estate in Buckinghamshire, England, in which many of the secret society founded by Rhodes participated. These were upper-class affairs attended by those often described as far right wing; probably far enough to the right to be categorized as fascist. The group started out with an antipathy for Germany during the WWI but paradoxically evolved into ardent supporters of German fascism during the run-up to WWII. This group met regularly at the Astor estate that was named "Cliveden house" in Buckinghamshire, England, and years later the group became known as the "Cliveden Set," a name we will see again in the next chapter.

Many of the extremely wealthy families that derived their fortunes from support from this secret society formed foundations that ostensibly were for philanthropic purposes. The Rockefeller Foundation would be a good example, and this foundation has indeed undertaken some noble causes and projects. It is also a major financer of both the Council on Foreign Relations and the Royal Institute of International Affairs from whence it came. It can be looked at as a tax-free shelter for the same causes promoted by Cecil J. Rhodes, and that would be to promote and establish Anglo culture throughout the world. Its stated mission, to "promote the well-being of mankind throughout the world," of course does not directly say that, but if one tracks where its money goes, to whom, and for what purpose, consistent patterns emerge. For example, one of its projects evolved into the so-called "Green Revolution," which it declared as a rousing success, but is generally thought of as an abysmal failure by most of the world. In a nutshell, the Green Revolution consisted of blasting nonindigenous crops with petrochemical-based herbicides, insecticides, and fertilizers to make them grow where they are not necessarily suited. Further, this process takes about ten calories of energy, mostly from oil, to produce one calorie of food energy. Not a good idea for an indigenous farmer whose most important resource is the knowledge of how to grow crops that his or her ancestors have been growing for thousands of years. We will be going into this subject in more detail in my next book, but for now, we will just mention that the stated objective associated with the

Green Revolution to "feed the world" had little to do with that. It was more about profit and control than anything else.

Just a cursory view of trustees and presidents shows the strong connections to the secret society groups previously discussed. For example, past trustee John Foster Dulles was a member of the Council on Foreign Relations as was John W. Davis, who was the founding president of the CFR and also J. P. Morgan's private attorney. Past trustees C. Douglas Dillon and John J. McCloy (whom we will be discussing in more detail in chapter 10) were also members of the CFR. A review of the other foundations produces the same results. Connections to known CIA fronts, such as the Agency for International Development, are commonplace. From the Ford Foundation (which Henry Ford walked away from because he said he could not control it) to the Carnegie Institution, we see projects that promote Cecil Rhodes's vision. We also consistently see nice-sounding projects that tend to make people dependent on Anglo-American agriculture that overthrow governments in resource-rich countries, and cause friction among minority communities. We further see support for the World Bank, which is in reality in the business of bankrupting countries and turning them into slave states for the "West." Cecil would be proud!

Along with the formation of a foundation of Anglophile power, we also see the machinations of this power. Along with the influence primarily wielded by the Ford and Rockefeller foundations in the Ivy League universities, we also have considerable influence in the creation of educational institutions. For example, by the time of his death in 1937, John D. Rockefeller had established the University of Chicago, the Rockefeller Institute for Medical Research, and the Lincoln School. These institutions ensured that Rockefeller influenced such fields as medicine, pharmaceuticals, food production, education, and behavioral sciences. These areas and others became excellent avenues for the vast oil empire developed by Rockefeller in the form of petrochemicals. Oil was and is used in a variety of pharmaceuticals, fertilizers, and herbicides to name a few. The products themselves and the oil used in their production turn enormous profits. Control of the industries and intellectual properties starts at the education level. The Rockefellers were also interested in eugenics, which promotes racism, discrimination, and class warfare. This pseudoscience has been studiously applied to keep the American people fighting among themselves so that they do not recognize who is stealing their money. In chapter 10, we will delve into how one foundation was able to virtually shut the city of New York down by dividing ethnic groups and classes. John D. Rockefeller, along with Mrs. Edward H. Harriman, funded and established the Eugenics Records Office in 1910. The Anglophile globalists are experts at creating "differences" between people and assigning characteristics to these so-called differences.

The press, or as it is now referred to as the media, became increasingly owned by big business and Wall Street. For example, NBC is now and has for a long time been owned and controlled mostly by General Electric, which was one of the J. P. Morgan-financed companies, and as such goes back to Cecil Rhodes's plans for a secret society. This trend started to become a problem at about the turn of the nineteenth to the twentieth century, and certainly has continued today. Corporate control of the media, which also had and has undue influence in the government, is probably not what the signers of the Constitution had in mind.

Character development seems to have been lacking in the American republic from the very beginning. We have already discussed some of this previously, and it is a foregone conclusion that one would have to have been lacking in character to have murdered and stole on a scale that the founders of the American republic did. It is interesting to note that two psychiatrists and authors, Dr. Steven J. Rubenzer and Dr. Thomas R. Faschingbauer, came to some startling conclusions in their book, *Personality, Character, and Leadership in The White House: Psychologists Assess the Presidents*.[156] Overall, they rated the US presidents, on the average, at the 42nd percentile in character development. This means that 58 percent of Americans have more character than the average US president. Further, they determined that high character was a detriment to going down in history as an effective leader. They found that to be an effective leader, and judged as such by historians, they determined that "the ability to lie and deceive is an important quality for success in the White House, and presidents who are less straightforward typically make better presidents."[157] This

---

[156.] Steven J. Rubenzer and Thomas R. Faschingbauer, *Personality, Character, and Leadership in The White House: Psychologists Assess the Presidents* (Potomac Books, August, 2004), Kindle Edition.

[157.] Ibid, Kindle Location 177-183.

is profound, and add to this that since Franklin Delano Roosevelt, the trend is toward even lower character. Some of the most recent presidents were almost completely devoid of character altogether. Also interesting was that Republicans scored higher than Democrats, and if it had not been for Jimmy Carter, who scored high, most recent Democrats would have been at the very bottom of the society when it came to character. This information does, however, track very well with Lobeczewski's model of idealists-starting movements that are taken over by "characteropaths" and ultimately psychopaths become predominant, who always screw things up so badly that they collapse, and the cycle starts all over again.

We could extrapolate a bit and surmise that the profiles of other politicians would probably not be significantly different than the presidents. Also, I doubt that those whom we have referred to as the global elite, the ones that put politicians in office, would score much higher either. An interesting documentary along these lines is available named "The Corporation."

Conclusions

The author is overwhelmed by the enormity of it all. The outright criminality of our so-called "Western heritage" is astounding. So-called "settlers" and "Pilgrims" supposedly landed on the American continent to escape persecution and practice religious freedom, and what did they do? They enslaved and murdered millions upon millions of people who were no threat to them whatsoever. This had nothing to do with religious freedom, and in fact these so-called "Puritans" would whip the flesh and cut the ears off their own should they not conform to the edicts of "Puritanism." They came here to *impose* their religion on anyone and everyone in their way and *eradicate* anyone that resisted them. They then wrote their history in such a way as to deny that it ever happened, or when this was not possible, they "documented" that either they had nothing to do with it, "disease killed the Indians," or that it was really their own fault, "they" just could not adapt to civilization. Prior to writing this chapter, the author believed that the United States had just recently, 9/11 attacks and so forth, entered a period of continuous warfare when in actuality, the history of the United States has been one of continuous warfare from the very beginning. Those who conquered the Americas wrote about "life, liberty, and the pursuit of happiness," but what they actually did was enslavement, genocide, and militarism.

It is a dark tale that needs some sunlight cast upon it. Much of this has been documented, but it does not, however, end up in the history books. What ends up in the history books is a sanitized and expanded version of what Rhodes put in his wills, which contained expressions such as "develop an appreciation for art, music, culture, and the rule of law of the English-speaking peoples and spread it throughout the world." Of course all this was considered "God's will," although one would be hard-pressed to find anything that was actually done by the founders of the United States that had anything to do with the ministry of Christ.

Today, one hears constant reference to "the American Dream," and what exactly would that be? Over the years, we hear less and less about what this expression means. Politicians used to at least make an attempt to shine a flashlight in front of us about this. Kennedy had his "New Frontier" that alluded to new challenges such as space exploration and so forth (although Native Americans might have had a different take on this expression, such as more of the same for them). The fact remains that he at least said something about the future. Today, we do not have even a cursory attempt to define the direction of the United States, just vague references that are actually meaningless. We hear inferences such as "America has lost its direction." Now how could we possibly have lost our direction when we seem to have no idea what that is? How could we possibly figure out where we are going when we do not know where we are and how we got here?

We have barely scratched the surface of these issues, and although there have been many that have documented what actually did happen in the conquest of the Americas, much of this vital information has been lost. We know how the native cultures were destroyed, but we know little about *what* was destroyed. For example, how did the at least eighteen million pre-Columbian people grow and store food? We know something about this but not enough, and it is crucial information. Apparently, they were able to live in fairly large cities, larger than those in Europe, and grow their food amongst themselves. In Europe, the food had to be grown outside the city and therefore required the city-state to conquer surrounding territories resulting in continuous warfare and theft of land and resources. This arguably is where nations came from. This concept may also be applied to other resources.

Somehow, the people of the Americas were able to live in fairly dense communities that were self-sustaining and self-supporting. Of course there were disputes and "wars," but nothing near the scale that went on in Europe, and largely not for the same reasons. Most of the Indians' "wars" were over honor—someone insulted someone else and things of the sort. Add to this the fact that hardly anyone got killed.

Other issues that we could have learned from native people are sanitation, medicine, resolving disputes, and a vast variety of things that are contained in culture and language. There were at least 1,500 languages that died in North America alone, and probably the actual figure is much larger. Each language has its own unique way of communicating ideas, concepts, and solving problems that often does not exist in other languages. When a language dies, a part of the human experience dies with it. What human and environmental solutions died with those languages? Perhaps the answers to questions that we badly need answers to right now died with these people, their cultures, and their languages. It is not a secret that our lifestyle is not sustainable. Less than 5 percent of the world's population cannot continue to use 25 percent of the world's resources, nor can it continue to create 25 percent of the world's pollution. These figures will change, with or without our cooperation. It might be very useful to know how these forgotten and destroyed people approached these problems.

This is not to say that the native peoples lived in absolute bliss. They certainly must have had their problems. There is, however, considerable evidence that they lived longer, more satisfying lives than those that replaced them. They were certainly less violent. Noteworthy is the previously mentioned fact that there was no record among the colonists of one of them that lived with the native people for any length of time and voluntarily returned to "civilization." Nor was there a record of a native person who stayed with the white settlers when allowed to leave.

We have seen in this chapter an arrogant culture that developed with an ironclad sense of superiority. It is ironic that there was absolutely no basis for these toxic beliefs. Over and over again, it is stated in American culture that destruction and mass murder is somehow "progress." Our industries take resources from the environment and turn them into toxins, which are sold for a profit and then eventually dumped back into the environment in the form of pollution. Add to this the fact that most of this is stuff we don't even need anyway. Does any of this make anyone happy? Why is it that we set records in production, wealth, and also the use of antidepressants? I am reminded of the bumper sticker that says something to the effect that "the woman who dies with the most clothes in her closet wins the game." Really? This author does not even think that is funny. Ridiculous would be more like it.

The fear that has its roots in the corrupted religious beliefs of America is also a concern. Fear of wild animals why else would bison replaced by cows be seen as progress? fear of the woods and the people that live in it; consistently used in white American writings are the terms *howling wilderness* and *uncivilized savages*. America is afraid of just about anything, everything, anybody, and everybody. How many nuclear weapons does the United States have at present? Over nine thousand! How many does it need? Arguably none. What is incomprehensible is the fact that there are plans to produce even more. This is a subject that we will discuss in the next chapter, but for now, it is safe to say that nuclear weapons have done anything but made us safe. It is this incredible fear that is the subject at hand, it is enormous, and it has been with us since day one.

It may be said that the First Nations peoples saw themselves as part of nature whereas Europeans saw themselves as separate from nature. Nature had to be controlled, managed, and used to serve man. European Americans had this "man against nature" mind-set that is still with us today. Mountains are not climbed, they are conquered." As if anyone could do such a thing. Marvelous Redwoods thousands of years old are cut down to be made into porches, toilet paper, and whatever. They serve no purpose just being beautiful and awe-inspiring. They need to be "harvested." Salmon need to be "genetically engineered" so that they can be grown in ponds. Never mind that for a very long time they did just fine by themselves, returning to where they came from to spawn, and ending up as hundreds of thousands of tons of food for raccoons, bears, and humans that dragged them into the forest. This is the only way that the forest obtained essential nutrients from the ocean hundreds of miles away. Why even mess with something as perfect as that? Harness the rivers for energy and harvest the forest for wood and destroy the entire ecosystem just because you can, and you end up destroying yourself. This is going on right now in the Pacific Northwest, and it has a lot of people really upset, especially those that used to make a living from tourism and fishing. The whole ecosystem is dying, and many just see the controversy as a bunch of "tree-huggers" that are in love with Spotted Owls. The Calvinists and the Puritans would be proud of us.

We saw this mind-set methodically destroy a way of life that had been highly successful for tens of thousands of years and replace it with one that had not been doing so well, except in the areas of mass murder, torture, slavery, and other forms of destruction. We also saw the development of some profound guiding documents as to what should be. No one can deny that the Declaration of Independence and the US Constitution are awe-inspiring and something to be admired. Too bad, America did not follow through with these most noble concepts and ideas. Whenever the "founding fathers" obtained power, they abused it, and they abused it horribly. We saw president after president abuse power and continue on a steady course of militarism, racism, and genocide. Any that even looked like they might change course, such as Lincoln, were removed from office one way or another. This held true all the way up to and including the Wilson administration. Heroes were made of racist murders, which included at least three of the four faces on Mount Rushmore. Washington, Jefferson, and Theodore Roosevelt were responsible for the murder of millions, and one could argue that Lincoln who presided over the Civil War could also join this club. It is almost incomprehensible that a serial mass-murderer such as Andrew Jackson can be written about by revered historians, such as Arthur Schlesinger in his book *The Age of Jackson*, and nothing at all mentioned about the "removal" of thousands of Native Americans, many of whom died during his administration. This was a disastrous act that easily qualifies as genocide, and Schlesinger wins a Pulitzer Prize without even mentioning one word about it. The Puritans and Calvinists would be proud.

There is a preponderance of evidence that the American bison was exterminated to destroy the Plains Indians. Both Sherman and Sheridan spoke and wrote of it, and after the Civil War, de facto slavery continued. No one knows what would have happened had Lincoln survived, but it is entirely possible that he would have taken a different tack. There is evidence that leads in that direction, and this could have been one motive behind his assassination. Presidents Theodore Roosevelt and Woodrow Wilson carried on the expansion of the USA past its borders at an accelerated rate and laid the foundations of a global empire, much of which was in collaboration with the

British. Largely hidden was the joint operation and control of the drug trade, which was and is to this day enormously profitable. Huge sums of money were made during the British and American Industrial Revolution that was concentrated into the hands of a few. This, along with increasing control of oil resources by the same wealthy elite, gave this small segment of the population disproportionate power.

We also saw this small group of elites develop the instruments of power. The enormous wealth these people were accumulating was put into tax-free foundations that were a subterfuge to avoid all taxes, including inheritance tax. Inheritance tax was established to prevent the concentration of wealth into the hands of a few, which if allowed to happen, will overpower and take control of any socioeconomic or political system. The Anglophile elitists came up with these foundations to do exactly that, and they did. These morally and ethically bankrupt people turn democracies into kleptocracies, plutocracies, and pathocracies; and they do not lose a minute of sleep over it. Quigley goes into much detail as to how these foundations linked Wall Street, the Ivy League schools, and the federal government. The universities Quigley mentions as being dominated by these foundations include Harvard, Yale, Columbia, and Princeton. Add to this the British universities of Oxford, Cambridge; and consider the influence gained by the Rhodes scholarship network, and we now see raw power wielded by these elites. Further, there is virtually no oversight of all of this. Even tenured professors at these and many other universities that go against these foundations and the power behind them can and do lose their jobs. Anyone who gets in their way is taken out of the picture one way or another. Any of them go up against Rhodes's doctrine of control of the "Holy Lands," and a storm of criticism will descend on them within hours that few have weathered. We will look closer into the machinations of these foundations in chapter 10.

We touched briefly on the control of oil being consolidated into the hands of a few, and the fact that World War I certainly was much to do about control of Iraqi oil, which is extremely high-grade oil just under the surface. Punch a hole in the ground, and there it is. The British were beside themselves with the prospect that Germany would be getting oil by rail, which would bypass the established British-controlled route through the Persian Gulf. Control the oil reserves of the world, make sure that all industries are petrochemical based, control the banking, supplement this with the most profitable of all products, namely drugs, and you control the world. Control these and you have just entered the most select club in the world, the "global elites."

Whether he intended or not, John F. Kennedy threatened all of the above, and he paid the ultimate price. For all the talk about the Kennedy family's wealth and influence, they were not the "biggest dogs on the porch" by a long shot. All the "big dogs" had to do was give a little nod, and the forces were put into play that resulted in what happened in Dealey Plaza on November 22, 1963. As previously mentioned, if Joseph Kennedy Sr. had not been incapacitated, he would have known that both Jack and Bobby Kennedy were literally in global elite's business and how dangerous that can be. The other factor is that neither JFK nor Bobby rubbed elbows with the Washington power-control group. For example, it is known that Lyndon Johnson, J. Edgar Hoover, Allen Dulles, and others played cards together. The Kennedys were not welcome, nor were they interested in attending occasions. They did not "fit in" with the global elites or their stooges. JFK's presidency was "Papa Joe's" play for the big time, and the Kennedys threatened the power base that had developed from the seventeenth century to the extreme power that started to come together at the end of the nineteenth and beginning of the twentieth century. This power base continued to develop even further from WWI to the post-WWII period, which we will discuss further in the next chapter.

The author does not put forth that the evolution of power described in this chapter is a "conspiracy theory" because a conspiracy is two or more people plotting to do something illegal. Taking control of the world's resources, political domination of the nations of the world, and controlling the world's economic systems is not, in itself, illegal. Rather than conspiracy, we need to recognize that this is how the global elite operate. They will network to take control and dominate everything they can. That is how they got there in the first place. Further, this is an exclusive club that, above all else, does not want the middle class moving up to their status. They will do just about anything to keep the masses out of their domain. They also consider the middle class as a threat and strive to keep the middle class just above the poor. If we really think about it, most of us are just a few paychecks away from losing all of our material possessions, including our homes. This is right where the power elite wants us, scared, and they want us so scared that we will keep our mouths shut out of fear of falling off that thin edge between the poor and the seemingly well-off middle class.

Just think about where you would be without a paycheck for a few months? Yes, I know some of us are already there. The poor are kept poor for two reasons, and both of these reasons have to do with keeping the middle class in line. The first reason is so that the middle class can feel superior to someone, "Well, at least I am not *that* bad off!" and the second reason is to keep the middle class scared that they could easily be *that* bad off! Everything the rich and powerful elite does is to keep the poor, poor and the middle class arrogant and scared. Race, religion, ethnicity, and "socioeconomic" class is used to divide people and keep them fighting with each other. Let us think about it, does not your average redneck have just about everything you can think of in common with your average black person? If the elite can keep the hatred going, no one is going to think about that. It is this author's contention that these silly so-called differences between people are created out of thin air just to keep everyone, except the power elite, off-balance and fighting so they, or we, can be controlled. Knowledge is power. We do not have to let these people do this to us.

Actually, freedom is scary. Everyone says they want to be free, but do they actually? The Native Americans were about as free as you can get, and somehow that terrified the Europeans something fierce. It scared them so much they killed virtually all of them and rationalized it. Rationalization is when you do something unacceptable but assign socially acceptable reasons for your actions. Just check a high school textbook some day. "They" had no resistance to disease . . . "They" were not here very long . . . "They" were not using the land effectively . . . "They" were a backward, Stone Age people that just did not fit into the "modern" world. You will either find a variation of the above or you will find hardly anything at all. And it is not only the Native Americans. Perhaps the Branch Davidians just wanted to be free? The author, along with everyone else, saw armored personnel carriers with US flags flying on them take them out. What were the flags there for? Were not these people Americans also? If "they" can do that to "them," they can do that to us.

In the next chapter, we will explore the further consolidation of global power from WWI to the Kennedy years. The emphasis will be on WWII and the postwar period, which resulted in a global power the likes of which the world had never seen before. It is the world we still live in, and we have to understand how we got where we are at if we can begin to understand where we are now. Chapter 10 will explore the deep politics of power, or what really happened behind the scenes in a way that we did not get from our history books.

Chapter Ten

The Age of Greed: World War I to the John F. Kennedy Assassination

Choose your enemies carefully, for you will become like them.

—**History's most ironic lesson**

The band U2 had some interesting lyrics in their song "The Cedars of Lebanon" that conveyed the same concept, and it went like this:

> Choose your enemies carefully, 'cause they will define you
> Make them interesting, because in some ways they will mind you
> They're not there in the beginning, but when your story ends
> Gonna last longer with you than your friends.

Enemies in Battle, Friends Everywhere Else

Although America thought that it was uniquely different, no people have ever become more like the British than the Americans. Certainly, many of the first settlers were English, but those that followed were far from being of British ancestry, and by the time of the Revolutionary War, America was very diverse. Gypsies, Jews, Berbers, Huguenots, Knights Templar—you name it, all came here by the tens of thousands. Many Anglicized their names, lost their native tongues, and hid their origins. Surnames thought of today as being typically from British Anglo-Saxon extraction actually were not. For example, the surname "Hale," as in "Nathan Hale," was likely to have come from Sephardic Jewish extraction with variations in spelling to include Hail, Healle, Hale, and Haile.[158] Many hid their pasts long after they had forgotten the reason they were hiding it. The author once knew a red-haired, freckled, big fellow with a surname that began with "Mac." One would assume, as he did, that he was of Scottish origin. He had a Y-chromosome test done from one of the several ancestry DNA-testing organizations and figured that it would come back "Celtic" or something of the sorts. His test identified that his male line had descended from a small village in Africa. Many Americans who have had these tests done are just as surprised as Mac was to find out that their ancestors origins, male and female, are far different than what they always assumed or thought they knew. It has been well established that the vast majority of Americans do not have British Anglo-Saxon roots.

As counterintuitive as it may seem, through war, people historically have taken on the characteristics of their enemy. We mentioned previously that the Revolutionary War may also be looked at as a family power struggle. Even considering the Declaration of Independence, the War of Independence, and a new Constitution, in many ways the British and the Americans became more alike through conflict and competition. As time went on, this became more and more evident. In fact today, the two may be looked at as one entity. Business and trade never stopped even during periods of conflict, and as time went on, more and more people found themselves "in the way" of the emerging "Anglo-American empire." "In the way" of this global juggernaut was not a healthy place to be, and millions upon millions of virtually defenseless people lost their lives at the hands of this constantly expanding empire that increasingly became more powerful and more arrogant.

America "got its feet wet" on the world stage in WWI with Germany. By that time, America had expanded south and west from its origins while the British had expanded south and east. US and British corporations had also expanded with the Anglo-American empire and had become inexorably intertwined. Even though Germany was

---

[158.] Elizabeth Caldwell Hirschman, *Melungeons, the Last Lost Tribe in America*, (Macon Georgia: Mercer University Press, 1st. Ed., 2005), 79.

chosen, or somehow developed, into the next evil enemy, there is no question that business prospered between the adversaries; and as we shall see, the main players in the two world wars also became much alike. Further, economic alliances and trade agreements developed and continued on well after hostilities began. Not only were the adversaries economically conjoined, but the governments and societies became more and more similar. Both sides learned from each other such things as how to effectively use propaganda to promote war. They also learned how to hide the devastating casualties, suffering, and misery caused by the horrific wars in the first half of the twentieth century. We were becoming like "them," and they were becoming like "us." Through war, the United States had become like the British, and then during two incalculably brutal world wars, both had become like the National Socialist Party, known as the NAZI party, of Germany. Germany was defeated during WWII, but the NAZIs were not. As strange as it may seem, "they" became "us."

Anglo-American Corporations

As discussed before, the Industrial Revolution fueled first by coal and then oil gave rise to increasingly larger corporations. These large-scale enterprises required more and more capital to get started; and the joint-stock companies, partnerships which drew start up capital from only a few entrepreneurs, just did not fit the bill. Increasingly, the combined capital of unlimited numbers of people was becoming necessary in both the United States and Great Britain. Publicly traded corporations became a necessity for the largest corporations. Middle-class people were needed to invest in these corporations, and the concept of "limited liability" became the practice and also the law. This simply meant that an individual shareholder was only liable for the amount they had invested in a company as far as corporate debt. Prior to this, it was possible to own only a few shares of stock, but then lose life's possessions, house, and all if the business failed. If the average person was to participate in these business ventures, this would have to change, and it did. Another change that came about was that smaller corporations were acquired by larger ones. Again, the laws changed to allow this, and it happened at an alarming rate. Between 1898 and 1904, 1,800 corporations were consolidated into 157 in the United

States alone.[159] With these larger and larger corporations owned by more and more shareholders who had less and less to say about the business, we now had the beginnings of our present-day publicly traded enterprise.

Additionally, the concept of a corporation as a person began to take shape and to be codified into law. In the United States, the Fourteenth Amendment to the US Constitution had been passed for the sole purpose of protecting the rights of freed slaves. In 1886, the Supreme Court took it upon itself to extend these rights into entities for which the Fourteenth Amendment was never intended. So we now have equal protection rights and also due process rights extended to corporations because they were "persons" under the eyes of the law. Later, other rights that were originally intended for human beings were granted to corporations such as owning property, entering into contracts, suing and being sued, and other immunities and privileges. It is noteworthy that the highest court in the land was most generous with granting human rights to corporations but more than a little shy when it came to demanding human responsibilities. A similar setup came about in Great Britain.

From early in the twentieth century on, the die had been cast, and we see a continuum of this to this day. We see enormous corporations comprised of managers that do not own and owners that do not manage the enterprise, and neither are responsible for its actions. How many of us jointly own stock in the form of annuities or other "financial instruments" but have no idea what we are doing? Many of us are sickened by the inexcusable destruction of pristine rain forests in Equator, but probably most of us have financed this very same destruction in our retirement funds and investments. Virtually, all of us are guilty of this in some way. We are not nearly as interested in corporate ethics, or the lack of such, as we are in making money. We are like the three monkeys: hear, see, and say no evil. In some ways, "we have confronted the enemy and discovered that he is us." This is the nature of the beast. The corporation gets sued, but neither the managers nor the owners are responsible; the corporation is guilty because it is a "person," you cannot

---

[159.] Roland Marchand, *Creating the Corporate Soul: The Rise of Public Relations and Corporate Imagery in American Big Business*, (Berkeley: University of California Press, 1998), 7

put a corporation in jail. As Andrew Jackson once stated on this very same issue, "It [the corporation] has neither body to punish nor soul to condemn." The author has portrayed Jackson in uncomplimentary terms, but he was certainly right on this issue. The unchecked power and lack of responsibility allowed the titans of these corporations to exercise undue influence not only in the conduct of business but also in government, education, health care, defense, and many other areas of everyday life. In fact, these corporations define who we are. They feed us, house us, clothe us, they define us socially and culturally, they influence what we believe and how we think; from cradle to grave, they are involved in everything we do. In short, they run the country.

Let us go back to WWI. A latecomer to WWI, the United States lost relatively few troops but defined itself as a major player on the world stage. Also by this time, the United States was the world's largest economy, with more than enough economic influence to let it be known that the twentieth Century would be America's time. International trade, banking, and business were becoming more and more concentrated into the hands of a few that had considerable influence in many countries. These relationships went on even during times of war. This is how we had seemingly incongruent facts such as IBM selling information-processing machines to the NAZIs, which they used to streamline the logistics of the Holocaust. Of course IBM denies this to this day, but the record is clear that IBM leased the business machines and provided custom-designed key punch cards that enabled the NAZIs to efficiently manage the trains going to the death camps. We will be discussing this and several more examples of US business trading with the enemy, even during declared war. The stark reality of capitalism is that a corporation will do anything to make a buck. It is like a shark cruising around looking for something to eat. That is what it is designed to do. It is the nature of the beast. Corporations are not immoral; they are amoral.

At the beginning of the twentieth century, this manifested itself into American capitalism with all the terms we are somewhat familiar with today. When we talk about international corporations, multinational corporations, Wall Street, the stock market, and so forth, these are the cogs in the wheel of capitalism, which is designed to make profit. Not only to make a profit, but a publicly traded corporation is bound by fiduciary duties and standards to maximize profit. Of course, this is not the same for a nonprofit business or one that is referred to as a "closely held" corporation, which means that the owners are a small group. In these and some other forms of corporations, the decision to do something for altruistic or benevolent reasons only affects those that are making the decision. However, in a large, publicly traded corporation, the executives just cannot go around spending money to do "nice" things. Shareholders do not want to hear it. They have invested in the company to make money, and the more, the better. If a lot of money is spent on community projects that do not contribute to the profitability of the company, this can make the stock "less competitive," which means shareholders just might sell the stock and buy something else. This would tend to drive down the price of the stock even more, and eventually, the company could go out of business.

Henry Ford actually was sued by his board of directors and the shareholders of the Ford Motor Company because he wanted to pay his workers more than the going rate for the type of work they would be doing. Ford was not doing this just to be a nice guy, which history shows he certainly was not. It was fundamental to his vision of what the company was all about. In a nutshell, his philosophy, as stated in his vision, was to make a quality automobile that an average worker earning a decent wage could afford. This was revolutionary in that any previous car was so expensive that only the rich could buy one. He intended to hire only the finest craftsmen to build these cars and pay them well for their skills and effort. Actually, he wanted his workers to be able to buy the cars coming off the assembly line. Further, he wanted the average American to put their families in them and travel around and see this great country. This was a novel idea for the average-working guy to travel with his family and have a good time. Henry Ford's vision created much for the American middle class, and it would not have happened if he paid his employees as little as possible. He was far from a perfect human being, but he had the vision thing down in spades. He created a middle class of people who work with their hands. Further, the effective way in which the work was designed allowed hardworking people to have enough time off so that they could enjoy themselves once in a while. This was something that was very rare, if not nonexistent, in the history of mankind. It is a tragedy that Henry turned very oppressive with his workforce and ended up at odds with organized labor, even to the extent of hiring goons with clubs and guns to suppress labor initiatives. He did, however, set forces in motion that resulted in the American working middle class.

Fascism and America

Most, if not all, of the owners of corporations did not share Henry Ford's view of creating a working middle class, even from the beginning. In fact, quite the opposite was true. The titans of industry, largely the product of J. P. Morgan & Co. and its offspring, came from the school of exploitation. These were antiunion, antiworkers' rights, and anti just about anything that empowered workers at all. They were philosophically more aligned with fascism than with Americanism. This is no exaggeration. American workers wanted their share of the prosperity that was coming to America at the beginning of the twentieth century. Wages was not the only issue. They also wanted a safe work environment and to not have to work from "can to can't." They wanted adequate health care, education and training, and a variety of issues that had to do with quality of life. Rather than looking at these issues as strengthening their workforce and developing employee loyalty that would improve profitability, the titans saw anything that cost them money as cutting into profit. This author has seen study after study that showed that American workers, including union workers, were dollar for dollar the most productive in the world. In most industries, the unions did the workforce training that resulted in increased safety and productivity, and that alone resulted in workers that outproduced anyone and everyone in the world.

Then as today, what "big business" is afraid of is the collective voice of organized labor and the challenge to the power of management. The titans do not want what they see as "conflict" in the workplace, even though stifled conflict is like a pressure cooker that will eventually explode and cause severe damage. What any smart manager wants to do is not to stifle conflict but to manage it. You want to have cooperation in decision making so that everyone has a sense of ownership in the direction decided upon, even if the parties do not always agree. You want collaboration, negotiation, different points of view, and mutual respect rather than threats, intimidation, violence, and sabotage. Anyone trained in conflict management knows that the lower levels of conflict can be used to benefit everyone whereas the more severe forms are destructive, and where you want to channel and keep the level of conflict at is decidedly the lower levels.

The most effective managers of conflict also understand that an organization is better off having avenues for workers to lodge a complaint, especially when they are complaining about someone that has more power than they do. If there is no avenue to redress a grievance and there is a power imbalance, the complainant will try to bring more power into his side or go around the person he has a problem with. Some people will act out in the form of sabotage or try to stir up trouble in the workplace among other workers when they perceive that they have no other way of airing their concerns. The descendents and "protégées" of Cecil Rhodes, J. P. Morgan, and all the rest had very little understanding of human behavior and human beings in general other than how to exploit them. They were crafty and manipulative but not smart, and they certainly did not understand the average worker. They fought against the rise of the working middle class then as they do today. In fact, they have all but destroyed unions, and with it, much of the middle class. As predicted in this author's graduate school business courses many years ago, the middle class is "going away" in America, and without it, the very foundation of the Republic will crumble and collapse. We will discuss this in more detail in my next book, but for now, we are seeing how American corporations fought against the creation of America as we know it.

They hired strikebreakers and violently suppressed any worker organization of any kind. It is well known that Pinkerton security had its roots in suppressing organized labor. They were hired to beat striking workers with baseball bats and, on more than one occasion, killed and murdered labor organizers. At times, the National Guard was used to suppress organized labor demonstrations and strikes. Less known, is that during the 1930s the American Legion was used as strikebreaker goons and even issued baseball bats to go out and bludgeon workers striking for collective bargaining rights.[160] Of course, the legionnaires were told that they were fighting Communism when in reality, they were fighting Americanism. They were being used by the wealthy to suppress and exploit the workers, workers that legionnaires had much more in common with than the wealthy elite.

Also not well known are the ties that the American Legion had to what may be construed as fascist objectives. Alvin Owsley, the legion

---

[160]. Jules Archer, *Plot To Seize The White House: The Shocking True Story of the Conspiracy to Overthrow F.D.R.* (Telson USA: Kindle Edition, August 3, 2007) Loc. 279-84.

commander in 1923, actually cited Italian fascism as a model for defending American against leftist influences and in that year even stated,

> If ever needed, the American Legion stands ready to protect our country's institutions and ideals as the Fascisti dealt with the destructionists who menaced Italy! . . . The American Legion is fighting every element that threatens our democratic government—Soviets, anarchists, IWW, revolutionary socialists and every other red . . . . Do not forget that the Fascisti are to Italy what the American Legion is to the United States.[161]

If that was not enough, the legion also invited Benito Mussolini to address their convention in 1930. Marine General Smedley Butler testified to a congressional committee that representatives of the American Legion tried to enlist his assistance in overthrowing Franklin Delano Roosevelt and installing a fascist dictatorship in the United States. Although Butler was largely portrayed as an "attention-seeking alarmist" in the press, almost all of Butler's claims were verified by the first congressional committee on un-American activities that concluded its investigation in 1935.[162] Butler's claims were more than serious. He went to Congress stating that he had been approached, through the American Legion, by some representatives of some of the biggest names in finance and business. Names such as J. P. Morgan, DuPont, Rockefeller, Pew, Remington, Mellon, Sloan, and others still have a familiar ring in high spheres of influence and were and still are connected to the previously mentioned Council on Foreign Relations. At the time, some of the above were on the influential American Liberty League and the National Executive Committee, which advanced many extreme right-wing views. Several of the members of these groups heavily sponsored, promoted,

---

[161.] Alec Campbell, "Where Do All the Soldiers Go?: Veterans and the Politics of Demobilization," in Diane E. Davis, Anthony W. Pereira, eds., *Irregular Armed Forces and their Role in Politics and State Formation* (New York: Cambridge University Press, 2003), 110-111.

[162.] Jules Archer, *Plot to Seize the White House: The Shocking True Story of the Conspiracy to Overthrow F.D.R.* (Telson USA: Kindle Edition, August 3, 2007) Loc. 3013-18.

and controlled the American Legion. In his book, *The Plot to Seize the White House*, Jules Archer established beyond a doubt that this plot actually took place and that the backers of it put up millions of dollars and were ready to up the ante to hundreds of millions to take over the US presidency and put their man in charge of the country. The plot was only stopped by the true patriotism of Marine Major General Smedley D. Butler, one of America's most decorated heroes.

It is interesting to note that fascist movements had already taken over Germany, Italy, Spain, Japan, and to a great extent Finland, Hungary, Romania, and Poland. Fascism also had a strong following in the United States that has been largely covered up to the present day. If one studies the fascists in Europe, there are common threads to what was going on in the United States between "the great wars." The Great Depression in the United States was actually a worldwide economic catastrophe, especially in Germany. Added to Germany's woes was the Treaty of Versailles that compelled Germany to virtually pay for all of the accumulated damage of WWI. This was not only unreasonable but also impossible for Germany, whose own economy and infrastructure had been devastated, to pay this astronomical figure. Most historians place the fundamental cause of WWII to be the crippling sanctions and reparations levied on Germany after WWI. These conditions are the wellspring from which demigods flow, and Hitler was the perfect match for these conditions. It is often overlooked that the Nazis originally passed themselves off as both nationalist and socialist, not fascist. The acronym NAZI stood for German words that mean National Socialist German Workers' Party in English.

Hitler gained power and support from the working class in Germany by using oratory that appealed to the working poor. This fact has been largely unreported in the United States because it can lead to some embarrassing places. One reporter who did go into this subject and many others that the mainstream media would not publicize was George Seldes, one of the greatest journalists of all time. Working for the *Chicago Tribune*, he interviewed many of the key players that later on would be center stage in WWII. Among these were Benito Mussolini, Vladimir Lenin, and Paul von Hindenburg. Much of his best work the *Tribune* would not publish. Disillusioned, he became a freelance reporter in 1927, and his first two books were *You Can't Print That!* (1929) and *Can These Things Be!* (1931). These books were based on articles he had written that publishers and editors refused to publish.

He was widely criticized in the press and was labeled a "muck raker" and worse. He reported on the Spanish Civil War and many other subjects related to the rise of fascism and abuse of power by wealthy industrialists. In 1940, he started a weekly political newspaper, *In Fact*, that contained information that the media would not publish. Some of the articles were from Seldes and also some from other journalists who had had their work rejected. The publication became the hallmark of a journalist who knew that what was being published in mainstream media was seriously flawed in that it catered to money and power. These articles became the foundation of his book *Facts and Fascism*, which Seldes published in 1943. In this work, Seldes explains in detail how Hitler duped the working people in Germany to support him. Seldes explained Hitler's promises to the German people as follows:

> Hitler was able to get thirteen million followers before 1933 by a pseudo-socialistic reform program and by great promises of aid to the common people. In the 26 points of the Nazi platform, adopted in 1920 and never repudiated, Hitler promised the miserable people of Germany:
>
> 1. The abolition of all unearned incomes.
> 2. The end of interest slavery. This was aimed against all bankers, not only Jewish bankers.
> 3. Nationalization of all joint-stock companies. This meant the end of all private industry, not only the monopolies but all big business.
> 4. Participation of the workers in the profits of all corporations—the mill, mine, factory, industrial worker was to become a part owner of industry.
> 5. Establishment of a sound middle class, Nazism, like Italian Fascism, made a great appeal to the big middle class, the small business man, the millions caught between the millstones of Big Business and labor. The big department stores, for example, were to be smashed. This promise delighted every small shopkeeper in Germany. Bernard Shaw once said that Britain was a nation of shopkeepers. This was just as true for Germany—and German shopkeepers were more alive politically. They were for Hitler's Nazism to a man—and

there supplied a large number of his murderous S.S. and S.A. troops.
6. Death penalty for usurers and profiteers.
7. Distinction between "raffendes" and "schaffendes" capital—between predatory and creative capital . . .[163]

Sounds pretty good, doesn't he? Hitler is thought of today as a solitary madman with great oratory skills that held the German people spellbound; however, the reality at the time was much different. Underreported is the fact than he was supported by global titans of industry from all over Europe and the United States. Seldes reported this, and that is why he could not get his most important work published. He hit too close to home on this and many other issues. Heavy industry did not support and finance him right off. He was largely seen as a "revolver-firing clown" by the elite bankers and industrialists until German industrialist Fritz Thyssen saw potential in him. Thyssen became Hitler's first big money supporter in 1923, and he groomed Hitler from then forward to take control of the nation and support Thyssen's agenda. Thyssen's main sphere of influence was the Steel Trust, which was a consortium of the major steel producers in Germany, roughly the equivalent of US Steel in its heyday. Anyone portrayed as evil has to be an "orphan." Whether it be Oswald or Hitler, connections to people in prominent positions become most uncomfortable. Hence we have the "lone gunman," "lone wolf," and the "lone madman" who single-handedly assassinates a president or takes over a country solely on their demented fanatical determination. This does not make sense now, and it never will.

According to Seldes, Thyssen put Hitler's show on the road and convinced other industrial leaders and bankers to support Hitler. Of course there was a catch. These industrialists had an agenda that was far different from what Hitler was supposedly promoting; in fact it was diametrically opposed to Hitler's and the National Socialists' stated positions. Destruction of the trade unions, collective bargaining, wage increases, and any form of worker rights at all was the hidden agenda of the industrialists. The German industrialists wanted what virtually

---

[163]. George Seldes, *Facts and Fascism* (In Fact, Inc.; 5th edition, Kindle, July 11, 2011) Loc. 244-258.

all top managers and owners of large corporations want and that is for the maximum amount of money to go to them and not the workers. This is what fascism is. It is corporate control of the government and the workforce to do whatever the owners want to do, and that would be to get filthy rich and leave everyone else poor and powerless. Hitler was dancing to this music and officially and publicly stating the exact opposite. Previously, we had Andrew Lobeczewski describe Hitler as not a great, spellbinding orator but appearing more like a clown.

The author has long thought that Hitler gave the appearance of a Charley Chaplin look-alike except he was not funny. The fact that this preposterous fool could arguably sway hundreds of millions of followers to follow him is incredible. Also to note the fact that even today he is widely known as this larger-than-life force for evil boggles the mind. Further, it begs the question as to who are the fools, Hitler and his backers who knew exactly what they were doing or the multitudes of followers that followed this braying jackass? Could it be that Hitler, and those of his ilk, are only masters at feeding back what the people want to hear? His power only came from the ability to set segments of the German population against one another. It came from the traumatic events that occurred in the beginning of the twentieth century that enabled him—with the advice, consent, and support of the elite industrialists—to whip-saw the population into a fear and hate frenzy. How else could this Mario Brothers look-alike be able to get millions of people to kill one another? Hitler was carefully taught by the power elite how to set people against one another to gain control of all the population. He certainly could not have done it alone, which is what most history books would want you to believe.

We also had much the same thing happening in Italy with Mussolini and his brand of fascism. Mussolini was chosen by the corporate power elite to pretend he was for the common man, and that once he was in power, he would redistribute the rich farmland owned by the upper class and so forth. Of course, when he did take control of the government, nothing of the sort happened. After lying right in the face of the whole country, he put the government at the beck and call of his rich corporate sponsors and brutally suppressed the rest of the country. Further, long forgotten is the fact that Mussolini became the darling of American fascists and their boot-lickers. The American Legion, a creation of J. P. Morgan bankers and corporations, all but worshiped "the Duce." They touted him, and also fascism, as a model of efficiency that was unencumbered by labor disputes and frivolities such as health care, education, training, and the like. They even invited him to almost every annual convention from 1922 to 1935 and actually did get him to come to their Chicago convention in 1935 where Col. William E. Easterwood, the national vice commander, made him an honorary member and pinned an American Legion button on him.[164] "The Duce's" ability to merge business with the government (read corporate control of the government here) not only received accolades from the legion, but he was also the envy of Wall Street and corporate America. News articles were published that marveled at his ability to get Italy's trains running on time. Fascism was the model of efficiency that these "geniuses" put forth as the cure for the Great Depression. "If only we had that here . . ." was the formula for getting the business world back on its feet, and they acted on it in the form of the previously mentioned plot to seize the White House.

Similar things were going on in Spain where Generalissimo Franco, unquestionably a fascist, took control of the government in October 1936. Some in the United States were wondering if all of Europe would turn fascist and some were not only wondering but hoping for such a transition not only in all of Europe but also in the United States. The Great Depression was a worldwide event, and extreme hardship is the wellspring from which extreme political movements flow, and flow they did. Hardship and fear can make simple, radical solutions attractive. It is also an environment in which shallow, insensitive, greedy, and manipulative people can prevail. Lobeczewski used the terms *psychopaths* and *characteropaths*, but there are also others such as the previously discussed Dr. Robert D. Hare, author of *Snakes in Suits*, who describe people who are not psychopaths or sociopaths but who can do horrible things to people, go home and kiss their spouse, play with the dog, and help their kids with their homework. Dr. Hare explains that these people are able to compartmentalize two completely different behavior patterns thus keeping their work world separate from their personal lives. They do not fit the pattern of the psychopath, but their behavior is very similar. Dr. Lobeczewski would probably label these people as "characteropaths."

[164.] Ibid, Loc. 1573-77.

"The Camel Never Sees Its Own Hump"

This is an expression in Arabic that roughly translates as above in English. The camel sees all of the other camel's humps but never his own. Repeatedly, we have seen the top Nazis, and those of their ilk, described as ruthless murderers that go home and lead normal lives, but apparently, the United States is totally devoid of ruthless mass-murderers, or perhaps we just cannot see our own hump. If one was to summarize our history books, the ledger would read something like this: The Native Americans just kind of got sick and died—too bad they just could not deal with a few germs—about eighteen million of them. We tried to free the Filipinos, but they just could not understand what we were doing, so we had to shoot them—about a million of them. The same thing happened with the Koreans and Vietnamese—somewhere between one and four million of them. And how about those Iraqis—about a million of them—Palestinians . . . Guatemalans . . . Cubans . . . Haitians . . . Panamanians . . . Nicaraguans . . . and the list goes on. All we are doing is trying to help people, and what thanks do we get? They shoot at us or throw shoes or rocks. What choice do we have? Some people you just can't help! And college kids that have the nerve to protest all of this? Why we have to shoot them too, to be fair. Stuff like that can spread: Marxism . . . Communism . . . disrespect for law and order. If it can happen at Kent State and Jackson State, it can happen anywhere and everywhere. You have to draw the line somewhere. If we don't get them over there, we will have to fight them here.

In mass-murdering civilians, we have probably far surpassed the Nazis, and it does not appear to have slowed down much at this writing. Having deliberately murdered at least a million Iraqis and displaced roughly five million of them, roughly half of whom are completely out of the country, we are currently setting sights on Iran, which could easily end up to be even more of a disaster than Iraq, Afghanistan, etc., combined. But the solution to the problem is to just not count the bodies. It did not happen. Recall George W. Bush's reply to the question of how many Iraqis civilians were killed? He did not know, but when a figure was put forth, he knew it was not *that* many! "Maybe about forty thousand or so, no more," was his answer as I recall. Odd that he has no idea how many, but he knows how many were not killed, very odd indeed.

Repeatedly, we see authors and researchers allude to an eerie comparison of Nazi Germany and post-WWII America. Not only Andrew Lobeczewski mentioned it but also Naomi Wolf, author of *The End of America*, delved into the similarities; and they are joined by Noam Chomsky, noted academic writer, researcher, and lecturer who also draws the same parallels. There are also many others who have drawn similar comparisons with a common thread of a people traumatized by war and militarism, who become reactionary in their thinking and their emotions. Let us not forget that both the vanquished and the victors are scared by the trauma of institutionalized violence and murder. Add to this the patently racist views of both societies and the overtly genocidal direction of both and we have two societies, ostensibly enemies, more alike than different. And as we shall see, they became even more alike during and after the war.

If one follows the connections that are never discussed in mainstream media, then or now, between the German elite bankers and industrialists, they lead right to the Wall Street and the National Association of Manufacturers or NAM. Most everybody is familiar with Wall Street bankers and the New York stock exchange, but few are aware of the economic and political power that the NAM wielded during the Great Depression. Since 1895, it has been the nation's largest industrial trade association, and its membership contained the very same business leaders that tried to entice Smedley Butler to overthrow the FDR White House and install a fascist dictatorship in the United States. George Seldes names two corporations as part of the Nazi cartel plot to establish a fascist government in the United States. Seldes identified the DuPont Empire and General Motors as the corporations involved and the executives of those two corporations that put forth this initiative as having been Lammot DuPont and Alfred P. Sloan Jr. respectively.[165] Again, we see connections to J. P. Morgan & Co. that go back to Cecil Rhodes, his Circle of Initiates, Round Table groups, and the rest of his Anglophile secret society to "spread Anglo culture throughout the world," or more directly, Anglo domination of the world. And the question remains as to why this was not widely reported at the time and is virtually unknown even today? Well, the answer is that the major media outlets are owned and/or controlled by

---

[165.] Ibid, Loc. 1078-84.

the very same corporations that were created by J. P. Morgan & Co. For example, General Electric, another J. P. Morgan creation, owns controlling interest in NBC; and we could draw the same lines for all major media outlets. This is why we did not see these connections in the run-up to WWII and why we do not see them now.

As mentioned in the previous chapter, Rhodes and Lord Milner were the main players in putting together the Circle of Initiates and the resulting Round Table groups, and these groups' membership consisted of what was and what became the Western industrial and banking elite. These financial and business centers were based primarily in England and the United States with connections throughout the world, including Nazi Germany. Most of the financial banking in England and Europe became known as Rothschild banking and in the United States the term was the House of Morgan or J. P. Morgan and Company. Many of the participants in Rhodes's secret society were also instrumental in growing and developing the international drug trade discussed previously. Names such as John Jacob Astor and his son Waldorf Astor, who was also chairman on the previously mentioned Council of the Royal Institute of International Affairs; John Murray Forbes of Boston, who was also a US agent for Baring Brothers, which was and is the primary bank of the opium traffic from 1783 to the present; and the Hathaway and Perkins families. Let us keep in mind that the Astor family owned and controlled major media outlets, such as the *Times*. So what are the chances that any of this would hit the front pages of newspapers?

The leading US banker for the above became the House of Morgan, and of all the money-making enterprises attributed to Morgan, rarely mentioned is the wildly profitable drug trade, which also fuels British banking. As discussed earlier, heroin and cocaine are worth about seven times their weight in gold. Further, one does not have to pay taxes or import duties on them because they are, and will remain, illegal. It is the perfect product, light and easily transported, the customers become addicted, and the profits are astronomical. Although the figures vary wildly, the annual street sales for heroin, cocaine, and marijuana in the United States was reported by the House Select Committee on Narcotics in 1986 to be about $233 billion per year. The worldwide trade has been reported to be about $350 billion. The true figures have been reported by nongovernmental agencies to be much higher, but even if we use the above figures, the vast majority of which goes through the above-mentioned banking and business enterprises, we see that drugs is a major player in propping up these banking and business systems. Add to this the fact that this is not money borrowed against a relatively small amount of real assets, sometimes referred to as "leveraged funds," nor is it money borrowed from our children's future, which the author refers to as "play money." This is cash on the barrelhead and can be used to "leverage" as much as ten to twenty times its face value. Simply put, it represents literally trillions of dollars per year. Take this money out of the Anglo financial system, and it collapses, as what almost happened when Al Qaeda and the Taliban shut down the opium/heroin trade in 2001. Coincidentally, the stock market started to crash, and we had the 9/11 attacks, after which, the US stock market was shut down. Drugs and the Anglo-American financial system go way back as we previously discussed.

The entire system of course includes the media, which has never, and probably will never, report this. Even the so-called progressive media does not touch this. There is so much power and money behind this pathological system that it is able to destroy anything and everything in its way. Any news outlet that even touches upon this either backs off or is destroyed. One example that we will discuss in more detail in my next book was the San Jose Mercury News, which published Gary Webb's series, "Dark Alliance," about the Iran-Contra affair and how drugs played heavily in the equation. US intelligence, law enforcement, and the rest of the media came down on them like a ton of bricks, and although Webb and the Mercury News had done a superlative job of citing sources and facts, this news outlet printed a retraction and got rid of Garry Webb. He was black-balled in the business and harassed to the point of suicide. This author tried to obtain copies of this series from the San Jose Mercury News, and the entire series had been removed from the archives, lock stock and barrel, just like it never happened. This is the power of the drug trade and the corporations and government agencies that "facilitate" it. They will stop at nothing to keep it going, and this financial system was developed and promulgated by the same Anglophile reactionary fascists that have used genocide, racism, and militarism to control the world. They became visible, albeit underreported, in the run-up to World War II, and many of the business interests were represented in the National Association of Manufacturers.

Most of the corporations of the NAM were J. P. Morgan creations, and they carried out traditions that can only be characterized as fascist.

Also, most of the major industries were members of the NAM, and collectively, they had a lot of political and economic power. They had considerable influence on the media in the form of advertising, and they would not hesitate to withdraw advertising money when the press did not report things the way the corporations wanted them to. This is in addition to the formation of the American Legion whose mission, not stated of course, was to intimidate organized labor. This went even further than intimidation to the point that these companies hired goons to bludgeon strikers and murder labor organizers. The legion actually issued out baseball bats and hard liquor and directed its members to severely beat up participants in organized labor activities. Police either looked the other way or even participated in the violence.

A typical example was Henry Ford and the Ford Motor Company. When the author studied him in graduate school business courses, he was portrayed as this marketing and manufacturing genius who invented assembly line production methods and paid his workers more than the going wages. Turns out that he was a brutal dictator who had people beaten up, fired, and even murdered if he believed they crossed him. Hitler and Himmler greatly admired his fascist leanings and especially his overt anti-Semitism. A man named Ralph Rimar, who was second in command of what was known as the intelligence department of the Ford empire, later wrote a book that was no less than shocking. The title of it is rather straight forward, *Heil Henry: The Confessions of a Ford Spy*, and the introduction is just as damning:

> International fascist tieups, gangsterism within the plant as well as support of the Fifth Column without; connections between Ford Company officials and vice rings; relationships between Ford Henchmen and city, state and government authorities, the use of criminals by the company, the protection of Nazis, the bribery of government witnesses, the torture, mutilation and murder of union men; the efforts to instigate race riots; the constant relentless plotting against tens of thousands of Ford workers.[166]

[166.] No publisher would publish Rimar's manuscript, although he gave a copy to Seldes with permission to quote from it. Seldes quoted from the

Rimar goes on to document all of the above and more, and the level of criminality is shocking. Seldes reports that Hitler even had a portrait of Ford on the wall of his office and raved about Ford's anti-Semitism. Another shocking revelation, according to Rimar, is that one of Henry Ford's executives, W. J. Cameron, published the notorious forgeries referred to as the "Protocols of Zion." Add to this that it was published in Ford's decidedly anti-Semitic company newspaper the *Dearborn Independent*.[167] Ford's paper certainly was not the only place where fascism was praised and anti-Semitism was openly advocated. Walter D. Fuller was president of Curtis Publishing Company, and he was mostly responsible for pro-fascist articles published in the *Saturday Evening Post*, a publication that was largely thought of as catering to the interests of small-town Main Street USA when the author was young. Between world wars, this publication produced a series of articles praising Mussolini and actually published two articles written by Nazi sympathizers. The titles of these articles do not call for any further explanation: "The Case Against the Jew," and "Will Labor Lose the War?"[168]

Hitler not only admired Ford's anti-Semitic views, he also appreciated that about one-third of his trucks, essential for his blitzkrieg war strategy, were manufactured by Ford Motor Company. In fact, Hitler put on a huge ceremony in Berlin, in 1938, where Hitler bestowed upon Ford the Grand Cross of the Order of the German Eagle.[169] Albeit this was prior to declared war, there is record of substantial complicity and assistance for the Nazi regime during the war. As late as 1945 a US Army report referred to Ford as "the arsenal of Nazism" with the "consent" of the company in Dearborn, Michigan.[170]

---

manuscript in his book as follows: George Seldes, *Facts and Fascism* (In Fact, Inc.; 5th edition, Kindle, July 11, 2011) Loc. 1814-20.

[167.] George Seldes, *Facts and Fascism* (In Fact, Inc.; 5th edition, Kindle, July 11, 2011) Loc. 1795-99.

[168.] Ibid, Loc. 1347-53.

[169.] Edwin Black, Nazi Nexus: America's Corporate Connections to Hitler's Holocaust (Kindle edition: Dialog Press, February 16, 2009), Loc. 292-99.

[170.] Ibid, 299-308.

Henry Ford was not the only American industrialist who gained the admiration of Adolf Hitler. Also in 1938, Hitler bestowed upon James D. Mooney, director of General Motors oversees operations, the German Eagle with Cross, which was the highest medal awarded to foreign supporters of the Nazi effort.[171] Seems that GM's Opel division also turned out trucks and built aircraft before and during the war. The profits were frozen until after the war. To add insult to injury, GM was awarded war reparations, by the US taxpayer, for allied aerial bomb damage to the GM Opel division plants during the war.

Prior to the two awards above, in 1937, Hitler bestowed the Merit Cross of the German Eagle with Star to Thomas J. Watson, IBM's president.[172] In fact, the medal was created for him. Of all the supporters of Hitler and the Nazis, Watson and IBM take first place. The Holocaust entailed much more information processing than one would surmise at first glance. The Nazis wanted to eliminate much more than a religion. Taking a cue from the Eugenics movement in the United States, the Nazis believed that humans had in their genetic makeup a substance called "germ plasm." They believed that inferior people had defective germ plasm and that this substance was passed on to their children, who in turn would be defective. Further, they believed that inferior germ plasm was dominant and so the defect would come to the surface in future generations even if no other ancestor was defective. It was along these lines that the Nazis first came to the conclusion that Jews had defective germ plasm that caused defects in character to be passed on, regardless of what the professed religion was.

This is why they categorized people as Jewish even if they only had one grandparent that was of that faith. One can see the information systems necessary to track down everyone with Jewish ancestry, not only in Germany but in all of occupied Europe. These kinds of tabulations are what IBM processing machines excelled at, and IBM and Watson knew exactly what was going on. There is no way that the Nazi regime could have euthanized six million people and probably much more without IBM. Let us keep in mind that substantial numbers of gypsies

---

[171.] Ibid, 1886-1904.
[172.] Ibid, 2738-46

and other people were also categorized and mass-murdered with the utmost of efficiency, thanks to IBM and Watson. Further, the efficiency with which the Nazi war machine was managed was greatly enhanced by IBM information processing machines. How many casualties resulted from IBM providing state-of-the-art information management to the Nazis? Why the above people were not held accountable for treason is unfathomable.

It was not only industrialists that were sympathetic to Hitler. *Fortune* magazine, owned by Morgan partner and reactionary fascist Henry Luce, praised Mussolini and fascism in its July 1934 issue, and lauded the manner in which great corporations had progressed under fascism.[173] It is interesting to note that two other publications owned by Luce, *Time* and *Life* magazines played key roles in convincing a large segment of the US population that Oswald was solely responsible for all of the wounds suffered by JFK and Texas Governor John Connelly in Dealey Plaza along with the "Magic Bullet Theory" and all the rest of the fairy tales associated with the JFK assassination. *Life* magazine is no longer published, but *Time* certainly is and, to this day, holds to the lone nut assassin theory put forth by the almost universally discredited Warren Commission. Virtually, all of the major media in the United States has supported fascism for well over one hundred years and has been consistently antiorganized labor. They are owned and controlled by major corporations and serve their agenda, which is unbridled and uncontrolled capitalism and everything that goes along with it, such as the destruction of the middle class, especially the "blue collar" working middle class represented by organized labor.

The fight for workers' rights, decent wages, adequate health care, and education has been a long, hard-fought battle. Corporate America has put billions of dollars into the destruction of all these. These greedy, selfish, and pathological sorry excuses for human beings could not stop the rise of the American worker and the American middle class even with all of their power. Add to this the fact that the economic creation and rise of the American middle-class is what made America the economic power that it was, up until roughly about 1973. At that

---

[173.] George Seldes, *Facts and Fascism* (In Fact, Inc.; 5th edition, Kindle, July 11, 2011), Loc. 530-36.

point, cracks began to form, small at first but increasingly larger and larger. Since that point, American workers' wages have been pretty much flat, although productivity has gone up year after year. Cheap oil, as we shall discuss in more detail in my next book, the development of computers, and the fact that Americans worked themselves to the point of exhaustion resulted in profitability never seen before. And what did corporate America do with these profits? They largely and legally stole them and used some to destroy the very systems that enabled these corporate profits in the first place. They also wrote books describing themselves as business geniuses for having looted the middle class. Beginning with Ronald Reagan as president, corporate America began dismantling unions. They began with the air traffic controllers and have not stopped since. Today, a very small segment of the private work force is unionized, and even that is under attack and dwindling. They have choked the goose that laid the golden egg.

The author vividly recalls Ronald Reagan when he was governor of California back in the early '70s. One of his brilliant moves was to throw all of the mentally ill patients out of hospitals. Ostensibly, he was freeing them from incarceration, but the truth of the matter is that he did not want to pay for their care. Virtually overnight, we saw a homeless population develop that did not exist prior to their "liberation," and today, many of the world record holding figures for prisoners is largely attributable to these mentally ill people that should be in hospitals being treated. Also recalled is the fact that plans were widely publicized to treat and care for the mentally ill in the community. Of course these plans never materialized because they would have cost money, more cost effective to let "them" eat out of trashcans or better yet, put them in jail where you can contract out services to the "private sector" so that the same people that put Reagan in office can make even more money off the defenseless mentally ill. Reagan was a finger-puppet of the rich who led the all out assault on the middle class. Yes, it was "successful," successful in destroying dollar for dollar the most effective and efficient workforce in the world, American organized labor. We will look at the facts and figures in my next book, but for now it is safe to say that the American camel never saw the fascist hump continually growing on its back. America saw Germany's hump, it saw Italy's hump, Spain's hump, and all the other fascist humps all over the world, but it never saw its own.

Fascism in the Aftermath of World War II

Much is widely known about the conduct of WWII such that we will not go into it in detail. Noteworthy, however, is the fact that Germany had advanced technology much of which is classified even today. That Germany had Supersonic jet propulsion, stealth technology, antigravity technology, and a rocketry program that was much further advanced than anything that was even on the drawing board in Great Britain or the United States was known to the intelligence services of all the allied nations. Both the US Office of Strategic Services, or OSS, and British intelligence, which is referred to as "M16," badly wanted this technology and was willing to go to extreme means to obtain it. Of course the Soviet Union was also a big player in this. One example of Nazi technology co-opted by the United States was the Ho-229, which had a radar absorbing surface, no vertical stabilizer, and the exhaust from the engines was discharged on top of the fuselage so to avoid detection by heat-seeking missiles, much like Northrop Grumman's B-2 bomber. The similarity between the Nazi Ho-229[174] and the American B-2 bomber is not a coincidence. Only a few prototypes were made, but if Germany had gone into mass production of this plane, the war could have had very different results. They simply ran out of time. Another Nazi aircraft, a long-range strategic bomber prototype, had also been made that reportedly flew to within a few miles of the coast of New York, took pictures, and returned to Germany, nonstop. There is credible evidence that the Nazis had an advanced nuclear bomb program, and that weapons grade uranium was transferred to the United States after the war. Jim Marrs, author of *The Rise of the Fourth Reich*, went into detail on this subject. Who got a hold of this technology and the engineers

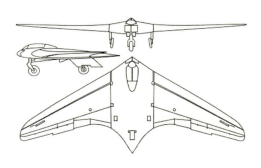

---

[174]. Source: Wikipedia, http://en.wikipedia.org/wiki/File:Horten_Ho_IX_line_drawing.svg.

that developed it would be masters of the world, and this was no secret to the Anglo-American Empire.

The development of the Office of Strategic Services, the OSS, during the war was another milestone in the transformation of the American republic into a pathocracy. Ostensibly created to coordinate espionage activities between the branches of the armed forces, the OSS was created, staffed, and funded by the same J. P. Morgan industrialists and bankers that tried to seize the FDR White House and install a reactionary fascist dictatorship in the United States. William "Wild Bill" Donovan was its first director, and there were other notable members such as Allen Dulles later to be director of the CIA. Instrumental in converting the OSS to the CIA was John J. McCloy. Many, including the above, had links to Wall Street, the Council on Foreign Relations (CFR), and other organizations connected to the Rhodes's secret society and J. P. Morgan establishment. Both McCloy and Dulles were members of the Warren Commission. Nearly every person instrumental in the transition from the OSS to the CIA was a member of the CFR, including the Dulles and Rockefeller brothers. Allen Dulles was a founder of the Council on Foreign Relations. The OSS certainly had its successes during WWII, but it was criticized within President Harry Truman's administration as a reactionary, fascist organization of dangerously unscrupulous radicals. For this reason, Truman decided to deactivate the organization. He did, however, allow for the creation of a central agency to coordinate all US intelligence under the direction of a National Security Council that would report directly to him.

As previously discussed, this became the CIA created by the National Security Act of 1947. There were some problems, however. To begin with this organization was financed into permanence by the Rockefeller foundation and the Carnegie institution. It was also staffed by the same reactionary fascists that were in the old OSS. Even while this transition from OSS to CIA was taking place, many thousands of Nazi war criminals were being taken into US corporations, the CIA and other intelligence agencies, higher education institutions, the National Security Agency, research hospitals, and other agencies. Notable among these war criminals was Warner Von Braun who was the director of the Nazi Peenemunde Rocket Research Center where the V-2 rocket was developed and manufactured. Von Braun was directly responsible for the mass murder of thousands of slave laborers at this site. MIT professor Noam Chomsky goes into some detail about how Von Braun directed that a certain percentage of prison laborers be executed when sabotage occurred in V-2 production. There are also photos of him in Waffen-SS uniform along with other Nazi officers. Von Braun was taken into the United States, and his past was whitewashed. He was portrayed as a scientist purely interested in rocketry and space travel that happened to be born in Germany. The inference was that he had no interest in the Nazi movement. This of course was a cover story and far from the truth. He was initially hired by the US Army to develop guided missiles and later became the Unites States' first director of the National Aeronautics and Space Administration, or NASA. He is credited as being largely responsible for putting the first American astronauts on the moon. He has received many awards from as high up as US presidents, but his murderous past has been totally ignored and denied. Here we have history recreated right before our eyes.

Von Braun was certainly not the only Nazi that was "sheep-dipped." In fact there were many thousands of Nazis that were taken into this country. Another notable example is Major General Walter Schreiber who was the head of the Nazi concentration camp prisoner experimentation programs supposedly for the purpose of medical research. These programs are known to have been responsible for starvation, torture, and the most repulsive kinds of experimentation known to man. He and his family came to the United States under "Operation Paperclip," and he was employed at the Air Force School of Medicine, Randolph Air Force Base, Texas. Journalist Drew Pearson exposed his past in 1952, and he was given a visa and a new job in Argentina in 1952.

The total extent of collaboration between the global power elite in the United States and Germany before, during, and after WWII is staggering. The Third Reich's minister of finance was none other than Martin Bormann, who was also the deputy führer. Apparently, he figured out that Germany was going to lose the war, and he planned accordingly. He executed a plan to finance the National Socialist Party's survival after the war and also the survival of most of its members. He knew that some would be tried and executed, but just as he planned, most of the wealth, power, and many thousands of key players not only survived but flourished after the war. When the German army was defeated at Stalingrad in 1943, the German industrialists along with Bormann realized that the defeat of Nazi Germany was inevitable. They made plans to move their wealth and, in reality, the wealth of much of Europe out of Germany and into myriad accounts, front agencies, and businesses all over the world. Bormann spearheaded this plan. Tons of gold and other precious metals, some of which had belonged to Jews and others that had been mass-murdered in death camps, were spirited out of the country. Funds were transferred to foreign assets and camouflaged on paper; and in 1945, two billion dollars—a lot of money in those days—that was in the Reichsbank treasury disappeared completely.[175]

This fortune that included much of the wealth of Europe was laundered into Swiss bank accounts, about forty of which have been traced to Argentina's Eva Perón. The man who controlled all of this was SS Commando Otto Skorzeny, Hitler's favorite officer. Skorzeny was a piece of work. He was six foot four inches, strong, intelligent, and absolutely fearless. Whatever mission he was assigned, he accomplished. He also had the survival skills of a rat and survived long after WWII ended. Skorzeny bought large tracks of land all over South America to be used by thousands of former SS officers. Although there were others, the main program to preserve the Third Reich and wait for a time when a Fourth Reich could surface was code-named ODESSA, the Organization der ehemaligen SS-Angehörigen or Organization of Former SS Members. This organization is the source of much of the talk about Nazis hiding in South America and undue influence with the various fascist regimes there. This group of international criminals took over entire governments and further consolidated their power through the international drug trade, gun running, front corporations, church fronts, and massive influence in multinational corporations and banks.

The US Department of State created Operation Safe Haven to hunt down hidden Nazi funds only to find their efforts thwarted by none other than Allen Dulles. Seems that Allen and his brother, John Foster, had done legal work for several Nazi banks and corporations, most telling was I. G. Farben which was one of Hitler's main financial supporters.[176] I. G. Farben was also the manufacturer of Zyklon B,

---

[175.] Richard Gilbride, *Matrix for Assassination: The JFK Conspiracy*, (Victoria, BC, Canada, Trafford Publishing, 2009), Kindle Edition, Loc. 781-9.

[176.] Richard Gilbride, *Matrix for Assassination: The JFK Conspiracy*, (Victoria, BC, Canada, Trafford Publishing, 2009), Kindle Edition, Loc. 802-10.

which was the poison used in the death camps. Other supporters, some of which have been previously mentioned, were Standard Oil, DuPont, Alcoa, General Electric, ITT, General Motors, Ford, Chase Manhattan, and Brown Brothers Harriman.[177] Allen Dulles was instrumental in the creation of the OSS, and he was a charter member of the Council on Foreign Relations. He also became its director in 1921. Apparently, he was not the only one in the OSS who had similar connections. As it turned out, most of the senior OSS staff was either related to the families of or employed by the above corporations.[178] Apparently this was not a surprise to Franklin Delano Roosevelt because he had the Department of State wiretap Dulles's phone and monitor his communications from the office directly below him in the Rockefeller Center.[179] The Department of State had been given the task of identifying US corporations that were aiding the Nazis. The conclusions drawn were that Dulles had continued to aid and work with his German business clients well after war was declared.[180]

In line with his character, Allen Dulles also facilitated the exodus of German industrialists, and their money, after the war. Dulles knew his communications were being monitored, so he used agents of the Vatican, with diplomatic immunity, to carry on the necessary transactions. Dulles also used the Vatican to obtain passports for Nazi officials to escape to South America.[181] These systems to get Nazis out of Europe and into South American were called "ratlines." Another ratline channel Dulles used was through the Knights of Malta, which is the smallest sovereignty in the world, occupying one city block in Rome.[182] Although small, the Knights of Malta have the power to issue passports, ostensibly to political refugees; but in these cases, they issued them to some of the worst criminals the world has ever seen. The Knights of Malta had some interesting members. On their rolls were Waffen-SS Commander Heinrich Himmler; Clay Shaw, the only person to be charged in the JFK assassination; and Kim Philby, the

---

[177.] Ibid.
[178.] Ibid.
[179.] Ibid.
[180.] Ibid.
[181.] Ibid. 716-21
[182.] Ibid. 727-31

British spy who defected to the Soviet Union. Philby was also involved with the ODESSA operation, ratlines, and all. Other members of interest were James Jesus Angleton, William J. Donovan, Reinhard Gehlen, John A. McCone, Benito Mussolini, and Juan Perón.

Assisting him in Rome was a father-and-son team, both of whom were also OSS agents. James Jesus Angleton and his father, Hugh, represented the company National Cash Register in Italy before the war. After the war, James Angleton held a variety of influential positions in the CIA, the last of which was the chief of counterintelligence. It is a certainty that Angleton was Oswald's handler and that he sent him to the USSR as a counterintelligence agent. Oswald was a U-2 controller who had access to top secret U-2 codes. Francis Gary Powers, the U-2 pilot downed over Russia, believed that Oswald had given the Soviets secret coding information that allowed them to take him down. Why would the CIA want to do that? Pentagon intelligence liaison chief, Air Force Colonial Fletcher Prouty, answered that question that President Eisenhower and Soviet Premier Khrushchev were planning to virtually end the cold war at an upcoming summit that was scuttled when the U-2 went down.

Angleton, Dulles, and others were also responsible for the escape of hundreds of top-ranking Nazis and the transfer of enormous amounts of money into Wall Street and South American banks. Yes, some of the technology came in handy, but these criminals who were embraced by their Anglo-American counterparts after WWII have caused irreparable damage to the free world.

Nazis Among Us

Operation Paperclip was the primary program to bring Germans with desirable scientific and technical expertise into the United States. President Truman approved of the program with the stipulation that no war criminals or persons with more than a minor affiliation to the Nazi party be included. Most of the individuals that Allen Dulles and the OSS wanted were, however, the most notorious criminals to have ever walked the face of the earth. The methods they used to achieve this have caused incalculable damage to the United States. They found that if they could classify these murders' past "top secret," compartmentalize this information on a "need to know" basis for access, and hide the whole thing under the veil of "National Security," they could do whatever they wanted to with these criminals and anything else they wanted to do. They could hide anything they wanted to from the American people, Congress, and even the president of the United States. Farewell to checks and balances, farewell to oversight, farewell to accountability, and farewell to America. The OSS/CIA took charge of the country. They now joined hands with their fascist brethren from Nazi Germany and ran wild with trillions of dollars from the US treasury and the international drug trade. Since WWII, they have started one war after another, overthrowing democratically elected governments, spreading murder and mayhem all over the planet, torturing and experimenting on their own people, and on and on. These are just a few of the Nazi psychopaths brought into the United States by their English-speaking counterparts. Let us take a look at a few more.

Josef Mengele, sometimes referred to as "the Angel of Death" was an SS officer at Auschwitz responsible for the murder, dismemberment, torture, so-called experimental operations and procedures of about four hundred thousand death camp victims. Mengele was one of the cruelest and most repulsive war criminals that ever lived. He had a medical degree as a physician and also a PhD in anthropology. He espoused a belief system commonly referred to as eugenics, which is the fraudulent and absurd pseudoscience, which purports to be the manipulation of a population to improve its genetic contribution. All sorts of evil sprang forth from this so-called "biosocial" movement, and it has been around a long time. This was the basis for involuntary sterilization of "undesirables," laws concerning who may marry whom, and a variety of racist views still around today. The first International Congress of Eugenics met in 1912, and among its attendees were Winston Churchill and Alexander Graham Bell. Early advocates of eugenics in the United States included President Theodore Roosevelt and J. D. Rockefeller. The Rockefeller Foundation funded all sorts of these initiatives in the United States and around the world. Mengele was never tried for his crimes, but the death camp butchers that were tried cited the eugenics movement in the United States as the basis for their ghastly experiments and mass murder.[183] He had a following in the United States.

[183.] The connections between US and Nazi eugenicists is discussed in: Edwin Black, *War Against the Weak: Eugenics and America's Campaign to Create a*

It is not certain how Mengele got out of Germany, but some researchers believe it was through one of the ratlines managed by the US Army's Counterintelligence Corps, or CIC.[184] Carol Rutz, *A Nation Betrayed*, writes that a Croatian priest and former Nazi collaborator operating out of the Vatican helped Mengele escape to Buenos Aires, Argentina, in 1949.[185] Seems the CIC hired a Croatian Catholic leader by the name of Monsignor Krunoslav Draganovic to run ratlines for the American-sponsored Nazis on the run. Carol also found evidence that Otto Skorzeny also used this channel for Nazi criminals to Paraguay and Buenos Aires.[186] According to Carol, Mengele not only made it out of Germany to Buenos Aires, but the CIA was flying him into the United States to assist with secret mind control programs and also genetic experiments. She tells an incredible story of being sold by her father to the CIA for MK-ULTRA programming involving torturous procedures and experiments to create multiple personalities for a variety of malicious purposes. Many of these horrifying procedures were conducted by a "Dr. Black" whom she is certain was actually Josef Mengele.[187] Carol also explains that she has had contact with several mind control survivors that have told much the same story. Some of the other aliases Mengele is believed to have used are, Dr. Green, Dr. Swartz, Father Joseph, or Vaterchen (*daddy* in German), and others.

The fact that Mengele was smuggled out of Germany by American intelligence, and the likely prospect that he was directly involved in the same sorts of torture and murder in the United States, under the protection of the US government, is simply off-scale. This scenario of an individual who has been presented to the world as one of the sickest of human beings to have ever lived, to have been brought to the United States to carry on his "work" on children, prisoners, and

---

Master Race (Kindle Edition: Dialog Press, Sep. 1, 2003)

[184.] Carol Rutz, *A Nation Betrayed: Secret Cold War Experiments Performed on our Children and Other Innocent People* (Kindle Edition: Fidelity Publishing LLC, 1st edition, August 1, 2001), Loc. 376-89.

[185.] Ibid.

[186.] Ibid, Kindle Loc. 385-93. Original Source: Burton Hersh, *The Old Boys: The American Elite and the Origins of the CIA*, (Charles Scribner's Sons, Macmillan Publishing Co., March 1992), 182.

[187.] Carol Rutz, op. cit., Loc. 426-31.

other powerless people is over-the-top. What he did do, in detail, is best documented by Carol Rutz.[188] Other authors had documented Mengele's atrocious acts as well. Jim Marrs,[189] Craig Roberts,[190] and others have substantiated that this fiend was brought into the United States to perform much the same criminal acts on Americans that he did in the Nazi concentration camps. There is no "operational necessity" or "national security" issue that would ever come close to rationalizing these criminal acts of epic proportions. It also clearly indicates that the OSS/CIA was run by "barely human beings" that were no better than the Nazis. Also clear is the fact that "national security" has nothing or little to do with national security but is more about hiding monstrous criminality. Would an organization run by psychopaths such as Allen Dulles, John McCloy, and the likes murder a president? Would they hesitate to smuggle billions, perhaps trillions, of dollars' worth of heroin and cocaine into the United States? The author believes that they not only could have, but actually did just that. And again we have the question, "What else would they do?"

Another Nazi sweetheart of a guy was Klaus Barbie, also known as the "butcher of Lyon." Lyon was a city in France occupied by Germany during WWII. Barbie, an SS officer, was assigned there as an occupation secret police officer known as "the gestapo." He was known by his schoolmates as a shy and quiet young man, intelligent but not brilliant. He had an abusive father, which might have played a part in the monster that came out of him in Lyon. He was known to have personally tortured many prisoners and civilian men, women, and children. It is believed that he was responsible for the mass murder of about fourteen thousand people, and he was known to have personally broken bones, sexually abused, and used electrical shock on his victims. This all came out and was documented at his trial in France in 1984.

---

[188]. Carol Rutz, *A Nation Betrayed: Secret Cold War Experiments Performed on our Children and Other Innocent People* (Kindle Edition: Fidelity Publishing LLC, 1st edition, August 1, 2001).

[189]. Jim Marrs, *The Rise of the Fourth Reich: The Secret Societies That Threaten to Take Over America*, (HarperCollins e-books: Reprint edition, (October 13, 2009).

[190]. Craig Roberts, *The Medusa File*, (Trilogus Books: Kindle edition, July 28, 2010)

Although convicted, many of the charges were dropped because of French laws designed to protect atrocities committed by French nationals in Algeria. Barbie received a life sentence, and he died in prison in 1991, of leukemia. There are photos of what Barbie did, and it is enough to make anyone sick, and there is no doubt that anyone who aided this monster needed to be in jail themselves. If this had been investigated, some of the top members of the US administration after WWII would have gone to jail because they were involved.

What is not widely reported was Barbie's escape from Nazi Germany and his reactionary fascist activities in South America for over thirty years. Alex Constantine reports that John McCloy arranged with the US Army's 970th CIC Unit for Barbie to be sheltered from prosecution.[191] At the time, McCloy was assistant secretary of war, and prior to WWII, he had represented several investors in the Nazi regime, including Standard Oil and Chase Manhattan Bank. Both of these were J. P. Morgan creations, and again we go back to Rhodes's Anglophile plan of world domination. McCloy was also a Wall Street lawyer who represented I. G. Farben,[192] the maker of Zyklon B, the gas used in the death camps. The 970th CIC was the army unit tasked with investigating Nazi war criminals hiding among the civilian population, and coincidentally the unit to which Sergeant Henry Kissinger, future secretary of state, was assigned.[193]

In Germany, the US Army's CIC used this sick, sadistic monster to supervise agents. This operation was labeled the "Petersen Bureau."[194] In 1950, Barbie escaped to Bolivia through the same Vatican ratline that Mengele used.[195] In 1998, the US Congress passed the War Crimes Disclosure Act, which revealed Barbie's activities in Brazil. Martin

---

[191.] Alex Constantine, *Virtual Government: CIA Mind Control Operations in America*, (Feral House: 1st edition, July 1, 1997) 85.

[192.] Ibid.

[193.] Mark Aarons, and John Loftus, *Unholy Trinity: The Vatican, the Nazis, and the Swiss Banks*, (St. Martin's Griffin: Revised edition June 15, 1998), 117.

[194.] Carol Rutz, *A Nation Betrayed: Secret Cold War Experiments Performed on our Children and Other Innocent People* (Kindle Edition: Fidelity Publishing LLC, 1st edition, August 1, 2001), Loc. 376-89.

[195.] Ibid.

A. Lee gained access to CIA documents and reported the following: "Klaus Barbie, for example, assisted a succession of military regimes in Bolivia, where he taught soldiers torture techniques and helped protect the flourishing cocaine trade in the late 1970s and early 1980s."[196] And again, we have narcotics used to finance torture, murder, and genocide with most of that cocaine going to the United States, and at the hands of one of the worst war criminals in history. Now we see why the CIA did not want Mike Levine investigating major cocaine traffickers in South America. Nazis, narcotics, war, torture, fascist regimes under the umbrella of "spreading democracy," fighting the "war on drugs," "containing communism," ad nauseam. Scratch the surface, and it opens up an "endless can of worms." What else would an agency that is capable of doing this do? And what would the same agency be capable of doing to protect these dark secrets? Murder? War? Lie? Cheat? Steal? Would they be capable of killing a president and many of the witnesses? The author believes so and would add that if they would do this, they would do *anything*!

Along with the above monsters were many, many others. One of whom was Werner von Braun's boss, SS General Walter Dornberger, who was the director of the V-1 and V-2 programs. The operation used about ten thousand slaves from concentration camps to manufacture and assemble the rockets. They worked under barbaric conditions, and consequently some would sabotage the operations. As a countermeasure, Dornberger, von Braun, and the rest of the leadership would randomly have prisoners strung up and eviscerated as a deterrent. Of course none of this was in their reports when they were not only given asylum in the United States, but given some of the most responsible government jobs in the country. Dornberger was first assigned to Wright-Patterson Air Force Base in Ohio and then went to Bell-Textron where he became chief lobbyist for Bell Helicopter during the Johnson administration and the Vietnam War.[197]

We also had SS Officer Kurt Debus who was responsible for using concentration camp prisoners as slave laborers at another V-2 factory at

---

[196.] Martin A. Lee, "CIA's Worst Kept Secret," (http://www.consortiumnews.com/2001/051601a.html, May 16, 2001), Accessed April 16, 2012.

[197.] Craig Roberts, *The Medusa File*, (Trilogus Books: Kindle edition, July 28, 2010), Loc. 1624-1636.

Mittelwerk. Thanks to Operation Paperclip, he became the first deputy director of the Kennedy Space Center at Cape Canaveral for NASA.[198]

Further we had Kurt Blome, another SS officer, who established the bioweapons research center for Himmler. He inoculated prisoners with plague and recorded his observations. He was hired by the US Army Chemical Corps to work on biological warfare weapons at Camp David, Maryland.[199]

And yet another was Nazi SS Major General Walter Schreiber who managed the doctors and funded the programs to experiment on prisoners. He was brought into the United States and worked at the Air Force School of Medicine at Randolph Air Force Base, Texas.[200]

Still another was Arthur Rudolph, who was director of operations at Mittelwerk where he oversaw the starvation and murder of about twenty thousand forced labor prisoners. He ended up working for NASA and worked on the Saturn rocket program.[201]

One more was Luftwaffe Colonel Hubertus Strughold, the director of the Luftwaffe's Institute for Aviation Medicine. During WWII, Strughold oversaw the experimentation on prisoners that entailed such atrocities as the deliberate freezing of body parts and keeping records on treatments and results. Instead of walking up the gallows steps, he was brought to the United States to head the air force's new School of Aviation Medicine at Randolph Air Force Base, Texas. After two years, he was promoted to the directorship of the new Department of Space Medicine.[202]

And another that thought freezing humans was necessary for Germany's war effort was Hans Trurnit who conducted freezing experiments at Dachau. Instead of walking to the gallows' steps, he walked into the US Army's chemical warfare arsenal at Edgewood, Maryland, to work in the toxicology laboratory.

Also matriculating to Edgewood to work on poison gases was Friedrich Hoffmann, who was a chemist for the Luftwaffe's Technical Research Institute where he worked synthesizing toxins and poison

---

[198.] Ibid, Loc. 1624-36.
[199.] Ibid, Loc. 1624-48.
[200.] Ibid, Loc. 1645-51.
[201.] Ibid, Loc. 1648-55.
[202.] Ibid, Loc. 1651-57.

gases.[203] Use of poison gases in warfare had been banned by the Geneva Conventions after WWI.

The last psychopath we will discuss that was given the red carpet treatment by Allen Dulles and company was Konrad Schaefer, an expert on desalinization who experimented on methods of making seawater drinkable. He tried some of the results of his methods out by force-feeding treated water to Dachau prisoners, killing several. He was rewarded for his efforts by being brought to the United States to join Strughold at the School of Aviation Medicine.[204]

Ends Justify the Means—Allen Dulles Personified

Allen Dulles, almost single-handedly, changed the direction of America and not in a constructive way. He had absolutely no moral or ethical compass with which to guide himself. All he understood and all he valued were certain goals based on his flawed view of the world, and he had no restraints whatsoever in how these goals were accomplished. He did not network or interact with anyone or any group other than those who shared his views and could contribute to accomplishing them. He had no emotional attachment to anyone of any particular religion, ethnicity, or political persuasion, other than the Anglo-American elites' march to dominate the world. He would use anybody or anything to accomplish this and he let no one in on this objective. He would lie right to anyone's face; in fact, that is exactly why John F. Kennedy fired him.

He and John McCloy ran the Warren Commission, the objectives of which would have been better served with these two on the suspect list. Earl Warren was a figurehead. These two fascists guided the commission onto thousands of small paths that lead to nowhere. The findings of the commission lead to no indictments, no charges, and no further investigations. Many, too many, witnesses of substantive information did not even testify before the commission. Many that did testify were either deemed "not credible" or were browbeaten by the likes of Arlen Specter, the author of the almost universally discredited

---

[203.] Ibid, Loc. 1658-64.
[204.] Ibid, Loc. 1658-70.

"magic bullet" theory.[205] This is not to mention the over one hundred witnesses and suspects that met an early demise.

Back to Dulles and post-WWII America. The fact that Dulles deliberately brought many, many thousands of high-ranking Nazi officers, scientists, businessmen, physicians, psychiatrists, bankers, of which nearly all were torturers and mass-murderers did not bother him in the slightest. He felt that he was justified because he had to use every advantage available to fight the most evil social system ever devised by man, Communism. This was a system so evil and so ominous that the "free world" (read Anglosphere) had to be at least as evil just to survive. In other words, we had to give up democracy to save it, and of course we were too ignorant to make that decision for ourselves; Allen Dulles had to make it for us. Even as ridiculous as this sounds, that was where Allen Dulles and those of his ilk were coming from, and this is not an exaggeration. The reader might find similar arguments today without going to much trouble. Take the word *Communism* out and substitute with *Al-Qaeda* and we have the same formula. Remember how seamlessly that happened? Almost overnight, when the Communist "evil empire" fell, it was replaced by the most terrible enemy that could possibly be, Al-Qaeda. Never mind that the same names of its members, exactly the same names, were the brave and courageous Mujahideen freedom fighters when the "evil empire," read Soviet Union, was around. When will we ever learn? When will we stop letting these pathological personalities lead us and define us?

Dulles and his cronies were not satisfied with thousands of Nazi murders put in charge of our most cherished institutions. No, those that he could not take directly into the United States were given

---

[205]. The names of witnesses and suspects that were not interviewed by what is commonly referred to as the "Warren Commission" number in the hundreds. Authors such as Mark Lane, Jim Garrison, Jim Marrs, Peter Dale Scott, Noel H. Twyman, Joan Mellen, Lamar Waldron, Thom Hartman, Mark North, Donald T. Philips, Richard Popkin, Michael Benson, Craig Jirbel, Dick Russell, and Mark Collom, Glen Sample, and many more, have clearly established the fact that the commission deliberately excluded those whose testimony did not lend itself to the "lone assassin," "magic bullet" story board.

free passage to major South and Central American countries, along with virtually the entire wealth of Europe. This money was largely transferred to Eva Perón's accounts where it was used to create sources of wealth and power all over South America. Much of it came under the influence of the Rockefellers, who had strong connections to Dulles, and was used to further their global ambitions. In addition to the prewar support and funding for fascist elements in Germany provided by Rockefeller influences, Nelson Rockefeller had obtained the intelligence position of coordinator of Inter-American Affairs in 1940. He also was selected as assistant secretary of state for Latin American Affairs in 1944.

The Rockefellers, Greed Personified

According to authors Loftus and Aarons, Nelson Rockefeller's main motivation was to gain control of Latin America's vast resources at the exclusion of European powers.[206] These authors also detailed the extensive business connections between American-based global elites and the Nazi regime that resulted in the financing of anything the Nazi's wanted in Latin America. From refueling stations to espionage bases, the Nazis were taken care of while the British had to pay hard cash. Further, Rockefeller would respond to any complaints by the British by cutting off vital war assets and resources causing a degrading of British war making effectiveness.[207] Rockefeller also took over much of Britain's valuable land and assets in Latin America while claiming that everything was being done to support British war efforts in the region. Rockefeller gained much control and influence in Latin America during and after the war and was only too happy to help war criminals to gain influence in several countries after the war, along with the looted wealth of Europe of course. Rockefeller influences helped several fascist regimes come to power in South America. He apparently went too far when he was able to gain United Nations recognition for fascist Argentina over the objections

---

[206]. John Loftus and Mark Aarons, *The Secret War against the Jews: How Western Espionage Betrayed the Jewish People* (New York: St. Martin's Press, 1994).

[207]. Ibid.

of President Truman, who promptly relieved him of his government position.[208]

This did not even slow him down a bit. In "polite circles," it was said that Rockefeller returned to the "world of business" and making money, where he teamed up with Allen Dulles, a trustee of the Rockefeller Foundation with whom he smuggled the wealth of Europe to South American banks. Recall that both were on the Council of Foreign Relations. These two had already done grave damage to the security of the United States, and probably considered themselves above the law. Dulles had learned how to hide the most evil crimes under the umbrella of national security, and he and Rockefeller, along with those of their ilk, had a field day smuggling guns, Nazis, and gold. With their influence in the government and the press, they were largely successful in keeping these facts from the American people. Anybody that "leaked" this information was likely to have problems as in getting or keeping a job and so forth. Anyone who took exception to these crimes was portrayed as a "conspiracy nut," or worse, and marginalized.

The fact that they largely were not held accountable for these off-scale violations of the Constitution, international law, or any other measure of common decency was not the end of the story. These criminal acts by public officials and prominent people professing to be patriotic Americans and pretending to be acting in the public interest opened the doors to blackmail on an unprecedented scale. Of course, all of this was classified, and virtually all of it has remained classified to this day. But this does not mean that it was not known. One group that came across these dirty not-so-little secrets was the World Zionist Organization headed by David Ben-Gurion. In the run-up to the creation of the state of Israel, it became evident that the Zionist movement did not have the votes needed in the United Nations General Assembly to pass the resolution for statehood.

In November 1947, with only a few days left before the final UN vote, David Ben-Gurion played his trump card. He knew that several fascist Latin American states contained the swing votes needed and that only one man representing one family had the power to put those votes in the Zionist corner. That man was Nelson Rockefeller. He called a meeting of his representatives with Nelson Rockefeller, and prior to

---

[208.] Ibid.

the meeting, Ben-Gurion's team put together a dossier of Rockefeller's criminal, actually treasonous activities. Authors John Loftus and Mark Aarons interviewed several intelligence operatives involved in this meeting that took place in Rockefeller's office and put together a composite of what was in the dossier.[209]

> In 1936 the Rockefellers entered into partnership with Dulles's Nazi front, the Schroder Bank of New York which was the key institution in the Fascist economic "miracle."
> In 1939, the Rockefeller controlled Chase National Bank-secured $25 million for Nazi Germany and supplied Berlin with information on ten thousand Nazi sympathizers in the United States.
> The Rockefeller-owned Standard Oil of New Jersey Co. shipped oil to the Nazis through Spain all throughout the war.
> Rockefeller's Swiss bank records with the Nazis.
> Rockefeller's signature on correspondence setting up the German cartel in South America.
> Transcripts of his conversations with Nazi agents during the war.
> Evidence of Rockefeller's complicity in helping Allen Dulles smuggle Nazi war criminals and money from the Vatican to Argentina.

The US Constitution defines treason as "giving aid and comfort to the enemy in time of war," and it looks like Ben-Gurion had the goods on Nelson Rockefeller. What they did not expect was for Rockefeller to turn around and blackmail them back. Loftus and Aarons interviewed what they described as "a very aged Israeli source" for his account of what happened next in Rockefeller's office.[210]

> Rockefeller skimmed through the dossier and coolly began to bargain. In return for the votes of the Latin

---

[209.] John Loftus and Mark Aarons, *The Secret War Against the Jews: How Western Espionage Betrayed the Jewish People* (New York, St. Martin's Press, 1994), 168.
[210.] Ibid. 169-70

American Bloc, he wanted guarantees that the Jews would keep their mouths shut about the flow of Nazi money and fugitives to South America. There would be no Zionist Nazi-hunting unit, no testimony at Nuremberg about the bankers or anyone else, not a single leak to the press about where the Nazis were living in South America or which Nazis were working for Dulles. The subject of Nazis was closed. Period. Forever.

The choice was simple, Rockefeller explained. "You can have vengeance, or you can have a country, but you cannot have both." His choice of the word "vengeance," not justice, left the Jews in no doubt where he stood. But the General Assembly would vote in only a few days. It was the last, best chance the Jews would ever have.

According to our Israeli informant, whose account was corroborated by several other sources in the intelligence community whom we interviewed subsequently, Ben-Gurion's representative was heartsick. Counterblackmail had not been in the game plan. He made a telephone call to try to obtain guidance. It took several hours before the reply came back: "Yes . . ." On behalf of the still-unborn state of Israel, the promise was formally given to let the Nazis go free. The men who murdered the Jews of Europe were effectively given amnesty, except for the unlucky few who had already been punished.

Once the deal was made, Rockefeller assured those present "that every country in Latin America will either vote in favor of Israel or abstain," and that is exactly what happened. According to both American intelligence and also Ben-Gurion's intelligence sources, Rockefeller called every fascist tin-pot dictator he had influence with and told them in no uncertain terms that they would either abstain or vote in favor of the creation of Israel, and that is exactly what happened. Brazil and Haiti switched their vote from "no" on November 26, 1947, to "yes" for the final vote on the twenty-ninth. Nicaragua, Bolivia, and Ecuador switched from abstaining to voting yes in these three days; and Argentina, Colombia, and El Salvador went from a "no" vote to abstaining. These votes were more than enough for the two-thirds majority needed for the resolution to pass.

Also during this time, there was a strong American diplomatic push underway to get several other countries, mostly European, to vote in favor of the creation of Israel. This effort was largely successful, and it is plausible that the Latin American votes were not necessary. The state of Israel was born but was it stillborn? What price was too high? Six million Jews tortured, starved to death, and otherwise murdered, and the crime went virtually unpunished because Zionists wanted to create a state that was safe for Jews? Add to this the fact that thousands of the world's worst criminals were placed into highly influential positions in the United States and Latin America and profoundly influenced medicine, education, intelligence, business, law enforcement, the military, and arguably created much of the world's illegal narcotics trade. These monsters, along with their fascist brethren already in the Americas, changed the very character of the so-called "free world," and to say that they changed it not in a good way would be generous. Choose your enemies carefully, "for they will be with you longer than your friends."

The Foundations

Largely seen as a means for the wealthy elite to fund projects that benefit society, these so-called "philanthropic organizations" function in ways that are far askew of their stated missions. They are not taxed, which makes them a convenient method of avoiding inheritance tax while maintaining family control of enormous wealth and power. For example, the Rockefeller Foundation was created by John D. Rockefeller Sr. in 1913 with largely Standard Oil money. At that time and even today, Standard Oil and its manifestations far surpass any other corporation's profits on the planet. Just one of its "children," Exxon Mobil, out produces most nations; and if the records were available, probably Exxon Mobil had a lot to do with the decision to invade Iraq again. Vice President Dick Chaney had a bad case of selective amnesia when questioned about this subject, and even went so far as to claim "executive privilege" when asked about secret meetings he had with the oil companies, ostensibly named the "Energy Commission," that some called the "fossil fuel commission." Although the vice president does not have executive privilege, only the president does, no one seemed to have the power to call him on this. On May 22, 2003, President George W. Bush signed Executive Order 13303 declaring that Iraq's oil was the "sole proprietorship" of the United States. This allowed US oil companies to operate with impunity and gave Bush control of Iraqi oil profits. This was roughly one month after the invasion of Iraq began. Further, the first industry secured by invading forces was the oil. Everything else could be and was looted. It appears that much of the early history of Western civilization recorded in museums and archeological sights was of little or no importance, but oil certainly was. The profits from oil and all the products that are made from it or that use it are what fuel the US-based foundations. These profits are used to further the interests of the people at the top and mostly do not serve the interests of mainstream America.

Enormous sums of money are funneled into these "philanthropic" organizations ostensibly for the "good of mankind," and the titles of the projects sound like really good undertakings, until we take a closer look. One of the most prestigious public research universities in the world is McGill University, Montreal, Quebec, Canada. During WWII, Dr. Donald Ewen Cameron pioneered brainwashing techniques at the Allen Memorial Institute at McGill, which was funded by the Rockefeller Foundation. Later, Dr. Cameron performed a variety of so-called mind control experiments and treatments on unsuspecting patients and children that rivaled what had been done in the Nazi death camps. Carol Rutz was one of his victims, and what she described as having been done to her by Cameron can only be one thing: torture.[211] He deliberately traumatized Carol and many others to create multiple personalities in them and also exact complete obedience. Carol also described that Dr. Josef Mengele, flown in from South America, directly participated in this sordid affair.

Dr. Cameron used electroconvulsive "therapy" that far exceeded, both in intensity and the number of applications, the protocols for even clinically depressed patients. He also was administering powerful electric shock to the genitals and anuses of very young children. According to Jim Turner, a lawyer who represented Cameron's victims, there was no question that these so-called treatments had caused profound damage to his clients turning some into "virtual

---

[211.] Carol Rutz, *A Nation Betrayed: Secret Cold War Experiments Performed on our Children and Other Innocent People* (Kindle Edition: Fidelity Publishing LLC, 1st edition, August 1, 2001).

vegetables."[212] Cameron was apparently trying to "wipe the slate clean" so that he could impose whatever personality variables he wanted into his victims and totally control their behavior. He was also working on creating multiple personalities that would perform whatever acts they were directed to do with no recollection of the events afterward.

Dr. Donald Ewen Cameron, c. 1967. Source-Wikipedia, http://en.wikipedia.org/wiki/Donald_Ewen_Cameron

What Dr. Cameron was actually doing was mind control operations for the Central Intelligence Agency under their MK-ULTRA program. During the Cold War, the CIA funded this program through a cover organization called the Society for the Investigation of Human Ecology in New York founded by Cornell University neurologist Harold Wolff.[213] Eight universities and several individual researchers received grants to do MK-ULTRA mind control experiments under the cover of this society. Dr. Cameron was elected president of the American Psychiatric Association in 1953 and became the first president of the World Psychiatric Association. Who would have known that this "prestigious," well-respected, and renowned psychiatrist had snakes in his head? He belonged in jail along with those of his ilk, such as Josef Mengele and Klaus Barbie. He experimented on the most vulnerable and powerless people in society, prisoners, mental patients, children, and others that could not refuse or defend themselves. This was a monster and criminal of the first order.

The program he was working on for the CIA, MK-ULTRA, was a powder keg in its own right and another portal into the American heart of darkness. Dangerous and damaging experimentation was done on thousands of prisoners, mental patients, children, college students, homeless, and minorities, most of whom did not know what was being done to them, nor did they have the power to resist

---

[212.] Ibid., Loc. 1037-1064
[213.] Ibid., Loc. 1023-1037

it. Carol Rutz's family was paid for their permission to experiment on her. Among other things, she was tortured by Cameron, Mengele, and others to create multiple personalities one of which was an assassin and another was created to commit suicide should the plot be discovered. Imagine how this sort of thing would go over with the American people if it was common knowledge? Also imagine how it would go over if the whole picture were also known? The "wheels come off the cart," or more plainly the republic is exposed as a Pathocracy. That is, the connections to politics, the power elite, corporations, banking, education, research, ad infinitum, all see the light of day. Should the whole picture be known, it is clear that the United States is run and controlled by psychopaths, characteropaths, and other abnormal personalities who are able to network on a global scale to control the world's money and resources. Further, they will do anything to maintain their power because this is all they know how to do.

Full disclosure of the MK-ULTRA program would unhinge the entire government let alone the CIA. For this reason, it was highly classified, but even CIA Director Richard Helms was not comfortable that it could be kept secret forever; so in 1973, Helms ordered all MK-ULTRA documents destroyed. Although the CIA thought they had destroyed them all, about twenty thousand documents stuck away in a warehouse somehow survived. These documents along with the records of the many victims of this barbaric program and also some of the CIA people that were aware of what was going on painted a pretty good picture, albeit an ugly one. In a strange turn of events in 1975, Vice President Nelson Rockefeller was appointed by President Gerald Ford to head up an investigation of the CIA's MK-ULTRA, and other such programs, as a result of a *New York Times* article. The formal title was "The US President's Commission on CIA activities within the United States," but it was commonly known as the Rockefeller Commission. Of course, both Ford and Rockefeller knew very well what the true story was and the commission did what is known as a "limited hang out," which is simply damage control. The commission had to go further than expected when they were confronted with overwhelming evidence of immoral, unethical, and outright criminal activity.

The cover story on this program was that it existed to understand and design resistance to Communist "brainwashing" techniques. Those of us that grew up during the '50s and '60s remember all too well the portrayal of the "Communist Bloc" countries as a monolithic group of the most evil societies that ever existed, and that the Western countries had to use extreme measures to counter these evil forces. POWs from the Korean War were presented as having been "brainwashed" to the point that they no longer thought independently. They believed only what they were told. Of course, the CIA heroically was "reverse engineering" these brainwashing techniques so that our POWs would be able to resist this insidious process. We all bought it. The author had some of this training, and there certainly is a legitimate need for captured soldiers to learn how to survive if captured. We all thought the training we received was good, and it probably was. It just was not the whole story.

This legitimate need apparently was the cover story. There were deeper, darker motives at work. We were the experts at brainwashing not the Communists. Hypnosis, electroconvulsive "therapy," and drugs used to promote suggestibility or induce amnesia were all experimented with on victimized persons. The results were deliberately portrayed to Congress and other investigative bodies as being almost worthless, but there is evidence that the CIA was doing this to hide what this program was really responsible for. They were successful in protecting the deepest, darkest aspects of MK-ULTRA which some say was the creation of "Manchurian candidate" type assassins and torture methods to extract information from unwilling subjects. The commission was also successful in portraying the program as having been completely shut down. Even today, one only has to go to the largely redacted news to see vestiges of MK-ULTRA and the roughly 150 separate programs related to or stemming from this program. Two examples that come to this author's mind are the interrogation methods used at Guantanamo, and all such facilities, and the search for a method of using drugs to eliminate memories causing posttraumatic stress in our soldiers. Both of these were subjects of the MK-ULTRA program that started back in the 1950s. The MK designates that the program was under the Technical Support Division of the CIA, and the cryptonym ULTRA goes back to the old Office of Strategic Services during WWII meaning the highest degree of secrecy.

So on the surface, we have one of the Rockefeller Foundation's "noble causes" of funding medical research, which in reality was torturing children to turn them into CIA slaves and murderers. When enough of these programs came to light in the late '70s, the CIA did another of its "limited hangout" tricks and passed the whole subject off as "totally ineffective." They also minimized the entire subject and passed it off as a small footnote of an off-the-worn-trail of intelligence programs, but was it really? Authors John Marks[214] and Ami Chen Mills[215] name over forty US colleges and universities that had CIA MK-ULTRA and other related programs on their campuses, and we are not talking about small, largely unknown institutions. Harvard Medical School, Princeton, and many state universities were known to have participated. We are also talking about fifteen research foundations, chemical and pharmaceutical companies, and at least three prisons. The total amount spent is not known to this day, but at least 6 percent of the CIA's total budget was allocated to MK-ULTRA in 1953, which was about $10 million, a lot of money in those days. This does not include funding from foundations and other CIA sources for funding, such as the drug trade. This was a major undertaking of which it is more than hard to believe that there were no results whatsoever.

Or were there? As discussed before, Jackson State Hospital in New Orleans, where Oswald applied for a job, was suspected of having had an MK-ULTRA program. In 1957, Oswald was stationed at Atsugi Naval Air Base, Japan, that had over twenty buildings housing the Joint Technical Advisory Group, which was the cover for one of the CIA's main operational bases in Asia.[216] Intelligence veterans such as Frank Camper, who had numerous FBI and CIA contacts, strongly suspect that Oswald was an MK-ULTRA subject at Atsugi Air Base.[217]

Several psychiatrists, attorneys, and researchers, including Lawrence Teeter who was Sirhan Sirhan's attorney, believe that Sirhan was under the influence of hypnosis when he fired at Robert F. Kennedy.[218] Teeter

---

[214.] John Marks, *The Search for the "Manchurian Candidate": The CIA and Mind Control*, (New York/London: W.W. Norton & Company, 1991).

[215.] Ami Chen Mills, *CIA off Campus: Building the Movement Against Agency Recruitment and Research*, (Boston: South End Press, 1991).

[216.] Dick Russell, *On the Trail of the JFK Assassins*, (Kindle Edition: Skyhorse Publishing, Nov. 22, 2008) Loc. 3786-89.

[217.] Ibid., 3789-92.

[218.] KPFA interview with Sirhan's lawyer, Lawrence Teeter, July 6, 2005, http://www.kpfa.org/archive/id/15830, accessed June 16, 2012.

linked MK-ULTRA techniques to Sirhan's bizarre behavior shortly before and during the assassination that was far askew of what people who knew him said he was capable of doing. There is a surprising amount of evidence that Sirhan had been a mind control subject, and we will be going into this is more detail in my next book. For now, it is interesting to note new information is still coming in on this subject. As recently as April 28, 2012, a key witness, who was never called to testify, has come forward to state that she was intimidated by the FBI and that they actually altered what she had told them in 1968. Nina Rhodes-Hughes gave an interview to CNN reporter Michael Martinez in which she emphatically states that there was more than one shooter and that "there were at least twelve and maybe fourteen shots fired . . ."[219] More than eight shots means someone else had to have been shooting at RFK besides Sirhan because the weapon he had was an eight-shot Iver Johnson .22 caliber Cadet 55-A revolver. There is other evidence that more than eight shots were fired, which we will be discussing in detail in the next book.

There is also credible evidence that Theodore Kaczynski, more commonly known as the Unabomber, was an MK-ULTRA subject at Harvard University from 1959 to 1962.[220] This was the university assistant professor who made many bombs for about a twenty-year period beginning in 1987. He used these bombs to blow up people associated with either academia or the airline industry, hence the name: *U*niversity and *a*irline *bomber*. He was responsible for killing three people and seriously injuring twenty-three more. Although the US major media widely covered the Unabomber story, one would be hard-pressed to find anything linking him to the CIA's MK-ULTRA mind control operations. Article after article goes into intricate detail on how he made the bombs, why he made them, his past life, and

---

[219.] Michael Martinez and Brad Johnson, "RFK Assassination Witness Tells CNN: There Was a Second Shooter," April 28, 2012, http://articles.cnn.com/2012-04-28/justice/justice_california-rfk-second-gun_1_sirhan-sirhan-federal-court-assassination?_s=PM:JUSTICE, Accessed June 15, 2012.

[220.] Alston Chase, "Harvard and the Making of the Unabomber," (The *Atlantic Monthly Online*: June 2000, http://www.theatlantic.com/past/docs/issues/2000/06/chase.htm, Accessed July 18, 2012.

endless theories on what went wrong with this "highly intelligent" and "gifted" academic, but almost no one publicly announced that there was even a suspicion or a possibility that this "troubled" academic had been in a government mind control program. If one would search hard and long enough, credible information is clearly there. For instance, the *Atlantic Monthly* published an article that presented hard evidence of this.[221] The question remains, however, as to how much traction one reputable but not very widely read news outlet would get with the public at large. Probably not very much, and this is precisely the point. As previously discussed, the US intelligence community quickly gained enough influence after WWII to suppress stories such as this. If things of this sort are reported in say "the newspaper of record," which would be the *New York Times*, the wheels start coming off the cart, so to speak. Anyone reporting about the drug trade, assassinations, mind control programs, and the like, open up a portal into the "American heart of darkness," and that is just not allowed. A little bit here and there is generally ignored because it will just sort of dissipate like a ripple on a still lake. But media stories that start to spread and grow like wild fire have to be put out, and that is exactly what has happened here with the Unabomber MK-ULTRA program. Let us just make a few obvious connections if this story were to get real traction: Unabomber—MK-ULTRA—Harvard—CIA—all on-campus MK-ULTRA programs—funded by Rockefeller Foundation—former Nazis operating in United States—Nazis and the wealth of Europe spirited out by the CIA and Rockefeller. As stated before, the "wheels start coming off the cart."

Occasionally there have been reports in major media outlets of well-known people that have been in mind control programs. These instances, however, are usually about people who have not committed notorious crimes. Ken Kesey, author of *One Flew over the Cuckoo's Nest*, was a subject of MK-ULTRA experiments while a student at Stanford University in 1960. He reportedly entered into the program at a nearby Veterans Administration hospital in Palo Alto, California, where he took LSD among other things.[222] He also got a job about six

---

[221.] Ibid.
[222.] John Marks, *The Search for the "Manchurian Candidate": The CIA and Mind Control*, (New York: W.W. Norton & Co. Inc. 1991), 129-130.

months later at this hospital as a psychiatric aide, and his experiences resulted in some of the most disturbing scenes in the movie. One has to wonder how much of the influence of Nazi-style "medicine" resulted in electroshock therapy, prefrontal lobotomy brain surgery, and psychotropic medications brought out in Kesey's movie and also common practice in psychiatric medicine after WWII. Some of these practices are still with us. In Kesey's case, these programs were funded directly by the Macy Foundation and indirectly by the Rockefeller Foundation under the umbrella of science and medical grants for the "benefit of mankind," etc., when actually, the hidden agenda was harmful experimentation done on students and mental patients by American fascists and Nazi war criminals for the "national interest." A search of the *New York Times* for the key words "Ken Kesey" and "MK-ULTRA" resulted in three hits, each of them excellent essays written by college students and published in the *New York Times* magazine. This is coverage, of sorts, but not enough for this issue to get any traction, lest the wheels come off the cart. Other personalities who have either stated that they were victims of mind control programs or are suspected to have been include Candy Jones, a fashion model and radio show host; mob assassin Whitey Bulger in these programs while in prison; and Duncan O'Finioan who appeared on a segment of Jesse Ventura's TV program *Conspiracy Theory* about mind control assassins.

O'Finioan stated that while he was in the MK-ULTRA (and other programs under its umbrella) program, he had had seven microchips implanted in his brain that were inadvertently discovered when his head was X-rayed after an automobile accident. He said that five had been removed but that two were inoperable. He met Ventura clandestinely in a parking lot and went into some detail about having been tortured to create multiple personalities, having been sent on assassination missions that he only became aware of through therapy, etc. Jesse Ventura stated on the show that he was convinced that O'Finioan was legitimate and that he believed what he was stating. If the O'Finioan segment of Jesse Ventura's program, aired January 6, 2010, was true, this would lead one to believe that these illegal programs are still going on and at least in part funded by these very same foundations that are represented to the world and the American people as only concerned with philanthropic motives for the "betterment of mankind" and so forth.

The reader is also reminded that Ike Atkinson, also known as "Sergeant Smack" discussed in chapter 1, "told fellow prisoners that he was used in CIA mind control experiments."²²³ The ramifications of this are startling given the fact that Atkinson was the leader of the previously discussed heroin smuggling gang that operated out of "Jack's American Star Bar" in Bangkok, smuggling enormous amounts of heroin into the United States over, roughly, a ten-year period. Add to this that the military, intelligence, and law enforcement government agencies had to have known what was going on. Some of the gang were arrested and prosecuted, but these were isolated events probably as a result of relatively low-level people doing an honest job. To think that the FBI and CIA claimed to have been powerless to shut this operation down because of excuses such as having to respect the national sovereignty of the foreign government of Thailand is incredible. Any casual observer will notice that the United States does not have any trouble trampling sovereignty rights when high officials seem to think it is "in the national interest" to do so. To think that at the same time these agencies were seemingly paralyzed, they had the leader of this drug cartel as a subject in mind control programs.

"But wait there's more!" Many readers will recall some of the bizarre goings-on surrounding events at Jonestown, Guyana, November 18, 1978, when supposedly one renegade preacher, Reverend Jim Jones, led 913 members of the People's Temple to create a whole city, from scratch, in Guyana. We will be going into more detail on this subject in my next book, but even a cursory look at the facts in this case make the official story preposterous. Research into this subject almost immediately brings up cracks in the official story, and the most definitive work that things were not as they were purported to be is a book authored by Michael Meiers, *Was Jonestown a CIA Medical Experiment?* Problem is, there are only about ten of these books available and the cost runs from $233.94 to about $2,000.00! When one sees pricing and availability like this, it usually means that the book is much in demand and the availability is being suppressed. Author Fletcher Prouty, *JFK: The CIA, Vietnam, and the Plot to Assassinate John F. Kennedy*, fully discussed how thousands of copies of his book disappeared out of bookstores when it was on its way to being a best seller. Carroll Quigley, author of *Tragedy and Hope: A History of the*

---

223. Alex Constantine, *Psychic Dictatorship in the U.S.A.* (Portland, OR: Feral House, 1995), 125.

World in Our Time also talked about how his first publisher bought the rights to his book and then would not print it. Quigley could not go to another publisher because the one he had signed with had sole rights to it. Even now, Quigley's book will run you about $300. Both of the above did not speak highly of powerful people and government institutions, so one can take an educated guess as to who suppressed these books. The cost of the Meiers' book screams that it contains explosive information that powerful people and institutions do not want anyone to know about.

Back to Jonestown. One only has to consider how difficult it is to plan a one-month family camping trip to appreciate how outlandish it is to accept that one "deranged" minister could pull something like this off. Add to this that Jones supposedly came up with what investigative reporters estimated as at least $26 million and possibly as much as $2 billion, and we are to believe that the whole thing was funded by Social Security and Welfare checks?[224] Where that money came from is very interesting. Several researchers have traced the People's Temple funding that financed Jonestown to a variety of CIA front and cut-out companies and banks that made money mostly in the arms and drugs trade. One bank mentioned that has been verified as a CIA cut-out and was discussed earlier by Fletcher Prouty was the Nugan Hand Bank of Australia. We also previously discussed how and why this bank was created by the CIA in discussing Paul Helliwell and Richard Armitage. It appears that some of these connections turned up at Jonestown, and several researchers noticed this. One of these researchers was John Judge who noted indications that Jonestown was built with money from narcotics, espionage, prostitution, and murder. He also mentioned Nugan Hand Bank as possibly one of the sources of funding for Jonestown.[225] Again, we have disturbing connections: CIA—drug money—mind control—mass murder (the first coroner on

---

[224.] John Judge, "The Black Hole of Guyana," "Ratville Times," 1985, 12, (August 16, 2012, accessed, last modified: September 11, 2012,) http://www.ratical.org/ratville/JFK/JohnJudge/Jonestown.html.

[225.] John Judge, "The Jonestown Banks," "Ratville Times," 1985, 5, (Last modified: August 16, 2012, accessed September 11, 2012), http://www.ratical.org/ratville/JFK/JohnJudge/JonestownBanks.html.

scene found puncture wounds on the back side of the shoulders of the victims)—and a massive cover-up.

Other persons alleged to have been subjects of MK-ULTRA, mind control, programs include Timothy McVeigh who claimed that "federal agents had implanted him with a microchip and left him with an unexplained scar on his posterior. 'It was painful,' he winced, 'to sit on the chip.'"[226] McVeigh had a notable similarity to Oswald in that he would do anything he was told to do, presumably from what he considered competent authority. He also had worked for what was named the "Advanced Technology Center" in Buffalo, New York, which had some interesting connections. This center was a part of Cornell Aeronautical Laboratory and given the acronym "Calspan." Cornell Aeronautical Laboratory was based at Cornell University, Ithaca, New York, where it was founded in 1946. It was funded by a CIA-front program named the "Human Ecology Fund," which was involved with extensive mind control programs. The laboratory was renamed "Calspan" in 1972 and was later acquired by Arvin Industries. Arvin-Calspan merged with Space Industries International (SII), and implanting telemetry chips is well within the capabilities of this organization.[227] Although the press just laughed off McVeigh's assertion, there are definite connections from McVeigh to known mind control programs that were not pursued. We also have yet one more of many potential manifestations of global fascism that were rationalized by American fascists using the old assertion that they were fighting forces so evil that they had to be at least as diabolical as their foe to prevail. We had to give up democracy if we wanted to keep it, or we had to "burn the village in order to save it."

The Carnegie Institution and Eugenics

Andrew Carnegie was the main sponsor and promoter of the eugenics program that started in the United States and eventually went international. The Rockefeller Foundation also provided funding and support for it. Although this movement had been around for some

---

[226.] Alex Constantine, *Virtual Government: CIA Mind Control Operations*, (Venice, CA: Feral House, 1st edition, July 1, 1997), 247.

[227.] Ibid, 252-253.

time, it became a viable operation when on April 21, 1902, Charles Davenport, esteemed for his Harvard degrees and "distinguished background," made a proposal to the representatives of the Carnegie Institution. This proposal, which was approved and funded, was to establish a Biological Experimental Station at Cold Springs Harbor, Long Island, New York, "to investigate . . . the method of evolution."[228] The startup cost was approved for $32,000.

Andrew Carnegie amassed a fortune in manufacturing and selling steel. He was another titan of business financed by J. P. Morgan. In 1901, he sold his ownership and interests to J. P. Morgan for $400 million, a lot of money in those days, and left the world of business and industry to devote the remainder of his life to "philanthropy." Again, let it be said that "for the betterment of mankind" was always at the end of his stated purpose, but these tax-exempt foundations and institutions were also a convenient means of avoiding taxes, especially inheritance taxes, and a means to wield power behind the façade of "science" and "research." Personal empires were also established, tax free. Carnegie apparently had some venomous racial beliefs that he believed it was his duty to act upon, and the eugenics movement seemed to fit well with his objectives. These objectives amounted to improving the United States and ultimately the world by eliminating people and groups of people that the eugenics movement and Carnegie believed were a drain on the rest of the population. Both the movement and its ultimate benefactor believed that a Nordic type of human being existed that was superior to all other "races" and "subraces."

As simply put as possible, the impetus for the eugenics movement was to create a master race by breeding human beings for certain characteristics, like farm animals. Those carrying desirable traits would be separated from those with undesirable characteristics and only bred with each other. While large families were to be encouraged for the "desirable," breeding would be diminished for the "undesirable" by a variety of methods. Encouraging desirable human beings to marry and have children was termed "positive eugenics," and extinguishing those with undesirable traits was termed "negative eugenics." If some of these

---

[228]. Edwin Black, *War against the Weak: Eugenics and America's Campaign to Create a Master Race*, (New York/London: Four Walls Eight Windows, Kindle Edition, 2003), Loc. 1039-55.

concepts seem familiar as Nazi ideology, the reason is that the United States of America is where these ideas flourished and spread to Hitler and the Nazis, and there is a clear record of this provided by Edwin Black in several of his works but most notably in *War against the Weak: Eugenics and America's Campaign to Create a Master Race.*[229]

Francis J. Galton, a cousin of Charles Darwin, published a paper in 1883 titled, "Inquires into Human Faculty and Development." In the paper, Galton coined a new word derived from two Greek words that mean "well born." His new word, *eugenics*, would have profound implications for millions of people in years to come. Families would be destroyed, tens of thousands of people sterilized, and ethnic and religious groups nearly extinguished over this one word. While Galton was cobbling together statistical support for his ideas, another scientist also coined a phrase. This two-word expression was *germ plasm,* and the man who came up with it was August Weismann, a German cellular biologist. Weismann put forth the idea that everything that makes up our being was passed to us by this germ plasm from our parents. His idea was that all emotional, physical, and even traits of character and morality were inherited from this germ plasm. We might call germ plasm chromosomes today, and some of the residue from this line of thought is still with us today. Many people still believe that intelligence, behavioral traits, values, ethics, and so on are inherited although there is no scientific evidence to support this.

What was created was a pseudoscience that took class and racial hatred and put a white laboratory coat on it. Fraudulent studies, bogus statistics, and genealogies with unsubstantiated and fallacious reasoning were done by "distinguished gentlemen" with impressive degrees. What the program needed to really take off was funding and structure, which was provided by the Carnegie Institution in 1902, only a few months after it began. The Carnegie Institution and Andrew Carnegie were not bystanders. They signed on wholeheartedly to the malignant goals

---

[229.] Author Edwin Black has more than adequately documented this in several books, two of which are: Edwin Black, *War Against the Weak: Eugenics and America's Campaign to Create a Master Race*, (New York/London: Four Walls Eight Windows, Kindle Edition, 2003). *Nazi Nexus: America's Corporate Connections to Hitler's Holocaust*, (Washington, DC, Dialog Press, Kindle Edition, Feb. 16, 2009).

of eugenics. Black's research is irrefutable and includes that Carnegie President John Merriam was regularly briefed on the status of the program.[230] Further, Carnegie statisticians went over the eugenics data for validity and reliability before submission to Congress. Yes, the US Congress was knee-deep in this horribly misguided project. The whole project was ridiculed in the press and most of academia, but still it continued.

IQ tests were developed that deliberately caused people that were not raised in a certain environment to come out "retarded," or "feeble minded." The terminology used in the tests and the results are still with us today: idiot, imbecile, moron, and so forth. Developed for the army were an alpha test for English-speaking people and a beta test for the non-English speaking. Both tests were culturally biased. For example, either in words or pictures a light bulb would either be described or a picture was shown of a light bulb without a filament. Now if a person had never seen a light bulb, before they would not know what was missing. Other pictures and descriptions depicted a bowling alley without bowling balls, and the question asked, "What is missing?" Someone not familiar with bowling would have no idea what the right answer was no matter how smart they were. Of course, these problems are still with us in intelligence testing, and this is portrayed as if they are inherent, but little or no mention is made that the tests were deliberately designed that way. Today, not as much can happen to you if you do not score well on these tests. However, less than a hundred years ago, you could have been involuntarily sterilized and or institutionalized so that you did not pass on your defective "germ plasm."

Even today, there are serious consequences for not scoring well on tests that were derived from these early "intelligence tests." As strange as this may seem, the Army Alpha test was adapted as a college entrance exam first used at Princeton University and later became the scholastic aptitude test used across the country for college admissions.[231] These

---

[230.] Edwin Black, *Nazi Nexus: America's Corporate Connections to Hitler's Holocaust*, (Washington, DC, Dialog Press, Kindle Edition, Feb. 16, 2009), loc. 715-20.

[231.] Edwin Black, *War Against the Weak: Eugenics and America's Campaign to Create a Master Race*, (New York/London: Four Walls Eight Windows, Kindle Edition, 2003), loc. 1902-7.

tests were deliberately designed to favor upper-middle-class whites and create a thriving environment for them. Conversely, the tests were designed to make life and procreation difficult for anyone not of that socioeconomic class. Even in the author's lifetime, this was evident. Let us take for an example the Vietnam War. If you could score well on the SAT, you could go to college and be classified by the draft board as "4F," which meant that you were deferred from compulsory conscription in the army, or at that time, even the Marine Corps. If you did not score well, it would be difficult to get into college, unless your family had enough influence to get you in anyway. If you were not in college and did not have some physical limitation, you were likely to be classified "1A" and very likely to end up in the infantry. We are talking about a frontline combat troop, and as such, you would have a good chance of getting shot or blown up. This is how a disproportionate number of minorities and poor whites get killed in wars. The deck is deliberately stacked against some people.

The goal of eugenics was to eliminate the most "useless" 10 percent of the population, and then do this over and over again until the goal was reached of having a master race. Tens of thousands of "undesirables" were sterilized as a result, and laws were passed to restrict who could marry whom. This is how Virginia came up with what is called the "one drop" law, that is, if you had any "Negro blood" at all in you, you were a Negro. Of course all of this necessitated detailed study of family history. Seemingly benign letters were sent out to gather information from birth records, marriage records, church records, and so forth, and the information was compiled. As one may imagine, this was an involved, tedious task that required a lot of human effort, especially to cross-reference information.

A man named Herman Hollerith worked at the census bureau, which had developed a process of tabulating information using a binary punch card system. He took this process with him and started a company we now know as International Business Machines or IBM. The punch cards were called "Hollerith" cards, and the processing systems were incredibly fast for those days. The author worked with these systems in the 1970s, writing and key punching programs as an air transportation systems analyst. They were not state of the art at that time, but they were still relatively fast and effective as an input/output instrument and infinitely faster than the old "stubby pencil" method. Cross-tabulating information at the speed that the IBM systems were capable of allowed for compiling of information that was unimaginable for those days.

The eugenicists took notice of this new tool and did imagine what they could do with this information-processing miracle. In fact as Edwin Black carefully has documented, years of work financed mostly by Carnegie went into developing the concept of eliminating everyone that was "mixed race" in the United States, first, and then throughout the world. Yes, you heard it right; that is what the eugenics project was about, and with the advent of IBM systems, they went ahead with the project. A man previously mentioned, zoologist and father of the eugenics movement, Charles Davenport, thought that New York would be an ideal location for the project. He later settled on Jamaica because it was not in the United States and would get less attention and had a "larger proportion of mulattoes."[232] The pilot study went ahead in 1926, with IBM's help, and entailed 370 Jamaicans. A vast amount of information was accumulated and codified as to heritage, physical traits, diseases and abnormalities, and so forth. The pilot study took place from 1927 to 1928 with the help of IBM programmers who had to have known the expected outcomes of the study to codify the information needed for the expected results. IBM was more than willing to participate in the lucrative "race-crossing" investigation.

As author Edwin Black reports, sex and race were in column 1, age in column 2, height in 4, cranial capacity in 18, foot length in 24, Army Alpha IQ testing in 33 . . . Family trees, bank account information, addresses, property ownership, etc., were also recorded on key punch cards. The whole affair bore a striking resemblance to the systems and methods used to inventory Jews and other "undesirables" before and during WW II. In fact, some of the information and the columns where the data were recorded were identical—not a coincidence! IBM to this day says that they unwittingly participated in the Holocaust. To have adopted the Jamaica study to the specific requirements of the Holocaust without knowing what the expected outcome would be is virtually impossible. IBM has not acknowledged guilt or apologized to this day. The Carnegie Institution was so proud of itself that it published a major paper on the project, and Davenport was so pleased that he put out letters throughout the world about

---

[232.] Ibid, loc. 6048-53.

how to do what he had done in Jamaica. One of the people he took the time to document and explain how and what he did was a man named Fischer, who was his counterpart in Germany, also funded by the Carnegie Institution. The rest is history, except for the American eugenics movement connections and, of course, Carnegie and Rockefeller money. Who would have thought . . . ?

Most of this information has been recorded . . . somewhere. At least it has been recorded by courageous researchers, authors, activists, and other courageous individuals who have gotten much of the information by doing interviews and following leads to get the facts. If this had not happened, we would not be thinking about this today. One probably would not find the above information in your average public school textbook. Further, and as we touched on earlier, after WW II and the advent of classifying anything embarrassing, whether it has anything to do with security or not, further spread the schism of what should be known in a free society and what is actually available. It is true that much of the above information is available, but you have to already know about it to be able to find it. One certainty is that one cannot "crack a cold one" in front of the TV, turn on the news, and plan on being presented with anything like what we have covered here. What we see and hear mostly about is just about every detail in the life of the likes of Kim Kardashian and her sisters, or maybe a dog caught on an ice flow on the Potomac, or whatever.

With the coming of much of the above power collecting at a hub now known as the CIA and the passing of the National Security Act of 1947, we now have the ability to classify most of activities of which we have been discussing. Further, much of this information since WW II that the people would have to have to keep power in check has not only been classified but put into about twenty underground acres in Suitland, Maryland. Most has not even been inventoried or indexed yet. Authors and researchers John Loftus and Mark Aarons visited this place called the Suitland complex just outside of Washington DC.[233] They said that aboveground is a one-story brick building about the size of a football field surrounded by acres of mowed grass. The brick

---

[233.] Information about the Suitland complex summarized from: John Loftus and Mark Aarons, *The Secret War Against the Jews: How Western Espionage Betrayed the Jewish People* (New York: St. Martin's Press, 1994), 1-3.

building is storage for the National Archives, which contains records from every war the United States has been involved in. Underneath the grass are about twenty acres of underground vaults, which contain classified records from WWII to the present, including captured records from the Third Reich and also from the British Secret Service.

You have to have special clearance to get in the elevator to go from the top floor, which is open to the public, into the vaults below. Vault number 6 is where a meager staff goes through each piece of paper and decides whether or not it may go upstairs to the archives. The Reagan administration cut funding for this operation to "save money," and it appears that the operation is a little behind. A little behind would be generous. They were at the beginning of WW II in 1994, and it is doubtful that they have completed it as of this writing. This is roughly about one-third of our modern history, and you can be assured that it is not the good stuff that has not been indexed yet. These vaults also contain nearly all the records of American espionage and covert actions. Add to this that when intelligence agencies do not want records to see the light of day, they file them in another agency's records. This way, they know where the records are, but no one else does. About one-third of the modern history of the United States is still classified and sitting, mostly not indexed, in these underground vaults, along with at least 1,171 CIA documents about the JFK assassination. What could be in those documents that would compromise national security if released? No wonder we do not know what has happened to us. We do not know our own history!

Hidden History

Perhaps in about a hundred years or so the operation at the National Archives will catch up and then release the history that the American people so desperately need. If these documents were to be released now, the American people would probably get a very different view of interventions, assassinations, and so-called "regime change" operations conducted since WW II. It is apparent that there is a lot more to some of the events since WW II that could make it clear as to why things are not going so well these days. The author wants "the rest of the story" on the following:

1950—It appears that there was a lot more to the Korean War than we have been told. Ostensibly, we have the war-mongering

North invading the free and democratic South just because they could. However, we now know that the country should not have been split in the first place, and that the US-backed leadership in the South consisted mostly of Koreans who collaborated with the Japanese occupation. They were considered traitors in the South and the North. Further, this war was more complex than the American people have been told and can be viewed as a surrogate or proxy war between the Chinese Nationalist Party, Kuomintang or KMT for short, and the mainland Communist China or the People's Republic of China. As we discussed in chapter 4, the KMT was not only on the island of Formosa, now Taiwan, but had several fully armed and combat-capable divisions in the opium-growing region of Southeast Asia.

These divisions attacked China in concert with General MacArthur's push way past the thirty-eighth parallel, threatening mainland China. Casualties skyrocketed as the Chinese counterattacked. Another fact that seems to be left out of the story is that these southern KMT divisions were a huge drug cartel and established the Golden Triangle as the major source of opium in the world. As discussed before, this Golden Triangle-opium-war formula would carry on with the French in Indochina and later the Americans. General Chennault's logistics airline, Civil Air Transport—which flew weapons, aircraft parts, and rice in and picked up opium for transport to market on the way out—would be a legacy for the same formula when the United States arrived. Actually it was the same aircraft, but the airline would be bought by the CIA and named Air America. If this were well known, we just might be a little more suspicious of the fact that we now have a war in Afghanistan and that country is now, last the author checked, responsible for 93 percent of the world's heroin.

1953—The CIA backs a coup in Iran that overthrows the democratically elected Mohammad Mosaddegh and replaced him with the Shah of Iran. The Shah is a brutal dictator who oppressed the Iranian people to the point that they could stand no more. Against a well-armed and brutal police state, about one million Iranians put on their death shrouds and marched to the capitol. The Shah was deposed, and the United States has been hostile toward Iran since. Mosaddegh's cardinal sin? He nationalized the oil reserves of the country and wanted to use a reasonable amount of the profit for the development of his people instead of deferring to the West. We need to see what really happened in Iran. If shown, we might see a marked similarity to Saddam Hussein of Iraq.

1954—In Guatemala, the CIA overthrew the president, Jacobo Arbenz, who was the democratically elected head of state. It has been well established that the reason for the coup was that Arbenz was planning to nationalize the United Fruit Company, owned by the Rockefellers. Cutting into the profits of the Rockefellers was and is unhealthy business. Guatemala ended up with a series of brutal right-wing dictators that murdered roughly one hundred thousand Guatemalan people in the next forty years. Nelson Rockefeller probably did not miss any sleep whatsoever. Also, the CIA was learning quickly how to overthrow governments on the cheap. All they did was to broadcast over the radio that there was this huge insurgent army marching to overthrow the government, and throw a few Coke bottles filled with gunpowder out of a small plane. Arbenz fell for it and surrendered.

1956—The CIA incited a revolt in Hungary and promised US aid and support. Nazi "master spy" Reinhard Gehlen's operation, riddled with Soviet spies, leaked the whole armed revolt. Instead of US aid, the Hungarians took to the streets and faced Soviet main battle tanks. Roughly thirty thousand Hungarians were killed. Not America's finest hour.

1959—CIA-backed Haitian President Francois Duvalier was elected president. He appointed himself president for life in 1964. Increasingly brutal and paranoid, Duvalier's private police force the "Tonton Macoutes" murdered at least thirty thousand Haitians, mostly using machetes. The United States did very little to stem the almost continuous slaughter. He died in 1971. The history of Haiti is mostly characterized by, at best, indifference to outright resistance to anything that could lead to development and prosperity. The only explanation for this could be to make sure a nation run by people of African ancestry does not succeed. Further, because Haiti and Honduras are the two poorest countries in Central and South America, if workers rights, fair pay, education, and health care come to these two countries, the people of every country in the region will want at least the same; less profit for the likes of the Rockefellers. Would not it be nice to know what is really going on?

1961—The CIA ran wild throughout the world. Because the Kennedy administration was an unknown quantity, the CIA did not keep JFK informed on what it was doing. He certainly knew about the Bay of Pigs invasion, but he did not know that the CIA had planned to force him into intervening with US conventional forces, which JFK insisted he would not do. Dulles was incommunicado during the invasion when he should have been in charge. Further, Castro knew when and where the invasion would take place and was ready for it. The CIA knew that Castro knew but went ahead anyway. They wanted to drag Kennedy into an invasion of Cuba and a good chance of nuclear war with the Soviets. The Joint Chiefs of Staff were all for it. The Pentagon, the CIA, and the many others were howling mad that Kennedy did not fall for it. Kennedy not only totally distrusted the CIA, but he also made plans to dismantle it. Kennedy (again, no saint) fired the CIA leadership and planned to shatter it "into a thousand pieces." Any organization will fight for its own survival. This was why President Richard Nixon referred to the JFK assassination as "the Bay of Pigs thing." The failed Bay of Pigs invasion was not the only reason for the assassination, but it was emblematic of everything else. We also have the Bay of Pigs, which also needs some explaining.

We also have a CIA assassination in the Dominican Republic of Rafael Trujillo, a US-backed dictator who seemed to be doing too well in business. His interests amounted to about 60 percent of the total economy, and American business did not seem to think he should have been doing better than they were. In Ecuador, the CIA forced elected President Jose Velasco out of office for reasons unknown. In the Congo, the CIA assassinated the elected president, Patrice Lumumba, on the pretext that he was a "Marxist." This was totally uncalled for. When the CIA identified someone as a Marxist, it usually meant that the leader had done something for the people and not allowed the United States and its allies to extract the wealth of the country for its own enrichment. What really happened? We need to know.

1963—Again in the Dominican Republic, the CIA overthrew elected president Juan Bosch who was replaced by a handful of right-wing military dictators. In Ecuador, much the same thing happened whereas President Arosemana was replaced by a right-wing military junta.

The above was not all of the sordid affairs involving coups, murders, and other illegal clandestine activities. The CIA was running wild. There has been much ado that Presidents Eisenhower and Kennedy gave the CIA a green light to go ahead with all of the above and much more, and in some cases, this was true. Probably this was the case more with Eisenhower than Kennedy. Eisenhower finally caught on when the CIA continued with U-2 flights over Soviet territory against his orders. The downing of the U-2 flown by Francis Gary Powers, which scuttled a major disarmament summit and made Eisenhower out to be liar to the entire world, caused him to reassess an agency that was supposed to be working for him that apparently was not. He said as much in his farewell address without naming the agency directly. Harry Truman issued a scathing letter and publicly dressed down the CIA, by name, exactly one month after the assassination in Dallas. The author does not believe it was a coincidence that Truman's letter was dated December 22, 1963. And of course, JFK had serious issues with this unbelievably arrogant and uncontrollable agency. This added up to three presidents in a row that were more than concerned about the CIA's unchecked power and the agency's outlandishly criminal behavior.

Reflections

In this chapter, we have discussed the assent of reactionary fascism in America that put power and financial gain, for a few, above all else. Profit was gained by financing and supporting fascism in Europe, namely in Italy and Germany. Leaders of major corporations paid unemployed soldiers from WW I to bludgeon striking workers, which was the beginning of the American Legion. There actually was a plot to seize the FDR presidency, which included about a half-million legionnaires. Wall Street bankers and the titans of industry invested heavily in the Nazi regime. Allen Dulles was a lawyer for I. G. Farben, the maker of Zyklon B, which was the poison gas used at Auschwitz and all of the death camps. Hitler went to war in vehicles made by Ford and General Motors Co., and his genocidal ideas had been funded by the Carnegie Institution. IBM applied their data-processing expertise to gas and cremate millions of Jews, gypsies, and other "worthless eaters." None of these sociopaths lost any sleep over their record-setting crimes and the money they made was used to solidify their power and influence.

These traitors did not miss one step after the war. Rockefeller, Dulles, and the rest tenderly cared for tens of thousands of the worst war criminals the world had seen. They were treated like royalty under

Operation Paperclip. The Vatican and the Knights of Malta were used for passports and visas to get them out. Even today, most Americans believe that this was necessary because of these monsters' scientific knowledge when the truth is that all most of them were good at was torture, murder, and other forms of criminality. Klause Barbie played a key role in fostering the South American drug trade that is destroying people and communities to this day. The lines of communication used to get the Nazi murderers to the United States and South America were also used to get most of the stolen wealth of Europe out also. Rockefeller pocketed most of that. Eva Perón's bank accounts were where most of this money went, and she and her husband skimmed off "their share."

In Asia, the endless wars started in Korea, but the real prize was China. While General MacArthur's troops fought and froze all the way to the Yalu River, the Kuomintang, fueled by drug money, attacked across China's southern border. This synergism of drugs and war continued on after Korea and the "Golden Triangle" opium also fueled the Vietnam War. This was the reason that the secret war in Laos was secret, after all. The formula was the same in every region where highly profitable drugs were grown. Look at a map and note these regions. Southeast Asia, the Andes in South America, and now Afghanistan are all regions where drugs and war have been married. Drugs have fueled every so-called conflict that the United States has been involved in since WW II.

None of this has done anything but cause useless destruction and misery, but for whom? We will not see any of the aforementioned people in a uniform. They are not the ones whose guts end up hanging off a barbed-wire fence, and not a drop of Agent Orange has ever shown up in any of them. They did, however, profit wildly.

This was the psychopathology that Kennedy was facing down, and he was whipping them. They had more power, but Kennedy was infinitely smarter than all of them put together, and he had the people clearly behind him. He was having a showdown with the same criminals in seven-hundred-dollar-suits that every modern president had to deal with. From FDR, Truman, and Eisenhower—all of them had faced the same people, by name. No one in history has damaged the American republic as much as Allen Dulles. He has been responsible for the senseless slaughter of millions of people, and he has also been responsible for the destruction of our most cherished institutions. The fight was on, and Kennedy was winning. The pathocrates knew this, and they also knew that Kennedy would be reelected in a landslide. This would have given him the authority to really clean house. Evelyn Lincoln, Kennedy's secretary, said that JFK told her that Lyndon Johnson would not be on the ticket as the democratic vice presidential candidate for the coming election, and Johnson was aware of this. She said that Kennedy had told her this right before leaving for Dallas. Well, as we all know, that was one thing that Lyndon Baines Johnson did not have to worry about. He came back on Air Force One, tail number 26000, as the President of the United States. The mask was off the pathocracy.

> The setting for Joseph Conrad's Heart of Darkness was on the Thames;
> From whence flowed the British Empire;
> Who would have imagined that the new age Heart of Darkness;
> Would emanate from the mouth of the Potomac?
>
> —*Bob Kirkconnell*

Afterword

Often times in conversations about subjects related to this book the comment is made that what we have just covered is just "human nature." The author recalls relatives telling him that the Native Americans were just as cruel, greedy, violent, dishonest, and so forth as the Europeans. The only difference being that Europeans were just more "advanced" and so they won. The implication in these discussions is almost always that Europeans were better at most everything and that the native peoples just could not "keep up" or adapt to "progress." "Primitive people" is often the phrase used with all of its negative implications. This view is almost universal. It is reflected in our textbooks, movies, and literature. As we have seen this point of view has been with us from the very beginning and has contributed to the virtual destruction of many cultures and languages, each of which are unique ways of looking at mankind's environment. How many ideas and concepts that we could use today died when these cultures and languages, at least 1500 of them, were destroyed?

As we have seen, religious beliefs (predominantly Calvinism) formed the basis for both capitalism and the genocide of the Native Americans. The notion that one has an obligation to God to use the land and resources for maximum profit was a fundamental assumption. Add to this the preposterous notion that since the native people were not doing this they had no right to the land and should be killed in the process claiming it for its "rightful owners." This mindset puts God on the side of racism and genocide, a corruption of the ministry of Christ that should have been obvious to people then and now. Unfortunately these ideas, ideas that Christ surely would have found antithetical to his teachings, have not been righted even today.

Priceless are the authors who documented what really happened in the conquest of the "new world," and this writer encourages the reader to explore this further. It is the only way that we can understand what we are dealing with today. Authors and their works such as: David E. Stannard, *American Holocaust: The Conquest of the New World*; Richard Drinnon, *Facing West: The Metaphysics of Indian-Hating and Empire-Building*; and Robert J. Miller, *Native America, Discovered and Conquered* are but a few of the outstanding works that are still available at reasonable prices. Book sellers such as aLibris, Google Books, and Amazon are excellent sources.

We have also seen the continuum racism, genocide, and militarism and how these forces shaped the American empire. Further, we can look at what is happening today and make the connections. Much of the destruction in Afghanistan, Iraq, and the occupied Palestinian territories has been rationalized in eerily similar fashion. School textbooks from the 1950s and '60s referred to what is now Iraq as being "the cradle of civilization." Hammurabi's code was the first well organized written law that put forth the concept that punishment should fit the crime. The last time the author looked at a high school history book there was less than one page of text describing Mesopotamia and most of that was a large picture of a stone horse. The "cradle of civilization" had somehow vanished and we are now left with ostensibly a people who do not understand civilization and need to be taught by being on the wrong end of an M-16. Palestinians are now not a people with thousands of years of civilization behind them, but somehow have turned into just wanderers with no history. In fact even today we have politicians publicly stating that they, Palestinians, do not even exist. And besides, "They were not making good use of the land anyway." Oh really! This line of thought is too similar to what was said about the Native Americans to be a coincidence.

We have also seen how early Europeans brought with them farming methods requiring a lot of land, and land that was not within their immediate living space. This means you now need to take someone else's land. Further, the human labor intensive farming methods created the need for slaves. So now we have the foundation of a nation built on stolen land by slave labor and we add militarism to make it all happen; the die is cast. As unpleasant as it is to confront, one cannot sugarcoat these seeds of destruction sown into America from the very beginning. One can write about equality, unalienable rights, liberty, and happiness for as long as one wishes but, the ship of state sailed in one direction and anyone who tried to change the course was met with extreme consequences, as we have seen.

Of course in a democracy you cannot just talk one way and behave in another and just leave it at that. The people have to be fooled into believing there is no disconnect between what is said and what is done. Hence we have the most sophisticated practices of propaganda developed right here in the land of the "free press." George Seldes, Noam Chomsky, James Loewen, and others have covered this subject for us quite well. The reader is also encouraged to look into this further.

Looking back on where we have been, it also appears that we Americans have an ever increasing sense of powerlessness about us. We have touched on the gains by the labor movement that did not come without a fight. The American people did stop the war in Vietnam, but since that time we have not seemed to want to "go to the mat" even over important issues. We need to ask ourselves the question, why? As powerless as most of us tend to feel at times this writer has had some surprising responses as the result of writing media outlets. Sure, you are going to get a "canned" response, but many do take notice when you know what you are talking about and you call them on their sloppy journalism, or worse. They do take notice. Occasionally the author has had responses along the lines of "Keep doing what you are doing . . ." and the like. Many in media really want to do a good job but also do not want to be unemployed. Kristina Borjesson's excellent book *Into the Buzzsaw: Leading Journalists Expose the Myth of a Free Press*, contains accounts of what happens to even nationally known journalists who do not tow the line. Writing media and also politicians that represent us is a powerful tool to let your voice be heard. The author has seen some important issues influenced by letter writing campaigns and petitions.

Let us remember that Oliver Stone's movie JFK provided the impetus for enough Americans to write, call, and otherwise insist that a reinvestigation of the JFK, MLK, and RFK assassinations be instituted, which resulted in the House Select Committee on Assassinations. One of the results of this was that it was determined that JFK was "Likely assassinated as a result of a conspiracy . . ." This would not have happened if the American people had not demanded it, and it also shows the power each of us has when we are informed and take action.

The author also would like to call attention to the virtually continuous warfare waged by America from that little colony in Virginia to the present. The long march "from sea to shining sea," ostensibly fueled again by God in the form of Manifest Destiny and codified by the racist Doctrine of Discovery, was an unprecedented event. This genocidal tide of destruction entailed stealing land, murder, and the destruction of priceless culture and knowledge. Then it had to be determined who was going to run it; slave south or the industrialized north? We have seen that this question was at least as important as the more advertised and altruistic battle to get rid of slavery. One indication as to what was really important was that the same generals that used "total warfare" to defeat the South also used the same tactics to annihilate the plains Indians. The slaughter of at least 30 million buffalo, virtually all of them, was an act that was unprecedented in human history and of such brutality that it had to have damaged the very soul of America. As we now know William Tecumseh Sherman stated in his own words that it was a deliberate act orchestrated because both the Northern and Southern forces combined could not have defeated the plains Indians such as the Comanche, an empire in its own right. That a people would do such a thing was absolutely inconceivable to Native America. They just could not understand it. Again, America looked at the Natives and the buffalo as "useless."

Once the conquest of the Continental United States was complete, we also saw war and conquest move to Philippines, the Caribbean, and elsewhere. As always, the US was doing people a favor by invading them. We were always "spreading democracy," putting down an insurgency, or securing our "vital interests," which most often were oil, drugs, gold, or some other resource. Of course, how you move these around also had to be secured. These war planners call "lines of communication" of which the Panama Canal, the Suez Canal, and the Strait of Malacca are a few examples. One has only to look at these war planning elements to not only see where the Anglo-American empire has been but also where we are now and where will we be in the future. It is not a coincidence that everywhere opium and cocaine have been grown we have had, or now have, a war going on. Check the map. The same holds true of oil, and when you have oil and drugs in the same region it is a foregone conclusion that we will be there. Let us recall Cecil Rhodes's empire roadmap.

Noteworthy also was the fact that the Anglo-American Empire went into turbo mode during the run-up to WW-II. In researching this period the author found information that was not only widely not known, but almost unbelievable in itself. The American Eugenics movement was one of these instances where one could almost not get one's mind around this appalling journey into the dark side of human nature. Add to this the fact that the US nurtured and shared these ghastly ideas with Nazi Germany. Who would have thought that the holocaust was born in the United States? Also, who would have thought that Hitler went to war using Ford and GM vehicles? Who would have thought that IBM would have already written the programs in the Haiti experiment that would be used to segregate people with Jewish ancestry and then exterminate them? To find out that the Eugenics movement was funded by the Carnegie Institution and the Rockefeller Foundation was another wake-up call. Add to this the fact that the elite power structure not only made money "trading with the enemy," but also was supportive of Fascism to a surprising degree, enough whereas the US President Franklin Delano Roosevelt had to take adverse action against the leaders and owners of large sectors of American business to force them into the war effort, on the American side that is.

Also unbelievable was the fact that support for the Nazis before the war was nothing in comparison to what was done afterward. The concerted effort made to smuggle the worst of the Nazi murderers out of Germany and place them in the US and South America is over the top. Add to this that the Vatican and the Knights of Malta were involved! Also noteworthy was the fact that many high ranking and/or influential Nazis, Americans, British, and Fascist Italy were members of the Knights of Malta. This would include Nazi intelligence Commander Reinhard Gehlen and Waffen-SS Commander Heinrich Himmler; American intelligence operatives Allen Dulles, James Jesus Angleton, John A. McCone, and William J. Donovan; British spy Kim Philby; Italian Fascist dictator Benito Mussolini; and the President Juan Perón of Argentina. All of the above and more also played key roles in smuggling the worst of the Nazi murderers out of Germany. It is also interesting that Clay Shaw, the only person to have been tried for the JFK assassination, was also a member of the Knights of Malta.

It should not be lost on any of us that these evil, barely human, beings were not only smuggled out but were given key positions in American government, education, research, and industry. We have also seen the profound damage they have caused here and in South America. What possibly could have been the motive for this? They were not scientists with invaluable knowledge this country needed, that is for sure. They were mass murderers that practiced barbarism and torture wearing lab coats. Somehow, they had to have had common goals and interests with their American sponsors. Could it have been visions of global domination dancing in their heads? The author's next book will explore these possibilities.

We also took a look at how intelligence, psychiatry, and education was co-opted by these American and Nazi Fascists to produce some of the most bizarre programs one can imagine, and in so doing caused immeasurable damage to our people and institutions. Electro-shock convulsive "therapy" and prefrontal lobotomies subjected many powerless people to profound and totally unnecessary damage. The total numbers might never be known because as we now know much of this information was classified. Further, that this was done in our most respected institutions has corrupted the very heart and soul of America. Add to this that the above was funded by so-called philanthropic institutes and foundations and we have a very ugly picture of what American leadership is really about.

No US president has dared take on the above ruthless monsters. These psychopaths have murdered anyone in their way. FDR sometimes put them in check, but he was too overburdened with fighting WW-II to take them on. Besides he needed them, evil as they were, to win the war. Harry Truman did not mind using them for his purposes until he saw the enormity of the evil he was consorting with, and he probably did not see this until JFK's head exploded in Dallas. One month to the day later he published a letter stating that the CIA was out of control. Dwight David Eisenhower used the instruments of pathocracy for his own edification up until a few days before he left office. He then whimpered about the out of control power structure he vaguely termed "the military industrial complex" and left the dirty work for his successor to deal with, and we know what happened to him. The reality that JFK was alone even in his own administration is profound. Investigative, intelligence, law enforcement, defense, and other agencies and institutions either were involved in the assassination or knew about it and just let it happen. Most were also involved in the cover-up, and all are culpable. Given all of the commissions, panels, investigations and the like and we end up with one person charged and he was acquitted? Hundreds of witnesses are not even questioned and those that were somehow ended up with immediate "health problems."

We also had the "crime of the century" solved by J. Edgar Hoover and the FBI in a few hours. At light speed Hoover determined that whole thing was planned and carried out by one 24 year-old madman. Of course, we will never know who or what Lee Harvey was because a South Chicago thug, gangster, and drug smuggler was so upset that his president was killed and that his (JFK's) wife would have to suffer through a trial so he felt duty bound to take Oswald out. Yeah right. The whole scenario is so preposterous that it would not even pass as historical fiction. Good true Americans who testified as to what they saw were harassed, harangued, vilified, threatened and even murdered; a lot of them. Jim Garrison who brought the only indictment was harassed to the ends of the earth. These were true patriots that were treated as if they were the murderers and traitors.

It is not lost on this author and hopefully the reader that things are the opposite of what they should be. The mask is off and it came off the day JFK was murdered. The pathocracy has shown its ugly face for all to see. The players in this most ugly scene are as evil as human beings can get and we identified them and what they have done. There should not be a Dulles International Airport or a J. Edgar Hoover Building in the United States. These were profoundly evil people that caused possibly irreparable damage to the country. Nothing needs to be named after James Jesus Angleton or Richard Helms, or anyone else who spent their life practicing treachery, treason, and murder. These people created and left us with a fascist dictatorship that is going to take some doing to change. The reader can be assured that, as has happened throughout history, it will fall. It is just a matter of how ugly it has to get for that to happen.

The author's hope is that we all rediscover the direction of Gandhi, Martin Luther King, Arch Bishop Desmond Tutu, JFK, and many others who tried to show us what power we actually have. The pathological individuals we have discussed only have the power we either give them or we let them have. The author is in awe and inspired by the above and many more. That a skinny and penniless Mahatma Gandhi could take on the British Empire and win is incredible. The author also recalls Arch Bishop Tutu saying in an interview that the hard part of liberating South Africa was to get the African people to make the decision that they actually wanted to be free. He continued that once they made that decision, the rest was easy. This writer and citizen of the planet will never forget those words. Does America really want to be free? If we all make that decision the rest will be easy. So I ask my fellow Americans, do we want to be free? If so, let us continue.

We are controlled by fear, and Americans are the easiest people in the world to scare. Most of us will do, or not do, just about anything to avoid a bad credit rating or maybe an IRS audit. We need to look at the courage demonstrated by those we actually revere and respect. JFK's *Profiles in Courage* provides excellent examples of people who did the right thing under pressure to compromise what they knew was right. Probably every one of them felt the fear in them leave and was glad they had done the right thing. The following are some perfectly legal and appropriate actions that many activists have found effective, and the more of us that do them the more effective they will be.

> ➢ Read and study the issues from different perspectives, and find out who or what is behind the issues. "Climate change is not happening . . ." and the "independent" study saying this was funded by big oil? Hmmmm.
> ➢ Write the president and other executives and also your congressmen and senators. Your voice does count and sometimes allows them to do what they already want to do anyway, but lack the support of their constituency. Make sure you are polite and respectful. Venting detracts from your message.
> ➢ Write news outlets for the same reasons, and write an op-ed now and then. You will be pleased when one or two are published. Local media tend to be more amenable to publishing editorials than you realize. Besides, it makes us think about the position we are taking when we put pen to paper.
> ➢ Join activist groups that support your positions and defend your rights. My favorites are: Academics for Justice, Veterans for Peace, Union of Concerned Scientists, The Green Party, Amnesty International, The American Civil Liberties Union, The International Solidarity Movement, Jewish Voice for Peace, and many more. Many of these activist and human rights groups have letter writing and petition signing campaigns that make contacting political representatives and news outlets very simple.

- Do not buy products and services from corporations that support objectives you do not agree with. You can get what you want somewhere else, and let the company know why you are not buying their product.
- Do not invest your money with any organization that is using your money against you. You would be surprised at how often this happens. Find out where your money is going and what it is being used for. There are activist organizations that can keep you up-to-speed.
- Go solar. My system did not cost me a dime, and the payments are less than what my electricity bill was anyway. It is also fun to watch my electric meter running backwards! And how about an electric car or a hybrid? Let's stop these oil wars.
- The author will assume that the reader feels that neither of the two major political parties represents their interests. Otherwise you would not be reading this book. Vote third party. Most progressive legislation was the direct result of third party movements. We might not have Social Security today if it were not for third party influence.

Actually we could all be doing the above and more without much effort at all, and it probably would not affect anyone's credit rating. In fact it might improve it.

Let us finish with some reflection on one current issue that also relates to this book. As we have seen, America has been virtually at war from the beginning to the present. One result is that public money that should go toward human development is transferred to the pockets of the wealthy elite. Without proper education the people are less likely to resist this process of looting the American treasury. Hence, we have the present all-out assault on public education funding. We also have had a series of mass murder episodes on school campuses. Is it possible that these two issues are connected?

Continuous warfare does not leave enough money left over to have a good education system, and the US cannot export as much continuous violence as it does throughout the world without it being returned to us. We cannot love our children and kill "theirs." They are us. This is not a novel idea of the author's. Michael Moore illustrated very well in his documentary, *Bowling for Columbine,* and Martin Luther King repeatedly warned that institutionalized violence, or war, erodes the character of the nation. Martin Luther King gave a speech one year to the day before he was assassinated at New York's Riverside church on April 4th, 1967. The title of it was "A Time to Break the Silence," but it is often referred to as his "Beyond Vietnam Speech." As JFK's American University speech can be viewed as his death warrant, Dr. King's speech was as powerful as any that has ever been given, and it certainly was a threat to the US pathocracy.

Below are a few excerpts from what Dr. King shared with the world that day. Notice the common threads from what he said in 1967 and what JFK had shared four years earlier at American University.

- The Western arrogance of feeling that it has everything to teach others and nothing to learn from them is not just. A true revolution of values will lay hands on the world order and say of war: "This way of settling differences is not just."
- Here is the true meaning and value of compassion and nonviolence when it helps us to see the enemy's point of view, to hear his questions, to know his assessment of ourselves. For from his view we may indeed see the basic weaknesses of our own condition, and if we are mature, we may learn and grow and profit from the wisdom of the brothers who are called the opposition.
- If America's soul becomes totally poisoned, part of the autopsy must read Vietnam. It can never be saved so long as it destroys the deepest hopes of men the world over.
- This business of burning human beings with napalm, of filling our nation's homes with orphans and widows, of injecting poisonous drugs of hate into veins of people normally humane, of sending men home from dark and bloody battlefields physically handicapped and psychologically deranged, cannot be reconciled with wisdom, justice and love.
- A nation that continues year after year to spend more money on military defense than on programs of social uplift is approaching spiritual death.
- The war in Vietnam is but a symptom of a far deeper malady within the American spirit, and if we ignore this sobering reality we will find ourselves organizing clergy—and laymen-concerned committees for the next generation.

> They will be concerned about Guatemala and Peru. They will be concerned about Thailand and Cambodia. They will be concerned about Mozambique and South Africa. We will be marching for these and a dozen other names and attending rallies without end unless there is a significant and profound change in American life and policy.
> Such thoughts take us beyond Vietnam, but not beyond our calling as sons of the living God.
> The Americans are forcing even their friends into becoming their enemies. It is curious that the Americans, who calculate so carefully on the possibilities of military victory, do not realize that in the process they are incurring deep psychological and political defeat.
> The image of America will never again be the image of revolution, freedom and democracy, but the image of violence and militarism."
> Then came the buildup in Vietnam and I watched the program broken and eviscerated as if it were some idle political plaything of a society gone mad on war, and I knew that America would never invest the necessary funds or energies in rehabilitation of its poor so long as adventures like Vietnam continued to draw men and skills and money like some demonic destructive suction tube.
> So I was increasingly compelled to see the war as an enemy of the poor and to attack it as such.
> We are called to speak for the weak, for the voiceless, for victims of our nation and for those it calls enemy, for no document from human hands can make these humans any less our brothers.
> Our only hope today lies in our ability to recapture the revolutionary spirit and go out into a sometimes hostile world declaring eternal hostility to poverty, racism, and militarism.
> We can no longer afford to worship the god of hate or bow before the altar of retaliation. The oceans of history are made turbulent by the ever-rising tides of hate.
> History is cluttered with the wreckage of nations and individuals that pursued this self-defeating path of hate.

The more one reads Kennedy's words and those of Dr. King the more one is struck with the commonality of these two transformational leaders. Both spoke of the concept that in listening to your enemies you gain insight into yourself, and both talked about recognizing the commonality of the human spirit. Notice also that both saw war as spiritually destructive, even if you win. These messages resonated with the American people, hence they were a threat to the power elite. This is why both men, and others, had to go. This is also why we do not hear these words today, even at events to commemorate these two leaders both of which, and their message, should be considered national treasures. The author recalls one Martin Luther King Day celebration that consisted of a parade that ended in a baseball stadium followed by wrestling matches. That was it. Not one word of Dr. King's was uttered the entire day.

We should be seeing, hearing, and discussing all of the above and everything else that we looked at in this book. Our history books should not be whitewashed. We should know the true cost of running a hyper-military state that sacrifices the needs of its citizens for weapons. We should know that the US Congress determined that JFK was "Likely killed as the result of a conspiracy," and that in 1999 a Memphis Tennessee jury found agencies of the US Government responsible for the wrongful death of Martin Luther King. The court room was almost empty at the time. Of course, these facts are a matter of public record, but ask around and you will find (as the author has) that most people do not know this.

It is the author's greatest hope that this 400 year march toward pathocracy comes to an end by the shared will and cooperation of the American people. There is no doubt that one way or another the sun will set on the American empire as has happened to all of them before. The only question is whether it collapses into chaos or transforms into a creative force that leads the world into a future where everyone has what was stated at the beginning as the American dream—life, liberty, and happiness. The choice is ours.

Acknowledgments

This book would not have been possible without the enormous help of a lot of dedicated people who work very hard to find and preserve hidden American history. My thanks to the *Mary Ferrell Foundation* for the incredibly comprehensive documentation provided of the assassinations discussed here and also permission to use their documentation. I am also indebted to the *The Col. L. Fletcher Prouty Reference Site* for the same. *Wikipedia* and *Spartacus Educational* were also an enormous help. Special thanks to the authors and activists at wanttoknow.info, and in particular to web site manager and cover-up researcher Fred Burks. They have done a wonderful job on not only disclosing cover-ups but also what all of us can do about it. Further, I want to thank the following newspapers for their permissions to quote from their articles: *Milwaukee Journal, Tuscaloosa News, Times Daily, Ellensburg Daily Record, New York Times, Washington Post, Tuscaloosa News, and Milwaukee Journal.*

This writer cannot thank ex-DEA agent and author Mike Levine enough for his courage and also his permission to quote him at length. He is an inspiration to us all. Thanks go to every author referenced in this work. There are too many to name individually, but these brave souls have labored against a lot criticism and outright harassment. They are all a special gift to the world. Please follow the works and authors referenced. They lead to some interesting places. All of them are a tremendous resource for information if we choose to take back the power that is rightfully ours. If they were brave enough to write it, we should be brave enough to act on it.

Along with the people and organizations above, the author wishes to thank all of the activist organizations that work every day to resist oppression and tyranny. There is not room enough to mention them all but just a few are as follows: Veterans for Peace, Academics for Justice, Union of Concerned Scientists, Amnesty International, American Civil Liberties Union, International Solidarity Movement, and Jewish Voice for Peace. We would be lost without them.

Thanks also goes to every relative and friend the author used as a sounding board. A lot of the content was hard to listen to and outright threatening to fundamental belief systems. Also appreciated are the people who sometimes disagreed with me. Their frank opinions helped to clarify my thoughts and get an idea of people's diverse view points. They also kept me on-course. My wife Leila was instrumental in doing this. Special thanks to Marcy Brooks and Gillian Delmonico for being the inspiration behind the cover design which Xlibris used to do the actual work. Special thanks also to Mary Deem and Diana Gall for proof-reading.

Lastly, I wish to express my gratitude to the hard working people at Xlibris for their outstanding assistance in publishing this book. From cover design to press releases, they did everything they said they would do and more. Thanks.

The Author

Index

A

Aarons, Mark, 87, 393, 398, 400, 419
African Americans, 19, 229, 268, 284–85, 287, 305–6, 319
Agent Orange, 73, 108, 158, 425
agents, 22, 24, 45, 48, 61, 120, 137, 186, 216–18, 230, 270
Air America, 10, 30, 34, 45, 106, 137
Air Force, 34, 119, 124–25, 128, 426
Alabama, 61–62, 167, 285
ALEC (American Legislative Exchange Council), 305
Algeria, 151, 195, 262
Alpha 66, 206–7, 250–51, 253
Al Qaeda, 287, 378
America, 10–11, 13–14, 19, 78, 88, 100, 104, 150, 152–53, 158, 277–87, 290–92, 295–96, 304, 307, 311–14, 318, 320–21, 323, 326, 330–31, 335–37, 339–42, 344–45, 352–56, 361–62, 367–68, 370, 380, 382–83, 390, 392, 402, 415–16, 424, 428, 430, 432, 434–35, 437
Americal Division, 93–94
American heart of darkness, 114–15, 130, 153, 235, 404, 409
American Holocaust, 293, 306
American Holocaust: The Conquest of the New World (Stannard), 292–93, 296, 307, 311
American Legion, 368–70, 373–74, 379, 424
American Legislative Exchange Council (ALEC), 305
American Liberty League, 369
American Psychiatric Association. *See* APA
American Republic, 3, 111, 153–54, 159, 168, 221, 258, 270, 281, 284, 287, 351, 385, 425
Americans, 9–10, 19–20, 34, 49, 78, 84, 88, 103–4, 118–20, 129, 131, 150, 169, 172, 230, 233, 235, 273–75, 278–79, 285, 317, 327, 330, 332, 337, 339–40, 351, 359, 361–62, 383, 392, 421, 429, 431, 434, 437
Anglo-American Empire, 339, 347–48, 362, 385, 430–31
antisocial personality disorder, 75
Antony, Mark, 260
APA (American Psychiatric Association), 75, 404
ARA (Inter-American Affairs), 398

Arbenz, Jacobo, 136, 146, 232, 422
Archer, Jules, 368–70
armed conflict, 95, 133, 135, 158, 206
Armitage, Richard, 139–45, 412
Arnold, Gordon, 187, 189
ARVN (Army of the Republic of Vietnam), 107
Asia, 101–2, 123, 129, 195, 263, 307, 348, 407, 425
assassination, 18, 20, 113, 131, 145, 149–51, 155–57, 160–62, 165, 167–68, 170–76, 180–88, 191, 193, 195–96, 206, 208–9, 211–12, 214–16, 218–19, 225–27, 230–31, 233–34, 238–47, 250–52, 255–57, 264, 266, 269–70, 273, 277, 279–80, 282, 290, 319–20, 356, 387, 408–9, 420, 423–24, 432, 439
  political, 116, 131, 137–38, 145, 206
assassination plots, 173, 207, 242
assassination teams, 137, 197, 208, 233, 244, 250–51
assassins, 155, 160, 165–66, 168, 181, 193, 219, 246, 251, 269, 405
Astor, John Jacob, 103, 349, 377
Astor, Waldorf, 349, 377
Atkinson, Leslie, 42–45, 57–58, 63–64, 113, 411
Australia, 139–40, 143–44, 296, 314

B

Bangkok, 17, 37–39, 43, 45, 68, 132, 140–42, 411
Barbie, Klaus, 392, 394, 404
Barns, Tracy, 235–38, 240, 250
Bay of Pigs invasion, 131, 166, 183, 197–200, 203, 206, 223, 234, 236, 238, 243, 248–49, 423
Beasley, 42–43, 46
belief systems, 33, 292, 320–21, 326, 390
Bell, Alexander Graham, 390
Ben-Gurion, David, 399–401
Black, Edwin, 380, 390, 414–16, 418
black operations, 140, 145–46, 231, 289
Blome, Kurt, 395
bodies, 15–17, 22, 25–28, 30, 33–34, 40, 43, 45–46, 52–53, 61–65, 69, 72–73, 80, 95, 101, 187, 192, 246, 289, 293, 322, 334, 365, 375
book depository, 157, 162, 166–67, 192, 196, 254–55
Bosch, Juan, 423
Britain, 103, 304, 338–39, 343, 371, 398
British Empire, 103, 282, 339, 343–44, 426, 433
buffalo, 322–24, 333–34, 413, 430
Bulger, Whitey, 410
Burma, 36, 106, 118
Bush, George W., 14, 30, 85–87, 90–91, 96, 122, 341
Bush, Prescott, 87–89
Bush administration, 84, 90, 95, 97–98
Butler, Smedley, 88–89, 369–70, 376

C

Cabell, Earle, 166, 207
Caesar, Julius, 268–69, 303

Calvinism, 326–27, 330, 427
Cameron, Donald Ewen, 403–5
Cameron, W. J., 380, 403–5
Canada, 268, 296, 302, 348, 387, 403
Carnegie, Andrew, 413–15
Carnegie Institution, 350, 385, 413–15, 418–19, 424, 431
Castro, Fidel, 125, 170, 172, 187, 197, 200–202, 204–5, 207–8, 211, 223, 232, 236, 241, 243–44, 248, 263, 275, 279, 423
CAT (Civil Air Transport), 106, 132–33, 421
CFR (Council on Foreign Relations), 348–50, 369, 385, 388
Chaney, Richard, 267, 402
characteropaths, 82–84, 98, 326, 352, 374, 405
Chase Manhattan Bank, 345, 393
Chennault, Clair, 106, 132, 421
Cheramie, Rose, 185–86
China, 102–4, 132, 290, 329, 343, 348, 421, 425
Chomsky, Noam, 328, 336–37, 341, 376, 386, 429
Christianity, 307, 326–27, 339
Christic Institute, 137–38, 143
Church Committee, 204, 216, 232–33
Churchill, Winston, 181, 249, 347, 390
CIA (Central Intelligence Agency), 30–32, 34–35, 48, 57–58, 71, 98, 106–12, 116–19, 122–23, 125–27, 130, 132–38, 144–46, 148–50, 154, 166, 169–73, 177, 182, 197–207, 209, 213–14, 217, 219–20, 222–27, 231–37, 239–43, 249, 257, 280–81, 287, 289, 385, 389, 391, 394, 404–7, 409, 411–12
CID (Criminal Investigations Division), 23, 46, 52, 57, 65, 114
Circle of Initiates, 347–48, 376–77
civil rights, 285–86
Civil War, 19, 284, 304, 316–17, 319, 321–25, 329, 356
Cleopatra, 260
Clines, Thomas, 137–40, 143–44, 146
cocaine, 31, 40, 101, 169, 305, 377, 392, 394, 430
colonies, 103, 283, 294, 298, 312
colonists, 297–98, 312, 314, 321, 327, 354
Commission on the Assassination of President Kennedy. *See* Warren Commission
communists, 78, 165, 175, 211, 213, 229, 275, 397, 405–6
Congress (US), 36, 39, 88, 107, 111–12, 135, 233, 252, 266, 270, 284, 286, 288–89, 295, 303, 316, 319, 332, 337, 369, 390, 406, 416
Connelly, John, 189, 254–56, 382
Conrad, Joseph, 294, 426
conspiracy, 61, 63, 66, 147, 155, 161, 170–72, 175–76, 194, 198, 210, 213, 227, 230, 235–36, 273, 313, 358, 368–69, 429, 438
Constantine, Alex, 41, 113–14, 393, 411, 413
Constitution (US), 9, 11, 14, 98, 108–10, 148, 284, 287–91, 301–2, 304, 332, 351, 399

corporate America, 18, 131, 133, 158–59, 266, 286, 374, 382–83
corporations, 73, 113, 143, 159, 267, 305, 345, 363–67, 371, 373, 376–79, 387–88, 405, 435
Corsicans, 218–19, 246
counterintelligence, 172, 242, 389
couriers, 22, 24, 43–45, 74
cover-ups, 70, 93, 126–27, 150, 155, 167, 171, 195, 234, 245, 432, 439
Criminal Investigations Division. *See* CID
Cuba, 9, 84, 146, 158, 165, 197, 199–202, 204–7, 210, 223–26, 236, 240–43, 249, 251, 263, 265, 287, 304, 307, 330, 333, 338
Cuban Revolutionary Council, 201, 238
Cubans, 9, 183, 186, 201, 204, 211, 227, 247–48, 263, 280, 375
  anti-Castro, 200, 211, 224, 236, 240–41, 249, 251
  exiled, 200, 205

D

Dallas, 20, 121, 126–28, 155, 160–62, 173–76, 186, 196, 198–99, 203, 205, 207, 209, 211, 213, 217, 226, 237, 243, 248–49, 251–53, 256, 269–70, 277, 424, 426, 432
Dal-Tex Building, 163, 251, 253–54, 256
Davenport, Charles, 414, 418
DEA (Drug Enforcement Agency), 29, 31–32, 45

Dealey Plaza, 149, 155, 161–63, 166, 207, 251–52, 254, 256, 269, 382
Declaration of Independence, 92, 283, 287, 291, 298–99, 302, 312, 356, 362
democracy, 13, 76, 109–10, 152, 159, 220, 228, 259, 270–72, 277, 303, 328, 335–37, 340, 357, 397, 413, 429, 437
Department of State, 25, 30, 35–36, 48, 388
Department of State Congressional Testimony, 38
Dien Bien Phu, 105, 262–63
Director of Plans, 234–35, 239
Donovan, William, 132, 287, 385, 389, 431
Dornberger, Walter, 394
Drug Abuse, 35–36, 39
Drugging America: A Trojan Horse (Stich), 133, 230, 305
drug money, 18, 107, 133, 152, 159, 204, 223, 412, 425
drugs, 10, 17–18, 24–25, 28–30, 40, 42–44, 47–49, 57, 62, 100–101, 104–6, 111–13, 116–19, 131, 133, 137–38, 145, 148, 151–52, 159, 168–69, 204–6, 219, 280, 288, 290, 335, 357, 378, 406, 425, 430
drug trade, 26, 39–40, 46, 58, 71, 100, 104–5, 112–13, 117, 119, 130–31, 133, 137, 147, 158, 180, 204, 206, 208, 223, 252, 357, 378, 407, 409
drug traffickers, 31, 223
Dulles, Allen, 111–12, 122, 124, 166, 200, 203, 207, 213–14, 225, 238, 269, 276, 358, 385,

387–89, 392, 396–99, 401,
   424–25
DuPont, Lammot, 369, 376, 388
Duvalier, Francois, 422

E

Easterling, Robert Wilfred, 182–84,
   254
Easterwood, William, 374
Eisenhower, Dwight, 113, 122,
   153, 158, 200, 203, 213, 220,
   424–25
elites, 135, 346, 357, 359
Elm Street, 163–64, 167, 209, 256
England, 103, 283, 297, 339, 342,
   347, 349, 377
eugenics, 350, 381, 390, 413–17
Europe, 81, 89, 102, 118, 128–29,
   132, 288, 296, 307, 336, 338,
   345, 347, 353–54, 370, 372,
   374, 377, 387–88, 398, 424–25
Europeans, 89, 307, 311–12, 323,
   326–27, 355, 359, 427
Executive Action, 136, 146, 213,
   231–32

F

*Farewell to Justice, Jim Garrison, JFK's
   Assassination, and the Case that
   Should Have Changed History, A*
   (Mellen), 185
fascism, 82, 89, 367, 370–74, 380,
   382, 384, 424, 431
Fatal Vision (McGinnis), 48, 52
Fayetteville, 41, 44–46, 62, 115
FBI (Federal Bureau of Investigation),
   17, 32, 44, 53, 57–58, 71, 130,
149–50, 160–61, 171, 173,
   175–76, 183, 186, 219–20,
   223, 228–31, 235, 239, 241,
   247–48, 252–53, 255, 270,
   280, 290, 408, 411, 433
FDC (Friends of Democratic Cuba),
   237
Ferrie, David, 181, 212, 236–38,
   241–42, 249–50
fingerprints, 193–94, 255
*First Hand Knowledge: How I
   Participated in the CIA-Mafia
   Murder of President Kennedy*, 202,
   224, 226, 237, 240, 249–50
Florida, 147, 171, 173, 186, 206–7,
   227, 244, 251, 305, 329
Forbes, John Murray, 377
Ford, Henry, 121, 350, 366–67,
   379–81, 388, 405
Ford Motor Company, 366, 379–80
Fort Bragg, 41, 43, 47, 57–58, 63, 69
founding fathers, 281, 284, 288–89,
   292–93, 296–301, 356

G

Galton, Francis J., 415
Garrison, Jim, 121, 155, 160–61,
   164–66, 170–71, 173, 181–82,
   184–85, 189, 236, 243, 248,
   250, 255, 257, 397, 433
Gehlen, Reinhard, 389, 422, 431
General Electric Company, 345, 351,
   377, 388
General Motors Corporation, 376,
   381, 388, 424
genocide, 14, 18–19, 95, 107, 292,
   299–301, 306, 311–14, 317,
   319–20, 322–23, 325–26,

330–31, 340, 353, 356, 394, 427–28
Germans, 78, 80–81, 119, 340, 371–72, 389, 391
Germany, 81–83, 87–89, 119, 136, 145, 330, 336–37, 339–40, 344, 349, 357, 362–63, 370–72, 381, 384, 386–87, 391–93, 398, 419, 424, 431
germ plasm, 19, 381, 415–16
global elites, 352, 358
Goebbels, Joseph, 328, 336–37, 340
Golden Triangle, 36–38, 100, 158, 204, 264, 421, 425
Gonzales, Alberto R., 90–92
Great Britain, 102–4, 223–24, 296, 298, 343–44, 347–48, 364, 384
Great Depression, 370, 374, 376

H

Halsey, William, 262–63, 273
Hare, Robert, 374
Harvey, William, 203, 208, 214, 216, 220, 232, 236, 239, 243–44, 246, 248
Hawaii, 22, 24–26, 329
Helliwell, Paul, 132–33, 412
Helms, Richard, 225, 231–35, 238–39, 246, 248, 278, 336, 405, 433
heroin, 15–17, 22, 25–26, 29–30, 33–34, 36–40, 42–46, 52, 58, 62–66, 69–70, 73, 101, 106, 114–15, 118–19, 137, 147–48, 151, 158, 168–69, 222–23, 377, 392, 411
Hersh, Seymour, 259
Hickam Air Force Base, 22, 24, 26, 28

Himmler, Heinrich, 379, 388, 395, 431
Hitler, Adolf, 81, 87, 118, 337, 370–73, 379–82, 387, 415, 424, 431
Hollerith, Herman, 417
Holy Lands, 300, 343–44, 348, 357
Hoover, J. Edgar, 57–58, 127, 161, 167, 173, 195, 227–31, 233–34, 239, 244, 248, 257, 280, 358, 433
Hunt, Howard, 197–99, 203, 235, 253–54
Hussein, Saddam, 85, 232, 300, 341

I

IBM, 365, 381–82, 417–18, 424, 431
I. G. Farben, 387, 393, 424
India, 103, 296, 331, 348
Indians, 101, 292–96, 316, 322–25, 327, 329, 354
industrialists, 88, 372, 382
International Congress of Eugenics, 390
Internet, 29, 76–77, 235
IQ tests (Intelligence Quotient), 76, 416
Iran, 140, 142–45, 281, 375, 421–22
Iran-Contra affair, 203, 378
Iraq, 9, 12, 77–78, 85, 95–98, 162, 267, 281, 300, 344, 375, 403, 428
Israel, 300, 347, 399, 401–2
Italy, 88, 243–44, 369–70, 373, 389, 424

J

Jackson, Andrew, 315–16, 335, 356, 365
Jackson, William Henry, 39, 49, 53

Jackson, William Herman, 39, 49, 52–53, 66
Jackson State Hospital, 407
Jack's Place, 48–49, 51–52, 61, 69
Japan, 16, 21, 26–28, 119, 122, 242, 245, 343, 348, 370, 407
Jefferson, Thomas, 283–84, 290–92, 297, 299, 302–3, 317, 321, 336, 356
Jews, 78–79, 82, 87, 328, 361, 380–81, 387, 398, 400–402, 419, 424
JFK, 117, 125–26, 128–29, 149–51, 153, 156, 158–59, 162, 166–69, 173, 175, 180, 183, 194–95, 197, 200–203, 207–9, 218, 220, 223–26, 228, 230, 232, 235–36, 239–41, 244, 251, 253–56, 259–64, 266, 269, 273, 278–79, 281, 284, 286, 319, 358, 382, 411, 423–24, 426, 429, 432–33, 436, 438
Johnson, Lyndon Baines (*see also* LBJ), 13, 173, 189–92, 194–96, 227–28, 231, 233, 239, 264, 266, 408, 426
Jones, Jim, 411–12
Jonestown, 411–12
journalists, 29, 234, 347, 371, 386

K

Kaczynski, Theodore, 408
Kennedy, Joe, 159, 279–80
Kennedy, John, 163–64, 176, 186, 200, 206–7, 269, 273, 279–80
Kennedy, John F. (*see also* JFK), 13, 15, 18–20, 150, 152, 157, 162–64, 166, 169, 174, 176, 180, 186, 188, 196–97, 200, 202, 205–7, 214–15, 221, 223, 226, 230, 237, 240, 243, 249–50, 252, 257, 259, 262–64, 270, 278–81, 286–87, 358, 396
Kennedy, Joseph, Sr., 223–24, 358
Kennedy, Robert, 204, 206, 208, 224, 257, 273
Kennedy administration, 14, 169, 202–3, 205, 207, 223–26, 235, 240–41, 285, 287, 422
Kennedy assassination, 195, 207, 222–23
Kennedy family, 152, 159, 224, 278
Kennedys, 158–59, 170, 175, 180, 206, 208, 221, 223–24, 230–31, 239, 246, 281, 286, 358
Kent State University, 109, 375
Kesey, Ken, 409–10
Khrushchev, Nikita, 153–54, 275, 389
King, Martin Luther, 131, 285, 287, 299, 435–36, 438
Kissinger, Henry, 139, 393
Knights of Malta, 388, 425, 431
Kohly, Mario, 200, 202, 205, 225
Kuomintang, 106, 132, 421, 425

L

Lansdale, Edward, 121–30, 133–36, 148, 208, 210
Laos, 36–37, 39, 106, 116, 136–37, 139–42, 144, 146–47, 425
Latin America, 146, 338, 398, 401
LBJ, 126–28, 189, 191, 194, 226, 234, 255, 286
LeMay, Curtis, 241, 265–66, 280
Lenin, Vladimir, 370
Levine, Mike, 32–35, 113, 394, 439

Life (magazine), 160, 234–35, 382
Lincoln, Evelyn, 226–27, 257, 304, 318–20, 356, 426
Lobaczewski, Andrew, 74, 76, 79–84, 86–87, 89, 93, 98, 271
Loftus, John, 87, 393, 398, 400, 419
Louisiana, 155, 212, 249, 335
Luce, Henry, 126, 129, 234, 382
Lumumba, Patrice, 232, 423

M

MacArthur, Douglas, 15, 175, 195, 263, 421, 425
MacDonald, Jeffrey, 41–43, 46–49, 71, 113–15
Macmillan, Harold, 275, 344, 391
Magsaysay, Ramon, 123–24
Mandela, Nelson, 276
Manila, 122–23, 130
Marcello, Carlos, 167–68, 170–71, 180–81, 204, 223, 232, 234, 236–40, 242, 248–50
Marine Corps, 154, 156, 242, 245, 417
Marrs, Jim, 187, 384, 392, 397
Maryland, 24–26, 45, 49, 395, 419
mass murder, 151, 262, 312, 339, 354, 356, 385, 390, 392, 412
McClellan, Barr, 193, 195–96
McCloy, John J., 269, 350, 385, 392–93, 396
McDonald, Jeffrey, 47
McGinnis, Joe, 46, 48
McNamara, Robert, 10, 129, 151, 225, 264–65
McVeigh, Timothy, 413
media, 35, 63, 72, 75–76, 79, 91, 112–13, 115, 131, 157, 233–35, 241, 257, 259, 270–71, 328, 335, 340, 351, 371, 378–79, 429
Mellen, Joan, 171, 182, 185, 397
Mengele, Josef, 390–91, 393, 403–5
Merriam, John, 416
Mexico, 294–96, 302, 338
middle class, 98–99, 358–59, 366, 368, 382–83
militarism, 14, 18–19, 134, 281, 287–90, 293–94, 300–301, 303, 306, 317, 319–20, 325–26, 330–31, 340, 353, 356, 376, 378, 428, 437
Milner, Alfred, 347–48, 377
mind control programs, 409–11, 413
minorities, 40, 99, 229–30, 268, 285–86, 298, 404, 417
Mitchell, Greg, 46–47
MK-ULTRA, 404–7, 409–10, 413
Monsanto, 73, 108, 112, 158, 264
Mooney, James D., 381
Morales, David, 137, 145–46, 208
Morgan, J. P., 345, 350, 368–69, 376–77, 414
Morrow, Robert D., 202, 224, 226, 236–38, 240, 247, 249–51
Mosaddegh, Mohammad, 232, 421
multiple personalities, 391, 403–5, 410
Mussolini, Benito, 369–70, 373, 380, 382, 389, 431
My American Journey (Powell), 94
My Lai Massacre, 93–94, 96

N

NAM (National Association of Manufacturers), 376, 378–79

National Archives, 88, 214, 243, 252, 420
National Executive Committee, 369
nationalism, 105–6
national security, 111–13, 116, 389, 392, 399, 420
National Security Act, 110–13, 220, 385, 419
National Security Action Memorandum. *See* NSAM
National Security Agency. *See* NSA
Nation Betrayed, A (Rutz), 391–93, 403
Native Americans, 19, 192, 228, 283, 291–93, 297, 299–300, 306, 315, 318, 320, 322–24, 327, 330, 332, 336, 353, 356, 359, 375, 427–28
native peoples, 292, 307, 312, 314, 316, 321, 326–29, 354, 427
Nazi Germany, 81, 223–24, 376, 386, 390, 393, 400, 431
Nazis, 19, 78, 82, 87–88, 257, 293, 306, 328, 363, 365, 370, 375, 379, 381–82, 384, 386–89, 392–94, 398–401, 409, 415, 422, 431
NBC (National Broadcasting Company), 351, 377
New Orleans, 89, 155, 160, 165, 232, 236–38, 247, 253, 407
New World, 297, 307, 314, 325
New York Times, 29, 32, 38, 61, 234, 409–10, 439
Nixon, Richard, 13, 116, 125–26, 200–202, 223, 240, 261
North Carolina, 41–42, 45, 52, 62–63, 69, 114–15
Northern Ireland, 314–15

NSA (National Security Agency), 125, 216–17, 385
NSAM (National Security Action Memorandum), 129, 151, 263–64
NSC (National Security Council), 110–12
Nugan Hand Bank, 144, 412

O

Odio, Sylvia, 210–11, 250
Office of Special Operations, 124–25
Okinawa, 16, 21–22, 25–26, 45
On the Trail of Assassins (Garrison), 165
Operation Mockingbird, 233–34
Operation Paperclip, 386, 389, 395, 425
Operation Phoenix, 137, 144–45, 203
Operation Red Rock, 115–16, 240
opium, 36–38, 100–106, 134, 137, 151, 168, 421, 430
opium trade, 102–3, 106
organized crime, 26, 41, 50, 113, 158–59, 167, 169–73, 180–81, 184, 200, 204–6, 213, 218–20, 223, 228–29, 233, 236, 240–41, 243, 247–48, 252, 263–64, 266, 279–81
OSI (Office of Special Investigations), 22
OSS (Office of Strategic Services), 132, 134, 220, 231, 384–85, 388–89, 406
Oswald, Lee Harvey, 53, 127, 154–56, 159–60, 162–68, 171, 173, 175, 181–84, 186–87, 190, 192–93, 196–98, 210–13, 219, 230, 242–43, 246,

249–50, 254–56, 372, 382, 389, 407, 413
owners, slave, 283–84, 296, 299

P

pathocracy, 74, 79, 81–82, 93, 97–98, 111, 133, 168, 259, 269–72, 287, 357, 385, 405, 426, 432–33, 438
Pentagon, 16, 84, 128, 173, 175, 220, 223–24, 241, 264, 266, 280, 287, 289, 423
Perón, Eva, 387, 398, 425
Perón, Juan, 389, 431
Philby, Kim, 388–89, 431
Philippines, 116, 122–23, 134, 329, 331–33, 430
PNAC (Project for a New American Century), 84, 86
Poland, 74, 370
politicians, 30, 98, 144, 152, 154, 172, 352–53, 428–29
politics, 73–75, 82–83, 87, 261, 279, 342, 369, 405
The Politics of Heroin: C. I. A. Complicity in the Global Drug Trade (McCoy), 38, 101, 114, 137, 147, 151
Powell, Colin, 93–97
power elite, 19, 259, 278, 346, 358–59, 373, 405, 438
Powers, Francis Gary, 153–55, 389, 424
power structure, 10, 239, 244–45, 257, 264, 279
propaganda, 104, 248, 272, 328, 336, 340–41, 363, 429

Prouty, L. Fletcher, 117–18, 121, 130, 134–35, 154, 209, 224
psychopaths, 33, 73–76, 78–79, 81–82, 91, 121, 154, 159, 168, 205, 214, 219, 221, 235, 257, 281, 352, 374, 392, 405, 432
Puritans, 327, 339, 352, 356

Q

QJ/WIN, 238–39, 243–44, 248
QJWIN, 217, 219
Quigley, Carroll, 342, 344, 346–48, 357, 411–12

R

racism, 14, 18–19, 278, 281–82, 293–94, 300–301, 303, 306, 312, 317, 319–20, 323, 325, 330–31, 337, 340, 350, 356, 378, 427, 437
Reagan, Ronald, 14, 122, 147, 261, 383, 420
Revolutionary War, 19, 297–98, 337, 361–62
Rhodes, Cecil, 342–44, 346–50, 353, 368, 376
Rice, Condoleezza, 93, 96–97
Rockefeller, John D., 350–51, 369, 385, 390, 398–99, 402
Rockefeller, Nelson, 350, 369, 390, 398–401, 405, 409, 422
Rockefeller Foundation, 349, 390, 399, 402–3, 406, 409–10, 413, 431
Romans, 77, 303
Rome, 243, 268–69, 303, 388–89

Roosevelt, Franklin Delano, 87–88, 261, 270, 276, 284, 352, 369, 388, 431
Roosevelt, Theodore, 224, 333, 335, 337–38, 356, 390
Rosselli, Johnny, 167–68, 180, 236, 243–44
Rothschild, 343, 345, 347–48
Round Table Groups, 348–49, 376–77
Royal Institute of International Affairs, 348–49, 377
Ruby, Jack, 160, 171, 173, 184–86, 198, 236, 240
ruling elite, 99, 135, 345
Rutz, Carol, 391–93, 403

S

sabotage, 207, 231, 367–68, 386, 394
Saigon, 34, 37, 122, 124–25, 137, 139, 143–44, 147–48
Sand Creek, 333–35
San Jose Mercury News, 378
Scholastic Aptitude Test, 416
Schreiber, Walter, 386, 395
Secord, Richard, 71, 139–40, 142–43, 147
secrecy, 34, 107, 109, 165, 167, 180, 229, 252, 290, 406
Secret History of the American Empire (Perkins), 112
secret service, 126, 161, 171, 173–75, 183, 187, 209, 219, 234, 239, 248
secret society, 342–44, 347–49, 351
Secret Team, The (Prouty), 71, 117, 140–44, 147–48, 153

Seldes, George, 370–72, 376, 379–80, 382, 429
Serles, 66–69
Shackley, Theodore, 136–44, 146–48, 207–8
Shaw, Clay, 155, 159, 171, 181–83, 212, 231, 236–38, 240, 242, 247–48, 388, 431
Sherman, William Tecumseh, 318, 321–22, 324, 356, 430
Skorzeny, Otto, 387, 391
slavery, 77, 228, 282–84, 287, 294, 299, 301, 303–6, 312, 317, 320, 340, 356, 430
slaves, 274, 283, 291, 303, 305, 312, 428
Sloan, Alfred, 369
South America, 204, 333, 343, 387–88, 393–94, 398, 401, 403, 422, 432
Southeast Asia, 21, 25, 30, 36–39, 43, 45, 47, 61, 64, 100, 102, 104, 106–10, 131, 137, 140–41, 145, 148, 150–52, 158, 168–69, 180, 204, 206, 208, 222, 263, 348, 421, 425
Southerland, Thomas Edward, 22, 24, 26–27, 45, 58, 61–65
South Vietnam, 37, 107, 124, 135, 147, 152, 232
Soviet Union, 153–54, 213, 241–42, 245, 265, 275, 280, 287, 338, 384, 389, 397
Spain, 84, 253, 307–8, 310, 313–14, 329, 370, 374, 400
Spaniards, 310–11, 313, 326
special operations, 116–17, 124–25
Standard Oil, 267, 388, 393, 400, 402

Stannard, David E., 292–93, 296, 307, 311, 428
State Department, 34–35, 48–49, 53, 71, 208, 287
Stoeckley, Helena, 42–44, 46–48, 57–58, 63, 113, 115
Sturgis, Frank, 197–99, 203, 254

T

Taliban, 378
TCMDs (Transportation Control and Movement Documents), 23–24
Tehran, 140, 142–43
Texas, 90, 127, 147, 155, 161, 171, 173, 186, 191, 205, 209, 213, 294, 386, 395
Thailand, 17, 21, 25–26, 36–37, 39, 43, 48–49, 57, 63, 65–66, 68–69, 106, 139–41, 147, 411
Thyssen, Fritz, 87–88, 372
Tinker Air Force Base, 67–68, 147
Trafficante, 167, 170, 180, 239, 241, 248
Treaty of Versailles, 370
Trujillo, Rafael, 232, 423
Truman, 122, 132, 172, 200, 203, 220, 385, 389, 399, 424–25, 432
Trurnit, Hans, 395
TSBD (Texas School Book Depository), 156, 163, 165, 168, 190, 192, 243, 251, 253, 255–56
Turkey, 118–20
Tutu, Desmond, 276, 433
Twyman, Noel, 146, 150, 174, 180, 214–15, 226, 243–44, 252, 264, 270, 397

Twyman, Noel H., 150, 174, 180, 214–15, 226, 243, 252, 264, 397

U

U-2, 153–55, 245, 389, 424
United States of America, 4, 11, 30–31, 37, 39–40, 43, 49–50, 52, 58, 62, 66–71, 73, 83–85, 88–89, 97–98, 104–6, 110–12, 117, 133–37, 143, 146, 148–49, 151, 154–55, 157, 172, 175, 180, 191, 194, 203–7, 211, 216–17, 219–20, 222–24, 226, 230–32, 239, 241–42, 244–45, 252, 257, 266, 268–69, 280–82, 287–88, 300–306, 312, 317, 319, 328–34, 336–37, 339, 341, 343–45, 348, 352–53, 355, 363–65, 369–70, 372, 374–77, 381–82, 384–86, 389–92, 394–97, 399–400, 403, 405, 409, 411, 413–15
USAID (United States Agency for International Development), 112, 165–66
US Army, 57, 64, 136, 176, 386, 393, 395
USSR (Union of Soviet Socialists Republics), 154–55, 184, 241–42, 245, 265, 276, 280, 389. *See also* Soviet Union

V

Valle, Eladio del, 249–50
Vang Pao, General, 138–41, 144, 147–48
Velasco, Jose, 423
Ventura, Jesse, 410

Vietnam, 10, 15, 21, 26, 30, 33–34, 37–39, 42–44, 47, 52, 61, 63–64, 73, 93, 106–8, 113, 115–17, 119, 124–25, 129, 138–40, 142, 144, 147, 151, 194–96, 203, 209, 262–64, 280–81, 288, 330–31, 335, 411, 429, 436–37
Vietnam War, 15, 18, 61, 71, 73, 100, 106–7, 117, 121, 134, 137, 139, 150–51, 158, 203, 394, 417, 425
Von Braun, Werner, 385–86, 394
Von Hindenburg, Paul, 370

W

Waldron, Lamar, 165, 167, 180, 397
Wallace, Malcolm, 192–94, 196, 255
Wall Street, 15, 44, 138, 158, 169, 266, 351, 357, 365, 374, 376, 385, 389, 393, 424
War Against the Weak: Eugenics and America's Campaign to Create a Master Race (Black), 415
war crimes, 89, 94–95, 318, 324
Warren Commission, 155–57, 161, 166–67, 175–77, 190, 203, 207, 211, 230, 232, 238, 251, 254, 270, 286, 385, 396
Washington, 62, 64, 124, 127–28, 141, 144, 209, 292–93, 299, 301, 318, 356
Washington, George, 289–90, 292–93, 301, 318, 325
Washington Post, 63–64, 234, 246, 439
Watson, Thomas, 381–82
Webb, Gary, 378
Weismann, August, 415

White House, 84, 91, 125, 128–29, 177, 202, 220, 225, 263, 320, 351, 368–70, 374
Willoughby, Charles, 175
Wilson, Woodrow, 143, 328, 336–38, 340, 342, 356
Wilson administration, 328, 336, 338, 340–41, 356
world domination, 345–46, 393
World War I, 80–81, 83, 87, 104–5, 133, 153, 164, 192, 220, 222–23, 231, 287, 336–42, 344, 349, 357–59, 361–62, 365, 370, 378, 384, 396
World War II, 83, 87, 95, 104–5, 117–18, 131, 133–34, 153, 164, 175, 192, 220, 222–23, 231, 287, 302–3, 328, 336, 339, 349, 359, 363, 370, 377–78, 384–87, 389–90, 392–93, 395, 403, 406, 409–10

Z

ZR/RIFLE, 203, 208, 213–15, 236–38, 243
Zyklon B, 387, 393, 424

Edwards Brothers Malloy
Thorofare, NJ USA
August 12, 2013